INTERPRETING SOCIAL VIOLENCE IN FRENCH CULTURE

INTERPRETING SOCIAL VIOLENCE IN FRENCH CULTURE

Buzançais, 1847–2008

Cynthia A. Bouton

LOUISIANA STATE UNIVERSITY PRESS BATON ROUGE

Published by Louisiana State University Press

Manufactured in the United States of America
First printing

Designer: Michelle A. Neustrom
Typefaces: Minion Pro, text; Bulmer BT, display
Printer: McNaughton & Gunn, Inc.
Binder: John H. Dekker & Sons

Library of Congress Cataloging-in-Publication Data

Bouton, Cynthia A.
Interpreting social violence in French culture : Buzançais, 1847–2008 / Cynthia A. Bouton.
p. cm.
Includes bibliographical references and index.
ISBN 978-0-8071-3686-7 (cloth : alk. paper) 1. Riots—France—Buzançais—History. 2. Violence—France—Buzançais—History. 3. Buzançais (France) —Social conditions. 4. Buzançais (France) —History. I. Title.
HV6485.F8B68 2010
303.6'230944551—dc22

2010007013

The paper in this book meets the guidelines for permanence and durability of the Committee on Production Guidelines for Book Longevity of the Council on Library Resources. ♾

CONTENTS

Acknowledgments vii

Introduction 1

CHAPTER ONE
The Riot and Its First Renditions 11

CHAPTER TWO
Repression and Reaction, Challenge and Response 31

CHAPTER THREE
Buzançais in Nineteenth-Century Politics and Literature 62

CHAPTER FOUR
Popular Publishing between the Wars 91

CHAPTER FIVE
Jacquerie as Cartoon and Television Drama 126

CHAPTER SIX
Buzançais Rendered in History, Patrimony, and Sound and Light 171

Epilogue 202

Notes 209

Index 251

ACKNOWLEDGMENTS

I received crucial financial support from the National Endowment for the Humanities and the Council for European Studies. The University of Michigan's Eisenberg Institute for Historical Studies provided me with a supportive environment and resources as I completed this project. Texas A&M University has supplied institutional assistance in the form of time and money, particularly from the College of Liberal Arts, the History Department, and the Melbern G. Glasscock Center for Humanities Research.

I have benefited greatly from the help of many librarians and archivists responsible for the collections I have plumbed, especially those at the Archives nationales, Bibliothèque nationale, Archives de Paris, Archives départementales de l'Indre (with special thanks to the director, Marc du Pouget), du Cher, de l'Indre-et-Loire, and de la Haute-Vienne, the Bibliothèque and Archives de l'Institut de France, the Institut Mémoires de l'édition contemporaine (IMEC), the Bibliothèque de la bande dessinée (Angoulême), Musée-Hôtel Bertrand in Châteauroux (especially Michèle Naturel), the Service historique de la défense, and the Archives municipales de Bruxelles.

In Buzançais, I found support and encouragement. I particularly thank Mayor Régis Blanchet for the information he supplied and his excitement about the project. Patrick Lepas invited me into his home and to rehearsals of the outdoor spectacle's performance. He and Léandre Boizeau graciously answered numerous appeals for information about their work.

I would like to thank especially Philippe Hénin, *France-Soir*'s archivist, for his assistance in finding a reproducible copy of *Crime ne paie pas,* and *France-Soir*'s management for permission to reproduce images.

Many people, colleagues and friends, have taken the time to read the manuscript in whole or in part and to share their comments with me. They include Julia Blackwelder, John Bohstedt, Kate Engel, Margaret Ezell, Manfred Gailus, Martin Geyer, Carol Harrison, April Hatfield, Melanie Hawthorne, Sylvia

Hoffert, Jeff Horn, Jo Burr Margadant, Ted Margadant, Pam Matthews, Peter McPhee, Jeremy Popkin, Jim Rosenheim, Rebecca Schloss, David Vaught, and Jocelyn Wills.

Further thanks go to panelists and audiences at multiple conferences where I have presented drafts of my work, who have offered helpful feedback, and my students, graduate and undergraduate, who have proved encouragingly insightful. My department heads at Texas A&M, Julia Blackwelder and Walter Buenger, have supported me throughout. I have received strategically important technical assistance from Steven Schloss.

I offer special thanks to the people at LSU Press who did so much to facilitate the process of turning a manuscript into book: Alisa Plant (acquisitions editor), Catherine L. Kadair (production editor), and Michelle Neustrom (book designer). Grace Carino expertly performed the crucial task of copyediting.

Penny Livesay has plied her amazing editorial skills and found *le mot juste* more times than I can count. I thank my family and friends for their encouragement and support. My son, Kevin, has grown up with French history with (mostly) good humor.

Introduction

On a beautiful bluebonnet Texas morning in March 2005, I received a telephone call from the mayor of Buzançais, a modest town of four thousand located deep in central France, three hours by train and bus south of Paris. "I understand from reading interviews you gave to local journalists that you're writing a history of my town," he said accusingly, "but you haven't talked to me." That, he said, wouldn't do. He had things I needed to see and hear in order to tell the story as I should.

The "story" told in this book began with a food riot in Buzançais on a bitter cold January day in 1847. The riot itself, provoked by the sight of grain passing through a town already suffering hunger, high prices, and unemployment and fearing worse to come, took the traditional form: interception of the shipment (*entrave*), invasion of granaries and mills, and forced resale of the grain at a "just price" set by the people, the whole fracas fired, fueled, and fanned by women. What started as a classic subsistence movement, however, triggered two days of rioting and class hostility punctuated by uncommon property damage. The son of a landowner shot and killed a protester; a crowd battered the shooter to death. Local authorities recoiled from the crowds and utterly failed to stem the riot's tide. Disorder soon spread throughout the region.

At the time, the Buzançais affair's resonance with memories of past collective violence quickly made it a national cause célèbre, a notoriety that distinguished it from the more than three hundred other riots that erupted throughout France during the Europe-wide crisis years, 1846–47. The July Monarchy (1830–48) responded fiercely with military occupation, highly publicized trials, and unusually severe sentences (three guillotinings) designed to punish a rebellious populace and to discipline cowering local elites. The riot also focused polemics in the political press, facilitated factional critiques of the government, and contributed to the debates preceding the Revolution of 1848.

Originally a local episode of horse-drawn carts, wind- and water-powered mills, cobblestone markets, pitchforks, blunderbusses, and guillotines, the Buzançais affair has survived the decades and lives on as a national cultural artifact in the France of the TGV, atomic power stations, hypermarkets, Ariane space rockets, and Tazers. Continuing to draw attention over a century and a half, it kept reappearing in local and national political discourse, the press, literature, visual culture, popular and scholarly historical narratives, and local spectacle: in the 1860s, 1880, 1919, the interwar era, the 1950s, late 1970s–1980s, and from the mid-1990s to the present. With each retelling, key representations differed substantively in detail and meaning. During these moments, competing political cultures in France found the story of Buzançais a useful weapon in their ideological arsenal as they sought to define themselves and to enhance their relative positions with the French public. That the nature of its telling concerned the town's mayor in the first decade of the twenty-first century, 160 years after the fact and in a France from which the food riot had long disappeared as a form of popular protest, validates the importance, not so much of the riot itself, but of the embedded issues that live on.

Kept alive through the years in a variety of media and formats—court documents, newspaper stories, novels, illustrations, popular histories, newspaper comic strips, television drama, scholarly histories, popular magazines—the Buzançais affair continues to draw attention in the twenty-first century through an annual sound-and-light spectacle presented in nearby fields to hundreds of spectators who come from near and far, by train, bus, and car. There, perched on bleachers and stools, locals and visitors alike witness the reenactment of the riot, followed by a dramatic adaptation of a 1990s historical novel based on the tumult and its aftermath.

Studying these diverse subsequent representations of the riot, as well as the immediate responses to it, and locating them in their respective contexts show how each version fashioned a narrative, or story, about the episode that performed particular functions for its teller.[1] The meanings that narrators derived from the episode, the media they chose to communicate these meanings, and the narrative choices they made, as well as their particular renderings, both reflected and participated in their respective eras. This frequent "return" to the Buzançais of 1847 reflects persistent ambiguities in the riot's origins and character that made it available for frequent renarrating. Its meaning was, and remains, unstable because the issues it invoked remain unresolved, rooted in fissures in French political and social discourse. Telling the Buzançais story has offered its narrators an opportunity to renegotiate the boundaries between such contested issues as moral and political economy, legitimate protest and crime, the right to existence and the right to property, collective and individual violence, and the proper exercise of authority. In the process, these narratives reveal shifting understandings of community, class, gender, ethnicity, and power relationships. By controlling the narrative of Buzançais, its narrators hoped to control the meanings it evokes.

The first half of the nineteenth century proved a volatile cultural and political era. In late-1840s France, industrialization, faster communication networks, growth in the reading population, and an increasingly democratic print culture combined with revolutionary uncertainty about how to describe and respond to these changes. The 1846–47 crisis had many traits common to past subsistence crises, but it occurred in a context different from that of its precursors. With the advent of telegraphs and railroads capable of speeding news about disorder and troops to and from riot sites, many contemporaries found themselves grappling both with multiple (and multiplying) discourses competing to represent the emerging society and political culture and with competing proposals for coping with these changes. Not only did the Buzançais riot give people copious material to think with, but thinking about it also helped them make the transition from one set of discourses and social organizations to another.

As news of the riot spread swiftly, the Buzançais affair captivated national attention as both familiar and exceptional. It seemed familiar because it drew upon a set of protest rituals that belonged to collective memories all over France; it seemed exceptional because the riot deviated in important ways from those expected protest "scripts." France—and even the town of Buzançais—had had a long tradition of food rioting, with recurring recourse to grain seizures, price-fixing, and public distributions. The tradition had varied over the centuries, of course,[2] and rioters had frequently incorporated new elements into their "repertory" of behaviors. However, collective protest that mounted during periods of food shortages and high prices rarely deviated significantly from a fairly well-established set of actions. Other forms of collective action to protest deteriorating labor conditions (such as low wages, the reorganization of the workplace, and the introduction of machinery) also depended on a relatively predictable set of behaviors. While most propertied contemporaries might deplore recourse to collective protest—with its threats of violence against (their) property and even their persons—they still generally recognized such action as part of the social and political fabric of their era. By 1846–47, however, the political climate of grudging toleration was changing, and the July Monarchy's sharply liberal political economy called for repression, not indulgence.

Most contemporaries would have located Buzançais and the department of the Indre (when they could locate it at all) in a usually orderly part of France: a small, provincial, unremarkable town in an unremarkable region in the country's center. With his novel *La Rabouilleuse* (translated as *The Black Sheep*), Honoré de Balzac had not long before the riot (1842) made literary capital out of "the spirit of immobility" that characterized life in the Indre.[3] The region had even more recently (October 1846) attracted national attention as the locus of horrible flooding and destitution, a region of victims, not rebels, and an object of pity, not fear.[4]

Despite this reputation, in January 1847, Buzançais exploded into violence, reenacting not just the classic behavior associated with past protests—medieval peasant wars (*jacqueries*), a centuries-old tradition of food riots, the revolutionary *maximum,* artisan protests, and frequent retributive violence against property—but also newer gestures associated with nascent industrial labor protest and starker hostilities that destroyed property and killed property owners. This unexpected bundling of several forms of protest together into a single episode warned that if such violence could occur in a place known for *immobilisme,* similar lightning might strike anywhere.

The Buzançais affair did have "cascading" regional and national resonances; it did provoke "a series of further ruptures that resulted in structural transformations" and made "repair difficult" and a "novel" outcome possible.[5] Buzançais ignited further disorder throughout the region, fed a crisis of communal and departmental authority, drew national attention in the press and among the intellectual elite, provoked debate in the Chamber of Deputies, and ultimately catalyzed political action. In the end, the July Monarchy government—previously aggressively committed to a liberal political economy—agreed to intervene to allay the crisis. Seen with a wider lens, the Buzançais affair had significant "lingering effects." The rich political discourses it generated ultimately put the state itself in play. It formed one of a series of "subevents" that constituted the crisis leading to the Revolution of 1848, and its legacy even played a minor role in the early days of that revolution.

Like Robert Gildea's *The Past in French History,* my study explores the interplay of political culture and collective memory by observing individuals shaping history and memory, as well as considering the dynamic role that market forces and media interests played in the episodic retelling of Buzançais and the remolding of its lingering narrative.[6] As Paul Cohen's *History in Three Keys* has shown of the Boxer Rebellion in China, Buzançais lives on in multiple modes: as event, as experience, and as myth.[7]

The key to this survival lies not primarily in its eventful character but rather in the very fact that its relatively "minor" status presents advantages for the student of French history and culture, just as it has for the French themselves. Unlike politically and culturally charged events such as the Bastille, the Dreyfus affair, or the 1961 massacre of Algerian War protesters in Paris,[8] the narratives of Buzançais have not spun off dizzying scholarly and popular battles waged to freeze its meanings. Aside from the local and departmental authorities and elites who lost honor and even their jobs over their handling of the affair—and who aspired to erase memories of their failures during the riot—no one tried to "suppress" memories of the entire event, as some sought to suppress shameful episodes of both world wars. People did, however, try to rewrite its narrative. Both at the time and subsequently, repeated efforts to reorder the disorder at Buzançais illuminate French attitudes and practices. In fact, the Buzançais affair has produced more narrative interest over time than the 1870 Hautefaye affair, told by Alain Corbin; the 1914 trial of Mme Caillaux, analyzed masterfully by Edward Berenson; or Robert Brasillach's 1944 trial, reopened by Alice Kaplan.[9]

Buzançais achieved a symbolic and synecdochical status for diverse interpreters of later eras and ultimately became what Pierre Nora has called a *lieu de mémoire,* a memory "plucked out . . . of history, then returned to it," "distorted and transformed," capable of resurfacing old meanings and generating new ones.[10] Long after the event, Buzançais retained an evocative power that authors utilized. As we shall see, for example, in the nineteenth century, Victor Hugo (1862) and Gustave Flaubert (1869) sympathetically invoked it in their novels, confident that the very mention of Buzançais would conjure memories of fury, riot, cowardice, pillage, mayhem, murder, and thumping guillotines (or at least memories of tales of them) that would produce the desired visceral effect in readers.[11] Economists, including Karl Marx (1850), wheeled it out to attack or defend capitalism.[12] Georges Clemenceau's newspaper, *La*

Justice (1880), gave it traction when he commissioned the exiled Communard Jules Vallès to write a serial novel for it.[13] These authors both drew upon and contributed to Buzançais's intertextual mosaic, which itself extended into and shaped twentieth-century constructions of the story.

In 1925, a court magistrate cum popular writer / historian, Pierre Bouchardon, commodified Buzançais for the growing mass market for sensational crime (and order) stories by serializing it in a commercial magazine, *Lectures pour tous,* and in a 1926 historical crime collection, *Crimes d'autrefois.*[14] In the 1970s, Buzançais appeared on research agendas for scholarly regional and local history, and in 1982, Philippe Vigier's contribution to the Editions Hachette's influential series on everyday life presented the riot as paradigmatic of the tensions of the 1840s.[15] By the 1990s, Buzançais had become the most frequently, and often the only, cited example of popular protest from the prerevolutionary midcentury era. Politically divergent but standard works such as François Furet's *La Révolution, 1770–1880* (1988), Hervé Robert's contribution on the July Monarchy for the widely read Que sais-je? series (1994), Peter McPhee's *Social History of France, 1780–1880* (1992), and Nicolas Bourguinat's preface to *Les Grains du désordre* (2002) all feature it.[16]

The 1980s and 1990s also resurrected Buzançais as local, popular history in new ways. Genealogists enthusiastically linked themselves to any individual associated with the affair; local historians and their societies eagerly tried to (re)implant Buzançais in local memory. A 1994 local magazine nostalgically insisted, contrary to earlier research, that, "still today, the memory of this tragedy strongly pervades the collective memory of Buzancéens," while an increasingly popular local performance and reenactment (a "sound and light" show) remapped it onto the modern landscape.[17] Whatever version of the original events resonated in the collective memory or memories (if any) of Buzancéens, such cultural forms as these created new memories and meanings, in part, by fabricating what David Lowenthal has called "heritage" through an affective reconnection to and dramatization of it.[18]

The Buzançais riot has found portrayal in diverse visual images as well: broadsheets, illustrations of fiction and history, a cartoon strip, and television docudrama. For example, Mario Simon's haunting, empathetic representations of Buzançais's common people for the first republication of Vallès's novel (1919)[19] contrast starkly with B. Leclercq's 1925 illustrations of them as cowering and craven in *Lectures pour tous.* In 1956, a captioned cartoon series in the newspaper *France-Soir* (owned by French media mogul Pierre Lazareff) entitled *Crime ne paie pas* (Crime Doesn't Pay) featured "La Jacquerie de Buzançais," which criminalized protest and contrasted dark, almost simian rioters with lighter, refined authorities.[20] In 1978, French national television's Antenne 2 dramatized Buzançais in a show entitled "Le Pain et le Vin" (Bread and Wine).[21] Unlike past renditions, this one, cloaked in deliberate ambiguity by the frequent, simultaneous use of contradictory aural and visual images, prodded viewers to make their own judgments of the rioters, the riot, and the repression.

Late twentieth-century mass-media culture refiltered nineteenth-century perceptions of class and gender, social and political relationships, through the contemporary prisms of race and ethnicity. Illustrators, in consultation with editors and writers, deployed images as signs to viewers seeking to interpret what they saw and read. Confronting images with their texts therefore reveals the ambiguous, disruptive, and complementary messages (intended and unintentional) they conveyed.

Buzançais has performed certain kinds of cultural, social, and political work at specific moments during the past 150 years. Through the 1920s partisans of the "Left" invoked it to warn about the perils of ignoring the "social question." Yet the riot's widely censured "excessive" violence held the Left back from elevating Buzançais to an iconic moment in its grand narrative of French history.[22]

"Liberals" invoked Buzançais to warn about the perils of a regulated economy unable to respond efficiently to shifts in supply or demand. But despite this "Right"'s fear and loathing of the "dangerous classes," its adherents largely avoided Buzançais after 1847 because the event also broadcast the cowardly behavior of elites. From the 1920s, however, the postwar Right—reinforced by the new crowd psychology's scientific imagery of savagery and irrationality—used Buzançais to emphasize broad "law and order" concerns that, by the 1950s and 1970s, intersected preoccupations with both the legacy of the fratricidal impulses seemingly embedded in French identity and current concerns about immigration and ethnicity. Rightists could mobilize the Buzançais affair as a case of crime, not social protest, and as a call to defend "civilization" against "barbarism."[23] The reproduction and marketing of the Buzançais riot thus changed over time as publishers, authors, illustrators, and local enthusiasts commodified the pliable tale to suit the growing media markets for history, crime stories, and commemorations of the local.

My study also demonstrates that the structures of each particular medium employed both constrained and empowered the messages conveyed by textual and visual narratives of Buzançais, perhaps as much as did the ideological positions of authors, illustrators, or producers. Through close readings of the texts and images produced, my work probes the relationship between medium and story, as well as the relationships between political cultures and production, marketing, and mediatizing cultures. In this Pierre Bourdieu's contributions to understanding cultural production (literature, visual culture, journalism, and television, for example) have assisted my analysis of the emergence of new media, their "mediating roles" vis-à-vis other fields such as politics and the professions, competition for recognition (and their specific capital) among the agents and institutions occupying these fields (*champs*), and the dispositions and rules that govern them.[24] My story of Buzançais's story further shows that not only did individual, local, and national "memories" rarely operate in the same way at the same time, but also the very nature of the media themselves as "vehicles of memory"—which ran the gamut from court records to cartoon strips, from novels to "sound and light" shows—transformed the modalities of remembrances.

Exploring what narratives of the Buzançais affair can tell us about French political cultures at particular moments in the past (and present) utilizes and expands upon Charles Tilly's concept of "contentious conversations."[25] Tilly argues that social identity develops out of and builds upon "contentious conversations" that "work, both through words and through a wide variety of nonverbal interchanges (not only gestures, body language, and deployment of physical objects, but also displays of symbols, spatial shifts, altered relations to physical settings, and interventions of third parties)" and even violence, to accomplish some end. Through these interactions, "us-them boundaries" form (involving such identities as class, neighborhood, gender, race, ethnicity, religion, nationality) that reinforce or challenge existing forms of exploitation.

The Buzançais affair not only served to denote political claims in 1847 but also helped suffuse them with historical legitimacy and enhance their political significance episodically ever since, thereby demonstrating that narratives of collective violence can also belong to continuing contentious conversations. For more than 150 years, the Buzançais affair has served various groups as a mobilizing symbol, as a call for solidarity, and as an exhortation to continue the struggle to defend or advance their legitimacy. In France these struggles, the ongoing *"guerres franco-françaises"* (as some have called them),[26] in which the French have confronted each other, often deploying some form of social violence—riots, strikes, and repression of them by the forces of order and law—have perpetuated the symbolic reference to Buzançais.

Buzançais's story has often served as a warning that social violence could threaten any given social order—a warning that could motivate either the forces of order or seekers of reform. I argue that in the long run (and especially from the 1970s) the persistent integration of such stories of social protest and demands for social justice into a widening variety of media has ultimately helped to shape French political identity into one in which the "politics of the street" has proved as customary as the politics of parliamentary assemblies.

As Bronislaw Baczko has observed, symbols remain "efficacious" only as long as they continue to resonate with communities that nurture them. When this resonance fades, the symbols tend to "disappear from collective life or are reduced to purely decorative functions."[27] In 1847 Buzançais experienced an eruption of collective violence; thereafter it remained an object of political contention as subsequent narratives deployed it in a contest over issues of continuing consequence in French society. Buzançais and subsequent renderings of it became part of the master narrative of French history, part of the ongoing process of national identity formation, one of the "stocks" of historical knowledge.

My study, like the narratives that engendered it, pivots on the telling and retelling of four key episodes in, or facets of, the riot: an initial interception of a grain convoy; the fatal shooting and beating incidents; several scuffles involving local women; and the responses of local elites and authorities to the disorder.[28] "Renderings" of all four elements involved gaps in the narratives and hotly contested aspects—about deeds and words, actors and acted upon, triggers and consequences—that invited leaps of imagination to resolve.[29] Narratives and images featured women and men, rich and poor, landlords and peasants, bourgeois and workers, authorities and people in different relationships of subordination and domination, and people as objects of honor or shame, empathy or antipathy. They positioned the figures in this event to convey important messages about roles (what are they doing?), the meanings of those roles (how do they look while doing it?), and the meanings of the event itself (what does it mean when women/peasants/workers, men/rich/landlords/bourgeois, or authorities involve themselves?).

This project also enables me to consider a particular event from a transdisciplinary perspective, applying methodologies from the realms of cultural studies, visual culture, and media studies to my work in history. It analyzes power relations embedded in texts and in images; the ways texts and images complement, complicate, and contradict each other; the ways history, memory, and fiction intersect and destabilize each other; and the ways each text or image portrays its story. I can also consider some continuing, powerful themes of political, gender, and class discourse, past and present, that form part of French culture. Extracted from its origins and integrated into various political cultures, collective memories, and academic discourses, Buzançais has served and still serves the needs of many different, and often conflicting, ideologies.

CHAPTER ONE

The Riot and Its First Renditions

> There are details that one would not believe if I wrote them down, for I would be accused of letting my imagination invent them. We are after all in the nineteenth century, we are in the heart of France.
>
> —"Assassinat de M. Louis Chambert"

On Wednesday, 13 January 1847, in a working-class faubourg of Buzançais called Les Hervaux, a group of women encountered a convoy of grain halted at an inn.[1] Determined to keep its cargo in Buzançais, they sought reinforcements among men working at the nearby charity workshop. Although the men hesitated, the women badgered them into action. Soon the mayor, Pierre-Charles Guesnyer, and several gendarmes arrived and calmed the crowd, the men returned to their work, and the carts continued on their way. However, the women soon recanted and again swooped down on the shipment. With the carts at bay, women returned to the workshop to rally the men once more. The latter, aware that they traditionally faced more severe post-riot punishment than women, seemed inclined to "listen to the mayor rather than give him a '*coup de pic,*'"[2] as one of the women observed. Women assaulted the reluctant men verbally and physically, "calling [them] stupid animals and cowards."[3] One man said, "Women forced [me] to march with them. They even hit me in the kidneys with rocks."[4] When the investigating magistrate later interrogated participants, he heard repeatedly that, menaced by "fear of going without grain," unemployment, and the pittance paid in charity workshops, desperate Buzancéens succumbed to the temptation posed by passing cargoes. For example, Jean Légeron, a twenty-seven-year-old with two young children, described himself as "in need." When the magistrate declared that employment at the workshop shielded him from real need, Légeron retorted, "I only earned 15 sols a day and one cannot live on that."[5]

Faced by this determined, concerted uprising, local authority faded away. The mayor and gendarmes retreated while men and women escorted carts and cargo uphill to the town hall courtyard and unloaded them. As the evening passed, several authorities—holed up in the town hall—debated ways to regain control. All efforts to rally the national guard having failed, the mayor dispatched a plea for help to the prefect, Ferdinand Leroy, twenty-three kilometers away in Châteauroux. However, word soon came that he had gone to quell a rumored disorder at Levroux and that his substitute refused to requisition troops without the prefect's permission. Left to fend for themselves, the mayor and the justice of the peace hunkered down for the night in the town hall while three gendarmes and their brigadier, Desiré Caudrelier, monitored the grain and its interceptors. For a while the parish priest circulated among the people to try to calm them.

As night fell, a crowd now swelled by curious neighbors, as well as workers returning from field and shop, spied another grain shipment, this one en route to Buzançais's bolting mill. They detoured this cargo to the courtyard, where it joined the earlier spoils, and its escort swelled the growing throng.

From the restive crowd emerged a few distinctive characters, some of them destined to live on in future accounts. Among them, a twenty-five-year-old unmarried, illiterate day laborer, Baptiste Bienvenu, joined the group escorting the second shipment. Although Bienvenu had no court record, he had a reputation as "excitable," having previously insulted and threatened a local proprietor for selling "worthless grain."[6] He also had a felling ax, which he carried everywhere and brandished when his anger mounted. Witnesses claimed that because of this fierce, ever present weapon they could spot him easily and remembered him vividly.

The courtyard congregants debated when and at what price to distribute the grain. Finally, they decided to guard it overnight and resolve the issue in the morning. As the January night grew colder, they lit a bonfire and fortified themselves with wine and eau-de-vie (brandy) supplied by François Moneron, a carpenter, window maker, and innkeeper. Thus fortified, the assembly mounted a campaign for support by dispatching small groups to roam the town, knock on doors, and rally locals.

By midnight, several among those assembled in the Buzançais courtyard decided to sound the town's tocsin. Repeated efforts to get the bell tower keys by bullying the sacristan and parish priest failed, however. When morning came at last, the municipal council convened at the town hall. The crowd—now numbering well over four hundred men, women, and children—positioned itself in the courtyard to observe the council's arrival. They insisted that authorities distribute the captive grain at prices set by the people. As tensions rose, restless protesters grew aggressive. Several among them, notably Baptiste Bienvenu, threatened and jostled one council member, Jean Brillault, a large property owner. Bienvenu later claimed that he had only wanted to scare Brillault, "a hard man who said he'd rather throw his grain in the water than sell it to the poor."[7] Another small group of men, including two twenty-year-olds, stonecutter Edouard Bataille and clog maker Louis Michot (a man generally identified as *le grand sabotier*), made one last assault on the bell tower. Eschewing the key in favor of Bienvenu and his axe, they broke down the door and sounded the tocsin themselves.

Seemingly simultaneously, approximately two hundred men, women, and children besieged the town's largest bolting mill, owned by Pierre Cloquemin. Cloquemin's modern mill just outside of town on the Indre River produced and exported large quantities of flour. Rumors circulated that locals had long pondered attacking the unpopular mill, and protesters claimed that Cloquemin categorically refused to sell to locals. When Caudrelier and one of Cloquemin's sons, Théophile, a local notary, tried to resist, the crowd threatened violence, whereupon the two men withdrew. The crowd then stormed the mill itself, breaking the waterwheel, sluice, and millstones. From there, they entered the main building, whose six stories included the apartment where Cloquemin himself lived. They threatened to kill him, seized his grain and flour, drank his wine, shattered windows and doors, smashed furniture, and divvied up almost 7,000 francs they found in a desk and an iron cask.[8] Twenty-three-year-old Pierre Trémine, a day laborer, smashed windows.[9] The ubiquitous Baptiste Bienvenu later admitted breaking items inside the mill but insisted that 25 francs of the 45 francs found on him by Brigadier Caudrelier constituted his entire household savings, and still only half of what he needed to support himself and his ailing mother.[10] Anne Bouchard, *femme* Coteron, a forty-four-year-old mother of two, collected items such as a mirror fragment, stockings, and some linens from Cloquemin's rooms in her apron.[11] Louis Michot claimed that he had "picked up" a sledgehammer at the mill and, when someone found wine, got drunk, a condition that set the stage for further violence and, ultimately, drink-induced memory loss.[12] In fact, despite the chaos, Caudrelier, in one of the few examples of effective authority, managed to rescue the mill's registers from the papers strewn around the office, deposit them at the town hall, and then return with another gendarme in time to extinguish several fires, as well as force a few rioters to return money they had taken.

After sacking the mill, some men paused at a nearby café, while others turned against Frédéric Gaulin, a Buzançais proprietor and grain merchant notorious among the common people for his hard-hearted trading. The axe-wielding Bienvenu and his cohorts searched Gaulin's granary, accosted Gaulin himself, and forced him to hand over a bag of 800 francs. Just when the crowd seemed poised to kill him and hurt his wife, who had interposed herself, the intervention of a cooler head in the crowd offered an opportunity to escape. Gaulin, his wife, and daughter thereupon abandoned their house to the rioters, who smashed furniture, doors, and windows and destroyed or seized other personal property. According to several gendarmes, Louis Venin—the man whose death soon changed the course of history at Buzançais—presented himself as the "leader of the brigands."[13]

As the day wore on, violence continued as rioters, including Jean Foigny, a forty-year-old day laborer, intercepted a cart laden with flour as it exited town.[14] Another group descended upon Jean Lecomte's grocery store and granaries, where a scuffle ensued. According to Brigadier Caudrelier, the self-proclaimed "brigand," Venin, halted before the grocery and heatedly told Michot and several others that they should spare the shop. Lecomte posed a dilemma for protesters; while he was not an export-oriented property owner or industrial miller, like the day's other targets, Lecomte's occupation as small-scale grain trader (*blatier*) had traditionally invited popular hostility. Venin ultimately capitulated to the rioters, who sacked Lecomte's shop, rifled its contents, inventoried his grain, and drank his alcohol. Etienne Billault, a thirty-five-year-old day laborer with two children, later admitted having eaten honey from the shop. François Légeron, a fifty-four-year-old widowed father, exited the shop with "mouth and hands covered with honey."[15] Jean Foigny testified, "I saw two *pains de sucre* hanging from the ceiling and I brought them down with a club. I found a piece of bread that was lying on the ground and I took it home."[16]

This done, one hundred people crossed a bridge over the Indre River and marched to Councilor Brillaut's house. It suffered as had the others. Billault admitted drinking wine from the councilor's wine cellar.[17] Foigny, however, claimed that he had refused to enter the house because Brillaut had done him favors in the past.[18]

A crowd also returned to the town hall, where a few members of the municipal council had retreated to ponder their options. By this time, many of the town's principal proprietors had also fled there to seek protection. Earlier in the day, the council had agreed to distribute the seized grain at 4 francs the double *décalitre* (even though it had cost 6 francs). The rioters now rejected this and demanded instead a price of 3 francs. They further insisted that everyone with surplus grain also agree to sell at this fixed price until the next harvest. They forced the mayor, the justice of the peace, and eventually more than sixty of the town's more notable citizens to sign just such an "engagement." It read: "I, the undersigned, agree to sell to the public all the wheat that I possess at 1 fr. 50 c. the *décalitre* and barley at 1 fr. The undersigned proprietors agree from now until the harvest to give grain to the people at 3 fr. the double *décalitre*." Those present signed; those absent soon received a visit from crowds bearing the engagement. The village drummer paraded through the streets proclaiming the concessions.

The presentation of the "engagement" already signed by the mayor and justice of the peace, and backed by a crowd swollen by peasants from neighboring communes who had answered the tocsin, persuaded most notables to sign. However, nine hesitated, and rioters responded with physical threats, occasional scuffles, and retribution against houses and their contents.

Rioters did spare one household, that of the proprietor Ratier. When they arrived before the house, they discovered the doors already open and the Ratier family standing in the courtyard. As the crowd prepared to enter, some women present cried out for them to stop: "Don't go into Ratier's house, he has always employed us fairly."[19] Accepting this assessment, the group turned away.

Only one of the besieged responded with violence, and he paid for it with his life: Eudoxe-Louis-Joseph Chambert, fils, the forty-year-old son of one of the largest property-owning families in town. Amid the turmoil of the morning, two men carrying the "engagement" arrived at the Chambert house seeking the head of household, Marie-Thérèse-Florence Moreau de Bellesourd, Mme Huard-Chambert, mother of Chambert fils. As she signed the engagement, Louis Venin, the "captain of the brigands," burst into the house and demanded money. A servant, Louis Bourgeot, intervened to stop Venin, and as the two scuffled, Chambert fils armed himself with a gun. As Venin pushed forward, Chambert fired point-blank. Venin collapsed, his shirt on fire. Hearing the shot, more people crowded into the house.

Immediately, shouts rang out that Chambert—a man many referred to as the "usurer"—had killed Venin. Some claimed that they had heard two shots, some that two men had died, and others that one had died and another had been wounded. Anne Bouchard, *femme* Coteron, admitted that when she had learned that Chambert had killed Venin she started yelling that Chambert, too, should die.[20] Hearing of Venin's murder, Jean Foigny grabbed his pitchfork, broke two of its tines to make it a better weapon, and ran to the scene. He claimed that he "intended to avenge his comrades."[21]

As the crowd swelled, a free-for-all ensued: Chambert first threatened to shoot anyone who approached but then dropped his weapon and ran upstairs. His pursuers ransacked the house, smashing and defenestrating furniture and possessions while a female servant, Madeleine Blanchet, whisked Chambert's mother away from the fray. Those who flushed Chambert from a large armoire on the second floor assaulted him with fists and clubs. François Velluet, a thirty-seven-year-old married day laborer with four children and a job as guard at the nearby forges of Bonneau, threw an axe at Chambert, hitting him in the forehead.[22] Chambert parried as best he could and finally managed to escape onto the main street, at which point *la femme* Coteron shouted to warn the crowd: "He is getting away."[23]

To escape his pursuers, Chambert dashed up the street into a saddler's shop, where he hid between two beds. Baptiste Brillant-Godeau, a thirty-seven-year-old widower with one child, dragged him into the street. Enraged men and women then bludgeoned him to death. Bienvenu struck repeatedly with his axe; Michot pummeled with his sledgehammer; Foigny stabbed with his pitchfork; *la femme* Coteron kicked repeatedly with her sabots. François Velluet boasted afterward that he had made a "cross on Chambert's face with his axe." Subsequently, François Arrouy, a thirty-six-year-old vine grower, admitted that he had struck Chambert with his pitchfork, first in the stomach, then in the face. When the fork stuck in the unfortunate Chambert's mouth, he had to put one foot on the victim's shoulder to extract it.[24] Scores of people watched the assault, but no one intervened.

Back at Chambert's house, the ransacking continued. Jean Baptiste took one of Mme Chambert's bonnets as a trophy.[25] François Velluet traded his sabots for a pair of Chambert's boots. Jean Foigny absconded with containers of walnuts and almonds, horsehair brushes, candles, and apples.[26] Pierre Trémine stood outside the house, while men, women, and children threw objects out windows, which others smashed into smaller pieces on the ground.[27]

Meanwhile, both the campaign to get universal acceptance of the "engagement" and the levying of violent reprisal against proprietors and property continued. For example, a group burst into the Dauvergne house. They demolished Dauvergne's property—a piano estimated at 3,000 francs as well as other expensive furniture recently acquired—and ripped apart beds and linens searching for stashes of money. As they ransacked the room where M. Dauvergne lay ill, he offered them 260 francs to go away. Jean Baptiste took another trophy: one of Mme Dauvergne's hats, which he wore together with Mme Chambert's bonnet, thereby making himself even more conspicuous.[28] When someone tossed a domino game out of the window, Velluet scooped up a "yellow coin," which he thought a louis d'or worth 20 francs, but so rarely had he seen money of value (he earned 15 francs a month as a guard, while supporting a family with four children) that he mistook as a louis a copper game token.[29]

At about one o'clock in the afternoon, news came that the prefect Leroy had arrived from Châteauroux, along with the *procureur du roi* (royal prosecutor) Edouard Girard de Vasson, the *juge d'instruction* (examining judge) Paul François Edouard Patureau-Mirand, and twenty-five dragoons.[30] Protesters and other townspeople ran to the town hall to watch the prefect arrive. When the protesters presented him with their signed "engagement" and declared that they had made "peace," the prefect refused to acknowledge either, whereupon several rioters pushed forward to accost him. Yet more violence threatened when the dragoons trotted in with sabers drawn and set up in battle formation around the courtyard, while rioters rallied to expel them by force. Witnesses accused Bienvenu of threatening to cut an officer's horse's hocks.[31] Gradually, however, tensions abated and the soldiers sheathed their weapons.

From within the pressing crowd, women stepped forward to plead their case to the prefect; they begged him to sanction the sale of grain at 3 francs. In the end, he largely capitulated: the soldiers downed their weapons—perhaps more readily because they had arrived in Buzançais with no cartridges[32]—and retreated to their quarters (a hotel); the prefect seemed to agree to grain sales at 3 francs (he later claimed he had categorically refused to sanction such an engagement); he handed over his purse to a group of women with small children and insisted that the mayor do the same; then the forces of authority retired to the town hall. Later that night the prefect decamped for Châteauroux, leaving behind a report about flagrant crimes and abandoning the people of Buzançais to work out their own troubles. The worst of the riot had spent itself, however. During the night, small groups continued knocking at proprietors' doors to demand handouts of money and food, but they steered clear of outright violence.

On Friday morning, 15 January, bands demanding charity continued their rounds. Two bourgeois women arranged a handout of money to supplicants. In the midst of this distribution someone snatched the purse from one woman's hand, but Brigadier Caudrelier arrested the culprit, and many of those present supported him. That afternoon, at the regular market, Buzançais authorities offered the confiscated grain for sale at the promised price of 3 francs. The school principal, in the presence of the mayor, recorded the name of everyone who received grain. Those who had money paid; those who had none received it on credit. That evening the mayor ordered a curfew. A national guard unit finally organized itself and, together with the gendarmes, patrolled the town. They arrested five individuals (for breaking the curfew), but fear of local reprisals resulted in their release.[33]

On the 16th, rumors of troublemakers from elsewhere heading for Buzançais caused such alarm that once again "the national guard took up arms." Fortunately, the rumor proved false, but, the mayor reported, he learned that during the panic some of the previous days' "most seditious" people from the rebellious faubourg Les Hervaux had rallied, armed with "their scythes turned around" for attack and their "iron pitchforks flying," to join the national guard to defend against these invaders. He saw this as further evidence of the town's dangerous and "unfortunate" position.[34]

On Saturday, 17 January, a small detachment of lancers arrived, followed by more on Sunday and Monday. The municipality reopened the charity workshops and sent workers to repair the road north toward Levroux. The mayor reported that this additional military force, added to the revived national guard, enabled him to pay the workers and to make the usual bread distributions to the needy without incident.[35]

After three days of turmoil, calm finally returned to Buzançais. However, the disorder had spread. Within days other riots erupted throughout the region: at Châteauroux, Niherne, Villedieu, Mézières, Vandoeuvres, and beyond. Protesters in these locations emulated those at Buzançais—stopping shipments, breaking machinery, and drawing up engagements to fix grain prices and to supply consumers, sometimes attacking the property and persons of those who refused to sign.[36] In a few places, they also demanded the raising and fixing of the price of agricultural labor. One other property owner was killed for reasons that remained murky.[37]

Even after order had returned and repression had begun, the disorder had produced some positive results. First, the municipal council at Buzançais continued to honor the engagement that its members had signed during the disorder. The investigating magistrates learned that certain members of the hastily assembled national guard had agreed to continue to police the town only with the provision that the council respect the engagement to distribute grain at 3 francs. Some proprietors continued selling grain at the lower price for several subsequent markets.

Second, public assistance improved. A new voluntary subscription raised 12,000 francs, and the council arranged for the purchase of grain which it then sold it to needy families at 2 francs below the market price for a double *décalitre.* A combination of local and government financing supported 150 workers in a charity workshop that paid 1 franc a day. The mayor also observed that this daily wage "could be raised according to need and ability."[38]

However, despite these measures, the mayor still worried about the possible resurgence of violence. Each week his report on the status of the Friday grain market credited the heavy military and police presence with assuring tranquility and asked that the force remain until the next harvest.[39] On 28 January, King Louis-Philippe ordered the dissolution of Buzançais's national guard and called for its reorganization: "Since its current composition is far from being a guarantee for the maintenance of public order and is instead a source of disturbance," the king proposed its reorganization "on a better basis, by calling only on that part of the citizenry devoted to public tranquility and offering serious guarantees against the return of the disorders that had bloodied the town of Buzançais."[40]

Even as these measures of relief and repression got under way, the story of the Buzançais uprising spread swiftly. Sensing that they had much to lose as the news spread, the local notables immediately generated their own versions of events.

THE FIRST ACCOUNTS

By 1847 France had developed a burgeoning popular press composed of both local and national newspapers. All of them hungered for news, ideally news that would not only sell papers but also suit each journal's particular political posture.[41] In fact, in this mid-nineteenth-century era of an emerging mass media for news of all kinds, no sooner had rioting ended in Buzançais than the press began to report it. Just as immediately, papers local and then national blurred the story with a flurry of divergent versions, many of them parroting unverified partisan local accounts. Not surprisingly, the initial reporting clearly reflected a lack of facts; the stories contained countless errors.[42] Of course, since all published stories emanated from accounts concocted by and for members of the local notability and the sitting administration, they evinced no sympathy toward the protesters in general and those soon to face trial in particular.

Damning the eruption of the common people, however, did not exonerate the authorities who had failed to control it. That the people rioted could have surprised few in France; that the authorities had failed promptly to suppress it alarmed many. In the aftermath, the fact that notables turned on one another revealed the disunity that permeated July Monarchy France. Whatever excuses they might muster, local authorities clearly had first failed to calm tensions and prevent violent eruptions and then cowered rather than rallied when disorder broke out. Efforts to control shame and damage to notables' reputations ensued immediately. While none condemned all authority or sought to undermine the entire system on which July Monarchy elites based control, each group—Buzançéen notables, the partisans of Chambert, and the department prefect and his allies—had a vested interest in the interpretation of events.

The July Monarchy notability actively generated and promoted a "civility" and honor code that distanced its members from those below as much as, if not more than, their property and wealth did.[43] In part this effort entailed an adaptation of ancien régime markers to the new situation; in part it necessitated creativity.[44] Against an image of the common people as irrational, victims of instincts and uncontrolled passions that led to brutal outbursts, and thus without honor, the new elite of male notables increasingly portrayed itself as rational, in control of its emotions, horrified by popular brutality, and thus honorable. On the one hand, a "myth" of the "dangerous classes"[45] associated the common people with a persistent, perhaps even increasing penchant for laziness and apathy punctuated by spasms of violence, drunkenness, improvidence, cravenness, and debauchery, characteristics of the emerging working class, as the bourgeoisie perceived it; on the other hand, an opposing myth of the new male elite emphasized its useful productivity, soberness, courage, foresight, and upright behavior, elements melding into an emerging class identity of its own for the nineteenth-century bourgeoisie.[46] While the common people bred criminals, the notability found itself compelled to moralize or repress them. The common people remained childlike; the notables had matured.

These social markers appear most clearly when used to distinguish male notables of capacity from their undisciplined inferiors of either gender. When applied to women of the notability, such markers were usually deployed to discipline women in the service of patriarchy. The increasingly elaborate rhetoric of gendered public and private spheres, honor, and character that dominated the era proved easier to articulate than to act upon, especially in a crisis, but it served to shame and motivate men who failed to follow their prescribed gendered scripts and risked losing their honor.[47] During the Buzançais affair, women and magistrates could and did turn "maleness" against both rioters and notables to provoke behavior changes and greater class solidarity.

Stung by such denunciations of their manhood and their competence, and fearing worse to come, various interested local parties published narratives during the four weeks between the disorder itself and the ensuing trial: first came a self-serving account authorized by the Buzançais notability; next, an avowedly partisan defense of Louis Chambert against charges that, in killing Venin, he had blundered or panicked. Then, only a few days later, defenders of the prefect published their own version. Each narrative manifested the interests of the concerned parties most clearly in the ways it did (or did not) address the four key aspects of the affair: the initial shipment interception; the fatal Venin/Chambert incidents; scuffles involving local women; the responses of local elites and authorities. All these public narratives appeared in the departmental press, which assured their dissemination to the people then most involved in shaping public opinion and the exercise of power. All these narratives showed how, even in the immediate aftermath of events, the "facts" could serve many masters, just as they would time and again in the future.

Thus, the notables' account,[48] clearly intended for dissemination in the local and regional press, highlighted the overwhelming odds confronting them and the bravery of the elderly mayor (with occasional references to the parish priest, the justice of the peace, and the brigadier of the gendarmerie). It dwelt upon the tardy and timorous support from department authorities, claiming that the prefect and his secretary-general ignored requests for troops to patrol the increasingly tense markets until too late. The notables' narrative further derided the prefect's handling of the affair, even after he did arrive.

Against accusations of not employing sufficient force to repress violence and violent demands, the notables responded that "even the first authority in the department, the Prefect himself supported by twenty-five dragoons and a brave officer, concluded that it was impossible to try any repression." Indeed, "cruel necessity" forced the prefect "to distribute his purse, and then the Mayor's, to escape the . . . rioters' . . . menacing clamors." The prefect, they claimed, beset by rioters in the square, had allowed them to believe that the engagement fixing prices had legitimacy. "Thus the cries to kill him changed to '*vivat*' . . . followed by . . . 'Peace is made.'" The notables concluded their savaging of the prefect by hinting at cowardice shown when "in the middle of the night the Prefect [retraced] his steps" to Châteauroux.

The notables summarized their defense with the following points:

> That M. le maire of Buzançais, despite his age, despite being deprived of his adjoint . . . had never backed down from any peril and never gave in to any fatigue.
>
> That several members of the municipal council had courageously seconded him.
>
> That the justice of the peace, despite threats, had circulated in groups actively hostile to him.
>
> That the brigadier of the gendarmerie had showed himself everywhere.
>
> That the noble priest had interposed himself everywhere in the fight, too often without results it is true, but always with paternal care.
>
> That all the generous citizens, for an instant blocked in their houses and separated by the furious masses, had united as soon as possible, and prevented, without any outside help for several days and several nights, incalculable evils and misfortunes.

Forty-five signatures from municipal councilors and local elites testified to the "veracity" of the narrative. The mayor and priest, noting "that they could not in all delicacy sign the present exposé because of the praise expressed about their conduct," declared that, "aside from what concerned them personally, they could attest to the rest of it."

Chambert's partisan declared that his "narrative is written by a relation

[and] devoted friend of this courageous citizen who was massacred in Buzançais."[49] Although this self-described "homage to the memory of a victim worthy of honor" focused most heavily on the personalities and events in and around the Chambert household, it also offered an account of the disorders that, from yet a different angle, attempted to weave a defense of the local notables in general, and Chambert in particular, into a thick blanket of unique contextual details.

In form, this narrative evokes the melodramas and romantic novels that predominated in French literature in the first half of the nineteenth century. Replete with asides directed to the reader, explanations grounded in individual states of mind, pleas for understanding and indulgence for the story's protagonist, Chambert, and semiveiled allusions to forbidden violent thoughts and deeds that "both propriety and the age's scientific spirit prohibit," it grimly documents excesses of horror. For example, the author draws upon these conventions when he writes that "there are details that one would not believe if I wrote them down, for I would be accused of letting my imagination invent them. We are after all in the nineteenth century, we are in the heart of France, in a region that remained pure even during the revolutionary orgies, when all of France ran with blood."[50] This version presents by far the most compelling tale because it provides the most passionate and perhaps the most memorable account.

This version omitted any reference to the voice or action of authority or of local elites, an absence that condemns by silence. Only Chambert's mother (pleading from within her house) and father (distant and unheeded from the street) exist outside the tight circle of actors in the drama that ended in their son's death. Yet ample evidence existed already that plenty of spectators, many of them proprietors themselves, had watched inertly. Chambert's defender's plea pitted rioters against proprietors as overpowering aggressors against hapless victims.

The prefect's allies' account, not surprisingly, differed substantially about the order of events and the events themselves, openly challenging the notables' version, which "produced forty signatures in Buzançais, of which only two or three could have witnessed the multiple events that occurred during the terrible day of the 14th. . . . With surprise . . . we find . . . such names as those of the Mayor and priest of Buzançais. With regret . . . we see them adhere to inexact perceptions, to calculated preteritions. . . . We are disposed to give great latitude to local susceptibilities, the love a citizen has for his city, but this exceeds all limits."[51] To "rectify flagrant errors" and "insidious attacks" contained in the notables' supposedly factual account, the prefect's allies' narrative offered "five principal facts." First, his partisans asserted that, although the administration in Buzançais had understated the gravity of the crisis, he had sped there forthwith.[52] Second, when he arrived, he found the mayor, "alone, abandoned by those who could have, who should have, helped him." When the prefect expressed his surprise, the mayor responded bitterly: "What can I do, *monsieur le préfet*? I have been abandoned by everyone." He had convoked the municipal council, he said, but "only three showed up and they left right away." When the prefect suggested that he once again "send for the municipal councilors and convoke the citizens, [the mayor] responded that it was useless." Third, the narrative contended that the prefect's arrival caused rioters to stop pillaging the Dauvergne household and "prevented [further] devastation . . . by the fractious rioters." He had, in fact, received at day's end accolades from the population and the mayor for his service in restoring tranquility.

Fourth, the prefect's defender denounced local notables' impotence as shown by their "highly unfortunate and regrettable act" of agreeing to the engagement: "The Mayor, justice of the peace, the municipal council, and the principal proprietors of Buzançais gave in to the violence. [They] signed the engagement to supply as much grain as they had, some of them until the next harvest, at the price of 3 francs the double *décalitre* [and] . . . distribute the six grain carts intercepted the previous day. . . . The Prefect energetically declared such a measure . . . illegal, dangerous. . . . It was entirely false that, while among the crowd, the Prefect had made any sort of concession." This version asserted his bravery and resolution as he struggled to gain control for two hours before the arrival of the twenty-five troops. It emphasized yet another blunder by Buzançais's administrative body: the commissioner of police had decided on his own authority to halt the troops outside town, thereby prolonging the threats to those already in town and inciting the undisciplined crowds to more audacious actions. Because of this misfeasance, the commissioner had his authority revoked on 4 February.

The prefect's allies' counterattack emphasized repeatedly that lack of unity among local notables and various levels of administration explained how the situation had spiraled out of control. Evidence of such disunity abounded: the municipal council had abandoned the mayor; local proprietors had locked themselves in their houses and refused to rally, even to stop destruction and death; no national guard had organized until two days after the violence had begun; inadequate communication occurred at all levels; and now the various parties had published spurious ex post facto narratives and counternarratives—all parading as truthful accounts—to justify their behavior. Such disunity explained why efforts to convoke the national guard had failed and elucidated the fifth "principal fact": why the prefect had decided against sending troops against the rioters. An "armed struggle" would have provoked the "most disastrous consequences." "In such circumstances, citizens must unite together to give moral support to the troops."

The incident that produced particularly revealing narratives and silences, the fatal confrontation between Venin and Chambert in the Chambert house and the battering to death of Chambert by a crowd in the street outside his house, represented two discrete events in time and space. To contemporaries, however, they intertwined inextricably but problematically. Obviously, the shooting of Venin provoked the violent attack on Chambert; yet to admit this meant recognizing that Chambert had provoked his own death, an admission that many found hard to make. The fact that Chambert's death occurred in broad daylight, in a public place, before scores of witnesses who did nothing to stop the attack, also raised difficult issues. Both the notables' exculpatory account and the prefect's defense studiously avoided this fact, while Chambert's partisan's version rehearsed it in detail.

The partisan "Chambertin" version of the killings explained that Chambert's "bravery" derived both from his concern for his charitable mother's welfare and from a preexisting condition that made him particularly volatile and sensitive, an *affection de mélancolie*. This provincial version of the *mal de Werther,* or so the author assured his (presumably male) readers, rendered Chambert wary of the "dark cloud" that loomed on the horizon, and pointed its brutal path to his door. Perhaps, the text speculated, this condition might explain his readiness to grab his gun when those of duller sensibilities had not. But rather than interpret this as a weakness, the reader should see it as a strength.

> In treating familiarly (*en tutoyant*) such a respectable lady, in insulting her in front of her son, they didn't realize that they had overstepped the boundary, that [the son] had used up his entire reservoir of calm, of prudence, and of resignation. They didn't notice that this unlucky young man clenched his

> fists and teeth, seeking vainly to control himself. They didn't understand that the nervous sensitivity from which he sometimes suffered during his life, was acting on him with an irresistible force.
>
> In effect, as anger exploded in his soul and he was lifted like a leaf during a storm he found his weapon, which he only intended to use as a threat, so that the people would understand and cease. . . . Venin advanced to disarm M. Louis Chambert, and, perhaps, to turn against him . . . the murderous weapon. But the explosion prevented him and Venin fell fatally wounded.

As the narrative explained, some might denounce Chambert's committing "a sudden impulse, an act of folly . . . but you lie scoundrels! It was heroism, because one must always avenge the dishonoring of gray hair, especially of a mother." The narrative ruled out self-interest: the son could not have resorted to arms in a mere defense of property because he held little of his own.[53] Even provoked beyond his ability to contain his emotions, the narrator asserted, Chambert had intended to use the weapon only to scare, not to wound or kill, but only a hair trigger turned a warning into a fatal shot. The account encouraged the notion that Chambert knew little of guns, not even his own. A man of peace, when brutally forced on to the defensive, turned dangerous.

Whereas the narrative granted contingency to Chambert's actions and empathy with his excess of sensibility, it denied both to the protestors, who, it contended, "had already destined his house for pillage" and only needed an excuse to indulge irrational rage. In fact, this account showed them lusting for Chambert's blood even before the incident. Moreover, while the narrator assumed that Chambert had no murderous motivations, he contended that Venin (indeed, the entire crowd) was capable of killing.[54] Further evidence of the difference between Chambert and Venin's avengers lay in the latter's excesses and bloodlust. As the narrative explained, Chambert's own death reflected popular irrationality: "so much fury and violence . . . Death, Oh! it was not enough for them. . . . There was a terrible competition in fury. Each tried to reach him, to hit him the hardest. Each wanted a part in the crime." The author targeted the faubourgs as the source of criminal disorder with a paralipsis: "God help me not to regard as accomplices the entire population of the faubourgs, the vast majority of whom played a part in the riot!"

By 7 February, several weeks after the riot had erupted, Didelot, the prosecutor general of the Cour Royale of Bourges, had completed the formal indictment that established an official version, based on witness testimony and interrogations of suspects.[55] When the trial opened at the end of February, Didelot delivered this version to the jury, thereby adding a fourth public narrative. Although the indictment's tone appeared carefully measured—less amplified by modifying adjectives—it relentlessly insisted that the Buzançais "crimes" posed "a permanent peril for society if not promptly and energetically remedied."

The prosecutor belabored the exceptional nature of the affair. The ten-page indictment recounted a detailed story of mounting "delirium" that revealed "perversity [and] an ignorance or scorn of the law" combined with "alarming talk" and "symptoms of agitation." He emphasized its violent and "atrocious" character and identified it as the trigger for a veritable epidemic of disorders. He also carefully linked it both to "prejudices" that resonated back to the *maximum* of the Reign of Terror during the French Revolution and to current hatreds "circulating among the workers . . . that emphasized the misery of the poor, the harshness of the rich, and spoke of pillage and vengeance against the bourgeois." The indictment quoted one older rioter's ominous threats to attack at the first sign because he had "already seen three revolutions."

Yet however exceptional it might be, the indictment also warned that the story of Buzançais carried a broader moral. The event demonstrated an "inflexible logic" that "the people, as soon as it ignores a single principle, tramples all of them under foot; as soon as it oversteps one limit, it oversteps them all and recognizes no break. . . . Property once violated by the interception and arbitrary tax of grain must continue even into the domiciles of citizens. A person's body and life itself are no long sacred to whosoever thus loses all notion of justice and injustice."

The prosecutor lingered over each act of "cruelty" with devastating descriptions. The indictment, like the Chambertin account, sought to elicit sympathy for the victim Chambert and remove any scintilla of doubt about the merciless barbarity of the attackers. Altogether, the indictment's compelling rendition provided context, motives, details parading as accurate facts, and narrative coherence.[56] The indictment supplemented its obvious purpose—to assure guilty verdicts with severe sentences for the accused—with a less transparent one that emerged more clearly during the trial itself. July Monarchy magistrates sought to castigate local authorities and elites for their failure to foresee and prevent such disorder and for their failure to quash it once it erupted.

While the four narratives all differed in some respects, all had some things in common. For instance, all found examples of violent, irrational women ("furies" in the notables' account) as well as men—during the shipment interception, during the assault on Chambert, or as beggars and shrill inciters to further destruction. No narrative could find unimpeachable conduct by any of Buzançais's elite men or its authorities,[57] but women supplied several clear cases of bravery and loyalty.

The notables' account, for example, eschewed details that cast their behavior in an unflattering light. However, their story did argue that the turning point in the disorder came not, as the prefect's allies' claimed, with his arrival on the second day but rather on the third day, in the wake of a particularly heinous maneuver that dishonored a "saintly girl." It recounted that after the "fatal night" passed from Thursday, the 14th, to Friday, the 15th, "a tight crowd pressed up to the door of a 'saintly girl' and exploited her charity by robbing her of her last *écu.* At the sight of this angel of virtue brutally trampled amidst the distribution of alms, indignation laid hold of several noble hearts. Generous workers threw themselves into the crowd of avid pillagers to separate them. They called 'to arms' and in an instant, honest people straightened up, rushed forward, and closed ranks. From this moment on, the riot receded."

The only women to appear in the prefect's allies' account came from the ranks of either the irrationally violent or the truly needy, underscoring both his bravery for confronting such irrationality single-handedly and his charity by offering aid to the deserving. The prefect's allies countered stories that he had surrendered his (and the mayor's) money to rioters in order to escape them, arguing that "it was not *at the clamor of a menacing crowd that alms were given,* it was when calm was returning. It was to women publicly known to be indigent, to several old, sick individuals to whom charity was distributed."[58] Such bravery and careful philanthropy (to needy mothers and the elderly infirm) honored the prefect, both as an administrator/magistrate and as a man.

Two acts of female bravery appear in the prosecutor's indictment. First, when confronted by angry rioters, the wife of one of the municipal councilors, Frédéric Gaulin, interposed herself between her husband and a man who had raised his axe to kill him. Second, the women of the Dauvergne household stolidly defended their ailing patriarch from assault. A third appears in the Chambert defense, which related what became the most publicized encounter. It told how Mme Chambert's servant, Madeleine Blanchet, valiantly protected her mistress from violence.

Although other stories emerged, the Chambert narrative provided the most detailed (and florid) description of the servant's actions: "In the middle of the fracas, the poor woman [Mme Chambert] was knocked down and trampled. Her faithful servant did not abandon her. Her maid [showed] the noblest courage. She told her that she would protect her with her own body. . . . When . . . Mme Chambert was once again attacked by cries of fury and vengeance [and] a multitude of arms rose up to strike her, . . . the intrepid servant preserved her as much as possible and she received almost all the blows destined for her mistress." In fact, this incident provided contemporaries with such a compelling example of selfless virtue that local notables offered the servant's story to the Académie française for consideration for its "prix de vertu." The academy found itself equally charmed by the story and awarded her the largest prize of the year. When in July 1847 Alexis de Tocqueville delivered the prize's "Discours" to the academy, the Buzançais affair had neither lost its public appeal nor seen its last recasting in narrative form.[59] Both Madeleine Blanchet and Mme Chambert emerge as embodiments of virtue. In them Tocqueville sees the promise of an endangered society healed and united. Tocqueville also used the occasion to contrast Madeleine's behavior with that of the local notability, who manifested a "weak, selfish and unintelligent feeling, that in the midst of revolutions often overcomes honest and timid souls, and causes good citizens to lock themselves in their houses and await their fate." In addition, he quotes President Mater, who presided over the Buzançais trial: "If there had existed in Buzançais twenty men who had the heart of [Madeleine Blanchet], none of the misfortunes that we now deplore would have happened."[60]

In all these incidents female bravery succeeded not only in deflecting violence, at least temporarily, but also in inspiring men to do what they had lacked the courage to do earlier—stand up to the rioters. Gaulin's wife's intercession on her husband's behalf inspired another man in the crowd to grab the rioter's arm and to tell him to "do no harm." Madeleine Blanchet's selfless defense of Mme Chambert not only saved her from assault but also inspired a neighbor, the locksmith Boistard, to hide the old lady in his cellar while the crowd ransacked her house and butchered her son.

The Chambert narrative even found signs of hope in the events at the Dauvergne household: "This honorable citizen, seriously ill and abed, had no defense to offer. His only daughter, his young and pretty daughter, prostrated herself before this armed and bloody crowd, daring to bar their passage. She [cried] 'kill me, but spare my father who is sick.' . . . This time, the scythes and axes backed down! This was a triumph about which humanity could boast. A noble and touching triumph of filial piety!" The episode resonated with literary and religious allusions of virtue and offered yet another turning point in the disorder in that it tamed and returned the perpetrators of violence to their humanity.

Thus women provided perfect foils for narratives of both disorder and virtue. All those presented above made ample use of both representations. Women shamed men at the *ateliers de charité* into intercepting a grain shipment; women's violence damaged furniture and bodies; their declamations of need provoked both menacing begging bands and expressions of charity. Yet women also evoked loftier emotions. Mothers pleaded for their sons; wives and daughters interceded for their husbands and fathers; maids shielded their mistresses with their own bodies. Consistent with the widely polarized notions of women's natures in the nineteenth century, women in Buzançais inspired both the worst and best in men. But in Buzançais, men's best did not suffice.

At the local level the Buzançais affair generated narratives that served the interests of multiple stakeholders: the local elite, officials charged with keeping order, and the investigating judiciary, as well as reporters and publishers of local and regional newspapers. None weighed in for the ordinary people, of course, though many inveighed against them. The people's voice, or at least vestiges of it, did get heard, however, as the mechanisms of repression inevitably came into play. As so often happens, the common people "spoke" only when interrogated by the forces of order, when hauled into court as witnesses or culprits, or through the proxy voices of the defense counsels who spoke of their hunger, their fears, and the commonplace injustices of ordinary life.

That the people's voices reached beyond Buzançais and beyond the Indre into all of France speaks to the historical nexus at which the uprising occurred. The Buzançais episode, with its disturbing mixture of old and new grievances and responses, resounded powerfully in a France itself in the midst of a swift (and to some, frightening) process of change.

CHAPTER TWO

Repression and Reaction, Challenge and Response

> Gentleness [*douceur*] is the distinctive character of inhabitants of this department. They appreciate the good that is done for them; they complain rarely about the ill caused them and they tolerate it with calm and resignation.
>
> —François-Jean-Baptiste Dalphonse,
> *Mémoire statistique du département de l'Indre*

> Buzançais is the epicenter . . . of an uprising of the poor classes against the rich classes.
>
> —Louis de Raynal, first prosecutor, Royal Court in Bourges

The Buzançais affair, as we have seen, began as a food riot that also expressed especially intense, broad class hostilities and political demands specific to the mid-nineteenth century. It mingled behaviors associated with classic food riots (appeals to authorities to police the market and prices, shipment interceptions, searches, requisitions, and popular price-fixing), with carnivalesque inversions (celebrations of society turned upside down, festive and purification rituals such as bonfires), with revolutionary protests (record burning, written petitions and contracts), with retributive violence (house and property smashing, assaults on persons, including murder), and with class warfare (poor against rich, workers against bourgeoisie, disempowered against powerful). The affair threatened July Monarchy notables because it attacked them on many fronts at once. It combined behaviors developed over centuries and in many different contexts and adapted them to the changing environment of the mid-nineteenth century. It mobilized both traditional and newer communities of consumers; it targeted both traditional and newer objects of popular anger.

From the first to the last day, Buzançais protesters aimed to ensure their subsistence needs in a time of crisis. History, however, had shown that the violent actions of food rioters merited recognition as political tactics, rather than as crimes. No French government could dodge the issue during the sixty years that separated the Great Revolution from the Revolution of 1848; no one could ignore how food riots had preceded and accompanied each revolution or virtually every change in regime: 1788–89, 1792–93, 1816–17, 1829–30.[1] Barely one generation separated those who protested in the 1790s from those who responded similarly in 1847. At least one rioter in Buzançais, the seventy-year-old Pierre Laumont, had lived long enough to see (and remember) both episodes. The mayor of Buzançais—along with several other municipal council members—was also in his seventies at the time of the riot. Many arrested rioters were in their late thirties and forties, old enough to remember several crises, regime changes, and the turbulence and debates they engendered. Moreover, as previous upheavals had taught, economic crisis could provide ample fuel for "contentious conversations" and revolution itself.

By 1847, conflict over work had also developed a long, rich, and varied history in France.[2] Workers challenged employers in manufacturing, service, and agriculture; they clashed over wages, control of the workplace, customs, and conditions of employment. Disputes could break out within one shop, a trade, or across several trades. Although work-related conflicts sometimes coincided with rising food prices, many erupted for other reasons: during monetary and credit crises, technological changes, shifts in workplace practices and relations between workers and employers, as well as changes in the law. These struggles took various forms, including violence such as machine breaking and other attacks on property and employers, strikes, and legal confrontations over charters and contracts.[3]

Buzançais rioters knitted these general strategies together, revealing different facets of popular protest and much about the dynamics of French society. First, they underscored the persistence of the "moral economy," a deeply rooted sense that entitlement to subsistence took precedence over property rights in times of actual or anticipated dearth and legitimized the seizure of food or its forced sale at a "just price" (*taxation populaire*).[4] Second, they reflected the local character of community politics that pitted local needs against the wider forces of growing regional, national, and international markets and of state making. Third, the behavior manifested popular understanding of an established political culture of reciprocity (which some referred to as paternalism) that assumed that elites in general and authorities in particular owed the people emergency assistance in exchange for social order and deference. The Revolution of 1789 had abolished the legal inequalities that underpinned ancien régime paternalism and had recast many of the claims informally (but no less powerfully) embedded in paternalist relations into the politics of rights. While politicians and intellectuals might debate the validity of such social rights as the rights to existence and to work (largely acknowledged by the Constitution of 1793), this legacy resonated powerfully throughout France in the 1840s, animated revolution in 1848, and in some senses is surviving in the France of the twenty-first century.

Buzançais reveals in particular what the widespread rioting of 1846–47 showed in general: that French people still retained a capacity to act on their norms and to act collectively to command food supplies by violent means if necessary. The riot was, in Buzançais as elsewhere, the product of mobilized communal networks and norms, engaging social relations and shared values. Collective action became possible because protesters could activate diverse communities located in the various networks of kinship, occupation, class, neighborhood, gender, age, friendship, religion, patronage, and even civic loyalty itself.[5] Not everyone in Buzançais rioted for the same reasons, and different episodes involved different communities, but they frequently created an intertwined web of action. These patterns, too, have persisted in France through the generations since Buzançais.

Buzançais also revealed the sharp, and perhaps even widening, fractures within its community. By 1847, the powerful machinery of commercialization, state making, industrialization, demographic growth, and revolution had destroyed, reconfigured, or created communities and severely tested their cultures, forcing their defenders to adapt their strategies to the changes they had wrought. Of course, by 1847, these same forces had also produced an ever larger and more powerful opposition, pitting a "free market" against a regulated one, private property against social claims on it, and individualism against mutuality. The July Monarchy had positioned itself on the side of property, the market, and the individual as liberal ideology conceived of them. However, a past record of revolution had revealed how all this could change, and the governing notability of the 1840s saw itself surrounded by challengers from both right and left, energized by the general economic crisis that beset Europe in 1846–47 and by a series of bad harvests in France itself.

If the riot in Buzançais had simply echoed long-standing traditions of food rioting, contemporaries might have treated it like the hundreds of other riots that erupted during the crisis. If the riot in Buzançais had embodied only conflicts that time resolved, its memory would have languished with that of others long forgotten. But succeeding generations have seen in it the clash of enduring issues, just as contemporaries saw something more menacing than a traditional subsistence uprising. For example, a mere four days after the worst of the rioting had ended at Buzançais, Louis de Raynal, the *premier avocat général* at Bourges, wrote to the minister of justice in Paris that events in the Indre, "of which Buzançais is the epicenter . . . present the spectacle of an uprising of the poor classes against the rich classes."[6] Within days of completing the investigation and making twenty-six arrests, Raynal emphasized further that "this movement, so curious in itself" but "so serious in its consequences for the future," would prove "one of the most important social events of our epoch." He declared that it "marked a new phase in the social question."[7] The indictment read at the trial declared that the events at Buzançais "distinguished themselves . . . by a special character of violence and atrocity, by the most audacious attacks on property and persons."[8]

Much of this anxiety arose from the fact that contemporaries feared the fusion of protest traditions over food and work into one movement. They often oscillated between calling the protesters "peasants" and calling them "workers," thereby revealing both the complexity of French society and their difficulty in constructing from their traditional vocabulary an appropriate language to represent the events they witnessed.

Buzançais exposed the worst fractures with its open violence, a violence against property and persons. Underpinning this "culture of retribution" lay demands for the punishment of those believed to have "betrayed" norms and neglected or refused to acknowledge rights. Such protests were, therefore, "punitive as well as corrective."[9] Rioters targeted persons because they sometimes "personified . . . abstract forces" but also because these persons did concrete, offensive things. For example, Cloquemin's bolting mill represented distant flour markets that sucked resources out of the community, but Cloquemin's own refusal to sell to locals threatened them directly.

Indeed, in the context of the mid-nineteenth century, authorities and elites feared the riot as "barbaric," "atrocious," and even "cannibalistic." Raynal himself wrote that "the murder of the unfortunate Chambert was committed with the ferocity of cannibals."[10] The account of the murder of Chambert related in the prosecution's vivid indictment seemed to validate the worst of such fears:

> These scoundrels indulged themselves in such cruelties that one would have trouble believing them if there were not witnesses and confessions. . . . They beat on Chambert as one would beat cattle. Michot ran after him, and struck him several times on the head and body, with blows from his heavy sledgehammer. Etienne Billaut struck him several times with a road worker's hammer, less heavy, but not less terrible in powerful hands. Foigny plunged his pitchfork into the body. The *femme* Coteron kicked him with her sabots. Arrouy tried to stab his stomach with a pitchfork, but . . . couldn't get it to penetrate, so he plunged it into [Chambert's] face so deeply that, in order to get it out he pulled on [the victim's] head and was finally forced to put his foot on [Chambert's] face or shoulder for leverage.[11]

Elites had long denounced and feared the wrath of the rioting "crowd" (*la foule*) as the "rabble" (*la canaille*) or as a "furious mob" (*une foule furieuse*). Yet they also acknowledged—even if reluctantly and with many qualifications—its legitimate role in the contentious politics of their era and sometimes even relied on it. However, during the nineteenth century, collective violence, and retaliatory violence especially, found less acceptance as the government attempted to criminalize it in all its forms.[12] In 1847, contemporaries denounced the Chambert killing as "horrible" and "savage." The indictment emphasized its "especially violent and atrocious character," its "furious delirium," and the "savage exaltation" of the rioters.

Perhaps most disturbingly to contemporaries, however, Buzançais revealed the vulnerability of the forces of order to popular protest, and the grim insecurity property owners faced. The rioting crowds numbered in the hundreds, but they had only the tools of their trades, hammers, hatchets, and metal bars—deadly implements, but not as deadly as firearms. Against such tools, Buzançais's notables had guns and knew how to use them. The rioters chopped, clubbed, forked, and kicked to death a property owner, but only after he had shot one of them dead.

Local authorities in Buzançais, however, did not turn their collective firepower against these rioting crowds. Instead, Buzancéen notables found themselves riven by internal dissension, seconded by only a puny, scattered force of gendarmes armed with bayonets (and apparently either unwilling or unable to shoot), abandoned by a deactivated national guard, and unable to requisition troops too dispersed for a quick response. This weak, fragmented, and conflicted local authority proved no match for the common people armed only with tools. The prefect Leroy himself chose to hand out francs, not fusillades, to distressed protesters. Consequently, during the post-rioting analysis, local and departmental officials confronted accusations of cowardice and lack of authority.

The menace of events in the Indre did not end with organized riotous crowds; collective action metastasized into small, wandering bands whose looming presence seemed to threaten that, if sufficient charity did not appear, terrible consequences might follow. Wandering bands of beggars had in fact sometimes combined in groups numbering in the hundreds to tramp the countryside during the crises of the seventeenth century, the Flour War of 1775, the Great Fear of 1789, in 1792 around Chartres, and during the crisis of 1816–17. Such experiences with begging bands contributed to the perception of them as "brigands" who might attack towns.[13]

For the July Monarchy elites of the national government, Buzançais clearly posed a profound threat. Briefly, they considered whether opposition politics had fomented disorder. Always sensitive to the threat of subversion, the examining magistrates at first suspected republican or communist influence. As one wrote on 22 January, "We have actively concerned ourselves with . . . knowing if a more general insurrection had been prepared in the communes which rose up, almost at the same time, and if republican or communist machinations had contributed to forming and triggering the explosion."[14] When no supporting evidence surfaced,[15] the magistrates conjured an even greater menace, calling Buzançais the "epicenter" of a "new *jacquerie.*" Raynal, the *premier avocat général,* wrote: "We should not delude ourselves," for "this is war of the poor against the rich, it is the maximum imposed by terror, pillage and threat; it is communism in practice. That such excesses are the direct result of social theories or political opinions . . . I doubt . . . but the evil, if it can be called that, if not energetically repressed could become imminent."[16] Such warnings registered powerfully with the profoundly insecure and anxious French bourgeoisie of the first half of the nineteenth century.[17]

The term *jacquerie* had taken on meaningful resonances in the postrevolutionary period. Historians, political commentators, and even theater evoked the late medieval *jacquerie,*[18] its violence, and the social demands of its rebels. In 1845, for example, one contemporary wrote, "What did the wild peasants of the Jacquerie want? Tired of seeing themselves decimated by famine, by leprosy, and by despair . . . [they demanded] a more equitable distribution of the profits of their labor [and] they demanded that people who did not work at all leave them the least part of the fruits of their sweat on which to live."[19] Such evocations reminded readers that even before the Revolution, France had seen popular risings against "gentlemen, their wives, their children," who "found themselves in great peril" during the "time of the *jacquerie.*"[20]

In provincial France during the July Monarchy, where aristocracy and landed bourgeoisie converged to form a powerful notability, and where protestations from below about social injustices had become more vocal and frequent, supporters and critics of the regime emphasized present connections with medieval and more recent revolutionary revolts. For example, the Orléanist J.-B. Monfalcon's influential *Histoire des insurrections de Lyon en 1831 et en 1834* worried that "guilty calls to the passions of the masses" could further "embitter the hate of those who own nothing against property owners, to organize murder and pillage, to provoke a *jacquerie* one hundred times more bloody than the one the memory of which has been transmitted by our annals."[21] Monfalcon's *Histoire* was one of the "first works" to argue that "the concrete details of a popular group's living situation explained its collective behavior,"[22] and its linking of July Monarchy uprisings with medieval *jacqueries* recoupled France's present to its past in powerful ways. Multiple commentators on the social question invoked the *jacquerie* as "armed and bloody misery" that resulted in "a war of the poor against the rich," a reference that carried contemporary as well as historical meanings,[23] including the fear that strikes might transform themselves into "industrial Jacqueries."[24]

For the political opposition, such connections became current and served as a caution to all. By 1847, the Fourierist Victor Considérant's *Principes du socialisme* warned that "yesterday's revolutionaries" might "today [be] full and satisfied" but that the current French working classes were not. He declared that, if the government and bourgeoisie did not wake up, they would soon confront "social revolutions" and "a European Jacquerie."[25] Thus act and text, both nationally and locally, had prepared the path to interpreting Buzançais as a *jacquerie,* and as such all the more disturbing. Resolving the Buzançais crisis seemed to call for a political as well as a judicial solution.

The events at and around Buzançais—events that occurred in a time of crisis and widespread disorder—proved especially disturbing and evoked particular attention from both the government and the politically concerned public of France. Much of this attention took the form of denunciation of the failure of Buzançais's elites and authorities to maintain control, a failure that forced intervention by greater authority and guaranteed a fierce application of order first and law second.

That the state responded forcefully came as no surprise, for however giddy the rioters may have felt at their apparent success, however shamed and craven the local elites by their failures, however frustrated the forces of order by their retreat, few could have imagined for long that repression and retribution would not soon arrive, and soon it did. The ministers of justice and defense, concluding that the exceptional, menacing nature of the disorders called for "prompt and energetic measures" by the "king's government," dispatched 450 men of the Seventy-third Infantry and 120 lancers to Buzançais to secure it.[26] On 19 January, only six days after rioting had begun, the prefect, the *juge d'instruction* (examining judge), Bazenerye, and the *premier avocat général* from the Royal Court in Bourges, Louis de Raynal, made a public entry with additional forces: the military commander in the department and a detachment of cavalry.[27]

In the ensuing weeks, as the judicial process ran its inexorable course, it produced a unique corpus of materials. Perusing these, contemporaries such as the national press, and then a succession of latter-day practitioners—novelists, polemicists, cartoonists, historians, impresarios of movies, television, and pageants, among others—found resources adaptable to a multitude of uses. Foremost among these, the judicial proceedings—interrogations before the trial and testimony during it—offered the only forum, albeit imperfect, in which the peoples' voices spoke. These voices emerged distorted by the agencies that elicited and transmitted them: the questions that the interrogators chose to ask, the transcripts of the trial, and the accounts generated by journalists. They nevertheless echoed long after death had silenced them all—the judges as well as the judged.

The judicial proceedings also vividly displayed the government's belief that Buzançais represented a menace to social and political order and its determination to inflict a potent symbolic retribution upon the culprits. Against this fierce commitment to order, the impassioned pleas of the defense attorneys posed the raw, compelling emotions fueled by hunger and despair and the traditional acceptance of these as causes (and perhaps justification) for popular resort to violence.

The *juge d'instruction,* Bazenerye, cast an intimidating shadow. Empowered to direct the preliminary (or preparatory) investigation, he heard witnesses, collected evidence, identified and examined suspects who faced him alone because they could not have defense counsel until formally accused, and detained suspects without having to inform them of the charges against them.[28] The task proved so overwhelming that the court appointed a second examining judge and assigned extra secretaries.[29] During the next seven days, the judges and their assistants took ninety-five statements, detained and examined forty-nine men and women, verified damages, evaluated injuries, searched suspects' residences, and collected other evidence.

During this investigation the judges shaped the case by both what they did and what they did not do. From the start, the government demanded swift and severe justice to halt the further spread of rioting and to protect property owners.[30] Yet assuring "exemplary" justice meant narrowing the case to target only those suspects whose trial would fall within the purview of the Assize Court, since only it could issue the death penalty and forced labor. The judges therefore did not concern themselves in a substantive way with the initial shipment interceptions of the 13th, except as preludes to the events that followed or as aggravating circumstances for the more serious indictments.[31] Instead, they concentrated on the next day's attacks on Buzançais's notables and their property, especially Chambert's murder. These acts fell within the Assize Court's jurisdiction, while any lesser charges would have fallen to the jurisdiction of the Correctional Court.[32] The *procureur général* (prosecutor), Didelot, specifically directed the examining judges to "stick to the most serious acts, so as to complete the [investigation] more rapidly and thus arrive at a repression that is more beneficial because all the more prompt."[33]

However much this intense preliminary examination may have taxed the judicial system, it proved—as its framers intended—more daunting for possible suspects. Not only did they have to undergo multiple interrogations, but they also faced house searches and detention—all in an atmosphere of secrecy and suspicion and in the presence of intimidating authority. In this uneven match of wits, the suspect struggled alone to mount effective responses.

For example, François Velluet's first interrogation on 19 January, the day the examining magistrate arrived in town, focused on reports that he had wielded an axe menacingly during the pillaging on the 14th, taken boots off the dead Chambert's feet, and stolen money from Dauvergne. Standing alone before Bazenerye, Velluet explained that he had carried an axe "to defend himself," had lost a sabot and replaced it with a boot he found "lying in the water," and had merely gleaned one piece of a domino game thrown out a window. Armed with physical evidence and other witnesses' testimony, Bazenerye reinterrogated Velluet later that day and proclaimed him a liar. He accused Velluet of throwing his axe at Chambert, stealing Chambert's boots, and boasting that he cut a cross on Chambert's face during the attack. Velluet admitted he had lied during the first interrogation "because I was troubled and didn't know what I was saying." He then resorted to outright denial interspersed with minor concessions. He had not thrown his axe at Chambert; rather, someone had taken it (implying that that "someone" had used it against Chambert without his knowledge) and only returned it later. Velluet vehemently denied that he had touched Chambert or that he had boasted that he had.[34] Whether the overmatched Velluet realized it or not, all these revisions and denials added up to further evidence of guilt.

On 27 January, Bazenerye interrogated Velluet a third time, citing multiple inconsistencies in his testimony and producing contradicting witness statements, especially about his axe attack on Chambert's face. After further denials, Velluet offered a tale that played upon contemporary understanding of workplace social relations as sites of competitive braggadocio: "Later [that day at work], we each recounted in our own way what had happened during Chambert's death. I might have said, that if I had been there I might well have done the same as the others."[35]

Anne Bouchard, *femme* Coteron, also endured three grueling interrogations: on 21, 23, and 27 January.[36] After denying any role in the shipment interception on the 13th, she admitted attending the next day's pillaging, but only as an onlooker, "with arms crossed." When Bazenerye asked her about the Chambert episode, she offered her own simple version. As a witness when Chambert had killed Venin, she said that "Venin and two others had entered Chambert's room [and] presented him with a list to sign. Chambert had fired a gun that killed Venin. They carried Venin to the hospice and we yelled that it was necessary to kill Chambert." Perhaps sensing that this admission might place her in greater jeopardy, she quickly revised her statement to say that she had arrived only after Venin had died. However, her initial version meshed well with her account of what happened next. She explained that "[Chambert] was not killed immediately. First, they pillaged [his house] and then they discovered him . . . where he had hidden himself. By the time he had escaped into the street, he was already injured. When he entered Rue's place, they went after him." She also claimed that Rue himself had ejected Chambert from his house, contradicting what would become the prosecution's position declaring the rioters responsible for dragging him into the street. Although she named several individuals whom she saw in the mêlée, she claimed that since "everyone was hitting all at the same time" she couldn't identify anyone in particular. She specifically denied kicking Chambert with her sabots.

The judge then questioned her relationship with Chambert's mother. He asked if she had not declared that they should kill the mother as well as the son. She swore she had not, but he pressed her and elicited answers that revealed social relations distinctly different from Velluet's. Bazenerye asked her if she had received charity from Mme Chambert, an allegation that, if true, would mark her behavior as particularly heinous, since it dishonored an active patronage relationship. Perhaps sensing this, *la femme* Coteron declared, "I have no knowledge of this, but my children, who go everywhere, may have visited her."

During the second interrogation, Bazenerye confronted *la femme* Coteron with various items found in her house: a fragment of a mirror, the skeleton of an umbrella, a cotton hat marked with the initials B.L.C., a pocket handkerchief with identifying markings removed. All these items—insignificant to anyone but the very poor—pointed, in the judge's mind, to something more than simply "watching" while others pillaged. As a defense, she explained that she had "no idea" how the mirror or the umbrella appeared in her house but that she had found both handkerchief and bonnet while doing the laundry. During the final interrogation before her indictment, Bazenerye squeezed out one more bit of crucial information. When asked if she could identify anyone who had hit Chambert, she claimed that Foigny had plunged a pitchfork into Chambert's mouth, testimony that later caused considerable problems during the trial when Arrouy, another of the suspects, admitted to this brutal act.

The decision to focus on only the most serious offenses saved twenty other suspects from more than a first interrogation. Most of the seventeen men and three women examined but released had profiles similar to those detained in age, occupation, marital status, and literacy, and most had clearly participated in the "lesser" troubles at Buzançais.

On 2 February, Bazenerye presented his written report and documentation to Raynal, who made his presentation on the 3rd to the Chambre d'accusation.[37] Raynal requested indictments for "murder, attempted murder, armed pillage in bands, incitement to such crimes, and arson."[38] The Chambre d'accusation ruled the next day to bind twenty-six over for trial before the Assize Court at Châteauroux. Raynal had long thought that twenty or twenty-five individuals brought to trial would make "a good impression." He thought this number "enough to make [the trial] a significant affair, but not too many given the seriousness of the facts."[39]

The judges had focused on the major crimes, indicting thirteen for "pillage, devastation, and murder" and the others for "pillage and devastation in a band and with open violence."[40] The accused included 14 day laborers, 8 artisans (especially masons and carpenters), and 1 innkeeper; 25 men and 1 woman; 8 single men, 2 widowers, 14 married men with children, 1 married woman with four children, and 1 married man with none. Their average age was thirty-six: the oldest, a seventy-year-old man; the youngest, three twenty-year-old men.[41] Only five could sign their name to their testimonies; none had been previously accused of any crime.

Since the central government demanded severe, exemplary, and expeditious justice in the Buzançais case, it convoked a special session of the Cour d'assises to meet at Châteauroux on 25 February instead of waiting for the regular session of the Cour Royale at Bourges in March.[42] The minister of justice urged Claude-Denis Mater, the *premier président* of the Royal Court and deputy to the Chambre d'accusation from the Cher, to respond decisively to this "call to his patriotism."[43] The minister reminded him that "an affair this serious had excited the attention of all of France and its result will have a great resonance, and a considerable influence on public security." He insisted that, properly conducted, the trial could have a "great moral effect on the country." Between 4 and 25 February, judicial authorities again leapt into action; they assigned judges and readied the roster of possible jurors, while the public prosecutor, Didelot, prepared his case with follow-up interrogations and defense counsel assignments.

By 14 February the men and women charged had already undergone multiple interrogations without defense counsel and awaited their fate in jail, most since 19 or 20 January. Despite retaining the revolutionary institution of the jury trial, the Code on Criminal Investigation still weighted the investigation heavily in favor of the prosecution.[44] Upon the completion of the preliminary investigation and the arraignment, the examining judge withdrew from the case and the prosecutor took over.[45] Until this point in the proceedings, the accused had had to weather the storm of charges, interrogations, and even the arraignment alone, without advice or legal counsel.[46]

Finally, on 14 and 15 February, the prosecution informed the twenty-six accused of the charges against them and assigned each a defense counselor.[47] A case of this magnitude stretched the resources of the jurisdiction, forcing the court to requisition two lawyers from Orléans, two from Paris, nine from Châteauroux, and two from Bourges. Nevertheless, most lawyers defended more than one individual. Despite such short notice, no lawyer protested the mere ten days left before the trial began, although during the trial one defender complained (fruitlessly) that he had not participated in the choice of witnesses for his client.[48]

The trial opened on Thursday, 25 February, and ran for seven straight days. No official transcript of it exists.[49] French law prohibited generating such a document because postrevolutionary jurisprudence insisted that jurors reach a verdict only on the basis of "moral certainty," arrived at by hearing oral testimony and "the totality of performances by defendants, accusers, and other interested parties."[50] Relying on a written transcript might diminish nonprofessional jurors' ability to arrive at fair verdicts and lead back toward the type of technical decisions made by magistrates during the ancien régime.

Nothing, however, prohibited the production of unofficial transcripts. Since French jurisprudence also insisted on publicity to encourage transparency in trials, the courtroom door was opened to the public—both in person and by way of the press. From the revolutionary era, when the principle of orality and publicity became law, journalists experimented with different methods of reporting courtroom proceedings.[51] The rush among the general press to publish criminal and civil trial proceedings (like the serialized fiction that often catered to this interest) testifies to the growing market for the genre.

In fact, despite evidence of growing revulsion against violence among French elites, nineteenth-century French readers regularly consumed stories of stark brutality in their newspapers and novels. The press abounded in detailed, gruesome accounts because horror sold papers. By the early nineteenth century, several newspapers, such as the *Gazette des Tribunaux* (founded in 1825) and *Le Droit, Journal des Tribunaux* (1837), dedicated themselves exclusively to reporting collective and individual violence and the responses of authorities and courts. The "market" proved so profitable that the political press and provincial papers jockeyed to report similar "news." Stories of horrible crimes, individual and collective, filled column after column not only of the emerging "penny" press, such as *Le Siècle* and *La Presse,* but even of the distinguished political press. Fiction featuring gruesome violence—often associating it with the depraved "dangerous classes"—filled the same papers "below the fold" (on the bottom half of the front page). It comes as no surprise, then, that the story of Buzançais both repelled and compelled and served wonderfully well not only the government's determination to deploy the trial for national edification but also the interest of the commercial press in selling papers.[52]

Consequently, although no official transcript documents the Buzançais trial, two unofficial ones exist. Migné, a publishing house in Châteauroux that did much of the official printing in the Indre, published a sixty-page pamphlet version.[53] Written in a seemingly apolitical style that feigned to reproduce the spoken word and had become increasingly common in court reporting in the nineteenth century, this transcript seems to have provided the basic template for the national press reports. Like the printing house that published it, it appears to have offered the more "official" version of the proceedings.

Between 6 and 13 March, *L'Eclaireur: Journal des départements de l'Indre, du Cher et de la Creuse*—a weekly left-leaning partisan newspaper published in La Châtre (Indre), edited by Victor Borie, and heavily supported by George Sand—printed a second version that sometimes differed substantially from the first. It introduced a dramatic tone by locating the trial deeply in its local and national context, revealing its more politically engaged tendencies, and deploying descriptions drawn from the increasingly popular theories of *physiognomonie* or phrenology.[54] Dipping into strategies of sentimental narrative, *L'Eclaireur* introduced each day's session with a note of dramatic anticipation.[55] For example, the very first sentence gave a foretaste of the trial's outcome by referring to "the funereal drama of Buzançais."[56]

In general, however, both versions offered similar and putatively literal transcriptions of what the judges, lawyers, witnesses, accused, and even the spectators said and did. Both resorted on occasion to simple testimony summaries that suggest that stenographers chose what constituted information worth reporting. Taken together, the transcripts offered insights into the trial that proved invaluable for those who publicized it and invoked it for various purposes, then and later.[57]

The first day's session opened with President Mater presiding, assisted by three other judges.[58] *Procureur général* Didelot and *procureur du roi* Vasson directed the prosecution. The transcripts emphasized that even before the judges had arrived, a huge crowd pressed to enter the courtroom, reconfigured specifically for this trial. The unusually large number of magistrates, jurors, accused, and lawyers required an enlarged venue. In addition, many high-status spectators—"magistrates, functionaries, lawyers, and several ladies"—sat in a reserved section, while more than sixty people "mostly from the working class or from the country" squeezed themselves into what space remained. The two transcripts diverge meaningfully in their descriptions of the courtroom atmosphere, however. The Migné transcript emphasized the spectators' "animated" demeanor, while *L'Eclaireur* noted the absence among the spectators of the "passionate interest that arises in trials of this sort" and described the attitude as "calm and gloomy," a result of the "profound impression this trial had produced in the region, one of those emotions that one never forgets."[59]

On this first day, the court picked twelve jurors and two substitutes from the forty names available. Exhorted by their superiors to conduct an exemplary trial and inflict draconian punishment, the magistrates worried whether the jurors would impose rigorous sentences, such as death and life at hard labor. Although jurors often avoided imposing the harshest penalties, the concern hardly seems credible in this instance, since jurors came from the same list of notables who ran the country.[60] After seating the jurors, gendarmes and soldiers arrayed the accused along three banks of bleachers. The transcripts described their physical (and emotional) appearances. The Migné transcript offered physical descriptions that could evoke ambiguous reactions among readers: "With the exception of Moneron, who was wearing a suit common to artisans in the region, all were dressed like rural day laborers in white or blue smocks. They had wide-brimmed hats or cotton bonnets, wooden clogs or hobnailed shoes. *La femme* Coteron wore the brown *capiche* [bonnet] worn by all women of the villages of the Berry. Their attitude, whether assumed or natural, spoke of beaten, consternated people: several cried, especially Michot, who attracted special attention. The features of some revealed intelligence, but many showed determination and resolution. Several, notably Bienvenu, Foigny, Brillant-Godeau and *la femme* Coteron, had a face whose expression seemed to indicate ferocious energy." The more sympathetic *Eclaireur* version countered the previous image of defeated barbarians by emphasizing the (gendered) disabilities that should have mitigated their situation: "All the accused looked straight ahead. With only a few exceptions, their faces revealed a limited intelligence, that education had not come to enrich and that misery had deadened. An older woman, found among them, stood out by the vivacity of her regard from which burst an almost instinctive sharpness that never leaves a woman regardless of her situation."[61]

After seating the accused, the prosecutor read his opening arguments (a restatement of the indictment): "The crimes that desolated the town of Buzançais distinguish themselves from other events of the same sort which occupy public attention right now by their special character of the violence and atrocity, by the most audacious attempts on property and persons." He continued that "nowhere had popular prejudices about the circulation of grain, nowhere had the bad passions that fermented at the base of certain souls exploded with such terrifying energy and brought with them such deplorable results." He added that Buzançais had kindled a much larger "contagion," proving that this "furious delirium" had exposed a "perversity, an ignorance or disdain for the law . . . that would become a permanent peril for society if [the court] did not bring prompt and energetic remedies."

In conclusion, Didelot reminded the jury about the vital, national importance of its duties. It had "a solemn mission to accomplish. The basis of human society has for an instant been shaken to its foundations, and to the jury is reserved the ability to steady it. All future security . . . is in its hands."

President Mater then interrogated the accused, beginning with Louis Michot, the twenty-year-old clog maker. Mater plied him with questions. On the second day of the rioting, had he not taken an "enormous sledgehammer" from Cloquemin's mill? (yes, he had); had he tried to destroy the mill? (no, he was too drunk to break anything). Mater then moved to the Chambert episode. Witnesses, Mater declared, said Michot had announced that he wanted to kill Chambert (he did not remember saying that). Mater followed with more questions that turned to statements. Did Michot remember having struck the first blow at Chambert? (no, he did not); did he remember saying later "it is I who killed Chambert and I don't regret it"? (no, he did not). Michot stuck stubbornly to three simple lines of defense: he had followed "the others," he was drunk, and he remembered nothing. Mater finally dismissed him, "since he remembers nothing." The prosecutor, Didelot, interjected, "You hit Chambert with your hammer and knocked him down. Then you struck blows to his stomach." Michot responded, "My dear sirs, as the good God is good, I remember nothing."

Baptiste Bienvenu, he of the omnipresent axe, began by defending himself more defiantly than Michot. When Mater asked if he had joined those who intercepted the shipment on the first day, Bienvenu explained that "no grain had dropped on the market. No one could have it for gold or silver, but nevertheless we needed it." Mater countered, "Grain is expensive, true. But you are not in misery. The government, the administration, the commune gives you assistance." Bienvenu responded, "No, monsieur, we do not receive assistance as you might mean it." Mater then attempted to prove that Bienvenu's status put him above need. He asked if the 45 francs found in his pocket had come from Cloquemin's mill. Bienvenu admitted the amount but claimed that 25 francs belonged to him. Mater pounced: "So you actually had money?" But Bienvenu parried with "I only had half of what I needed. I have to fast far too often." Mater pounced again: "It appears that fasting does you good, it gives you strength, because it pushes you to break everything." Again, Bienvenu stuck to a defense based on need: "I took care of my sick mother for a year. I still owe everything I had to spend during that time." Mater concluded this part of the interrogation with a moral argument: "You are not alone in having debts, but that does not give leave to break things."

The rest of the interrogation listed other violent threats and deeds. For example, Mater asked Bienvenu if he had threatened the proprietor Gaulin, raised his axe as if to strike the municipal councilor Brillault, and similarly threatened Cloquemin's son as well as the prefect. Bienvenu insisted that he never intended to strike them, only to scare them. He explained that Gaulin had tried to sell worthless grain. To Mater's suggestion that he could have simply not bought any, Bienvenu retorted, "We still had to eat."

Inexplicably, although Mater sought to establish a record of threatened violence against people and actual violence against property, he steered clear of the Chambert episode except to establish Bienvenu's presence at the house. The president's interrogation over, the prosecutor provoked an objection from Bienvenu's defense lawyer by making a speech, not about the Chambert murder, but about Bienvenu's character. Didelot told the jury to "fix well on the position of the accused Bienvenu. He is a lazy idler, a vagabond by habit, who works rarely. His mother supplies all his needs. However, at the time of the riot he had work at the charity workshop. . . . He was seen everywhere doing evil."

Bienvenu's defense, based on need and the desperation that followed from his situation—debts arising from caring for a sick mother, insufficient assistance to meet basic needs, and frustration at his inability to communicate his crisis to those in positions to help—stood in stark contrast to the picture of a violent, able-bodied shirker painted by Mater and Didelot. Even during the preliminary investigation, Bienvenu had consistently denied any part in the killing of Chambert. Witnesses linked him to the Chambert affair, but never as convincingly as they implicated others. Nevertheless, the indictment of premeditated, aggravated murder stuck to him, through guilt by association with other violent threats and deeds. In his closing statement, Didelot simply named Bienvenu as "among those who beat and killed Chambert; drops of blood were found on his axe." He asserted Bienvenu's premeditated guilt by connecting his actions with his words: "Remember the threat he addressed to M. Gaulin: 'My axe is newly sharpened; it is for the *bourgeois.*'"

Others among the accused embraced defenses based on desperation, not depravity. For example, Jean Foigny asked Mater, "Do you think that with 15 sous a day one can feed six people these days?" So many others claimed drunkenness as an excuse that Mater chided *la femme* Coteron: "Had you not been drinking? Women, they do not drink?" François Légeron, père, also admitted having gotten drunk, a fact he hoped would shield him against accusations of having uttered some of the most inflammatory lines of the affair. In question after question, Mater quoted what witnesses had heard Légeron say: "I've seen three revolutions, at the first sign I'll swing my pitchfork around"; "Chambert is such a tough man. . . . I had to jump on his head with two hands"; and "Today is mardi-gras and tomorrow ash Wednesday: we will kill the bourgeois and bury them like carnival." Légeron declared he remembered nothing except having said, "I had already seen pitchforks turned around."

Although many of the accused stumbled as they struggled to defend themselves, only François Arrouy buckled completely under the pressure of the interrogation and confessed the worst crimes. He admitted trying to break the mill's wheel by throwing a paving stone into it, to running the streets of Buzançais yelling that "Chambert must be quartered," and to having to put his foot on Chambert's shoulder to pull his pitchfork out of Chambert's mouth. Such an admission provoked "expressions of horror" from spectators.

By the end of the first day, Mater had interrogated all the accused and turned to two important witnesses for the prosecution: Desiré Caudrelier, the brigadier of the gendarmerie, and Jean-Baptiste-Pierre Ambroise Berton-Brunetière, the secretary for the justice of the peace at Buzançais. As well as recounting events and identifying the accused who participated in the disorders, Caudrelier's testimony offered the president a choice opportunity to attack the local notables' failure to defend themselves and their town from riot. When Me Luneau, the defense lawyer for Barraud and Laumant, asked Caudrelier about the "attitude of the inhabitants of Buzançais during the troubles," Mater erupted: "My God, the brigadier's deposition reveals that during the insurrection most bourgeois were hidden in their cellars." Caudrelier admitted that he "had had no one by his side." Mater finished the day with a statement that starkly demonstrated that his public role included educating the notability as much as punishing (and warning) the common people. He applauded Caudrelier's "intelligence and courage," declaring, "If men of heart and honor in the town where you reside had acted like you, we would not be here to deplore such great and irreparable misfortunes." During the next three days, the court heard testimony from eighty-nine witnesses for the prosecution, two medical experts, and thirty-two defense witnesses.

Witnesses for the defense—mostly sharing the same social backgrounds as the accused—struggled to make their voices heard in the courtroom, where an imposing, occasionally hostile, and frequently dismissive climate withered their unsophisticated efforts either to plead extenuating circumstances or to counter previous testimonies for the prosecution. For example, several witnesses on Michot's behalf emphasized his good nature but reduced mental capacities, calling him "an imbecile" and "a lunatic" and claiming "he preferred playing with ten-year-old children" to socializing with his fellow workers, who often mocked him.[62] Witnesses for Brillant-Godeau claimed he had said repeatedly that he had "returned all money taken during the rioting" and had "done all he could to save Chambert."[63]

Many defense witnesses foundered under sneering commentary from Mater. For example, when a female witness tried to provide an alibi for Pierre Barault on the first night of trouble, Mater chided her for sitting around "chatting."[64] When another tried to testify that he had met with Barault as he left the previous witness's house, and walked with him for another hour (until midnight), Mater retorted that midnight seemed "late for a man who has to get up early to work."[65] Mater also implied that several witnesses were as guilty as the accused because they had spent the days of the riot "walking through the streets, watching what was happening, or hiding so as not to be seen" but doing nothing.[66] Even the courtroom joined in the derision by laughing at several testimonies, as when one witness vowed that all the accused were "good people" (*braves gens*).[67]

Given this environment, a few subsequent witnesses so completely bungled their testimonies that one rattled defense lawyer, Me Berton-Pouriat, declared himself ready to excuse all those he had slated to appear.[68] But the prosecutor

—obviously enjoying testimonies that seemed more likely to indict than exonerate—urged continuing on the grounds that "we seek the truth and we do not want to neglect or omit anything that could serve this end." Thus, he continued, "No one should silence witnesses the minute that they no longer speak for the accused." Mater concurred and reminded the frustrated Berton-Pouriat that the "court must assure that you complete this duty whether it be the accused's choice or by assignment."[69] Although further witnesses offered support for good character, good intentions (Georges Coulon-Cormier), and extenuating circumstances (Pierre Trémine), in the end, most witnesses failed to sound convincing. Several ended up testifying against those they had been called to support, or further inculpating others.

At the end of the fourth day, prosecutor Didelot's closing summary (*réquisitoire*) largely reprised his opening statements, but his emphasis on the singular importance of the case struck an ominous chord. His first words declared that "such pillage and devastation, which carried such serious threats to property, could also bring civil war in its wake." Events in Buzançais constituted "communist doctrines in action that, with their reliance on the axe and the poignard, aimed to level all conditions, to overturn society." According to the Migné transcript, this statement produced a "sensation" in the courtroom. Didelot reminded the jury that, "in the presence of such powerful interest, we [the government as represented by the prosecution] are certain that you will find yourself up to the social mission that we have confided in you." He concluded, "The country has its eyes on you; on your decision depends perhaps its security."

The last word of the day went to Me Prothade-Martinet, defense lawyer for Michot and Arrouy, who made his summary (*plaidoirie*) with an eye not simply to defend his clients (Michot "with his terrible hammer" and Arrouy, "the man with the pitchfork") but also to set the tone for a general defense based on poverty and ignorance. He countered the prosecution's thesis that "suffering had played no part" but only "bad passions and the love of pillage." He asked the jury how could anyone "deny the presence [of misery] in face of the crisis we now experience?" He claimed, "To learn if misery exists, one has only to descend to our streets full of beggars, to travel through our faubourgs, our countryside, where so many families fight against dearth, against the high price of food." A second cause lay in "popular prejudice" about "the exportation of grain." Do the people care if commercialized agriculture might yield long-term benefits, he asked? "No, the people only know and see one thing:

their grain, their only nourishment . . . taken away from them!" He caused a sensation in the courtroom when he declared, "The people do not believe . . . shortages [exist]; they believe . . . hoarding [does]."

Prothade-Martinet further shocked the courtroom by asserting that Chambert had committed a "fatal recklessness" when he killed Venin. When "this crowd drunk with pillage and wine" learned of Chambert's killing one of their own, "it sentenced him with five hundred formidable voices that made them judge and executioner." For the people, "this was not a murder, this was an execution!" Not only did extenuating circumstances exist, the defense lawyer asserted, but he decried the injustice of indicting only a few individuals when "so many guilty parties were still free in Buzançais!" He concluded with a call for the jury to respond with "humanity." The day's session ended with a crowd of "magistrates and spectators surrounding Prothade-Martinet to congratulate him" on his "remarkable closing statements."

Over the next two days, defense speeches continued. Only one other defense lawyer, Me François Rollinat, achieved the immediate (and ultimately national) attention captured by Prothade-Martinet. As counsel for five of the accused, Rollinat had his hands full. He, like Prothade-Martinet the day before, argued that, while Chambert may have "exercised his rights when he killed Venin," "he also committed a fatal imprudence." And, like his colleague, Rollinat dedicated most of his defense to expounding the consequences of poverty.

He pondered what a "humble peaceful request" (rather than a violent "great popular movement") to the "rich proprietors of Buzançais" might have sounded like: "You are rich and I am poor, I must accept without protest the social place providence has given me. You enjoy in peace all these goods, all these gifts of fortune. To you material well-being, and what is better, to you moral well-being, all the pleasures of the mind, happy leisure, science, enlightenment, and government. To me work, fatigue, sweat, misery, and what is worse, to me ignorance, the deprivation of the benefits of education, intellectual and moral abjection. I only ask one thing of you: the right to live and I only ask for bread in exchange for the work that I offer and which is my only means of survival." Rollinat asked "what heartless man could answer: No, you do not have the right to live, you only have the right to die in silence!" But, he continued, exactly this happens during a dearth, "when on one hand the price of grain rises indefinitely . . . and wages decline indefinitely." One had only to look into the cottage of the poor Foigny, Rollinat argued: "Foigny, earning only

75 centimes a day, could with great difficulty share a morsel of bread among his four famished children and their tearful mother."

Rollinat argued that no one should have trouble understanding Buzançais because "to ask why the people . . . exceeded the limits of legality . . . is to ask why storms form in the air, why thunder cracks, why oceans flood their banks, why torrential rains send so far their devastating floods." His words provoked a "profound sensation." Like Prothade-Martinet, he asked for understanding for the accused, when "those who found themselves in the crowd, who remained passive spectators of this horrible drama that occurred around them" face no consequences for their association with this "murder by execution." And he pleaded for "mercy" for a people so "ignorant and miserable." He urged "education" for the poor so that, "finally convinced of the disinterested views and the eminently philanthropic spirit of the laws that govern them, . . . they will say, if I suffer it is because it is not in the power for the government that protects me to ease my suffering." Upon the completion of his statement, "which had a powerful effect on the courtroom," Rollinat also received the congratulations of "a large number of people."[70]

On the sixth day President Mater gave his summary. The Migné transcript described his function as that of an "impartial organ of the law, called to calm the impressions that passionate words can make too vivid, charged with stripping away from the prosecution and defenses' statements all that which eloquence gave them, and [seizing the] real and positive . . . to lay them bare before the jurors." Neither transcript quoted directly from his concluding remarks, but the Migné version described their effect: "As his exposé progressed, the accused bowed their heads and appeared plunged into a deep sense of being overwhelmed. It seemed that this serious and imposing voice succeeded in destroying the last illusions that many of them had nurtured up to now." Finally, two hours later, Mater charged the jury to consider the 320 charges detailed in the indictments.

The defense lawyers had asked that the court allow the jury to consider extenuating circumstances because, they claimed, the women who had originated the 13 January shipment interception had provoked the men in the charity workshop. This first act, they argued, had set into motion everything that followed.[71] Moreover, they claimed, only after Chambert had grabbed a gun and shot Venin did those accused of murder respond, virtually instinctively. Pleas for leniency fell largely on deaf ears, however, for when the trial ended on 4 March at two in the morning, after nine hours of deliberation the jury found all but one of the accused (Louis Bézard) guilty as charged, charges that in three cases clearly carried the death penalty.

Upon hearing his fate, Louis Michot was "seized with a frenetic agitation: he slammed his head against the iron bars around him, tore his hair with both hands, cried with a broken voice, "Adieu, my dear family! It is thus over. I'll never see you again." Bienvenu and Velluet "wept and trembled." Mater then asked if the defense wished to add anything before the magistrates ruled on the penalties. Only Berton-Pouriat, defense for Jean-Baptiste Rouet-Bézard, asked for clemency for his client; Michot begged for his own life.

No sooner did the magistrates retire to consider the final penalties than the courtroom erupted as "these twenty-five unfortunates, finally seeing in . . . horror where their crimes had led, abandoned themselves to despair. The curses and blasphemies of some mixed with the tears and protests of others. . . . The three condemned to death cried out 'Mercy! Mercy!'"

Two hours later, the magistrates returned and pronounced decisions—decisions clearly meant to carry symbolic force as well as punitive consequences for the convicted, for they had rejected all pleas for clemency. They condemned three rioters to the guillotine (Bienvenu, Michot, and Velluet), four to hard labor (*travaux forcés*) for life, three for ten years, two for eight years, twelve (including the one woman) for five years, and one (the seventy-year-old) to prison for five years. The court also pronounced a fine of 1,000 francs against those accused of "pillage and damages."[72] Although the harshness of the sentences impressed those who pondered the trial then and later, the defense had mitigated the verdicts to some degree, since ten of the thirteen indicted for capital crimes avoided this ultimate punishment. Calls for mercy, for understanding, for a greater sensitivity to the context of suffering and ignorance, and for an awareness of the uncertainty of evidence may have played a part in this. The lawyers submitted appeals for fourteen of their clients, but the Cour de cassation rejected all of them.[73]

No sooner had the session ended than several jurors—themselves overwhelmed by the severity of their verdicts—signed petitions requesting that the government commute the death sentences.[74] Each lawyer sent clemency requests to the king. In Buzançais, the police commissioner wrote that, even among the disorders' victims, "the general will asks for the generous intervention of royal clemency."[75] (Didelot, the prosecutor, argued strongly against clemency, claiming that "the execution of the sentences would print a healthy terror, not only on the department of the Indre, but also on all of France.")[76] The Indre's deputy to the Chamber of Deputies, Muret de Bort, also wrote to ask for mercy, a letter that eight jurors cosigned.[77] Others, including family members, sent appeals for clemency to the king, but he rejected these on 6 April.

The forces of order and property had prevailed, and the ceremonies of power ensued.[78] On 20 March, the four condemned to forced labor for life first suffered display in the stocks (*carcan*) on the public *place* of Châteauroux. Then troops marched them off, chained together, dressed in the convict's gray tunic, and dragging a ball shackled to one ankle. The court distributed the other convicted Buzançais rioters to various prisons: Fontevrault, Melun, and Limoges. For the woman sentenced to forced labor, the penalty meant having to work inside a prison.

Appeals to the king continued to arrive as late as 14 April. Two particularly eloquent examples came only days before the executions on 16 April. One from Emile Mathieu, a proprietor located in the region, argued that the fault for the excesses at Buzançais lay with the local elites because "no one opposed the disorders," so the "peasants at Buzançais . . . believed that the inhabitants had turned local authority over to them." He argued that "they did not believe that they had committed a crime by avenging the death of Venin [killed by Chambert]." He admitted that the peasants of Buzançais were ignorant, even stupid, but had the bourgeoisie not "stayed hidden in their houses," the protest would never have gone beyond a demonstration to ask for grain at a reduced price.[79] On 12 April, Frère de Dieu de Magallon, *religieux de la Charité,* in a letter to Queen Marie-Amélie, also defended the condemned as more "misled than culpable" because "local authority and the written consent of the notable inhabitants had persuaded them that [by circulating the engagement] they were doing something legitimate." When Chambert shot one of their number, "the rioters thought that they had the right to pronounce a sentence, because they had been persuaded that they were the legitimate masters." This, he concluded, showed that the men "were not corrupt, that they were not criminals in their hearts."[80]

Despite these importunings, on Friday, 16 April, troops and cannons escorted the three condemned men to Buzançais, where executioners guillotined them on market day in the public square.[81] Although the prefect had worried that this exemplary punishment might spark more disorders and had arranged for a large military presence,[82] execution day produced a very different reaction. Crowds formed and watched in silence as the procession, including the condemned men and their confessors, made its way from Châteauroux to Buzançais. The *premier avocat général,* Raynal, reported that he witnessed "no manifestation of hostility, no cry of sympathy for the condemned, no word indicating anger." However, "the part of the lower class who had taken part in the troubles remained closed up in their houses."[83] After the execution, the three priests kneeled on the guillotine's steps and prayed together, and then the priest from Buzançais raised his cross to the spectators and gave them a benediction. The mayor's weekly report on the day's market said that, despite shortages, higher prices, and few transactions, "the most perfect calm reigned and sales took place freely." He never mentioned either the executions or the unusually heavy military presence.[84]

No sooner had the execution taken place than rumors arose that a "deplorable negligence" had caused a gap of an hour and a half between the time that the condemned men had arrived in Buzançais and that of their deaths. The prefect explained that the men building the guillotine discovered at the last minute an essential part missing and the executioners refused to act without a fully functional machine. Although they ultimately fixed the problem, "the condemned men were forced to listen to and to see these last operations and were subjected to an even greater suffering, which profoundly affected everyone."[85]

Once the prosecution had completed its criminal cases, the civil cases began. In accordance with revolutionary law, victims could hold the inhabitants of a commune civilly responsible for attacks on their persons and property.[86] The commune of Buzançais found itself slapped with a huge (71,789 francs 75 centimes) civil suit by the riot's victims.[87] The case lingered throughout much of the rest of the century. A 4 April 1848 decision by the civil court of Châteauroux reduced the indemnity to just under 30,000 francs, with interest accumulating from 12 October 1847, plus the cost of the trial.[88] Debates over how to pay the debt led to squabbles over taxation methods and timetables that dragged on for years. The community had not managed to regulate its debt even in the late 1870s, when heirs still battled over payments awarded their parents.[89]

Of course, long before the court had completed its work and had issued its sentences, rioting in the Indre had abated. The Buzançais repression had proved unusually severe, and subsequent prosecutions of the other outbreaks in the department during the regular session of the Assize Court in March and the lower Correctional Court resulted in the lighter sentences rendered. Two men received twenty years of hard labor and one ten years for their roles in riots at Vandoeuvre; two others got ten years each for the Villedieu riot. But all had their punishments reduced substantially after review by the king.[90]

Similarly, except for the unfortunate three men executed, few of the Buzançais convicted rioters actually completed their terms. In August 1847, Louis-Philippe's Ministry of Justice reduced sentences for many rioters caught in the subsistence movements that the crisis engendered throughout France.[91] The Revolution of 1848 liberated several Buzançais rioters from their long confinements. After hearing the news of the abdication of Louis-Philippe on 25 February 1848, demonstrators in Limoges demanded the release from prison of the Buzançais incarcerees as part of a series of revolutionary demands. The provisional committee charged with departmental administration acceded on 29 February by issuing a "pardon in the name of the French people."[92] Buzançais defense lawyer Prothade-Martinet wrote to support this action and asked that the remaining condemned receive similar clemency: "Return these unfortunate people to their families in the name of the magnanimous nation you govern. The victory of the Republic has excited the enthusiasm of the people, its generosity will receive benedictions and acknowledgements."[93] By April, most of those detained had received pardons on the grounds that the Limoges example called for similar responses elsewhere.[94] "The Republic should not have two weights and measures" wrote the commissioner of the department of the Indre to the minister of justice.[95] Although it took some longer than others, all, even those sentenced for life, eventually regained their freedom. For example, after twenty-five years of repeated pleas by the rioter Arrouy and his family, the Third Republic government finally released him on 2 March 1873.[96]

The Buzançais affair created a cast of characters drawn from the ranks of the high and the low, the rich and the poor, the oppressors and the oppressed, the villainous and the virtuous, the mean and the munificent, the brutal and the benign, the cowardly and the courageous. It also provided a narrative—several narratives—of events that lent themselves to illustrating the best and worst of human nature, the power and the perils of authority, and the tensions new and old coursing through France. The thriving national press of France, growing in reach and impact, ensured that these narratives and the characters who peopled them would circulate far and wide.

Refracted through the lens of the mid-nineteenth-century French press, the riot and its aftermath produced accounts that spanned the political spectrum of the time. The result not only showed the fluid qualities of the event itself but also added a freshet to the reservoir of contemporary materials from which future generations could draw. The press articulated a range of opinions—those of reporters and editors, as well as those extracted from outside sources—on such topics as class hostility, property versus personal rights, and the legitimacy of "contentious conversations" embodied in old and new forms of popular protest, especially when they involved violence.

Buzançais provided a crucible in which the combustion of a traditional form of popular outcry, long seen as a legitimate expression of the right to subsistence, commingled with a newer menacing uprising, the workers' revolt against authority and property. This amalgam provoked in some quarters fears of an emergent, ominous conspiracy that threatened the very basis of order in French society. Newspapers perceived it as a contretemps on which they could air their particular political views—and sell a lot of papers in the process.[97] Newspapermen who saw political journalism as a "field" (in Bourdieu's sense) seized Buzançais as a chance to amass "capital" that might advance themselves and their papers.

By the time of the Buzançais affair, therefore, the French reading public had already savored a panoply of widely publicized criminal and civil trials.[98] So the political press swiftly zeroed in on it. For three months, the story remained in the public arena: as riot and repression (in January), as trial (in February), and as punishment (in March and April). Some papers even returned to the affair in May. By quickly focusing polemics in the political press, Buzançais served to facilitate political critiques of the government.[99]

The national press began by reprinting often flawed local reports, most of them taken from the department paper, the *Journal de l'Indre,*[100] but soon began to draw its own conclusions from the "evidence" it received. Debates over elements of the narrative or disputes about the identity of the participants arose first and foremost not in the pursuit of truth but in each newspaper's need to support its own political position. Newspapers from the socialist left, republican left, Orléanist center right, and religious/legitimist right all manipulated narratives of Buzançais to articulate their political positions.[101] Those on the "socialist left" included the communist *Le Populaire* (mid-1840s, circulation 13,500), edited by Etienne Cabet; the Fourierist *Le Démocratie pacifique* (1,665), edited by Victor Considérant; and *L'Atelier,* a paper produced by a group of Saint-Simonian artisans (1,050). All three represented leftist political positions often as much at odds with one another as with more conservative papers, especially about the place of property in the new social order.[102] More centrist but still defiantly left, *La Réforme* (1,860) expressed the radical republican and mildly social-reform-oriented opinions of Alexandre Ledru-Rollin and Louis Blanc.

The *Constitutionnel* (25,000) and *Journal des débats* (9,300) leaned toward the center right and largely supported the Orléanist regime. Papers on the right included legitimist and Catholic journals such as *L'Univers* (4,500) and (after 1847) the *Union monarchique* (5,000), which circulated to the Ultras and socially and doctrinally conservative Catholics. Within certain boundaries of verisimilitude, every paper felt free to publish imagined plots, dialogues, and characters. This journalistic license emerged most clearly as time passed from the original event itself. The greater the distance in time, the more flexible Buzançais became.

Papers of every political persuasion opposed violence; most found the executions at Buzançais excessive, and their editors distanced themselves from the government. They did not, however, share similar positions on the disturbances themselves or their meanings. The Left (of the socialist or republican sort) sympathized with the starving poor and indicted the government and landed elites for failing to respond quickly, sufficiently, and compassionately. Guizot's government and its affiliated newspapers defended property, free circulation, and a grain trade that protected proprietors from low prices (the *échelle mobile*). These papers therefore castigated the people and exonerated Chambert.

Rioting in Buzançais and elsewhere underscored the urgency of issues simultaneously under debate in the Chamber of Peers and Chamber of Deputies, issues including government intervention in the grain trade, public assistance, and the reorganization of the national guard in the provinces. Even as riots broke out all over France in early 1847, both houses debated a free trade agreement with England, suspended the *échelle mobile,* voted for incentives to import grain into the country, and increased resources for struggling charity workshops and food distributions to the poor. The first page of many newspapers discussed the broader problems raised by these issues, while subsequent pages reported on Buzançais and elsewhere. Sometimes Buzançais even made the front page as evidence in the larger debate. Thus, the political press made the Buzançais "Jacquerie" the focus of more and more national attention.[103]

For Orléanists, focusing on the heinousness of the acts and the feral behavior of the masses of rioters deflected attention away from what, to the July Monarchy forces of order, surfaced as the two most disquieting aspects of the affair: the breakdown of authority's ability to enforce order and the lack of solidarity among elites. The central government found itself on the defensive against accusations of a lack of preparedness (for an economic crisis as well as for domestic disorder) leveled by many of its supporters in the two chambers. At the local level, the whole affair smacked not only of cowardice but also of an absence of both public spirit and bourgeois class solidarity.

For the opposition on the left, while conflation of both acts carried certain dangers, it also proved compelling. On the one hand, highlighting the unruly, dangerous, violent potential of the desperate poor sounded a warning to the government. On the other hand, such a link also risked associating the "people"—considered inherently good—with wanton, violent murderers. Faced with such a dilemma, the left opposition newspapers generally elided the grim details and carefully deplored violence, focusing instead on the larger context and issues.

Buzançais's widespread notoriety had many immediate consequences. For example, the perceived failure to call forth armed repression at the first sign of disorder may have encouraged a more aggressive reaction later in the national crisis. When a demonstration by thousands of workers to reduce bread prices morphed into a violent attack on bakeries, grocery stores, and wine shops in Mulhouse in June 1847, the mayor requisitioned troops that opened fire several times, ultimately killing eight rioters.[104] Yet, as we have already seen, outrage at the injustice protesters had suffered in Buzançais resurfaced in the early days of the Revolution of 1848 in Limoges, when demonstrators demanded the release of prisoners held there.

The claims of a regional newspaper, *Gazette du Berri,* that "the name of the city of Buzançais . . . has had a great effect: all eyes are fixed on us, all mouths want to tell of our misfortunes" might have borne little weight, but then a national paper, *La Réforme,* declared that "France will never forget this episode."[105] Indeed, the press (local and national) had found in Buzançais a useful synecdoche for the social, economic, and political tensions that exploded during the crisis years.

Eventually, by the end of May 1847, the press's attention turned to other events and ultimately to the 1848 Revolution itself. However, by then the political press had made rich use of Buzançais as a symbol around which it could organize debate of the issues that concerned it: the economy, popular violence, justice, and the social question. The memory did not fade quickly. While debates died down in the press, they persisted well into the summer in other forms of print culture and in the Chamber of Deputies. The image of executions at Buzançais resonated well beyond the town market.

Pamphlets and books from the right and left invoked Buzançais as a symbol of the government's shortcomings. For example, Marcellin de L'Estang, a moderate legitimist, dismissed a government that responded to "famine in the streets, misery at home, and despair of the soul" with "dramas of saturnalias, sterile vaudevilles, and the unbelievable complicated plots and bad taste of feuilletons" instead of real freedom of the press, which it suppressed. He warned that "the success and fortune of the novelist [and the government] will be assured until, finally, the people tire of eating paper and realize that they are hungry and want to eat . . . the bread of Buzançais!"[106]

On the left, journalists and pamphleteers found the "scaffold of Buzançais" a potent symbol for social crisis and government failings. Charles Robin cynically congratulated the minister of justice for "avenging society" with the "deaths of the guilty at Buzançais." Robin indicted the government itself as more culpable, guilty of "wasting the resources of the country" through corruption "to the point that a bad harvest suffices . . . to destroy all security and open everything to doubt" while the "victims . . . only wanted bread." He reminded the government that "the people . . . hardly revolt for pleasure . . . not for fun [do] they let themselves get stuck by bayonets and stomped on by the cavalry, [or] leave their jobs, their families to expose themselves to death!" He concluded, "For the people to fly off their hinges, they must be forced, outraged, pushed over the edge."[107]

Likewise, Georges Mathieu-Dairnvaell juxtaposed the honest, struggling working man with the scandal-ridden, immoral speculators associated with the Guizot ministry. The corrupt government and its cronies go unpunished: "Not for them the scaffold at Buzançais. . . . They did not know how to prepare for misery, but they punish it severely." He complained, "It is prohibited to steal a bread when one is dying of hunger, but one can steal by gambling [with public resources], sell promises and privileges, [and the minister of justice] sees nothing criminal in that!"[108]

Georges Duchêne associated the government with "a new famine pact." He lamented that "strikes and riots over a few centimes might seem petty and ridiculous to government officials with pensions accustomed to voting their special favors in thousands of francs at time," but how could the government not understand the cause of the hatreds that divide society "when it responds to all this with . . . the dragonnade at Anzin, the fusillades at Saint-Etienne, and the scaffold at Buzançais"?[109]

Even in the Chamber of Deputies, republicans like Alexandre Ledru-Rollin kept the public eye on Buzançais. In a lengthy speech on 18 June, he castigated the government for its failures on the subsistence question. He declaimed, "When it comes to the poor proletariat's bread, what you call free trade, I call brigandage!" Invoking the ancien régime Controller General Turgot's response to widespread food rioting in 1775, Ledru-Rollin granted that violence should not go unanswered, but he pleaded for clemency and even amnesty for the protesters. He claimed that "the simple country people . . . pushed by the fear of hunger" did regrettably respond with savagery, but, he asked, how could a government that so failed them not pity them? He asked, "How could you raise the funereal scaffold at Buzançais?"[110]

By exploiting the ambiguities surrounding the riots themselves and pitting claims for social justice against those of property and public order in terms that embodied and validated particular stances, the journalists, editors, and politicians of midcentury France had mined the Buzançais affair for malleable, ductile materials. After midcentury, artists in many media found these qualities enabled them to invoke the Buzançais drama and its cast as shorthand to make a point, strike a chord, stir an emotion, because even as the actors faded away, the memories and the issues survived.

CHAPTER THREE

Buzançais in Nineteenth-Century Politics and Literature

> The social idea invades everything, literature as well as politics, . . . ever since men have begun to talk of the Social with a weapon in their hands.
>
> —Jules Vallès, "La littérature sociale"

Throughout the second half of the nineteenth century, the story of Buzançais remained in the memories of some who had lived through it and of others who had perhaps read about it in the press's widely circulated stories about the riot and the trial that followed. Evidence of these memories appears in polemics and popular culture, in debates over economic policy, and in the references of several major French writers. The first representations appear synecdochically—as quick allusions to Buzançais—suggesting that the writers themselves believed that a simple evocation of the affair sufficed to convey meaning.

Even before the Revolution of 1848, the story of the *jacquerie* of Buzançais and the subsequent repression had entered at least one genre of popular culture, song, if somewhat obliquely. Songwriter Pierre Dupont, decrying the pervasiveness of privation and the dire straits of the starving, alludes to the executions at Buzançais in his 1847 "The Song of Bread." Following a poignant description of popular hunger, misery, and recrimination (including collective violence), the fourth verse invokes the injustice and futility of repression:

> Arrest among the populace
> The carriers of guns and scythes
> Cause there in the public space
> The scaffolds' skeletons to rise
> Before the eyes of the dismayed crowd
> After the falling blade's thud

Has decapitated their futures
A cry will rise up for blood

The refrain continues:

One cannot stop the murmurs
Of the people, when "I'm hungry!" they've said
Because it's the cry of nature:
We must have bread: We must have bread![1]

During the Second Republic, memories of Buzançais remained vivid. In 1848, Benoît Voisin referred to Buzançais directly in a lyric satirizing an erstwhile July Monarchy proprietor who, after the February Revolution, presents himself for election as a worker / man of the people. This seigneur cum candidate identifies himself as

Once a usurer, a great hoarder
During the days of famine,
The Republic scared me,
As you can see by my demeanor;
Forget, Français,
Lille and Buzançais,
And their starving terror.[2]

The refrain emphasized the candidate's new status:

Since February
I'm a worker
Long live the Republic!"[3]

The song played upon the all-too-real popular concern that elections would return control to the very property owners who had let the people suffer and punished those who had protested, as well as fears that recently awakened "friends of the people" would revert to oppression at the first opportunity.[4]

These concerns appeared throughout the Second Republic. During the 2 November 1848 constitutional debates in the National Assembly, Félix Pyat, spokesman for an amendment to add the right to work to the document,[5] provoked outrage when he invoked Buzançais. After enumerating a long list of occupations that found themselves as vulnerable to "competition, bankruptcy, and usury . . . , [and] as oppressed by capital . . . as the worker who struggles against unemployment and hunger," he attacked any government that first ignored such suffering and then handed out "vouchers for bread in Paris and vouchers for the guillotine at Buzançais."[6] Violent protests erupted in the hall: many damned his remark as a "glorification of murder." Despite Pyat's protestations that his comment "attacked not the verdict, but the necessity to make such a verdict," enraged colleagues accused him of "preaching insurrection." Pyat retorted that "undoubtedly the sentences condemned the men for murder, but the cause of the murder was famine, and the cause of the famine was the Government."[7]

Thus, the mere reference to Buzançais could still provoke violent reactions. Throughout the Second Republic and into the early 1850s, pamphleteers and pundits from the political right and left frequently marshaled memories of it in their battles to rally opinion. A moderate republican and economist, François Ducuing, admitted that "without large-scale property, we would not have had the executions at Buzançais."[8] In 1848, Gustave Du Puynode, another moderate economist and author of many books on slavery, banking, and economic policy, argued for public education and cited events in the Indre to support his argument: "Primary instruction . . . lessens the perils that come from social differences. . . . Last year, during our time of dearth . . . abominable troubles . . . the horrible cries, pillage, and murder at Mézières, Vendoeuvre, and Buzançais happened only in the most backward and ignorant part of France."[9]

Karl Marx himself cited Buzançais as an example. In *Class Struggles in France, 1848–1850,* Marx juxtaposed the "shameless orgies of the finance aristocracy" and "the struggle of people for the first necessities of life." He complained, "At Buzançais, the hunger rioters [are] executed."[10] In the explanatory notes, he exaggerated the episode's casualties: "In 1847 in Buzançais, in connection with the incipient famine, two rich landowners were killed by an excited crowd as grain usurers; five persons were executed on account of this murder.

During the Second Empire, Buzançais attracted commentaries from literary giants like Victor Hugo in *Les Misérables* (1862) and Gustave Flaubert in *L'Education sentimentale* (1869). Hugo used Buzançais to think about the nature of disorder. He wrote: "Insurrection flows from the mind, riot from the stomach. In cases of famine, riot, Buzançais, for instance, has a true, pathetic, and just point of departure. Still it remains riot. Why? Because fundamentally right, it was wrong in form. Savage though right, violent though it struck haphazardly; it walked like the blind elephant, crushing; it left behind the corpses of old men, women, and children; without knowing why, it poured out the blood of the inoffensive and the innocent. To nurture the people is a good aim; to massacre it is an evil means. . . . In the beginning insurrection is a riot."[11]

While Flaubert's socialist character, Sénéchal, feasted on oysters, exotic delicacies, and homemade bread, he "spoke of the murders at Buzançais and the food crisis" and warned that if the "deplorable theories of laissez-faire and noninterference" continued to foster a "feudalism of money . . . far worse than the old feudalism . . . the people would lose patience and might well avenge their sufferings on the capitalists, either by sanguinary proscriptions or by the looting of their houses."[12] Songwriter and poet Emmanuel Delorme carried imagery and continuing memory of the Buzançais affair into the Commune. His song "The Social Republic" sympathizes with the perpetually suffering worker and condemns the "three heads cut off at Buzançais" by those who "gaily pass their time partying" and who "negotiate with gun shots."[13] The storm of commentary on, and references to, Buzançais continued to box the political and intellectual compasses well into the 1860s and beyond.[14]

Not, however, until the 1880 publication of Jules Vallès's serial historical novel *Les Blouses: La Famine à Buzançais (1847)* did the affair receive substantial narrative attention. By the time Vallès (1832–85) penned this first full-length novel about the Buzançais episode, France had witnessed multiple occasions for violent protest. The Revolution of 1848 had resulted in the short-lived Second Republic, which ended in the installation of the Second Empire in the hands of Louis Napoleon in 1851–52. Republican and socialist protest continued. Humiliating defeat in the Franco-Prussian War (2 September 1870) culminated in the "année terrible" of trauma associated with the Paris Commune of 1871. During this period, the Second Empire collapsed, the Third Republic was proclaimed, and, in retaliation, the invading German armies put Paris under siege (September 1870–January 1871). After armistice in January, elections in February brought a monarchist victory at the polls (February) and set off an insurrection in Paris that a revolutionary government in March proclaimed the "Commune." Short lived (a mere seventy-two days), the Commune ended in violent suppression at the end of May. As many as 30,000 Communards and workers were summarily executed, 38,000 others imprisoned, and 7,000 forcibly deported as the vengeful government pursued three goals: punishing the Communards; discrediting the Commune's principles; and demonstrating the "price of revolution to those who might contemplate it in the future."[15]

The painful legacy of the Commune and the arduous process of instituting a lasting republic dragged on for years. The government executed a Communard as late as June 1874, and it took until 1880 to install a stable, functioning system of government. Former Communards and their sympathizers commemorated the Commune as an attempt to achieve the cooperative agenda of 1848 and tried to nurture the memory of its dreams and repression. The victorious Right tried to tarnish that legacy and suppress all its memories.

By 1880, militancy among socialists and striking workers had reemerged in the new Third Republic. Working-class congresses had started meeting again in 1876, and the Fédération du parti des travailleurs socialistes formed in 1879. The Radical Republicans emerged as the most important parliamentary political party on the left. Committed to a republican government and a secular state, the Radical Republicans included social reform on their agenda. Moderate by socialist standards, they nevertheless seemed radical at the time, mounting such demands as an income tax, a reduction in work hours, pension plans, and the legalization of unions and strikes. Journalist, editor, and future prime minister of France Georges Clemenceau (1841–1929), elected deputy in 1876, emerged as an important spokesman for the Radical Republicans. As they scrambled for political support, they confronted the handicap that many allies on the left still languished in exile.

In 1880, Clemenceau stepped up his agitation for a general amnesty for those condemned for their roles in the Paris Commune of 1871.[16] While visiting Brussels in January, he met exiled Communard and activist writer Jules Vallès. Whether they already knew each other is unclear, but Vallès's father had taught Clemenceau at the *lycée impériale* in Nantes.[17] Clemenceau asked Vallès to collaborate with him on his new Radical Republican newspaper, *La Justice*.[18] He clearly hoped that a contribution from a major exiled Communard would boost his campaign for amnesty and his search for political allies.

In Vallès, Clemenceau found a logical collaborator. Forty-eight years old (nine years older than Clemenceau) when *La Justice* published his serial historical novel *Les Blouses: La Famine à Buzançais (1847)*, Vallès had by then established an impressive record as a political activist, journalist, novelist, literary critic, and autobiographer.[19] He had written articles for such papers as

L'Evénement, L'Epoque, Le Figaro, Le Progrès de Lyon, Le Réveil, and *Le Siècle;* founded papers such as *Le Peuple, La Rue,* and *Le Cri du peuple;* and written several serialized novels such as *Les Réfractaires* and the semiautobiographical trilogy *Jacques Vingtras,* still in progress in 1880. The first two volumes, *L'Enfant* and *Le Bachelier,* had already appeared, and the third, *L'Insurgé,* based on his experiences in the Commune, came out after his death in 1885. In 1878 he had written, "I would like to write a great social novel with the misery of the silent, crushed people."[20] Vallès undoubtedly hoped that *Les Blouses* would contribute to fulfilling this aspiration.

Vallès had lived through the crisis of 1846–47 while at school in Nantes (where riots flared throughout the region), and when the Revolution of 1848 ignited, he joined the "youth republican club of Brittany and the Vendée." In 1851, his father, alarmed by his son's political activities and repeated academic failures, interned him in a mental hospital. Revolutionary agitation later led to short prison sentences in 1853 and 1868.[21] Vallès thus knew intimately the physical hardships associated with alienation, and they haunted him most of his life; his semiautobiographical trilogy dwells on long periods of misery and suffering, as well as struggles with his place in society.[22]

Vallès clearly saw writing as part of his activist mission, remaining profoundly committed to the belief that "social description" could sustain a political combat and that it performed a "revolutionary" function.[23] He also saw history writing as an important political tool in the activist's arsenal and intended his literary works especially for an audience of "petits esprits."[24] In 1881 he wrote that he did not aspire to political power but rather preferred to write history: "I like best being the spokesman for the past. I want to be the historian of the great anonymous crowd which revolted and which was crushed in 1871. This role is worth more [than politics]—I will be the deputy of the *fusillés* [the executed]."[25]

For Vallès, the Buzançais episode offered an excellent opportunity to evoke history in the service of the "People" and the "Social."[26] By 1880, he had already developed a particular vision of French society, drawn as much from his life experience as from the current political and social discourse. His understanding of the identity of the "people" owed more to the first half of the nineteenth century than the second; more to romanticism than to realism; more to Michelet than to Marx; more to the era of a France still largely composed of peasants, artisans, and day laborers than of the proletariat; more to the Revolution of 1848 than the industrial revolution to come. Vallès drew all his life upon the legacy of 1848. "The People . . . was not destroyed by the cannons of June

[1848], and socialism emerges to threaten from its nest of cannon balls. . . . The *Social* arrives, hear it! It arrives with giant steps, carrying the name, not of death but of salvation."[27]

Vallès frequently used visual markers (often clothing) in his writing to distinguish the two classes, workers and bourgeoisie. He usually collapsed them into oppositions—such as *la blouse* (worker's smock) and *la redingote* (bourgeois frock coat), but he sometimes qualified these oppositions.[28] Frock coat wearers at times traded their coats for smocks. Vallès described certain *redingote* wearers who "worked behind the counter," "went to the shop in [a] worker's cap [*casquette*]," and "walked around the muddy factory floor in *sabots*."[29] Many of the social categories, and the language Vallès used to express them, current in 1848 (and 1847) had less direct resonance in 1880, when he wrote his historical novel on Buzançais,[30] but they retained idealized and mythologized connotations.

Vallès had frequently written that among the people initiative lay with the women. For example, his *Insurgé* declared that, "when women get involved, when the housewife pushes her man, when she grabs the black flag to stick it between two paving stones, it is like the sun rising on a city in revolt."[31] In 1878, he had written: "Women have taken their place in history. On 5 and 6 October [1789] they went to Versailles to demand to see the baker's boy and show him a loaf of bread on the end of a pike. They began the Revolution. Flying over the classic insurrections of July 1830 and February 1848, we find, in June [1848], a poor man's wife sitting at the barricades. She has stuck a soup pot between two paving stones, where she cooks soup and makes bullets. Bourgeois revolutions hardly see her. But once a social storm erupts or gets ready to erupt, she appears. 18 March [1871], she appeared with red scarves."[32] Vallès drew upon the long-standing ideology that gender differences existed, rooted principally in women's maternal role, and he therefore assumed that men still performed more important (because less "interested") roles; nonetheless, he granted women a vital, if not essential, role in popular movements.

Vallès, spending his exile for his participation during the Commune (for which the *conseil de guerre* had condemned him to death in absentia on 14 July 1872) wandering between London and Brussels, responded to Clemenceau's proposal with *Les Blouses: La Famine à Buzançais (1847).* It appeared in twenty-four installments between 21 June and 28 July 1880.[33]

The advance advertisement for the feuilleton established both the author's credentials and the import of his writing.[34] Identifying him as "Jules V.," rather than by his full name, the first-page, first-column announcement referred to "the famous writer who has recounted misery with a superbly bitter and vivid style. . . . Under the Empire, the author saw misery intimately. . . . In *Les Blouses,* the drama of hunger is mixed with the grandiose drama of popular movements and the faces of these new resistors are illuminated by the spark of the barricades." By conflating France's past and present, its legacy of food riots and political revolutions, its dramas of hunger and barricades, the paper established the story's relevance.

Vallès, as a contributor to *La Justice,* made sense in many ways. The paper, as an advocate for amnesty for the exiled Communards, found in Vallès a symbol. The announcement further identified him as "the writer, mixed up in the most poignant events of that terrible year, who has had to live abroad for several years." Exile might remove his person, but never his words. Vallès, a veritable "écrivain engagé,"[35] had remained in regular contact with French public opinion, despite his exile. With the Assembly then debating an amnesty, the editors "counted on soon seeing his energetic face" and dedicated the rest of the first page of the paper to exhorting the government to move forward swiftly and decisively to resolve the status of the exiles. *Les Blouses* was still running in *La Justice* when the government finally adopted the general amnesty law on 10 July 1880. Freed from exile after ten years, Vallès returned to Paris on the 13th.

Les Blouses belongs to a lengthening popular tradition of the serialized novel, the *roman-feuilleton.* During the nineteenth century, two of the fastest growing sources of reading, the novel and the newspaper, combined to produce the *roman-feuilleton.*[36] In 1836, for the first time in France, Emile de Girardin published a novel, *La Vieille fille,* by Balzac "below the fold" on the front page in his new "industrial" paper, *La Presse.*[37] The practice had spread widely by 1880. Indeed, "the *roman-feuilleton* was the dominant literary genre of the 19th century."[38]

The serial novel of the nineteenth century drew inspiration from the growing fascination with history. From this convergence emerged the historical novel.[39] Departing from the assumption that traditional history could never render the past in its fullness, historical fiction could supply the spirit of the age, the drama of the past, and the complete character of past figures without sacrificing authenticity.[40]

However, serialization imposed a battery of constraints on the structure and cadence of novels, as shown in the unevenness of *Les Blouses*'s plot and the infelicities of its style. A story had to sustain interest from one installment to the next in a mere half page of newspaper a few times a week. Successful writers refrained from overburdening the reader with information (such as detailed description or too many characters) or a complicated plot that risked "losing" readers or made it difficult for them to pick up the thread in midrun. Each short installment usually relied heavily on dialogue rather than description, on action, on repetitive situations and characters, and on a "stock of ready-made clichés and images."[41]

Serialization required collaboration between editor and author. Editors sought novels that would advance their papers' particular agenda; therefore, editors dictated the rhythm of publication. This dynamic meant that most novels remained works in progress, even after publication had begun; changes in the number and frequency of installments often occurred in medias res. Editors sometimes urged authors to increase the number of installments of wildly popular novels, such as Eugène Sue's *Mystères de Paris* (1842–43), or to reduce the number when readers balked. Authors sometimes altered their narratives or characters to respond to changes in the current political situation or current events, making the serial novel one "evolving, creating itself with each installment . . . essentially in *status nascendi.*"[42] All of Vallès's novels appeared as *roman-feuilletons,*[43] and most underwent considerable editing before appearing later as bound novels. *Les Blouses* (which never appeared independently in Vallès's lifetime) also suffered from a last-minute reduction in length, which improved neither its literary merits nor the coherence of its narrative.

Vallès may have also chosen Buzançais as a subject because he knew that many of his contemporaries might still remember stories of 1846–47. By invoking Buzançais, Vallès could create a chain of memories that led through the Revolution of 1848 to the Commune and its brutal resolution. Subsequent amnesties accorded by the Second Republic to Buzançais's accused might foreshadow the fate of the exiled Communards. The story itself intersected with current concerns for amnesty for exiled Communards and the reemerging social agenda.

Vallès's moving account mixed "history," based on his research in several 1847 newspapers (mostly official/government papers) held in the Brussels Royal Library, and "fiction" by linking popular protest over subsistence and work to the formal politics of republican agitation on the eve of 1848. In his version a secret republican society seeks to exploit popular protest for political ends. No evidence suggests that such a secret republican society ever existed in Buzançais.[44] Otherwise, his streamlined and selective narrative of events of the disturbance adhered fairly closely to the records he consulted, and he matched several characters to similarly named historical counterparts. In some instances, he retained actual participants in the struggle but renamed them. In others, he retained names but reconfigured their roles. However, his main characters had no counterpart in the historical Buzançais, and his narrative of the episode itself extemporized on the official record by highlighting certain events and particular episodes within them.

What follows looks at three different aspects of this work. First, it considers Vallès's approach to four critical episodes: the initial interception of the grain transports, the Venin/Chambert fatal shooting and beating incidents, the three incidents involving women, and the responses of local elites and authorities to the disorder. Second, it explores the problematic interplay of the fictional and historical dimensions of the novel. And finally, it asks what Vallès and Clemenceau might have expected *Les Blouses* to achieve and how it could have participated in the particular debates of the era.

Vallès begins the narrative with an encounter among the principal characters, setting the stage for action by emphasizing both the hardship that the crisis had wrought among the peasantry and workers of Buzançais and the character of republican politics among the local elites.[45] His four main characters belong to two households that represent the dilemmas of the day and the book: one a peasant, the other a bourgeois, republican household. The peasant household includes a middle-aged (fifty years old), honest, hardworking man, Jean Fombertot; Marianne, his equally hardworking, honest, pragmatic wife; and their young granddaughter, Jeanne. Vallès often manipulated character names to generate contemporary resonances and may have done so in this case. The name Fombertot recalls Fombertaux, a Parisan communist in the years 1840–48. Marianne's name could simply suggest a common peasant of the era or, more powerfully, invoke the symbol of France. Jeanne could evoke Jeanne d'Arc, but this name carried more complicated and contentious political meanings. Despite Vallès's narrow view of female political rights, these women's names not only carry symbolic political significance but also, perhaps, acknowledge the power of women to effect social and political change.[46] A local, apparently unmarried doctor (and republican agitator), Bonnel, presides over the bourgeois household, where his young adopted son, André, is entering adulthood.

The story opens with the Fombertots' suffering. The crisis has made grain so expensive that they cannot buy food for Jeanne. We learn that Fombertot fasted the day before in order to afford bread for her, but today he has no alternative but to ask for charity from André. Fombertot literally embodies the suffering wrought by the crisis. His voice "trembles," his face is "sad," and his eyes "brim with tears." He is "crushed" by his struggle to find bread and "almost devoid of imagination" from the effort. He explains, "It is horrible to find that in making oneself sick, in killing oneself with work, one still cannot feed little children." He communicates his misery with his body: "head bowed, shoulders bent, as if . . . it were his fault that bread cost 24 sous for 4 livres." Fombertot is generally deferential before his social superiors ("a man made for work not struggle"[47]), but sheer desperation drives him to voice his plight. At such prices, he despairs, "how can anyone expect the poor folk to survive? We have given our last *liard* to the baker. Today nothing, nothing at all."[48]

Marianne, Fombertot's wife and Jeanne's grandmother, "the strong head of household," expresses her mounting frustration as a vulnerable member of the peasantry but also as a woman. She declares, "Bread! Ah! If I were a man, I, myself, would certainly find some!" She demonstrates her skills in improvising solutions as a dexterous practitioner of an "economy of expedients."[49] "I sold a memento from my mother. I promised her I would keep it forever, but bread didn't cost 24 sous [then]. I have money for a little bread in the pocket of my apron. There is some for today; we will see about tomorrow." She and her husband still muster enough pride to delay what appears an inevitable recourse to the humiliations of charity. When André offers money, they both defer. "Charity again, she murmured painfully, I know that there are good people on earth . . . but if you had to help everyone, the fortune of a millionaire would not suffice . . . it is so hard to hold out one's hand." Fombertot echoes his wife: "Let me have one more day without offering me charity . . . without having to ask for it."[50] Despite not having eaten for two days, when asked whether he is hungry, he "lies heroically" and says no.

Vallès's Marianne and Fombertot represent the honorable, worthy, struggling peasantry of France, characterizations diametrically opposed to prosecutor Didelot's representation of Bienvenu and his fellow protesters in 1847. Inclined to accept their difficult lot and willing to work hard, they find themselves miserable victims of a crisis created by dishonorable and unworthy "hoarders" and ignored by society. Vallès offers a striking example of the heedless, rich hoarders when André remembers stories of M. Brenas, a millionaire flour merchant whose son threw gold out of windows in Paris while "those who worked the earth and brought in the harvest did not even have water to drink." Although Brenas had no real counterpart in Buzançais in 1847, accusations of "hard-heartedness" occurred commonly, such as those leveled against miller Cloquemin for refusing to sell his flour to local consumers or those against Chambert for usury. Introducing the plight of Fombertot and Marianne at the beginning of the story compels sympathy and respect. Their mounting frustration at their inability to feed a small, defenseless child no matter how hard they work propels them to assert themselves and perhaps to revolt.

With the departure of Fombertot and Marianne, André joins his protector, Doctor Bonnel, at his "modest house" in the faubourg. Bonnel recounts André's legacy to him. He describes a father exiled from France for his republican convictions, forced to die in England, and who had left his only son to his trusted comrade in arms, Bonnel, to raise.[51] As they discussed how to make the current crisis serve the republican cause, they heard "a clamor" outside. A "great crush of men and women crammed together, milling around huge carts." They yelled, "They are ours!" The crowd had intercepted a shipment of grain.

Describing the interception, Vallès anthropomorphizes the grain itself. "The crowd speaks to the sacks as though they were men." Of the interception Vallès writes, "One might have called it the application of the Lynch law. These men and women seemed to have caught criminals. . . . On the carts they had heavy captives . . . with a rope around their necks like the hanged. . . . The sacks of grain were the prisoners!"[52] His analogy between the seizure of the grain itself and the capture of criminals further underscores the grim seriousness the people have attached to the object of their survival (and death).

Vallès introduces another fictional character into the narrative of the interception: *la vieille,* the Old Woman. She quickly emerges as one of the leaders of the disorder. This otherwise nameless widow, "with a marked face, yellow like copper under her black headdress, gray eyes, wrinkled lip, [who] stood erect on legs as thin as spindles" and whose voice "grated like the hinge of the guillotine," claimed command based on her experience of many earlier protests. Vallès clearly compresses into this striking female character the words and deeds of multiple participants from 1847. When she defends her right to lead with "I saw the Great Revolution!" she echoes 1847 rioter François Légeron's claim that he had "already seen three revolutions."[53]

In fact, as "the image of stubborn and heroic work, who had scraped the earth with her fingers to sustain life," *la vieille* holds impeccable credentials for an insurgent. A daughter of a jacobin,[54] she has lost one of her sons in combat in Africa and another during a coal strike in the Loire. "From this had come her hatred of everything associated with the government, those she called the hoarders and assassins, the hoarders of children and of grain." When authorities question her right to command, this "general in a wool dress and widow's headdress" orders her son to cock his scythe for defense (or aggression), "wielding it like a hunchedback bayonet."[55] Vallès contrasts the Old Woman's authority to that of the mayor of Buzançais, who "did not speak with the accent of command."

Around the Old Woman assembled many other honest and hardworking but miserable people. When the mayor challenged her authority to command the disposition of the grain carts, she drew on her memories of past revolutions, which also served as an education for others in the processes of popular government. She quickly organized a "tribunal . . . as in 1793" that included "as many women as men . . . because it involved soup and the cooking pot." When she asked for nominations, the assembly greeted this "novel idea" with a curiosity "that is a hunger as well." This education in the (by 1847 in historical time and 1880 in Vallès's time) art of democratic practice resulted in the election of the Old Woman, the mayor, the honest peasants Fombertot and Marianne, and a man named Monneron (Vallès named some of his characters after individuals involved in the historical Buzançais affair, though he altered the spelling of their names).

In 1847, Monneron had played a visible role in the events surrounding the interception and sequestration of the grain carts. Witnesses had reported that the forty-three-year-old carpenter, glazier, and inn owner had spent the night after the interception distributing free eau-de-vie and exhorting locals to "pillage and beat up the bourgeois."[56] Vallès's Monneron played a more laudable role. A largely self-made, rich man (whom the poor called "Monneron l'Aisé"[57]), he remained honest and a "best friend to the poor," to whom he readily extended credit and honorable assistance. He defended the needy, lecturing the mayor that "it was not fair that brave people who only asked to be able to work die of hunger instead . . . [and] that the famine was intentionally created by [those who] claim[ed] that there was no more grain so that the price of bread would rise."[58] He insisted that "It was imperative that the hungry have food." A *redingote,* he still made common cause with *les blouses.*

Throughout this episode, Vallès has the people receive lessons in democratization and social justice. For example, the Old Woman taught the assemblage of people to call the five chosen leaders "delegates" because "that was how one designated those who would speak for them when they went to find the bosses and the authorities." When the people debate what to do with the shipment they have captured, Monneron suggests taking it to the seat of local government, explaining that "the *mairie* is everyone's house . . . we will be the government and what we do will be legal."[59]

By the time the townspeople install the grain in the courtyard, night has begun to fall. The mayor orders the gendarmes (*les pantalon bleus*) to "put themselves in the service of the people," and they help build a bonfire for the bivouac. Thus, "they install on the *grande place* a source of heat—and of revolt!" Vallès further connects this scene to the bonapartist legacy. "It flattered the men of the village that they were camped like a battalion around a bivouac fire such as they had seen on the engravings of the eve of Austerlitz, with Napoleon sleeping astride a straw chair set before dying embers. However, instead of Napoleon, they could see the Old Woman sitting on a piece of dead wood, looking like a visionary."

The interception episode ends with an explanation supplied by Monneron to Candulier, the newly arrived brigadier of the gendarmerie: "We have stopped a convoy of grain, because the faubourg needs bread. The mayor understood our reasons, our rights: the reason of misery, the right of hunger. This grain will be distributed to the poor." When Candulier hesitates, doubting that the mayor would acquiesce to these demands, "the Old Woman, standing before the fire and radiating its red light, raised her right hand toward the sky and said, 'I swear it.' With her right hand she pointed to the sacks, 'Let's go, distribute it!'" Upon a second hesitation, the Old Woman announces, "It is Revolution!" and orders the sounding of the tocsin.[60] Monneron explains that once "we have gotten into it, we have to go all the way. If we give an inch, it's the end! They will know we are cowards, and they will sell us bread even more dearly . . . if they don't make us eat grass!"[61]

Vallès's account bristles with foreboding, perhaps playing to memories of his older readers as well as to the sensibility of his contemporaries. As Dr. Bonnel watches the mounting tensions, he worries ominously that "it smells of massacre and not insurrection."[62] When the crowd escorting the grain carts arrives at the house where the Fombertots live, Marianne's "instinct emanating from her race, tells her that this band of starving people would reassemble before nightfall, a herd of bulls who had seen red flags . . . and that there would be calamity." Nevertheless, she has no choice but to make common cause with them because "they were her sisters in misery." As the carts pass through town on the way to the courtyard, they move like "hearses." As day breaks over the courtyard, it illuminates "sad and cruel faces" and an "empty bread bin" put there "as a sort of symbol," which seems like "a standing coffin, ready to receive into its shadowy [interior] a murdered man."

Vallès leaves the scene at the town square to recount, in the next chapter, the struggles of local republicans to manage the rapidly deteriorating situation. When he returns the reader to the square, it has filled with those who responded to the call of the tocsin. They are planning an attack on the bolting mill belonging to the Coquelmin family.[63] Locals denounce this infamous clan, which includes one knave who loaned money at ruinous rates and another who hard-heartedly installed machinery that eliminated needed jobs. Their pasts make them ready targets for people now rendered increasingly desperate by a dawning realization that the mayor had abandoned them and broken his promise to distribute the seized grain. The crowd storms the mill and attempts to destroy this "damned pig, Capital."

In Vallès's version, after the attackers found money in the miller's office, only a few individuals took coins as souvenirs, and one took 40 francs because the miller long owed it to him for the purchase of his house, "but most flouted the money that rolled around on the floor. They scorned and spit on it. . . . They didn't consider that the money would make them rich for a year or even a day. They hoped to ruin a rich man, to bleed the purse of a hoarder—not to collect the drops of blood from the bloodletting, but to create chaos in his account books, where their sweat and tears were entered."[64] The attack on the account books echoes the Great Fear of 1789 and the assault on the land registers of the seigneurs. The capitalists of the 1840s (or 1880s) have supplanted the aristocrats of the ancien régime.

After destroying the mill and the account books,[65] they declare that "now we are all the same, the bourgeois and the poor! No more mill to bolt the grain and no more money to buy it in Châteauroux. Now they'll see what a famine is all about!" As the attack winds down, word arrives of a "convention" ordering an immediate reduction in the price of grain and a promise to sell at lower prices until the next harvest. Although many proprietors have signed it, several households have not.

Thus, Vallès leads readers to the mortal events in the Chambert house. The Chamberts remain one of the last households that had not signed the "engagement." Yet rich and poor alike are already congratulating themselves on an agreement cordially contracted, and "everything seemed over. Everyone intermingled, the bourgeois, the delegates and the crowd. And everyone shook hands. The poor thanked the rich and the rich seemed good friends with the poor."[66] The Old Woman knows better. "Through clenched teeth, she spits out bits of the "Carmagnole": "With lead, iron, and then bread." Nevertheless, this spirit of social unity results in choosing three delegates to go to Chambert's house and request compliance from him. When they arrive, they find one of the engagement's escorts, Velin, already there.[67] He enters with Fombertot while the others wait outside, "in order not to appear too threatening" and because neither Fombertot nor Velin "had ever had trouble with him." When they enter, "an old woman is there and even before they speak to her, she holds out a paper at the bottom of which are signatures. She has been forewarned and has added her name. 'And your son?' [they ask.] She . . . stammers, 'It appears that he has already sold all his grain and that he cannot accept [the engagement].' 'Then he will give money!'" This version imposes a coherent logic on the demand for money, attributed in the records to Venin's largely criminal predilections. Vallès has Velin demand money because Chambert has sold his grain and the proceeds could help the hungry crowd buy grain elsewhere. When the men begin to search for Chambert, Velin encounters resistance from the proprietor's servant, who fights back. In the midst of the struggle, Chambert appears with his gun and asks, "'Who goes there? . . . Who struck my servant? . . . ' [He then exclaims,] 'It is you!' The bourgeois raises his weapon at Velin and takes aim at him. The latter does not respond, but goes straight at the gun, grabs it, and tries to lower its barrel. A detonation! Smoke! . . . The man spins around, his entrails hanging from his stomach. 'I am dead! . . . ' [says Velin.] He falls backwards, his arms in the form of a cross. His smock is on fire. The gun blast has set it aflame." Fombertot leaps to put out the fire and save his friend, whose death (as Vallès's recourse to the symbol of the crucifix signals) represents either an expiation of the people's sins or a sacrifice to advance the popular cause, or both. He looks at him and cries, "It's a crime!" and turns toward the shooter and repeats: "It is a crime!"[68]

The minute the people in the street hear the shot, they charge into the house. They find Fombertot covered in his friend's blood, raising his arms to the sky and repeating, "It is a crime!" The crowd immediately begins calling for Chambert's death. The Old Woman gives her son a sign to brandish his scythe, and many others follow suit, "breaking the teeth of their forks to make the injuries more horrible and mortal." Although Monneron tries to make peace by counseling Chambert to put down his gun and surrender, the man flees in terror.

Vallès paints the vengeful crowd vividly. They track Chambert into a deserted shop "like a dog following the trail of a wounded boar intending to devour it." Just at that moment, André arrives "leading a half dozen men half in suits, half in smocks." They plunge into the "pile" of people, who exclaim, "They are republicans!" With that twist—a twist far removed from actual events at Buzançais—Vallès whisks the reader to a different scene altogether, which concerns only the actions and concerns of the republicans. In fact, Vallès never returns to the disorders at Buzançais. When the novel does consider what happened after the narrative shifted from the boutique where Chambert hid to the republicans, three months have passed and the guillotine's scaffold is under construction for the execution of three men for their part in the rioting.[69] Only then does the reader learn that Chambert had died. "Such rage was theirs! [The rioters] had plunged a pitchfork into his entrails [and] broken his skull with sabots."

With respect to the role of women, where the narratives of 1847 found evidence of brave women who either defended or were bourgeois, Vallès focused mainly on bravery among dispossessed women. Bourgeois women figure only briefly in his account, and then only in the republican story line. However, Vallès does invent two extraordinary major female characters, the peasant Marianne and the Old Woman, who offer important, if different, models of bravery and honor in the face of suffering and danger. Although the records of 1847 frequently reported women as leaders and active participants in the events at Buzançais, they had revealed the actual identity of only one, Anne Coteron. This forty-four-year-old widow and mother of two children had played a visible role in the Chambert household, threatening to harm Mme Chambert and kicking the prostrate body of M. Chambert with her sabots, contributing to his death. Vallès not only blends aspects of Coteron's identity into his two main female characters but also has them play considerably broader parts in his story. Among the protesters, only two men, Fombertot and Monneron, play equally important roles. Even then, the Old Woman distinguishes herself, especially as the leader of the entire popular movement.

Although age, stage in life cycle, and, at least superficially, personality separated these two female characters, by juxtaposing them Vallès asks us to consider them as parts of a continuum of historical development. Marianne performs the roles of a nurturing and assertive parent (of her grandchild), an honorable voice of duty, a loving (if critical) wife, but a reluctant insurgent. At middle age, she has seen hard times but holds on to hope.[70] She sustains feelings of "tenderness" toward her husband and grandchild "that one wouldn't have expected from someone so frustrated." When the people chose delegates to represent them "as judges of the hoarders . . . against the rich," they immediately named Marianne and her husband, Fombertot. Upon seeing the crowd arrive to collect them so that they can assume their new responsibilities, Fombertot defers to her judgment about whether to participate.[71] Although unable to find a caregiver for the little Jeanne—who thereby becomes, herself, "an unwitting delegate for little girls for whom the old people are unsure they can find bread"—Marianne feels herself too bound by solidarity with their "sisters in misery" to refuse. However, rather than perform the role of battle commander or agitator, Vallès's Marianne provides a more symbolic function. For example, when Fombertot expresses mounting frustration with his lot and when he marches with the crowd as their delegate, Marianne's forceful will has given him the courage to assert himself. Although she leaves the crowd (to put Jeanne to bed) as soon as they sequester the grain in the courtyard, her influence remains. The Old Woman wishes Marianne were present when she orders the popular delegates to the Chambert household, "in order to spur on Fombertot."

In describing Marianne's role as largely identifying what to do and motivating others—mostly men—to do it, Vallès depicts a reality often observed in the politics of provisions. For example, the records from Buzançais emphasize the shaming role performed by women from the faubourg during the grain interception. They twice pressured the male workers in the charity workshop to take action. Vallès describes Fombertot struggling with his fears: "But he had Marianne's words in his ear, 'Tomorrow it will be your turn to find [bread]!' He remembered her tone and gesture. She had done everything she could. . . . She counted on him for Jeanne's bread. She would need more as soon as the loaf bought with money from the sold memento was gone. He was scared, not knowing where to find what she demanded with such urgency."[72]

However, Marianne never appears again—except as a voice in Fombertot's ear—until the end on the day of the executions. As the executioners "threw the three cadavers without their heads in a basket . . . someone shouted, 'They murdered them! and they sent my husband to the galleys.' It was . . . Marianne, who carried Jeanne in her arms, screaming and crying. The little girl opened her mouth and said, 'Grandmother, I'm hungry!'"[73] With the experience of the recent months behind her, Marianne resembles the tougher, more pragmatic, and politically adept Old Woman in tangible ways. Now effectively a widow herself, Marianne has at least one "revolution" behind her, the experience of suffering that attends such traumatic events, and the prospect of more, if not greater, misery and injustice ahead.

The Old Woman, as an experienced revolutionary with sixty hard years—and their attendant revolutions and travails—finds herself in a situation unlike Marianne's. Her husband has died and left her the head of the household. Her remaining son has assumed the role of comrade in arms. She coordinates the interception of the grain shipment, arranges for the election of the delegation to represent the people, forces the gendarmes to back down when they try to discipline the crowd, organizes the visit to the Chamberts, and authorizes the exercise of summary justice against Velin's killer. She represents both the revolution of 1793 and the Inquisition. She derives her models of severity, discipline, and awe from both the Terror and the Catholic Church. Yet in her "hatred of everything associated with the government" she expresses Vallès's desire to fight against all forms of oppression—monarchist, bonapartist, or jacobin—and to embrace violence as the means to win. In 1879 he had written, "Only by violent blows has the idea of justice has been forged that will save the weak and poor from servitude and hunger."[74]

Both Vallès's female characters reflect his general assumptions about women's roles in society and contentious politics.[75] In 1870 he had declared, "Hunger? When mothers see that their children are hungry, the children must eat. Then it is possible that, when the children cry, there will be such attacks on granaries and casernes, that cannon will not be able to drive them back."[76] Women, she argues, derive their revolutionary impulses first from their status as mothers. In *Les Blouses,* Vallès has his republican doctor Bonnel explain, "Something tells me that blood is about to flow. . . . Women will cry 'Bread!

Bread!' When women get involved, when mothers take their children by the hand before the *mairies* or hospices, the casernes open and vomit soldiers. The red pants [soldiers] will advance, and first prayers will be thrown at their heads, then stones, and finally, the captain will order the troops to fire and cadavers will pile up on the pavement."[77] Women's maternal roles give them courage to act and speak that men often lack.

Portraying the common people at Buzançais, Vallès presents two strong female characters in Marianne and the Old Woman as insurgents and a much weaker, hesitant male character in Fombertot. While Fombertot offers a model of probity that counters many contemporary representations of peasants and workers as malingering and potentially violent brutes, without overromanticizing him (as Vallès accused George Sand of doing), he appears highly deferential before authority, easily cowed, and entirely too hopeful that current notables will offer assistance in time to prevent actual starvation. He still struggles with an unwillingness to accept that local elites and his government have abandoned, and will again abandon, him, his family, and his fellow peasants and workers to their suffering. He tells Bonnet, "We have only lacked bread for a few weeks, but that will not last . . . one has to hope that the bourgeois will take care of it. And there is the good God."[78]

Perhaps Vallès suggests that, for men like Fombertot, the burden of formal status as head of household makes risk taking more difficult to contemplate than for women, who can act on a different set of imperatives. Whatever the explanation, Marianne proves able to move beyond the boundaries of deference more readily than her husband and sees their situation more lucidly. She suspects more than he that the system of paternalist charity dispensed by the current regime will not suffice to allay suffering. And Marianne, not Fombertot, decides that, despite the risks, they both must assume their responsibilities as delegates and march with their neighbors.

In the end, neither woman suffers as harsh a fate as their male counterparts.[79] Marianne never faces arrest or prosecution; Vallès leaves her to face future injustices wiser, angrier, less hopeful, and alone. When, at the end, little Jeanne again cries for bread, the reader wonders about their fates. The Old Woman avoids prison (or even the guillotine), but only by feigning insanity and submitting to incarceration in an asylum.[80] Her ability to claim this defense in order to avoid punishment, probably execution, lies in persistent gendered assumptions about women's irrational nature, assumptions that society denied to men.[81] In the end, reflecting a historical pattern of punishing women less severely than men after subsistence movements, Vallès leaves a picture of brave women of the people. Despite the odds, they risked "dying riddled with lead, rather than from an empty gut."[82]

The mix of history and fiction in *Les Blouses* offers a new and nuanced picture of the interactions between elites and common people and among elites themselves in Buzançais. As we have already seen, many of the previous accounts and the debates they provoked—available to Vallès as he researched the project—highlighted the local failure to prevent and then quell the disorders. Vallès portrayed local elites and authorities (apart from the secondary, parallel, and entirely fictional story of republican agitation) in order to represent local social and political relations in a small town in nineteenth-century France.

When he describes social relations in Buzançais, Vallès focuses in particular on the gulf separating the bourgeoisie from the poor, the character of the exploitation fostering tensions, and the damage wrought by the dependency embedded in paternalism. Vallès's Buzançais—much like the town presented in the 1847 documents—harbors a polarized society. Aside from the self-made artisan, inn owner, and newly rich Monneron, no one from the middle ranks of society appears in the story to fill the social space or to mediate between the desperate, hungry working poor and the hard-hearted rich property owners. The mill owner Coquelmin and his family control access to food, jobs, and credit; the property owner Gaulier has publicly declared that "he would rather throw his grain in the river than give it for less than five francs the *hectolitre*"; and the fictional "hoarder" Brenas wastes money on his profligate son while ignoring local needs. The Old Woman calls the property owners "aristocrats," thereby linking the ancien régime with her contemporary society, signaling the need for yet more revolution. Frustrated but honorable poor, like the Fombertots, cannot afford food. Vallès has, however, accentuated the social polarization by neglecting to note the recent establishment of a charity workshop meant to allay, if insufficiently, the worst suffering.

In such a society, riven by powerful tensions, the role of authorities could prove crucial. But neither in Vallès's Buzançais nor in the 1847 town itself did authorities acquit themselves with the right mix of compassion and discipline to halt the excesses or to relieve distress. Although Vallès has again taken the artistic license to streamline the local administration, to reconfigure certain actions, and to focus most heavily on two characters—the mayor and the brigadier commanding the gendarmes—he presents a reasonable approximation of their dilemmas.

Both officials appear overmatched by the situation. As in 1847, the mayor arrives in the faubourg Les Hervaux just as the women have rallied men to intercept the grain shipment passing through town. As he arrives, leading some gendarmes (the "blue pants"), the Old Woman and crowd ready for a fight. But "the blue pants hesitate. The mayor himself does not speak in a commanding voice [and] invokes the law with a weak voice."[83] The Old Woman further outflanks him when she welcomes him to join the "delegation" that will speak for the people: "You will be the fifth member with your tricolor scarf. You will be the president, as my father was in the district [in 1793], and what we five decide will be done."[84]

The mayor suffers a further failure of will later, when orders come from the justice of the peace to dissipate the crowd, "by force if necessary." As the small brigade of gendarmes prepares to comply, the mayor begins to protest the order, but "suddenly, he realized that he had in this an opportunity to flee responsibility and peril." "Affecting energy and anger," he announces he will seek a counterorder and leaves the scene. The gendarmes find themselves "not mistreated, but annihilated, stifled, and caught up in the whirlwind." Upon the mayor's return, the crowd and carts have already arrived in the courtyard. He declares that he has orchestrated a magisterial coup. "Instead of obeying the justice of the peace, the blue pants will put themselves in the service of the people."[85] They will supervise the distribution of the grain as soon as the brigadier arrives in town. This said, "the poor mayor, broken with fatigue and emotion," announces that he needs rest "and asked for permission to withdraw." After extracting his support for the popular distribution, the delegation grants his wish. He leaves, never to reappear.

The brigadier of the gendarmerie, Candulier, finds himself in a similarly difficult situation. He arrives from a mission in Châteauroux to discover the people camped in the courtyard around the captured grain. Monneron explains to him, "We have stopped the grain convoy because the faubourg lacked bread. The mayor understands our reasons, our right. . . . This grain will be distributed to the poor, and he designated you for the distribution."[86] When he protests, the Old Woman inquires, "Would you rather amass your men and fire on us?" He swears he does not want to fight, but the alternative—to distribute the grain—paralyzes him. The ringing of the tocsin saves him from having to act.

Vallès suggests that because the mayor and brigadier "know everyone" in the crowd and have long ties to the community, they find it difficult to act decisively. The mayor "knew that there wasn't a dishonest person . . . in the entire mass of rebels." Similarly, the brigadier has lived many years in the locality and even married a woman from the region. "No one looked at him as an enemy, because he had never been malicious to the honest people."[87] In this passage Vallès represents the ways in which such community ties could facilitate the protesters' capacity to act and inhibit authorities' reactions, whatever the criminal code might say.

The ultimate repression comes from outside Buzançais, not from within. Soldiers arrive from Châteauroux, led by the *commissaire de police* and the *procureur de roi*. Arrests, trials, then death, galley, and prison sentences follow. In Vallès's story the wrath of the Orléanist government falls heavily and implacably on the common people but spares the republican conspiracy. When Bonnel defends those destined for the guillotine as less guilty than many others, Albert Delacamp, the prefect's secretary and Bonnel's comrade from school, explains, "Yes, we are going to suppress three men who are . . . only accomplices in an attempt against authority and the Code. The [Code's] texts decree death for this. . . . We need an example. . . . The defense of society demands it."[88]

Furthermore, the very ambiguity inherent in the politics of provisions complicates even more the application of martial law and force. Faced with actual suffering by working people—and not malingering vagabonds—local authorities had long found it easier to negotiate than to repress. As Monneron had reminded the mayor, "It is not fair that decent people who only ask to work die of hunger . . . poor people must eat." Confronted with the face-to-face reality of misery and bound by traditions of patronage that shape mutual obligations, Vallès's characters hesitate before turning to repression.

As the documents derived from the event itself reveal, negotiation and conciliation might appear as weakness and cowardliness. Was the mayor weak or pragmatic? Did he act tentatively and placatingly, out of craven fear or because he found himself forced to acknowledge, as Monneron said, that the poor had "the reason of misery and the rights of hunger"? This sort of dilemma of authority appears in other novels of the era, such as Emile Zola's *Germinal* (1885).

As it turns out, however, Vallès's novel seems to have foundered precisely on his representation of local authority—and of the mayor in particular. In his postscript, which offered a brief explanation for reducing the number of installments and shortening his story, he explained: "I [did] not have . . . all the necessary documents. I have conserved, I believe, the true character of this hunger riot; but I have, it appears, attributed to a hero of this painful drama a role marked by weakness, when on the contrary the man was full of devotion and humanity. This is . . . information . . . that honorable people, witnesses to the riot, have sent to me in the interest of truth. I refer to the mayor of Buzançais in 1847. I hasten . . . to restitute the portion of courage and honor to the person whom I have poorly sketched from my exile."[89] Vallès implied that Buzancéens themselves had written, thirty years after the fact, to complain about his portrayal of the mayor. No records of this correspondence remain.

That hard memories of the episode remained, even this late, should not surprise. When prices rose during the crisis of the 1850s, the gendarmerie watched public affairs carefully. In 1853, a police report detailed how both Buzançais locals and authorities behaved when the price of grain spiked in October: "Tranquility still reigns in the city of Buzançais, despite the high price of bread, which never stops worrying the municipal administration. The population watches with a certain fright the state of things, particularly since threats have already been heard. M. the mayor is in a position to open public works and wants to keep them open this winter in order to aid the needy."[90] In fact, the mayor, a member of the mill-owning family, the Cloquemins, might have had reason for particular vigilance, since he had witnessed firsthand the disorders of 1847. The Cloquemins dominated municipal office for much of the nineteenth century. The son and notary, Théophile Cloquemin, served as the mayor of Buzançais after the Revolution of 1848 until 1857. Another member of the family, Fernand Cloquemin, served from 1865 until well into the 1870s.

Civil suits over compensation for property destroyed during the disorders also lingered into the late 1870s.[91] The Cloquemins themselves remained persistent parties to the claims throughout the century. In addition, families relentlessly petitioned for the release of their relations who still languished in prison. The Third Republic government finally released the last rioters in 1873.[92] Tensions must still have smoldered long after the fact,[93] and the appearance of *Les Blouses* in 1880 clearly threatened to reignite them.

Thus thirty-three years after the original episode, controlling the narrative had again become a priority. Vallès wrote to the editor of *La Justice* on 20 July 1880, while installments were still appearing, that he was going back to work on it and "finish it . . . at the theater of the intrigue [Buzançais]," but apparently he never made it to the Indre and never, himself, took up the novel again.[94]

Whether the novel could have benefited from more development and nuance does not detract from the fact that its mixture of history and fiction had already interwoven multiple themes that linked the years 1847, 1848, 1870–71, and 1880. An intent to create these connections helps explain Vallès's interjection of the fictional republican story line. This serious departure from the emerging traditions of historical fiction—which usually stayed closer to actual historical events—helped elaborate axioms that had long sustained Vallès's political thought: that the "people" furnish, and should continue to furnish, the proper and sufficient sources for the fight for social justice and freedom; that the cause of social revolution demanded unity rather than factionalism, and simple pragmatic principles rather than complicated, abstract theories; that desperate people will commit desperate acts; and that the proper response to desperate acts in the name of social justice is forgiveness.

Vallès constructs a narrative of an active, secret republican conspiracy in Buzançais that, by 1847, had long hoped for the proper moment to strike at the Orléanist monarchy. Although apparently no such conspiracy lurked in Buzançais, his portrayal of the tensions between two republican factions and the larger concerns of the Orléanist government about the threat they posed, does not depart far from the history of the era. Only six months later, a series of republican banquets in fact bolstered a mounting assault on Louis-Philippe's authority.

In the novel, Vallès explores two strands of republican ideology. One, represented by Doctor Bonnel and his comrade in arms, Professor Juliard, embraced a social agenda that sought alliances with the common people—"a battalion in *redingotes* and in *blouses*"—to demand social justice. Bonnel described an ideological lineage that connected back to "Babeuf, the Carbonari, and the Secret Societies," linking his political agenda back to the failed revolutionary efforts of Babeuf's Conspiracy of Equals of the late 1790s, the republican Carbonari (in French, Charbonnerie) of the Restoration, and the mostly Parisian secret societies of the 1840s. This form of "radical republicanism" shared a great deal with the socialist and communist movements of the 1840s associated with Auguste Blanqui, Charles Fourier, and Etienne Cabet.[95] The other strand, represented by the Captain, an army officer, endorsed a political republicanism that had little affinity for either socialism or the common people. Vallès cast the two factions in terms of the political newspapers that most clearly represented their views in the 1840s: Bonnel with the *Réforme* and the Captain with the *National.*

At every turn Vallès uses debates among republicans to emphasize the legitimacy of "the protest of the hungry" rather than to celebrate republican ideology. More than halfway through the novel, as the republicans deliberate what to do, Bonnel puts the events in Buzançais in their wider context:

> In all the poor departments in France, everywhere the price of bread rises; and the people's anger ends up rising, too, because their suffering is horrible! . . . I have seen bands of men and women running through the countryside, shoeless, in rags, holding out their hands to ask . . . for charity [and] presenting their skinny children. I have seen . . . these processions of the hungry, these promenades of ragged penitents, these "chains of misery" sadder to encounter than a chain gang heading for the galleys. . . . I have also seen bands of workers in tatters, walking with their heads lowered, feet bleeding, stopping before the gates to châteaux, before the doors of the rich, raising their arms and asking for bread as one would ask for a pardon for a crime.[96]

He argues that the republicans must make common cause with the hungry for justice, no matter what the cost. The uprising at Buzançais provides "a unique occasion for a social war": "A man has been killed at the very moment when he came to ask, unarmed, that [the proprietor] sign a promise about the price of grain. Will the crowd dismember the killer? Possibly. But that is precisely why [we should] go to the side of the rioters at Buzançais. . . . The Revolution demands that we expose our honor, that we commit ourselves to solidarity with crimes, when those crimes are public crimes born of famine and the product of despair. . . . We have to go to the side of the unfortunate . . . we must cover [them] with the mantle of an idea."[97] Bonnel worried some about the risks for people on the margins—who, with their families, already balanced perilously close to famine and annihilation—if they joined with the republicans, who believed that even "defeat would constitute a step for the right to work and bread." But, having no family himself, except his protégé André, he gave less thought to immediate, concrete consequences than to the long-term, abstract principles at stake.

The Captain's position, however, prevails long enough to paralyze the republican movement. He renounces efforts to make common cause with the protesting Buzancéens. After hearing news of the violence at the Chambert household, he refuses to participate, explaining, "The movement has turned into a massacre. It would sully the flag to associate it with murder. . . . I refuse to associate myself . . . with a company of miserable carriers of pitchforks. . . . I wish to be shot in combat; I would hold my head high on the political scaffold, but I do not want to go to the galleys or be guillotined as an accomplice to a whirlwind that will obey neither you nor me, but only obeys its instincts like a wounded and ferocious animal." Bonnel retorts that the Captain does not have the "courage necessary" for such a combat, that he opts out "because the *blousiers* . . . have started the action with scythes and pitchforks." He concludes, "You love the Revolution, perhaps, but you do not love the poor."[98]

The debate between Bonnel and the Captain reflects real tensions present —in the politics of the century—during the Revolution of 1848 and again during the Third Republic when Clemenceau's Radical Republicans embraced social reform against the moderates who resisted. Moreover, the Captain had pointed out a further complication—the people seemed to refuse republicanism of any stripe. Fombertot had already refused Bonnel's attempts to recruit him to the cause. When, during the heat of the disorder, André tried again to rally him with "big words of Justice and Misery," Fombertot responded, "It is wrong to side with the republicans. There may be a few honest hearts among them, like your adoptive father, but the base is bad, full of convicted criminals! . . . I have a wife and child. I don't know what the Republic is!"[99] Honest peasants logically feared association with frequently imprisoned political agitators.

Vallès casts Fombertot and his neighbors as believing that they acted legitimately, a belief rooted in their traditions of "moral economy." Fombertot repeats frequently that "We have done no wrong" in claiming rights to grain when it was scarce or cost too much for working people. Yet they also recognized perfectly well the illegal character of seditious political conspiracies. In the end, why would *blousiers* risk their necks for the republican *redingotes*?

Attempts to recruit other Buzancéens to the republican cause find no traction either. They categorically refuse to participate. Already suspicious when they see a young man "dressed like a monsieur, in the middle of workers' vests and smocks," they respond with revulsion and threaten to hurt André when they discover him speaking of republican politics. Bonnel tries to explain the disconnect: "The *porte-vestes* cannot know as much as the *porte-redingotes*. They do not understand that we want to have republican insurrections because we want to prevent their decimation by famine."[100] Efforts to bring the republican cause and the cause of the people together in any meaningful way fail over lack of communication. The people find it hard to understand the principles of republicanism; they see only men who speak too abstractly about politics when the cupboard is bare and who cavalierly risk lives for uncertain, future ends.

In the end, the people's suspicions seem well founded. Both the republican and the popular causes fail, but the government represses the popular revolt with a punitive harshness the republicans escape almost completely. The bourgeois republicans turn out to have defenders in high places, among others of their class. Bonnel, wounded in the fracas, discovers that his "former schoolmate" and "friend from childhood" Albert Delcamp has become secretary to the prefect. Now Delcamp "is for the white flag. He believes in the king, God, force, dogma, the fatality of misery, and the necessary enslavement of the people."[101] Despite the enormous gulf that separates their political beliefs, Bonnel and Delcamp have always remained cordial because they share the same memories. Delcamp explains, "My precepts order me to be pitiless toward any insurgent . . . but my friendship orders me to come to your aid." He proves faithful to his word. He makes the common people pay the price with the guillotine and galleys, with prison and the insane asylum; but no republican faces trial. Delcamp allows Professor Juliard and André to escape abroad.

The Captain—Bonnel's comrade in conspiracy—"the republican who cares only for revolutionaries with white hands," guards the guillotine, ready to "kill the people, if the people let out a cry of pity in favor of the unfortunate ones who will die." With the execution of the poor, the ties of class have prevailed. Bonnel dies of his wounds, André and Juliard will return to fight another day, but three working men will never see another day. Many others (Fombertot included) will see the future from the galleys or prison, and the Old Woman will spend the rest of her days in an insane asylum. Her son fled town to avoid arrest but can never return.

Les Blouses resonates powerfully with Vallès's concern to show the relentless tribulations of the struggle for the "Social," the need to find means of communication between the *redingote* and the *blousier,* and the tragic consequences of social injustice and exploitation. The very message that desperate people's sheer misery can drive them to desperate acts calls for readers to understand and, ideally, to act on the behalf of those who suffer. It warns against blithely exploiting the people's misery and frustration without considering the risks they will run. It also calls for clemency, even appeals for amnesty for those who act out of that misery. *Les Blouses* does not justify violence, but it does contextualize it. It evokes memories of France's revolutionary past. The plight of the Buzançais rioters and the republican agitators resonates with both 1848 and 1870–71. Roger Bellet has observed that Vallès had always sought to write "for the people, even if, before 1870, he understood them only vaguely . . . after 1871 and even more so after 1883, Vallès learned that writing for the people meant neither writing as the people nor writing to be read only by the people. . . . [He decided] to put his writing in the service of the Revolution."[102]

When Vallès returned to Paris, he quickly plunged back into political journalism and literary criticism. In 1883, he resumed publication of his paper, *Le Cri du peuple,* which he had founded in 1871 to contribute to the political debates of the Commune. The paper combined news reporting with political commentary and several genres of serialized literature. Each page of the paper featured a different feuilleton, but the front page often featured Vallès's own works.[103]

When Vallès died in February 1885, not quite five years after his return to France, his colleagues continued to publish the paper. In April the editors announced that they planned to publish *Les Blouses,* "one of the most powerful and least known works by Jules Vallès."[104] They further described it as "a grippingly current novel . . . of the rising price of bread, of famine, the battle for survival, the struggle of the poor who have not yet become insurgents, but who, as new resisters, revolt against death. One will read terrible scenes revealed by the light of the barricades, poignant episodes which make this work truly human and social, where under the title, *Les Blouses,* the dramas of famine are mixed with the grandiose tragedies of popular movements."[105]

When the novel appeared, however, the editors had changed the subtitle. In place of the original subtitle, *La Famine à Buzançais (1847),* it now read *La Famine à Charançais, 1847.* The novel appeared, almost daily, in twenty-five installments from 15 April until 12 May 1885. Aside from the name of the town, they changed nothing in the text. Yet this decision to give the town a fictional name underscores the political significance contemporaries still attached (or the editors feared they still attached) to the interpretation of the events themselves. The editors believed that the story itself still mattered as a "social novel," even as they eliminated its role as a (semifictionalized) history of protest in France.[106] In the end, this small alteration signaled a belief in the story's continuing power to evoke issues of social and political relevance in early Third Republic France.

CHAPTER FOUR

Popular Publishing between the Wars

The question of expensive bread and grain are [again] today on the agenda. This is not the first time that such a threat of dearth has occurred in France.

—Pierre Bouchardon, "La Jacquerie de Buzançais"

Soon after World War I, two new narratives appeared, in 1919 and 1925, respectively, an era by which living memory of 1847 had died out. Each narrative presents a dramatically different version—textually but also, for the first time, visually—of the Buzançais affair. In 1919, a Paris publisher, Edouard-Joseph, produced the first book version of Vallès, *Les Blouses,* and engaged Mario Simon to illustrate it.[1] In 1925, the Librairie Hachette's monthly popular magazine *Les Lectures pour tous: Revue universelle et populaire illustrée* included in its section "Récits historiques" a two-part history of the Buzançais riots.[2] The author, Pierre Bouchardon, and illustrator, B. Leclercq, offered a different twist both textually and visually. This chapter looks at the historical context for each narrative and the particular character of each version. It explores the contributions that visual images made, compares the images, and speculates about how they reflected and contributed to French culture and politics in the interwar years.

BUZANÇAIS, 1919

The year 1919 proved a turbulent one. While the Paris Peace Conference dragged on from January to June, the world did not stand still. France itself, exhausted from four years of war, witnessed the resurgence of anarchism, the acquittal of Socialist leader Jean Jaurès's killer, continued support for the Socialist Party and the affiliated labor union, the Confédération générale du travail (CGT), mounting labor unrest, several serious threats of a general strike, and anti-immigrant violence—all combined with the general horror at recent losses and devastation.[3] Moreover, the twentieth century had witnessed a renewal of food riots,[4] some with revolutionary potential, as in 1917 Russia.

The wartime Union sacrée French government, formed to encourage cohesion against the enemy, had never eliminated the tensions fracturing France in 1914, but it had, at least for a while, muted them in the interests of the common good and encouraged a subsequent memory of a "national sentiment" of unity.[5] Even before the war ended, however, conflict reemerged to challenge the myth of unity.

Specifically, the subsistence issue continued to prove explosive in France. During the war, conscription and casualties had siphoned off most adult peasant males, as hundreds of deserted villages testified; agricultural productivity had consequently declined.[6] Everyone suffered; yet persistently rising prices made many urban consumers feel that farmers benefited, perhaps excessively, from the demand for food for the civilian and military populations.[7] The resentment had some basis in experience. Because agricultural prices had remained high throughout the war and inflation benefited debtors most, many rural proprietors had in fact managed to pay off debts, buy more land, and enjoy a higher standard of living.[8]

Although wages rose, they failed—at least until 1916—to keep pace with prices. Middle-class consumers—such as those in the liberal professions, civil servants, and those living on *rentes* and other incomes hurt by inflation—found their standards of living threatened, even after the armistice. During this period, the newspapers reported daily on the *vie chère* (the high cost of living).[9]

On several occasions, the French government intervened to fix and then freeze grain prices (in 1915 and 1918) and to impose rationing in many towns. After 22 January 1918, Clemenceau's government even compelled the heretofore privileged city of Paris to undergo bread rationing even more stringent (300 grams versus 600 grams daily) than that long in effect in many other cities in France.[10] After February 1918, the French government pursued an increasingly aggressive policy of economic controls.[11] Despite these measures, however, the government "remained loyal to the values of liberalism" in principle and "had only reluctantly, and in an *ad hoc* manner, taken the most urgent measures."[12] At the time of the armistice, prices had reached two and a half times their level in 1913.[13] The exchange value of the franc continued to fall.[14]

The suffering wrought by the war had not ended with the armistice in November 1918; chronic scarcity and real hunger continued to haunt many. On 2 February 1919, the French government ordered that trials of price gougers take place before courts-martial rather than the civilian criminal courts.[15] The rising labor movement, marked by the formation of the Third International in March 1919, the "spectacular growth" of membership in the Socialist Party and the CGT in France, and widespread work stoppages led the government to grant certain concessions, such as collective bargaining (March) and the eight-hour day (April).[16] Despite these concessions, the massive Paris May Day demonstration organized by the CGT in 1919 ended in repression that included two deaths and more than seven hundred injured, suggesting that, "aside from organizing the peace, the fundamental problem that confronted the government was social agitation inextricably linked to the Russian Revolution."[17]

This general climate of tension again accentuated the ambiguities the Buzançais saga illustrated so well in the past. The problem of hunger, misery, and revolt—the politics of subsistence and social rights—reinforced by a more articulate and assertive labor movement, found a potentially broad audience after the war.[18] In some ways the Vallès novel's fictional republican story line might have played just as well (if not better) in 1919 as in 1880 because, after years of wartime government intervention in more and more aspects of French society, restoring a functioning peacetime republic in France ranked high on the political agenda. External threats notwithstanding, internal concerns about authoritarianism from the right and left, the role of the presidency in the Third Republic, and the vote for women, among other issues, kept the debate alive. In February 1919, an assassination attempt on "Tiger" Clemenceau's life by anarchists stoked the fire.

The same prolonged war whose long-awaited peace witnessed continued suffering had also released new passions for living and new ways to express and market them. While many French (and Europeans in general) still struggled in 1919 to make ends meet, others—those who had avoided the worst effects of the war and those who had even profited from it—translated these passions into consumption. One scholar (and contemporary) of the book trade in the interwar years described "the luxury of the book" as "only one element of the rampant desire for luxury that seized hold of society, and which was manifested in the least trinket, in fabric, clothing, furniture."[19] "Having experienced agony, Europe took up again a taste for living [and] pleasure in all its forms. A beautiful book was one form of pleasure." Another observer emphasized the pent-up bibliophilia imposed by the war: "People went on reading" during the war, he explained, "and by Armistice Day four years of scrubby volumes on bad paper had built up a powerful longing for decently published books of any sort."[20]

New publishers rushed to serve this hungry postwar market.[21] Before the war, twelve to fifteen publishers had supplied the small French market for fine illustrated books (*livres de luxe*)—limited editions printed on special paper and accompanied by illustrations; after the war, more than one hundred supplied a market that had grown tenfold.[22] These books sold to several categories of bibliophiles who paid from 40 to 100 francs for "mass-produced" editions limited to 3,000 copies and as much as 5,000 francs for printings of no more than 150 copies.[23]

A flourishing market existed for books called *demi-luxe,* serviced by publishers who targeted the less wealthy French book enthusiast but still supplied, for a price of around 20 francs, special paper, illustrations, and stylish finishing. Publishers aimed to "satisfy the artistic needs of the average client," "to develop their taste for the beautiful,"[24] and to encourage market growth for their products. One contemporary commentator lamented this trend: "New publishers are springing up like mushrooms . . . [they] dream of money, not reputation. Unrestrained by modesty—or by taste, knowledge, and conscience—they abandon themselves to a flood of publications which swamp the market."[25]

Even these publishing tyros—ignorant of the trade but nonetheless eager to profit in it—feared market instability (and the uncertain value of the franc) in the period immediately after the war. Soon both new and experienced publishers probed the market with books by known authors with a following. Many also turned to illustrations made of wood engravings, which they could print at the same time as the texts, reducing the costs of printing.[26]

In 1919, a small Paris publishing house, Edouard-Joseph, published a short list of illustrated novels, including the first book edition of Vallès, *Les Blouses.*[27] Although this *maison d'édition* never produced more than a handful of works annually until its disappearance in 1923, its brief existence reflects many characteristics of the era's publishing history. It published limited editions, some portion of which appeared on special paper.[28] The printer numbered each copy, starting over with each paper type. The advantage of a small print run lay in the fact that the quality of the type and illustrations deteriorated as the run continued.

Edouard-Joseph's decision to include Vallès's story of the riot at Buzançais in its 1919 catalog typifies the publisher's business strategy of focusing on recent but largely unknown works by known authors. It also published books by two Nobel laureates and three books by a winner of the Académie française's Grand prix de littérature.[29] While all three authors clearly had a significant critical following, Edouard-Joseph chose works recently completed or not yet disseminated in France. For example, the Nobel laureate Maurice Maeterlinck had just finished his play *Le Bourgmestre de Stilmonde* in 1918, and although he had written his comedy *Le Miracle de Saint Antoine* in 1904 (previously translated and performed in German and English), this 1919 edition made it available for the first time in French. Romain Rolland's *Voyage musical aux pays du passé* collected for the first time several essays on music history written between 1900 and 1910. Francis Jammes had only recently completed the three short stories—*Le Noël de mes enfants, La Rose à Marie,* and *Une Vierge*—that appeared in 1919. *Les Blouses* stands out as the only book published posthumously. Although Vallès had an established reputation as an author and essayist of the late nineteenth century, his work certainly did not carry the public recognition of Balzac's or Zola's.[30] Recognition came as much from his notoriety as an exiled Communard as from his literary qualities. Many critics had complained that his work rang too loudly of politics to rise into the realm of truly great writing.

Reviewing several authors published posthumously in 1919, literary critic Fernand Vandérem, writing for *Revue de Paris,* defended Vallès's qualities as a writer, observing that "if a little melodrama spoils the ending, certain silhouettes such as the old jacobin woman [and] certain episodes such as the attack on the grain, attain grandeur."[31] Vandérem applauds the possibility that the publication of *Les Blouses*—"this history of a modern Jacquerie, of villagers thrown into revolt by famine and the lack of grain"—will put Vallès back on the literary "agenda." He compared *Les Blouses* favorably with the late nineteenth-century novel of a different sort of *jacquerie,* Eugène Le Roy's *Jacquou le croquant.*[32]

The review highlights a difference between *Les Blouses* and the rest of the books on Edouard-Joseph's 1919 list but also helps to contextualize it. Most of the other novels on the list—Maeterlinck's *Bourgmestre* and Jammes's *Rose à Marie,* for example—either speak directly to questions posed by the Great War itself or else avoid obvious political engagement. Despite his declared intention not to discuss Vallès's political career, "which was that of all rebels: agitated, painful, sensational," Vandérem finds himself drawn back to its because of its contemporary relevance. He admits that Vallès's politics have adversely affected sales of his books because "politically at this moment, Jules Vallès is a sort of bolshevik, a sort of Sadoul, only yesterday a militant communard, a survivor of Satory. He stinks worse than a cigarette butt: he smells like a wall [used by firing squads]. And the social outcry that attaches to his person extends, by contagion, to his literature."[33]

Vandérem observes that Vallès's very political position makes him even less palatable in the postwar nationalist climate because "Vallès is [in effect] guilty of the crime of parricide. He has attacked the Alma Mater, a capital crime that one would make him pay for dearly." Vandérem nonetheless urges those who share his [Vandérem's] opinions to read *Les Blouses.* He argues, "It would do them no harm to reread . . . all of Vallès . . . to learn about what a great writer, the great novelist our literature has lost—and conserved—in him." The review seemed at once to validate the publisher's relegation of *Les Blouses* to the category of "curiosities" and, still, to resurrect it. Certainly 1919 was not 1847 (when the riot actually erupted) or 1880 (when Vallès wrote his novel), but some issues of 1847 (and 1880) might readily resonate in 1919: scarcity, social justice, and republicanism.

The publishing house distinguished *Les Blouses* from its other 1919 works by commissioning an obscure book illustrator, Mario Simon, to produce images that differed in style and content from the other books' illustrations. For its other publications, Edouard-Joseph had employed woodcuts from distinguished artists who had had, and continued to have, important careers as artists and especially as illustrators.[34] Mario Simon, however, appears to have illustrated no other book during this period.[35]

Whatever his provenance and destination, Simon's 1919 illustrations illuminate both tone and subject in Vallès's work for an audience certainly unfamiliar with either the novel or the historical riot at Buzançais. Although critics often worried that illustrators who produced images for works of another era risked introducing inaccuracies ("He is a designer, not an archeologist"), Simon's work seems, instead, to complement the tone and politics of Vallès's story.[36]

Of course illustrations, no matter how seemingly "appropriate" or "faithful" to the text, always introduce another level of interpretation. As Philip Stewart has argued, "Illustrations cannot be a direct transcription from language to image."[37] Furthermore, he observes, the insertion of illustrations into a text constitutes a "sort of defiance . . . an assertion of a coequal viewpoint." Think, he urges, "of illustration as being 'against' rather than 'to' the text, probing its tacit ambiguities if not its weaknesses. Although both image and text can be metaphoric: they cannot always—and perhaps cannot usually—adopt each other's metaphors and thus are tempted to substitute, literally or otherwise transmogrify the metaphors they feed upon in the other medium." Stewart argues that "illustrations are a form of representation that refers simultaneously to the world (for recognition of its visual signs) and to the text."[38] Text and image depend on each other for meaning; both influence the reader/viewer's interpretation of things read and seen. Illustrations can profoundly influence the interpretation of texts by directing attention to specific gestures, characters, and episodes while excluding others. This impact might in fact distort the author's purposes, but with Vallès dead and gone, Simon had only to please himself, the publisher, and (ideally) buyers of the book.

For the Edouard-Joseph edition, Simon provided eleven full-page and three small images. For the eleven major illustrations he chose seven episodes from the popular movement itself and four from the republican conspiracy. Most of these depict moments pivotal to Vallès's drama. For example, Simon portrays the protest organizers trying to convince Marianne to join the "delegation" with her husband, Jean Fombertot; Fombertot confronting his fears to assert his right to food; the people deciding to attack the bolting mill; and deciding to visit the Chambert house. Only one image, which depicts a hunger march (a "chain of misery"), shows a suffering people bowed and miserable. The others show a grim but determined and assertive people who know they face risks but nonetheless decide to act. None of these images portrays the oppressors against which the people revolt.

The frontispiece (Fig. 4.1) is a dark, intense image of the bonfire, the *feu de bivouac,* around which those who guarded the intercepted grain convoys spent the night. The fire reinforced their courage to assert their right to subsistence and encouraged others to rally together as a community. Vallès's related text reads:

> It was almost midnight. They had been in the courtyard of the *collège* many hours. There reigned a sort of discipline of silence and rest. . . . Some were gathering their thoughts, others had dozed off on this spot that resembled a corner of the bourg in the Vendée where a battalion of Chouans might have stopped. Except, however, no one was making soup: this was a bivouac of hunger.
>
> But when the Old Woman said, "We will sound the tocsin!" memories of

> history awoke among those whose fathers, during the time of Robespierre, had been guillotiners or guillotined. . . .
>
> The bivouac fire now illuminated a spectacle capable of scaring eyes used to seeing only fires of branches and dry leaves in the desert of the fields. The least certain and the most calm from the faubourg of Les Hervaux were there with the look of people who aren't afraid of rifle shots. The growing light of morning and the agonizing light of the embers which no one fed any more, mixed together to create a pale and sad day which showed sad and cruel faces. The scythe of the Old Woman's son, the hunchbacked bayonet, seemed to disembowel the low sky.[39]

In the illustration, gaunt, grim, and resolute faces crowd around the fire. Some hold their tools—pitchforks, scythes, axes, and clubs—which will also serve as weapons and flagstaffs the next day. Men and women—the old and young sit nearest the fire while others stand close by—face (what must be) the Old Woman's son, who lifts his scythe as standard and battle blade in visual representation of the scythe turned for attack (*à l'envers*) that troubled witnesses and authorities in 1847. Its shadow in the background further emphasizes its ominous potential. The text reminds readers that, for some of the people assembled, the bonfire evokes memories of past revolts—both revolutionary (the time of Robespierre) and counterrevolutionary (the Vendée and the Chouans)—while it signals less political, but still real, danger for others. The people personify no particular political sentiments, although the scythe seems vaguely political, like a battle flag, and the people do project the concentrated intensity of those who have suffered and will stand it no more.

This illustration reinforces Vallès's intention to depict the sober determination of an honest but tormented working people to no longer bear the injustices that prolong their misery. Together with the text, this image stands in stark contrast to the official testimony of 1847, which made the bonfire the center of a carnival-like celebration of drunken irresponsibility and violence. The viewer sees an assembly of people meeting around the fire as a deliberative body—staring out at the viewer. They seem poised to act, though their grim faces portray little hope of success.

Yet only the viewer who has already read the book knows what the illustration means. In 1919, few could know the story of Buzançais in advance: the generation that could remember the event itself had died, and few of the living

Fig. 4.1. *Bivouac, Bonfire, and Battle Standards.* From Jules Vallès, *Les Blouses: La Famine à Buzançais* (1847), illustrations by Mario Simon (Paris: Edouard-Joseph, 1919).

had heard firsthand stories of it. A world war had intervened to divert attention from events of the nineteenth century. Only the edition's adjacent title page gives any signal for interpreting this frontispiece. As Stewart has suggested of illustrations, "the picture is 'worth a thousand words' only when you already know the words." Unlike a picture hanging in a gallery, an illustration never appears "without a verbal context, and the more that context is complete, the more it 'means.'"[40] Simon's frontispiece sets a mood to accompany the title, but only reading the story could locate the mood in its appropriate context.

The edition's final illustration (Fig. 4.2) of the popular movement provides few clues for situating it precisely in the text. Even after reading the text, this depiction of a more general moment—with the crowd held back at the behest of the Old Woman—does not mark a particular episode in the plot but rather a state of expectation. Her son/lieutenant—his scythe / battle weapon / standard at the ready—joins her at the front. All the figures but one stare directly out at the property owners / authorities / viewer, challengingly, seeming to wait for a response. The figure on the Old Woman's left—perhaps Fombertot, with a gun in a less menacing position as he rests upon its upturned barrel—looks back into the crowd. Is he looking for signs from among those in the crowd for what will happen next? Does he look to the multitude for reassurance?

Above the crowd hovers a skeletal, Valkyrie-like form. For whom does she

Fig. 4.2. *Specter of Hunger; Specter of Death.* From Jules Vallès, *Les Blouses: La Famine à Buzançais* (1847), illustrations by Mario Simon (Paris: Edouard-Joseph, 1919).

wait to spirit away to Valhalla, the hall of fallen warriors? For those viewers who might miss the allusion to a Valkyrie in the skeletal figure that looms above the crowd, the effect was still haunting. An earlier image of Fombertot struggling to decide whether to continue and risk possible repression by supporting the protest or yield to traditional habits of deference shows him in the embrace of yet another skeletal specter of doom. Combined, the two images suggest that protesting Buzancéens were driven by the specter of death.

Figure 4.2 captures a moment just before the repressive force of the state descends, expressed in the grim expectation on the faces looking directly out at the viewer. Simon seems to invite the viewer/reader into the story, perhaps as if the protesters were asking whether the viewer would join ranks with the people or stand against them. The story's dénouement (the guillotine) suggests that the viewer has failed the protesters just as completely as did the property owners and authorities, by permitting and participating in repression and not supporting resistance to the injustices of hunger. Simon visually reinforces the contemporary relevance of issues that Buzançais has served in its past.

Two other images of the popular movement merit note. The first depicts an active (rather than expectant) crowd before the bolting mill (Fig. 4.3). Only this illustration directly indicates the goals and concerns of the protesters. No other image refers specifically to hunger or work; no other image signals the targets (human or material) of popular wrath. But Simon has located the mill at the center, clearly the focus of the people's attention. Most have their back to the viewer as they lean into the hill they will charge to "capture" the mill. On higher ground, the Old Woman leads and animates the crowd, which presses toward the mill. In the foreground a man with an upraised sickle (perhaps evoking bolshevism) urges those behind him (including the viewer?) to join them.

Simon's depiction of this episode takes more liberties with the story than do his other illustrations. Vallès's text supplies a context for the assault on the mill by describing the debate over the hard-heartedness of the Coquelmin family. After one member of the crowd explains that "the youngest son has installed a machine that does the work of twenty men and has put us out of work," another responds that "the machine has broken our arms." Vallès's description of the gestures that followed are at odds with the image presented on the next page: "One of those [in the assembly] who had had his arms broken had an idea . . . he raised his useless arms above the people: 'Let's go demolish the mill!' It was like the vertigo that makes cattle crazy at the fair. 'To the mill,

Fig. 4.3. *To the Mill!* From Jules Vallès, *Les Blouses: La Famine à Buzançais* (1847), illustrations by Mario Simon (Paris: Edouard-Joseph, 1919).

to the mill!'"[41] Yet the raised arms that animate the crowd in the illustration are neither broken nor male; they belong to the Old Woman, who thus plays an even more substantial role as an icon of popular protest in Simon's illustrations than in Vallès's novel.

As in the novel, Simon's images locate women in more central positions than they actually took during the event itself. As we have already seen, women had often played important roles in early modern and modern French subsistence movements; by the late nineteenth and twentieth centuries struggles over food had become even more exclusively a female, or housewife's, domain. By 1880, when Vallès wrote *Les Blouses,* he tended to interpret women's roles in protest movements as mostly emanating from their familial responsibilities; by 1919, this assumption drew strength from an increasing female predominance in more recent subsistence movements.[42]

Earlier chapters of this book have focused on *textual* renderings of four particular episodes central to the story of the Buzançais affair: the initial interception of the grain transports, the Venin/Chambert fatal shooting and beating incidents, the three incidents involving women, and the responses of local elites and authorities to the disorder. The *illustrations* reflect a different set of choices about which episodes to emphasize. For example, Simon offers no depiction of the initial shipment interception, which figured as crucial in the records from 1847 and in the Vallès text.

He does supply an image relevant to the Chambert episode (Fig. 4.4). However, the viewer can "recognize" its relevance only by the illustration's physical location in the text, not from the image itself. Rather than some aspect of the confrontation with Chambert, Simon portrays a moment of anticipation. The Old Woman, the delegates, and several others (numbering "10 or 12" in Vallès's text) assemble outside and prepare to visit the Chambert household to collect its signature on the engagement to lower and fix grain prices. The Old Woman—with her son (holding his scythe[43]) at her side—stands, staring out at the Chambert residence / the viewer, holding her hand out to halt the men and women designated to march with her. They have just sent Fombertot and Velin forward into Chambert's house, declaring they will wait outside ("so as not to appear threatening" to the Chamberts[44]). Again, by capturing the moment just before one of the story's major dramas occurs, Simon seems to invite the viewer into the story, to join ranks with the people or stand against them. The illustration leaves the viewer uncertain about what will happen next.

This image, together with Fig. 4.2, presents dark, straight-on views of serried ranks of common people, armed only with tools or flags, resolutely facing or perhaps marching toward a grim encounter of some sort. Simon's depictions powerfully evoked the work of the most compelling socialist illustrator of the prewar generation, Théophile-Alexandre Steinlen (1859–1923), particularly his front-page illustration for an 1894 issue of *Le Chambard socialiste,* in which his work regularly appeared, and for the 1902 musical rendition of Eugène Pottier's

Fig. 4.4. *At Chambert's: The Calm before the Storm.* From Jules Vallès, *Les Blouses: La Famine à Buzançais* (1847), illustrations by Mario Simon (Paris: Edouard-Joseph, 1919).

1887 poem/song "L'Internationale." While the illustration for "L'Internationale" portrayed only men carrying flags, the drawing for the Marxist newspaper *Le Chambard* places Marianne in the center of the front rank of men wielding tools.[45]

In the spirit of Vallès's novel, Simon has also placed two women at the center of his illustrations: Marianne and the Old Woman. Marianne negotiates her and her husband's participation in the protest; the Old Woman animates the assault on the mill and disciplines the crowd before Chambert's house. Other women appear with men in the illustrations at the center of the protesting assemblies. Against this representation of strong, assertive women, however,

Simon supplies another image of women as the principal mourners in the "hunger processions," in the "chains of misery" walking barefoot, as in a Lenten religious ceremony, behind a life-sized crucifix (Fig. 4.5). Again, Simon elaborates on Vallès's text, which describes hunger marches of "tattered penitents" of both men and women, to create an image of a religious procession of women. Drawing on long-standing cultural and iconographic traditions, Simon's gendered image associates women with the "Passion of the Cross," mourning for the dead, the miserable, and the innocent. He deploys images of women to "figure moments of breakdown or crisis" and to "embody death and survival, horror and heroism."[46]

Fig. 4.5. *Tattered Penitents in Chains of Misery.* From Jules Vallès, *Les Blouses: La Famine à Buzançais* (1847), illustrations by Mario Simon (Paris: Edouard-Joseph, 1919).

Simon's illustrations completely separate the plot of the popular movement from that of republican revolutionary agitation, which Vallès intertwines in his novel. No Buzancéen elites or authorities appear in any of his representations of the popular movement. None of the republican illustrations engages the viewer as directly as those about the popular movement. No figures stare out at the viewer or seem to ask him or her to choose a side. The republican figures appear completely absorbed in their own worlds, mirroring Vallès's portrayal of their callous disregard for the problems of subsistence and existence troubling the popular protesters.

Simon's illustrations largely complement the spirit of Vallès's work without substantively misleading the reader about plot or details. Perhaps most important, the majority of his images call upon the viewer to participate, to position him- or herself with or against the cause. They seem to ask: What would you do at this moment? This active involvement of the viewer in the story, before the story's next action is known, calls upon contemporary sensibilities to confront the issue of social justice and the proper role of protest, a call entirely appropriate to the turbulent new era in which Edouard-Joseph issued the novel. The publisher may or may not have had an overtly political mission in publishing Vallès's novel; even a purely commercial motive could explain the choice. Just as the war itself and anxieties about the war dominated much of the literature of the postwar period, so too did concern for social justice, social revolution, and the nature of republicanism.

Soon, however, the political atmosphere changed in France, as did the functions of stories like that of Buzançais. In 1925, Pierre Bouchardon (1870–1956), a career magistrate with a lifetime of service in French civil, criminal, and military courts, wrote a two-part history of the Buzançais affair entitled "La Jacquerie de Buzançais." He published it in the successful, popular monthly illustrated magazine *Lectures pour tous.* A year later he reprinted the story—this time without illustrations—in his 1926 collection of infamous "true" crime stories drawn from the nineteenth-century records, *Crimes d'autrefois.*[47] Bouchardon's emphasis on the criminal character of the Buzançais affair clashed with Vallès's version. Far from a paean to the repressed, Bouchardon's story of Buzançais constituted just one of more than twenty histories of famous crimes, or *affaires célèbres,* for which he established a significant reputation in the 1920s and 1930s.

After a brief stint (1893–95) as a journalist for the daily paper *Le Matin,* Bouchardon followed his father, a defense attorney, into law. He chose the magistracy, and during the decade preceding World War I he had held the posts of head clerk (*chef de bureau*) for criminal affairs for the Ministry of Justice (1908–12) and investigating judge (*juge d'instruction*) in the department of the Seine (1912–14). Immediately after the war exploded, the newly formed Union sacrée government under President Raymond Poincaré called Bouchardon to serve as *capitaine-rapporteur* (the military equivalent of the civilian investigating judge) for the Third Conseil de guerre, whose jurisdiction included not only the peacetime responsibilities of assuring the general execution of military justice in cases such as desertion and insubordination but also extended to jurisdiction over investigating and trying wartime incidents of treason. Bouchardon thereby found himself playing instrumental roles in the treason investigations of Mata Hari, the Bolo affair, and, most important, the Caillaux affair. The last targeted Joseph Caillaux, a prewar pacifist, Radical finance minister (1899–1902), and prime minister (1911–12).[48]

After the war, the government assigned Bouchardon to the presidency of the Cour d'assises in Paris, where he served from 1920 to 1928. He deplored the weakening of the president's role in the Assize Court, a change that dated from the early Third Republic. To Bouchardon, the "reform" had turned the president, once "an absolute monarch," into a "constitutional kinglet."[49] The law (19 June 1881) had removed the power of the court's president to issue a summary of the trial just before sending the jury off to deliberate. Bouchardon explained that this authority, limited only by the president's "conscience," had empowered the president to "direct personally the jurors in the exercise of their functions." He had seen this role in action before 1881, when he attended trials as a child, and Bouchardon clearly thought it essential for public order and the proper management of the jury. Expressing a widely shared view, he disdained juries for their "dangerous omnipotence," which sometimes produced the "spectacle, as scandalous as it was paradoxical, of a correctional court condemning the perpetrator of a slap, while an Assize court acquitted a murderer."[50]

Bouchardon sneered that one often found in the jury "equal doses of silliness, malfeasance, and fear," which made it a "flawed" and unreliable instrument of justice.[51] He admitted that if juries were "eliminated . . . I would not mourn them." His memoir, written in 1953, reflected a pronounced sympathy for the Vichy government's vitiating "reform" of the jury system.[52] He also declared in his memoir that the 1881 reduction of the president's power effectively meant that the incumbent had, "especially in Paris, abdicated" his position, as demonstrated by his "fear" of and "capitulation" to the defense lawyers who "usurped" his power and controlled the jury.[53] Bouchardon's lifelong attitudes about the moral and disciplinary authority of the courts and the roles magistrates should play in public order emerged repeatedly in his stories about crime and the dispensation of justice.

Bouchardon increasingly cast himself as a last bastion of judicial independence and a brave defender of the prerogatives and dignity of the magistracy. His dogged investigation of the Caillaux affair (as well as his political affiliations with the Union sacrée government and the one that followed it, the right-leaning Bloc national) ultimately resulted in his political marginalization in the mid-1920s, when the political climate changed and the elections of 1924 returned the Cartel des gauches—a loose alliance between the Radicals, Socialists, and several smaller left-wing parties. This new government restored Caillaux's civil rights and then named him finance minister.

Bouchardon certainly believed himself the target of political retribution. Caillaux had, after all, openly despised and condescended to his interrogator, describing him as "stout, always unshaven, and rarely bathed."[54] Caillaux also accused Bouchardon of partisan politics and right-wing extremism, pronouncing him a "reader of *L'Action française*" and "saturated to the marrow with the religion of the state." This, Caillaux believed, had led to his merciless persecution at Bouchardon's hands.[55] Caillaux's loudest defenders came from the left: Radicals, Socialists, the Ligue des droits de l'homme, "who considered his sentence iniquitous, called his case 'the new Dreyfus affair,'" and agitated for an amnesty.[56] Bouchardon could then cite Caillaux's rehabilitation as "evidence" of his professional marginalization by the Cartel des gauches. He described in his memoirs his "time of disgrace" wrought by the elections of 1924, which had "brought into power . . . the friends of those against whom I had had to investigate. . . . I quickly understood that they intended to make me pay dearly for the independence that I had manifested with regard to certain lackeys of the regime, which our capacity to forget had reintegrated into their former posts. Only [the law of] irremovability of judges . . . protected me from revocation."[57]

Instead, he watched "all my colleagues pass me by."[58] He believed firmly that the Cartel des gauches continued to block his advancement until the elections of 1928 "gave the Chamber of Deputies another political orientation" by returning a government, the Union nationale, headed by Raymond Poincaré, under whose wartime Union sacrée goverment Bouchardon had fared well. Then "the ban was lifted," and he received a promotion to the Cour de cassation, France's highest court of appeals.[59]

During the 1920s a receptive audience emerged for Bouchardon's conservative morality tales of crime and punishment. The situation in France did not settle happily after 1919, as many had hoped it would; moreover, the "social malaise" that emerged in the postwar period continued to haunt many sectors of French society. The concessions granted to workers immediately after the war (rights to collective bargaining and the eight-hour day) did not quench their demands. In February and March 1920, the CGT organized strikes among the railwaymen and miners in the Nord, which triggered repression. On 1 May, bloody violence broke out in Paris between strikers and police. The government called out the troops, sent in strikebreakers, and fired workers. The severe suppression of a series of strikes in 1920 and the birth of the French Communist Party in December 1920 prepared the ground for the emergence of a vocal and increasingly powerful labor movement during the interwar years.[60]

When elections in May 1924 returned the Cartel des gauches, the new government undertook a series of domestic measures that included amnesty for deserters and those condemned by the Haute Cour. The transfer of assassinated prewar Socialist leader (and pacifist) Jean Jaurès's remains to the Pantheon (and the toleration of a Communist Party demonstration in Paris), combined with other measures aimed to advance social solidarity, generated heightened fears on the right of communism and revolutionary disorders. The pursuit of *laïcité* flew in the face of significant Catholic opposition. All these changes aggravated France's financial instability and heightened virulent debates about how to solve it. It also provoked a conservative reaction that bolstered Bouchardon's audience.

While stewing about his failure to advance, Bouchardon got an opportunity to write for the popular magazine *Lectures pour tous.* He explains in his memoirs how he came to write about "causes célèbres" for this widely disseminated monthly publication from one of the largest publishers in France, Hachette: "One day . . . the *directeur* of *Lectures pour tous,* the kind M. Jacquin, asked me if I could evoke, for the magazine, my memories of the spy trials [from the war]. I decided to try and, under the title, 'Dramas of Espionage,' I wrote a brief article for the July 1920 issue. . . . [Meanwhile], in June 1920, the *Revue de France* began to publish 'The Murder of M. Fualdès' by Armand Pravel. . . . What a difference from the inept police novels that bad public taste had [heretofore] made fashionable!"[61] Noting the success of this genre, Jacquin convinced Bouchardon to submit another contribution to his magazine in 1921, this time the story of a murder at the château of Chamblas in 1840. But Bouchardon complained that the editors had "mutilated" his work "because of the rules of the publishing house." They demanded illustrations inserted "right in the middle of the text, which often required leaping twenty lines at a time and last minute cuts . . . not always done with discernment."[62] Although Bouchardon fretted about assaults on "propriety" and the "juridical errors" that such publications permitted in the interests of fashion, he thought himself an appropriate author because he could avoid the traps awaiting those less well versed in the law and historical sources.

Most important, his position as magistrate gave him access to the actual dossiers of past cases, supplying a documentation lacking in most similar works and enhancing the verisimilitude of his own contributions. His narratives brim with information and quotations culled from the original documents; he frequently cites historical studies and draws upon the genres of legal narrative, fictional narrative, news reporting, and historical narrative to lend authority to his voice to substantiate his work. Beneath this cloak of documentation, however, Bouchardon cavalierly manipulates the evidence. He alters quotations, realigns the sequences of events, and even assigns culpability to historical actors when no corroborating evidence exists. Bouchardon's skill in summarizing the "facts" of a case before sending the jury out to deliberate enhances the apparent authority of his work. He intersperses his narrative with magistrate-like judgments about appropriate behavior and proper procedure. Clearly he thought that tales of crime could edify as well as entertain.

Bouchardon deployed tales of crime and repression in the service of both entertainment and moral order. In style and vision, he hoped to emulate Balzac, for whom he declared a life-long reverence. Balzac's work "has always seemed as vast as the world. . . . Every time I write a book, I always ask for an epigraph from him."[63] He took inspiration from Balzac's description of the crime stories published in the *Gazette des tribunaux*, as "novels published in blood rather than in ink."[64] Even reviewers saw an affinity between the two, noting their passionate interest in "criminal psychology" and masterful investigation of it.[65]

Bouchardon found the genre appealing and smugly thought himself entirely suited to it.[66] He consequently began to write more frequently, especially after the Cartel des gauches blocked his promotion to the Cour de cassation (Appeals Court). During the hiatus in his public career, from 1924 until May 1929,

Bouchardon wrote some fourteen books containing at least one and sometimes multiple "truthful" accounts of past, infamous criminal cases, stories of terrible crimes that editors and Bouchardon believed would titillate readers.[67] He explained that editor Albin Michel encouraged him to substitute the word "crime" for "mystery" in his titles, a signal that crime stories had great commercial appeal.[68] He also became a regular contributor of stories to *Les Lectures pour tous,* and his name often appeared on the cover as a writer recognizable to their readers, a surefire indication that both the author and his work had the kind of marketability that appealed to the relentlessly profit-motivated Hachette.[69]

By the time Bouchardon began writing for *Lectures pour tous,* it had already gained an important place in French culture.[70] Before and during the war, it had appeared twice a month as a small-format, illustrated popular literary magazine, founded in 1898; after the war Hachette published it only once a month but increased each issue to approximately 150 pages of serial novels, plays, historical narratives, travel and exploration narratives, and news items. Seeking the broadest audience, male and female, young and mature, from all classes, *Lectures pour tous* informed its readers on matters of current interest: from fashion advice to commentaries on *la vie chère;* from descriptions of the "new" man or woman to keys to identifying the female American tourist in Paris; from travel stories of Africa or Japan to details of future technology. Each issue also included photographic essays, and a steady stream of house illustrators provided images for each entry. At a cost of 3 francs 50 centimes an issue (slightly more than a two-kilogram loaf of bread in 1925), it reached a wide audience.[71]

In the June and July 1925 issues, Bouchardon published a two-part history of the "Jacquerie of Buzançais" under one of the regular feature headings, "Nouvelles et récit historique" (Short Stories and Historical Narratives). One of Hachette's regular illustrators, B. Leclercq, provided six images of various sizes.[72]

An introduction establishes the story's timeliness: "The question of expensive bread and grain is today on the agenda. This is not the first time that such a threat of dearth has occurred in France. [A situation] exploited by a band of rioters, it even provoked, seventy-five years ago, a Jacquerie. . . . Our eminent collaborator, M. P. Bouchardon, helps us relive the bloody scenes of this poignant historical narrative. Nothing is more tragic than this rigorously exact reconstitution of a country uprising that bathed the little city of Buzançais, in the Indre, in blood."[73]

By 1925, monetary crises and flash inflation had several times rattled postwar France, so that high prices remained prominent in the news and memories of the recent past. Yet here the editor emphasizes not claims for justice for those consumers, or struggling peasants and workers, menaced by high food prices (as Vallès's novel had) but rather a bloody tragedy exploited by a "band of rioters." The term *jacquerie,* as Vallès had employed it, resonated in the popular culture with peasant revolts against medieval seigneurial oppression. As used by elites in 1847, it had connoted a threat to the propertied. Bouchardon, seconded by the editors, clearly thought French readers in 1925 particularly sensitive to stories of public order restored by gendarmes and troops of the line. Bouchardon proclaims the crimes at Buzançais "so atrocious that the judicial annals have never had to record a memory of such an agony."[74]

Even the illustration that opened the story (and preceded the text) (Fig. 4.6) could foster a different set of expectations than the frontispiece to Vallès's novel. Peasants and workers (dressed in smocks and carrying pitchforks, scythes, and axes) assemble on one side of the bridge that crosses the Indre in Buzançais. They appear to be heading, with some hesitation, somewhere on the other side. Even after one reads the narrative, the particular moment illustrated remains unclear. Perhaps the illustrator, Leclercq, has chosen to represent the start of another workday, perhaps a moment when peasants and workers see a grain cart passing through town and ponder whether to let it continue its route or intercept it, perhaps the moment before the assault on the mill, or perhaps the moment when the forces of repression arrive. The viewer/reader has few clues but can clearly sense something afoot in Buzançais. A dynamic different from that in the Simon illustrations for *Les Blouses* operates in these illustrations. Leclercq's images emphasize motion, as the perspective and pointing gestures lead the eye across the bridge. Simon's illustrations, in contrast, suggest restraint—e.g., the Old Woman holding the protesters back.

Although the viewers cannot tell what will happen, they might infer a mood from gestures, postures, and facial expressions—ranging from curiosity to intense determination—of the peasants and workers. But the illustrator represents another aspect as well: a mean suspiciousness, best seen in the face of a man in the foreground carrying the basket near the bridge. He glares back at a child who bends to pick up a jug, which he has perhaps dropped. Overwhelmingly, men compose the crowd. Their hunched and grasping appearance may signal either the physical costs of labor, a cowardly disposition, or a lack of

Fig. 4.6. *The Bridge to Destiny.* From Pierre Bouchardon, "La Jacquerie de Buzançais," *Lectures pour tous* (June and July 1925).

good breeding—in character—which contrasts sharply with the "upright" posture (and character) of the well-bred.

Bouchardon begins his narrative with a story of a fictional *jacquerie* against a cruel aristocratic landlord on the eve of the Revolution of 1830, derived from the aforementioned popular novel *Jacquou le croquant* by Eugène Le Roy (1899). In Le Roy's story the court ultimately acquits those who rose up against their oppressor. Bouchardon comments that this outcome could happen only in fiction, unless it came "from some terrifying scene from the revolutionary period, that the author of Jacquou has transposed in time, after having changed everyone's name." Bouchardon regularly peppers his story with literary allusions. Apparently, however, he does not know (or perhaps disdains) Vallès's version of the Buzançais affair, since he never mentions it.

Bouchardon follows the fictional story of Jacquou's *jacquerie* with another tale of an actual event in Hautefaye, when a crowd assembled on market day and brutally murdered a local notable during the early days of the 1870 Franco-Prussian War.[75] He concludes that "these country uprisings that arrive like a groundswell and, in an instant, turn into some sort of hideous scene, were not all that rare during the last century." But, Bouchardon declares, "the Hautefaye affaire was a flash in the pan [*un feu de paille*]; the Buzançais affair was a great fire [*une grande incendie*]."[76]

Bouchardon supplies context for his account of the tragedy to follow: a succession of bad harvests, poor transportation, rising prices. He invokes the historian Thureau-Dangin's work on the July Monarchy for his conclusion that its "palliatives were insufficient . . . and certainly too late." He continues, "Misery was widespread," "the wind of *jacquerie* blew and serious disorders erupted in many places" because "the peasants and workers were convinced that grain was being transported out of France." He explained that "to manage these riots, troops had to be called in. They repressed. It would have been better *to prevent* it."[77]

Bouchardon applauds the efforts of the municipal government and the propertied for opening a charity workshop to "relieve the suffering of the poor class." But, such "excellent" efforts "were not understood." Workers who "could have found higher paid labor elsewhere" "invaded" the workshop. Instead of working, "they made speeches. They made too many speeches." Not only did they "incite hatred," but they also spoke of "particular revenge" that targeted specific property owners. Bouchardon harks back to the revolutionary club movement when he concludes that, "in less than a month, the workshop had become a club, a veritable foyer of insurrection." The lifelong magistrate, now entertainer and edifier, substantiates his denunciation of the workshops by quoting some of the threats witnesses had reported hearing, such as Légeron's remark that "I have seen three revolutions. Let them make another one. *I'll turn my scythe around* and we'll see."[78]

Bouchardon's narrative heavily emphasizes a movement with overtly revolutionary intent, not a riot of desperate people seeking relief from their misery or a protest movement for the right to subsistence or existence. Many times during his account, he invokes the word "revolution" to interpret events. For example, he hints that had authorities thwarted the first shipment interception, they "could have stifled the incident from which the *revolution* began." He declares that "even before the people from the countryside respond [to the tocsin] call to war, *revolution* had already begun to rage, aware of its force and ready for the worst excesses." Bouchardon declares that, when the prefect decided to return to Châteauroux and leave Buzançais to its fate, this departure "left *revolution* the master of the little town."[79]

Bouchardon supplies a brief but telling narrative of the shipment interception that occurred on the first day of the protest. Leclercq follows the narrative with an illustration. The narrative begins by closely following the actual 1847 dossier, especially the act of indictment. It contains many details: two carts, each pulled by two horses, carrying ninety-one sacks of grain headed for Issoudun stopped at an inn owned by Roulet Isidore in the faubourg Les Hervaux. Bouchardon characterizes the neighborhood's population as "miserable and turbulent." Not surprisingly, then, "immediately, a crowd formed, composed principally of women."

As the crowd gathers, Bouchardon takes the opportunity to launch into another judgment about proper behavior: "The most elementary prudence would have told the cart drivers to whip up their horses and depart swiftly from this dangerous zone. But . . . not only did they unharness their horses, but they took a table at the cabaret where they had a leisurely meal . . . , accompanied by coffee and liqueurs."[80] While they dallied, rumors arose and sped throughout the town. Women ran to the charity workshop to gather reinforcements, and "riot began to organize itself."

When the drivers—"weighed down by feasting"—reemerged to head on their way, they found they had missed the window of opportunity. Neither the mayor nor the three gendarmes, who had by this time arrived, could open a passage for them because more and more "workers from the charity workshop were constantly arriving."

Leclercq's illustration appears two pages after Bouchardon's description of the interception. It depicts the moment when the mayor (his official sash at his waist) attempts to negotiate with the crowd assembled outside the inn. Two huge carts of grain line up behind him, along with the drivers and at least one gendarme. While the mayor (clearly unarmed) holds his hands open at his side displaying a gesture of conciliation or at least nonviolence, the two men who confront him appear more aggressive. One even has a weapon elevated, seemingly to initiate an assault. Several groups of men and women listen to the exchange. Leclercq has chosen to illustrate an exchange between the mayor and two men, although the records (and even Bouchardon in a backhanded way) suggest that women not only started the interception but also mounted the most vociferous and assertive protests that day. Perhaps Leclercq assumed that representing men rather than women as spokespeople for the protesters would seem more convincing to twentieth-century viewers. Or perhaps representing men in this position seemed more politically threatening and therefore more consistent with Bouchardon's assertions of the violent revolutionary significance of the protest.

In the end, Bouchardon asserts that "hundreds of demonstrators" escorted the carts to the courtyard in the main square. They built a bonfire and prepared to guard "their conquest." When the brigadier, Caudrelier, finally did arrive "at a gallop on his horse," he thought he had found himself "in the middle of a gypsy encampment."

Bouchardon harshly assesses the nonchalant behavior of the grain cart drivers, but he judges most severely those who intercepted the grain. He makes no reference to claims for rights to existence or social justice. Instead, he immediately criminalizes their behavior, characterizing them as "pillagers." Leclercq's illustration of the interception foregrounds what might look like plotting, further underscoring criminal premeditation. Bouchardon's description of the assembly around the bonfire captures his attitude: "The burning logs lit evil faces red. The women, especially, were scary to see. One would have called them a band of witches at the hour of the sabbath."[81] Bouchardon conflates evidence culled from the dossier with imaginary witness accounts that enhance his representation of events at Buzançais as criminal and dangerously revolutionary. Such elaboration on the testimony actually present in the dossier appears even more clearly in Bouchardon's narrative of the Venin/Chambert fatal shooting and beating incidents.

According to Bouchardon, by the time the "brigands" had smashed and pillaged their way through Cloquemin's mill, "the band had developed a taste for pillage and turned to sack some other houses." Bouchardon, in terms redolent of Tocqueville's, recounts in detail their attacks on the property and persons of "bourgeois," who, "either because of a lack of courage or decisiveness, preferred to hide in their homes and wait for the attack that individually each could not repulse." Again, he echoes the disdainful, shaming tone leveled against Buzancéen local elites by the magistrates in 1847. He reminds his readers that the property owners in 1847 "had forgotten that union [would have made them] stronger."[82] "House after house was sacked," and local authorities had no choice but to "resign themselves to promising to sell grain to the people at 3 francs the double *décalitre.*" Thus, Bouchardon concludes, "power passed into the insurgents' hands."[83]

Bouchardon draws detail from and embellishes upon the 1847 dossier for his narrative of the Venin/Chambert episodes. He observes that, although the declaration of the "engagement" might have appeased "the shock troops," it would not stop the rampage. By now, they had "gorged themselves with wine and liqueurs," indulged themselves with "orgies," and consequently "worried little about such treaties; destruction and theft had become their friends."

And so, at "11 o'clock in the morning," they arrived "at the corner of rue Porte-de-Luçay and the Grand'Rue, where four people lived in a vast house: an old woman, Marie-Thérèse-Florence Moreau de Bellsourd—who lived apart from her husband, M. Huard-Chambert who also lived in the same town—their only son, Eudoxe-Louis-Joseph, 39 years old, their male servant, Louis Bourgeot, and female servant, Madeleine Blanchet."

In Bouchardon's account, Mme Chambert's hand shakes as she signs the engagement at the urging of her son. Its carriers withdraw from the house, "even touching their hats" as they depart. Just as they leave, the "column" bursts in "like a whirlwind." Venin, "the captain of the brigands," marches at their head. Venin demands money (twice he declares: "I need money") and wrestles with the servant Bourgeot. Chambert "follows the peripeteia of this scene with growing emotion." He sees his house under siege, the life of Bourgeot in danger. "He trembles for his own life, certainly for that of his mother."[84] Chambert gets his hunting rifle and, in a struggle with Venin, whom Bouchardon blames for the situation, Chambert kills the intruder. Bouchardon wonders, "Did M. Chambert intentionally pull the trigger? Did he respond by reflex when his assailant grabbed him by the throat and jostled his weapon? We will never know." Although Bouchardon expresses justifiable uncertainty, he simultaneously introduces new embellishments. While the trial dossier contains witnesses who saw Venin reach out toward Chambert, no one could say with certainty if physical contact had occurred.

But in Bouchardon's account, once Chambert had shot Venin, "the wild beasts" prepared Chambert's "torture." Bouchardon recounts with impressive detail the pursuit and murder that followed. He describes Chambert, "whose forehead is damp with the sweat of agony," hiding in the armoire on the second floor of his house.[85] At one point Bouchardon shifts to literary reference to convey a sense of the scene: he compares Chambert to Matho the barbarian, who, in (Flaubert's) *Salammbô,* is released to the people. "Who doesn't remember these last pages . . . ? There was nothing, except his eyes, that gave the appearance of being human."[86] After detailing the crowd's revenge on Chambert, Bouchardon concludes that, "when the body of M. Chambert was nothing but a wound, the batterers stopped. Weary from striking, they backed up several steps, formed a circle, and savagely contemplated their work." In case the reader lacked a clear enough mental image of the condition of Chambert's body, Bouchardon describes it precisely: "M. Chambert . . . lying on his back, all smeared with blood, his left eye hanging from its socket, his face mutilated, blood escaping in floods from his mouth. And the poor man was still breathing."[87] By the time the gendarmes could carry his unconscious body to the hospice, he had died. But the "horde" turned to the Dauvergne house, where the bedridden seventy-year-old M. Dauvergne "ransomed" his bedroom for 260 francs, leaving the fractious to destroy the rest of his house, including "a piano that had cost three thousand francs in 1845."

Bouchardon's narrative itemizes virtually every act of atrocity and denigration the dossiers listed. For example, he lingers over the story of the "disproportionately large" wheelwright, Baptiste, "who played the clown." During the pillage of the Chambert household, he "coiffed himself with one of Mme Chambert's ribbon caps and now put one of Mme Dauvergne's black hats on top of it." He concludes, "If the criminal dossier did not prove it, one could barely believe that such refinements of cruelty were possible."[88] He recounts Arrouy's struggle to pull his two-tined pitchfork from Chambert's head, where he had plunged it, and Anne Coteron's kicks to Chambert's body with her clogs. He quotes a witness who told of rioters bludgeoning Chambert "like one would beat cattle."

Bouchardon left so little to the reader's imagination that he rendered any illustration unnecessary, and none exists for this episode. Part I of Bouchardon's narrative ends with a warning of retribution to follow: "It was about two o'clock . . . when a cry was heard: 'The troops! Here are the troops! The Préfect has arrived.'"

Bouchardon's account makes little room for women of the common people to play important roles in the events of the *jacquerie* at Buzançais, and when they do, he usually uses them as images of disorder and unreason. They start the shipment interception but quickly disappear from the narrative of it. They appear briefly as witches plotting evil around a bonfire on the Sabbath. The illustrator Leclercq follows the narrative in denying an active strategic role to women during the protest, for they do not appear in his illustrations in assertive positions.

Poor women reappear as shameful beggars in Bouchardon's story on the third day of the disorders. On 15 January, during the "last convulsions of the riot," another form of popular behavior emerges. Bouchardon recounts that "bands, where the feminine element dominated, continued to travel the town insolently demanding what they called charity at the doors" of the rich.[89] Only

Mme Chambert's loyal servant, Madeleine Blanchet, wins praise for her "admirable courage" when she "covers her mistress with her body and cries out 'you will kill me before you do harm to her!'" But Bouchardon awards her a mere two sentences, preferring, instead to dwell on the cowardly side of those who dared to so threaten such a powerless elderly woman.[90]

Bouchardon focused mainly on men as the real actors in his crime story. His narrative even streamlines responsibility by heavily emphasizing two men in particular: Baptiste Bienvenu for a prominent leadership role, and François Légeron for his colorful and evocative declarations. Bouchardon's account finds Bienvenu everywhere. He had threatened the proprietor Gaulin days before the riot erupted; "led the expedition" to sound the tocsin; menaced an elderly proprietor and the parish priest with his axe the morning after the shipment interception; and led the assault on Cloquemin's mill. After the mill, when the "band . . . turned to go sack some other house," Bienvenu "again put himself at the head of the attack column." Bouchardon repeated and then exaggerated the characterization supplied by the prosecutor during the trial in 1847, when he described Bienvenu as a "vagabond, who had never really worked in his life, even though he was in the prime of life. He slept here and there, often in barns, barely supporting himself, scorned by all. Now, in an instant he had become the master and made a whole town of four thousand souls tremble."[91]

Although Bienvenu himself claimed that he had had to support his sick mother for a year, had trouble finding steady work, and had not played the role the prosecution imagined, neither the court nor Bouchardon accepted his version. Bouchardon further claimed that Bienvenu had "rivaled Venin in ferocity." He had helped to drag Chambert from his hiding place in the saddler's boutique and then had helped to break all the shop's windows, bashed Chambert with his axe, and ultimately even accosted the lieutenant of the dragoons sent to quell the disorder. Bouchardon—this experienced late nineteenth-century magistrate—mounted a more damaging case against the twenty-five-year-old illiterate man than had his judicial counterpart in 1847.

Bourgeois women figured more prominently than in Vallès's account but served mostly to accentuate the reader's horror at the atrocities committed. Bouchardon follows the original dossier in identifying several bourgeois women who crossed paths with the protesters, but he emphasizes their victimization more heavily than their brave resistance. For example, he explained that when Bienvenu had raised his axe against M. Gaulin, Mme Gaulin had "thrown herself between the two men." But rather than praise her courage, Bouchardon mentions that Bienvenu had been startled and this "second of hesitation saved the husband," but then "he turned his weapon against the woman." Only the "happy" intervention of the gravedigger, Lagoutte, held back Bienvenu's arm and, "under his protection, the Gaulin family, could flee, safe and sound." At the Dauvergne household, Bouchardon ignored the strategies by mother and daughter to protect the ailing elderly husband and father, which had attracted fulsome praise in accounts from 1847. Instead, he emphasized their victimization. He recounted that "while some pillagers descended to the cellar to steal wine, others surrounded Mme Dauvergne, threatened and mocked her, [and] neither her tears nor her age could impress them."[92] The daughter does not even appear in his narrative.

In order to leave the reader with a lingering image of bourgeois woman as victim—and thereby heighten outrage at the irrational, criminal crowd—Bouchardon saves for his last story the tale of the Mlle Uranie Liniet, a "saintly and dignified" elderly maiden lady. Widely recognized as the "guardian angel of the misfortunate," she becomes the victim of "brutality." As she advanced with a sack of alms money in her hand toward a group begging at her door, "two or three maniacs tore it from her."[93] This action even provoked "many bourgeois to come out of their cellars and the same cry emitted from one hundred mouths: To arms!" Even the national guard found the courage to respond to the mayor's call to order showing that the victimization of bourgeois women, especially of their apotheosis—the virginal, charitable, elderly maiden—still had in the interwar years impressive symbolic power to represent virtue and provoke outrage. Bouchardon, however, did not acknowledge women as potential agents of courageous behavior.

Bouchardon does permit working-class and peasant women to figure in his account in another way, however. He employs them to mark the consequences of the protesters' heinous criminal acts. Bouchardon recounts that, during the three day trial, "a poor woman had slipped into the back of the courtroom and no one could refuse her their pity. It was Louis Michot's mother, . . . who for the past fifteen days, had had masses said to spare her son's life." Her religious piety, more than her misery, merits sympathy. In another example intended to affect readers with the severity of the repression, he observes that, when the line of gendarmes and troops escorting the carts carrying the three condemned men to their execution pass through the town of Villedieu on their way from Châteauroux to Buzançais, several inhabitants appeared on their doorsills to watch. "No one said anything [but] the women crossed themselves." After the executions, Bouchardon again emphasizes the religious message received by local women as he explains that "only a few women in mourning bonnets [*capiches*] followed the bodies of the executed to the cemetery."[94]

Leclercq's illustrations also focus heavily on the repression that followed the disorder. His drawings for the second installment of the story provide only images of police and occupying troops. In the two major images, the forces of repression occupy the central space, and worried locals figure only on the periphery. Leclercq also deploys gendered images to convey the message of the devastating consequences of the repression. In one of these (Fig. 4.7), in the foreground, a peasant woman shields a boy with her body while mounted soldiers patrol the town looking for suspects. Two other peasants holding pitchforks huddle cravenly off to the side, apparently hiding behind trees.

Bouchardon locates his discussion of what happened in Buzançais in 1847 within a context of economic hardship and popular turbulence but also administrative incompetence, at both the national and local levels. His critique of insufficiency and the tardiness of relief efforts and, especially, the short-sighted recourse to repression rather than prevention of the disorders that erupted set the stage for him to indict the July Monarchy's administration. This lifelong Third Republic magistrate, an avowed advocate of social order and respect for authority, showed no pity for the protesters in 1847, but neither did he manifest any sympathy for the local officers' mismanagement or the craven behavior of local elites.

He opens his narrative from the perspective of the only local figure for whom he manifests some sympathy, the brigadier of the Buzançais gendarmerie, Desiré Caudrelier. Describing Caudrelier as a "young" man, "still full of bravery," Bouchardon speculates, "Had he been in Buzançais the day the unrest began, [he] might have been able to stifle it." Instead, however, he had left the town in the hands of three undistinguished gendarmes and the mayor, Guesnyer, whom Bouchardon dismisses as a man who, "despite his respectable age and hoary head, was no longer listened to and even less obeyed."[95]

Bouchardon repeatedly echoes the disdain for local authority and elites that oozed from many a page in the dossier compiled by the July Monarchy magistrates. His narrative records malfeasance and nonfeasance. The mayor had "abstained from calling the national guard"—a "body with neither organization nor discipline" that "had no desire to confront the riot." "No one budged. Sensing worsening danger, the majority of bourgeois had locked their doors,

Fig. 4.7. *Repression: The Storm before the Calm.* From Pierre Bouchardon, "La Jacquerie de Buzançais," *Lectures pour tous* (June and July 1925).

and then many hid themselves in their cellars or in their attics." Bouchardon recounts the arrival of the prefect and a small collection of magistrates in Buzançais. They immediately found themselves vastly outnumbered and disrespected by the crowds assembled to confront his arrival: "The mutinous crowd closed in on M. Ferdinand Leroy, almost touching him; their breath reeked of wine and alcohol; they threatened him. . . . Protected by the gendarmes, the Prefect managed to extract himself, but not without having emptied his purse, and then the mayor's as well, into the hands of the most insolent."[96]

To elucidate the prefect's situation, Bouchardon alludes to the plight of Louis XVI when, during his ill-fated flight to Varennes in 1791, the king took refuge from the hostile crowd that had identified him and sought to stop his escape with violence if necessary. When the hussars appeared, M. de Choiseul told the king that the best he could do with the force available was "to clear the King's way with a charge," but they would have to move swiftly and, by implication, without dignity, or the crowd would overwhelm the troops.[97] Bouchardon lets the reader conclude that a similar fate awaited the prefect.[98] After the belated arrival of the dragoons, the lieutenant finds himself compelled to admit, "I can clear the place and hold a position before the city hall as long as necessary. But beyond that zone, I cannot promise anything. My men risk massacre if they try to arrest the leaders, send patrols into the narrow streets. . . . Moreover, I have to confess that we left without cartridges." Too few men, and those who finally arrived have come unarmed. Bouchardon sees no need to elaborate beyond stating that the prefect decided "at one o'clock in the morning to return to Châteauroux and leave revolution the mistress of the little town."[99]

Only after the assault on the saintly Mlle Liniet (and the worst of the unrest) had ended did local authorities and the bourgeoisie find the courage to emerge from hiding. Bouchardon explains that "the national guard finally assembled and occupied the town hall . . . with more zeal than discipline." He concludes that although the guard "rendered a few services, it was obvious that . . . only the regular army could assure order and then punishment."[100]

Bouchardon supplies a lengthy narrative of the Assize Court magistrates' savage indictment of local ineptitude. He attacks administrative incompetence by describing the final execution of the three rioters, Bienvenu, Michot, and Velluet. After lengthy debates over the date and the context of the execution, squabbles over precedence, and finally over who would attend, the whole execution culminated in a "deplorable" failure to construct a functioning guillotine in time for the publicized event. Even Bouchardon found it inexcusable that the three men had to wait for several hours while the builders found the right pieces to complete the job. Bouchardon could not resist a final embellishment: "The three unfortunate men . . . came to love this horrible noise [of the guillotine under construction] and feared no longer hearing it, since they guessed that it granted them their last minutes."[101]

Bouchardon recounts Mater's "severe words for all those who had hidden themselves in attics and cellars, when the union of several good citizens would have sufficed to force the riot to back down," leaving no doubt about Bouchardon's desire to convey a message about the need for unity of elites in the face of disorder. He claims to quote prosecutor Didelot's admonishment in his final statement: "It is unbelievable, gentlemen, that this brigandage was not stopped by the national guard. It should never be forgotten that citizens must defend themselves. [The national guard] should never forget its slogan: liberty, public order."[102] Bouchardon's story of the *jacquerie* of Buzançais contains a moral for all who favor public order and who wish to defend themselves and their property against popular claims. They must stand bravely united to protect their interests. Cowardly disunity results in devastation. This magistrate and now writer, a man who, as we have seen, had, in other publications, expressed his profound displeasure with the weakening of the authority (both judicial and moral) invested in the magistracy during the Third Republic, reflects the conservative commitment to public order of his class and profession.

Not surprisingly, then, Bouchardon focuses more on the reimposition of public order than on the issues of social justice or moral ambiguity and depicts the protesters in harsh terms: "wild animals," "sinister faces," and "breath stinking of wine and alcohol." Although he quotes several pleas for clemency and understanding, he refuses to grant either. He declares that he cannot accept the notion of mercy for Chambert's murderers: "The peasantry did not limit themselves to [simply] killing Chambert; they *tortured* him, with savage refinements."[103]

Bouchardon's narrative of the *jacquerie* at Buzançais stands in stark contrast to Vallès's account. Vallès had opened a space for explaining the popular movement in terms of exploitation, suffering, and claims for social justice and the right to existence. Bouchardon closed that space by emphatically criminalizing it. Both sought to negotiate a particular reading of the story consistent with their political ends, and to this purpose both authors and the illustrators whose images accompanied their work employed particular episodes and images in particular ways to support their narrative ends.

Each of these versions fits best with an interpretation that considers the cultural context in which it appeared. In 1919 and 1925, contentious eras of contrasting political tinctures, these works well served their purposes and eras as well as those of the individuals who wrote and published them. The publishing houses of Edouard-Joseph in 1919 and Hachette in 1925 responded to particular market opportunities and offered very different publications for very different audiences: the first, an illustrated limited edition of an unknown novel by a politically engaged, recognized author aimed at consumers with some means who sought cultural capital in an era of sympathy for the suffering; the second, a crime (and punishment) story in a widely disseminated, popular magazine (read also by those seeking to acquire cultural capital) written by a politically conservative defender of public order in an era deeply concerned with it. Thus in a France far removed from the France of 1847, authors of starkly contrasting outlooks and publishers with an eye to exploiting evolving markets and finding profitable niches in the field of cultural production found in Buzançais's tractable plot and characters a usable past serviceable to many masters.

CHAPTER FIVE

Jacquerie as Cartoon and Television Drama

Crime doesn't pay: The Jacquerie of Buzançais!
—"La Jacquerie de Buzançais," in *France-Soir* (1956)

Bread and wine: Social drama, or the unbridling of the criminal instincts of the crowd?
—*Le Pain et le Vin,* television movie (1978)

After World War II, the Buzançais affair reappeared not only in familiar genres—such as the political press, historical fiction, and crime stories—but also in other media that renewed its importance to the general public: the cartoon strip, television, historical scholarship, local history, genealogy, and theatrical performance mined the affair in new ways. These innovations presented images of social conflict to a mass audience, demonstrating Buzançais's continuing relevance to traditional issues, as well as its ability to attract an increasingly apolitical general interest. The different media, by their very nature, approached their audiences through different processes, mechanisms their creators knew and used. The crudity and boldness of cartoons, designed for readers to absorb in a glance, evoked strong emotions based on visual stereotypes. Television dramas, which unfolded over many minutes, juxtaposed historical images with fictional personages to produce complex effects that might educate as well as entertain.

LE CRIME NE PAIE PAS IN 1956

In 1956 the newspaper *France-Soir* recast the Buzançais story in its famous popular cartoon series *Le Crime ne paie pas* (Crime Doesn't Pay). Dedicated to reporting "authentic, sensational, criminal affairs" from the past, it focused nineteen consecutive issues on the "Jacquerie of Buzançais."[1] The paper's widespread circulation assured greater public awareness of the episode than ever before. In 1956 *France-Soir* proudly emblazoned on the first page: "The only French daily paper with a circulation of over a million."[2] It had achieved this success by appealing to the broadest French audience.

Its owner and guiding force, Pierre Lazareff (1907–72), had worked for several papers before the war, and in 1932 he joined *Paris-Soir,* helping to make it the most widely read daily newspaper in France. During the war, Lazareff moved to New York to escape the persecution of Jews during the occupation. There he worked for the Voice of America. With the Liberation, he returned to France and took over the French resistance movement's paper, *Défense de la France,* quickly transforming it from an underground tract into a successful daily, renamed *France-Soir.* By 1948, the paper had gone from a quarter of a million issues a day to 630,000. In 1954, it leapt the million mark, and by 1957 it sold 1,350,000 copies a day.[3]

After the war Lazareff's paper swiftly seized the attention of French readers. Having learned the newspaper business both during France's interwar era (the apogee for the press[4]) and during the war in the United States, Lazareff sought to make *France-Soir* both a *grand journal* ("a national 'paper of record'") and a paper with mass popular appeal—in effect a hybrid of the *New York Times* and the prewar *Paris-Soir.* To accomplish this journalistic equivalent of squaring the circle, Lazareff combined a bold presentation style (eye-catching print format, widely dispersed photographs) with aggressive reporting of both national and international affairs, sports news, unusual or common interest stories (the *faits divers*), gossip columns, serialized novels, self-improvement advice, and cartoon strips. *France-Soir* included advice columns for women (on fashion, home decoration and repairs, child rearing, exercises to keep fit, and romantic relationships), crossword puzzles, television and radio guides, and horoscopes.

Under Lazareff's enterprising direction, *France-Soir* became the first daily paper to run a full page of cartoons every day.[5] His ambitious, dynamic strategies received a much needed injection of capital in 1949, when the Librarie Hachette acquired control of the paper. Thus bolstered, *France-Soir* built a staff of highly skilled national and foreign correspondents and photographers, often by raiding the ranks of competitors. The strategy worked. During the height of its success, the paper printed as many as eight daily editions, often displaying different headlines and lead stories. From a total of twenty-six national newspapers published in the period immediately after the Liberation, only sixteen remained in 1950 and twelve in 1953. *France-Soir* was first among them.[6]

For the *France-Soir* project, Lazareff enlisted his longtime mentor and powerful ally, Paul Gordeaux (1891–1974), whom he appointed the paper's literary director. Before the war, Gordeaux had directed the theatrical section of one of the "Five Great" papers of the 1920s, *L'Echo de Paris,* an influential organ of the conservative Right.[7] Almost twenty years Lazareff's senior, Gordeaux had given him his first newspaper job and had nurtured his talent.

After the war, when Lazareff asked him to direct *France-Soir*'s cultural desk, Gordeaux not only managed the paper's theater, literary, and cultural sections but also initiated several columns (including the popular "Potins de Commère"—gossiping on gossip—column that often ran on several pages of the same issue), and he originated and wrote for several highly acclaimed "vertical" cartoon strips. The "vertical" strip constituted a new departure in format, which some cartoon aficionados might define as "illustrated stories" rather than "pure" cartoon strips; in the latter, "speech" appears in "balloons" inside the frames themselves, while "illustrated stories" usually relied on explanatory text beneath or outside the frames. During the 1950s, both kinds of strips appeared frequently. Even before Gordeaux's participation, *France-Soir* had already published several well-received "illustrated stories" beginning with *Les Misérables* in 1946. Adapted from Victor Hugo's novel by Marijac (one of the most famous French contributors to cartoons in the 1950s, real name Jacques Dumas) and illustrated by Gaston Niezab, it was the first daily cartoon strip published in France. Encouraged by this success, the paper tried another Hugo novel, *Notre Dame de Paris,* also adapted by Marijac and illustrated by Niezab. These illustrated stories proved so popular that the agency for cartoon illustrators, Opera Mundi, developed several others, some based on Alexandre Dumas's novels (illustrated by Francis Josse). *France-Soir* published many of these as well.[8]

Gordeaux's first experiment with a daily vertical strip format appeared under the title *Le Film du ½ siècle.* It offered a history of the past fifty years, emphasizing those events most important to France. Jean Bellus illustrated the text, usually providing five panels for each day's strip. Gordeaux clearly drew inspiration for his novel approach from the cinema, which by the 1950s had emerged as a wildly popular and innovative genre in France. The vertical borders of each strip replicated the perforated edges of the moving picture film, and the alternating text and images might encourage cinema lovers to appreciate the blurred boundaries between movies and cartoons.

In 1950 *France-Soir* announced that it planned to follow the *Film du ½ siècle,* "whose success has been so great that thousands of readers have asked us to publish it as a book," with a new series, "*Le Crime ne paie pas,* which will bring alive History's great criminal affairs." The paper listed some of the illustrators who would collaborate on the series and some of the early titles projected: "L'Affaire des poisons, Le Courrier de Lyon, L'Auberge de Peyrebeille, Mme Lafarge, Lacenaire, Pranzini, Jack l'Eventreur, Le Vampire de Dusseldorf, Ravachol, La Malle à Gouffé, Landru, Mestorino, Petiot, etc. etc." On Tuesday, 14 February, a front-page announcement for the new series appeared in a bold black box, proclaiming that *Le Crime ne paie pas* would debut the next day. On the 15th, the editors ran another large black box at the top of the first page, emblazoned with words in white: "Le Crime ne paie pas; En page 8, les grandes enquêtes criminelles de l'Histoire; Aujourd'hui: l'Affaire des Poisons; Une nouvelle série de bandes dessinées."[9] In this new series (and his other popular serial *Les Amours célèbres*), Gordeaux abandoned the word "film" in the title along with the special border, but he kept the vertical format. Henceforth he referred to these two series as *bandes dessinées,* or illustrated strips.[10]

France-Soir put neither of Gordeaux's new strips on the same page as other cartoons until late in February 1956; subsequently it changed location several times. By the time "Le Jacquerie de Buzançais" ran in January and February 1956, Gordeaux's two series, *Les Amours célèbres* (Great Love Stories, as opposed to Great Crime Stories) and *Le Crime ne paie pas,* ran on opposites sides of the same page. Below *Les Amours,* the paper often wedged an advice column called "Unhappy Hearts"; below *Le Crime,* it put another column called "Advice from Philomène," which provided recipes and other useful household information. Between *Les Amours* and *Le Crime,* the paper ran a subtitled photographic series of sensational stories entitled "Le Film du jour de *France-Soir.*" On the first day "La Jacquerie de Buzançais" ran, the other series, *Les Amours,* featured the story "La Fornarina."[11] The "Film of the Day" included photographs from the opening ceremonies of the Winter Olympics in Cortina D'Ampezzo, Italy.[12] On the same page, then, readers/viewers got advice, read stories of love and crime, and saw photographs of national and international affairs: famous stars, violent protests, exciting adventures, terrible tragedies, and unusual moments captured on film.

For example, over the nineteen days of "La Jacquerie de Buzançais" readers/viewers saw photographs of the American expedition to Antarctica; Queen

Elizabeth's visit to Lagos, Nigeria; a deadly fire in Baltimore, Maryland; the celebration of carnival in Nice; protests at the University of Alabama against desegregation; the return of the sultan of Morocco to Casablanca; a clash between police and demonstrating former combatants before the Monument aux Morts in Algiers; a lifeboat sinking in the turbulent North Sea; frozen waterways and electric lines during the cold snap in Europe; and the two dogs who won first prize in the Westminster Kennel Club's exposition in New York.

Gordeaux's *Les Amours célèbres* and *Le Crime ne paie pas* ran virtually every day from 1950 to 1965, when editorship (and the narrative work) passed seamlessly to Robert Mallat, who continued it for five more years.[13] Such longevity at a paper so nakedly on the make as *France-Soir* testifies to the readers' embrace of Gordeaux's format, content, and message. For more than twenty years, Gordeaux cycled a stable of renowned illustrators—such as Alberto Uderzo, illustrator of *Asterix,* and Jean-Claude Forest, creator of *Barbarella*—through his seemingly inexhaustible supply of stories of love and deception, crime and punishment. Unlike literary novice Bouchardon, Gordeaux, as a doyen of French journalism and confidante of Pierre Lazareff, had encyclopedic knowledge of French illustrators. He could and did pick and choose among them. Few would have missed a chance to appear in the pages of *France-Soir.*[14]

The success of *France-Soir* largely reflects certain developments in the postwar media that also helped shape such cartoon strips as *Le Crime ne paie pas* in general and the narrative and visual story of "La Jacquerie de Buzançais" in particular. After the Liberation and during the early years of the Fourth Republic, the government proved deeply committed to the democratization and moralization of French culture.[15] In an effort to prevent the recrudescence of fascist politics in France, initiatives from many sectors sought to extend access to culture, both classic and modern, and deploy it to edify a public with growing resources and leisure time to imbibe it. Contradictions riddled many of these efforts. On the one hand, French policy makers hoped to encourage and reinvigorate a historically vibrant French culture by enhancing its accessibility and expanding its potential audience. On the other hand, they feared that an uneducated mass culture already being depleted by changes that threatened traditional society might be transformed into a nonculture through American and media influences. Under the combined weight of their hopes and their fears, French policy makers tended to use a heavy hand in defining and then nurturing culture. France thus found itself "an old society . . . constrained to partake of the present and to protect its historical, religious, and political values from the onslaught of the standardized norms of the age of mass communications."[16]

Before World War II, American writers/illustrators had dominated the French cartoon market.[17] During the war, the German occupation in the north and the Vichy government in the south resisted the American influence and gave preference to French and other European illustrators. Many of the French cartoon creators who dominated the era after the war got their start through collaboration. The first French wartime journal to favor French illustrators, *Le Téméraire,* was an open propaganda instrument for the Nazis.[18]

After the war, the contest for journal space resumed, manifesting itself particularly through the emerging culture of the "ninth art," the cartoon strip, when a "new invasion of cheap stories threatened the journals that used exclusively the services of French illustrators and writers."[19] This "invasion" followed the May 1946 Blum-Byrnes trade agreement, which restructured French war debt and, in exchange, permitted American cultural products—such as film and cartoons—free access to the French market.[20] This agreement sparked controversy among the French cultural critics (though many confessed admiration for American cultural products) and ultimately galvanized a reaction, from left and right, against American cartoon strips. The French Catholic and conservative Right bewailed the commercialism and immorality of many American cartoons. The Communist Party deplored American imperialism. The French Union des artistes dessinateurs protested over its marginalization by American (and even Belgian) competition.[21]

A law passed in July 1949 sought both to protect children from immoral literature and to limit foreign (implicitly American) imports by subjecting them to special scrutiny and tariffs. At the same time, it defined the cartoon strip exclusively as a product intended for a youth audience.[22] This definition limited access to the French cartoon market, since any magazine or journal that published cartoons now fell under a law that banned "the slightest rubric or drawing in which the contents seemed an apology for banditism, lies, theft, laziness, cowardliness, hate, debauchery, any crime or misdemeanor, or any act that might demoralize children or youth."[23] A further law, in November 1954, updated the list of banned subjects to include material that might "inspire or sustain ethnic prejudices."[24] The legislation also created a "surveillance commission" to monitor compliance.

Although this legislation explicitly targeted only publications for children, it resonated more widely, just as many critics of mass media had hoped. The laws' proponents hoped that "suggestion and persuasion" rather than repression would serve to instill moral order in the images and texts. The law ultimately seems to have led to "autocensure" by both French publishers and importers of foreign materials.[25] The surveillance commission never actually brought any publisher to court, but its apologists asserted that its existence served to uplift subject matter and tone.

Paul Gordeaux's *Crime ne paie pas* series seems to have adhered generally to the law's mission, even though the National Assembly had not specifically targeted daily newspapers like *France-Soir* because they aimed at an older audience; nevertheless, the law applied to their cartoons as well. Moreover, *France-Soir,* in particular, did hope to encourage sales by including stories and activities designed for younger interests and abilities. Gordeaux may have conceived of *Le Crime* as a way to comply with the law's general purpose and to cultivate favorable opinion among a public that had overwhelmingly supported such a law. Gordeaux had long affiliated himself with the conservative Right's social agenda of law and order—while working for both the *Echo de Paris* before the war and *France-Soir* after it. This new cartoon strip, faithful to the editorial stance of *France-Soir* as well as to the legal proscription, roundly condemned crime (as Gordeaux understood it) and openly supported the forces of order. Over the next sixteen years, beginning with its first episode, *Crime ne paie pas* unambiguously denounced all "banditos, lies, theft, laziness, cowardliness, hate, debauchery, [and] any crime or misdemeanor," instances of which it found rampant in French history. While it and *Amours célèbres* may have taken certain visual liberties in their representations of sexually attractive women (often featuring gaping, if not ripped, bodices) and violent behavior, they did so largely by way of condemning those portrayed as too sexually provocative or physically aggressive.

Just as in Gordeaux's other series, *Amours célèbres,* each story in the *Crime ne paie pas* strip ran from five to thirty weekly episodes and employed a vertical strip, with long narrative texts placed beneath each of five images. Gordeaux introduced each new story with a brief narrative and began each day's episode with an update. The first *Le Crime* story, "L'Affaire des poisons," appeared in February 1950; illustrated by Jean Ache, it ran for eight days.[26] The story told of mysterious poisonings in the 1670s at the court of Louis XIV, the inquiry into their causes, and the ultimate prosecution and execution of both the murderers and the band of alleged witches, abortionists, and poisoners who had, through devious and alchemical means, produced and distributed the poison.[27]

Gordeaux drew his stories from both French and international sources. Although he wrote the texts himself, he generally adapted the work of others to this new format.[28] Colleagues claimed that Gordeaux did research in the Bibliothèque nationale before he wrote and that he prided himself on his "historical accuracy" (Lazareff told Gordeaux, "'Le crime ne paie pas' and 'Les Amours célèbres' made you the most read historian in France."[29]) In the 1950s, Gordeaux had a mountain of histories/stories of famous crimes that he could mine. The police story (*policier*), detective story, mystery story, and historical novel, which had emerged as genres from the second half of the nineteenth century, had exploded in popularity in the twentieth.[30] The acquisition of the newspaper by Librairie Hachette in 1949 facilitated access to this literature through Hachette's catalog and its publications that often serialized this sort of literature, including Bouchardon's contributions. Not surprisingly, Gordeaux's narrative of the "Jacquerie of Buzançais" shows his familiarity with Bouchardon's interwar version.

Gordeaux's choices and the interpretation he brought to them expose common themes. First, he avoided chafing the unhealed sores of France's deeply politicized past. He did not adapt tales of revolutionary *journées* or political trials that contemporary politics continued to debate heatedly, such as the Dreyfus affair or trials of collaborators from the recent war. Second, he adopted an unambiguously conservative approach to social norms. Property, social order, and female virtue enjoyed his highest respect. Gordeaux condemned all assaults on them and celebrated punishment of their perpetrators. Although he permitted his texts and their illustrations to cater to an adult audience's greater tolerance for violence and sexuality, he balanced these with texts and images that emphasized the repercussions of violence and sexuality when unleashed. After all, the very title of his series headlined that crime did not pay; therefore, criminals must pay. Third, he made his "criminals" and their "criminal acts" appear aberrant, outside the boundary of normal society. Cruelty or excesses of hard-heartedness among his characters might bring a stern rebuke, but such attitudes never justified unlawful retaliation.

Finally, with the notable exception of the Buzançais affair, Gordeaux used no stories of popular protest. He had introduced many tales of criminal behavior by bands of outlaws and gangsters and even stories about political killings, such as the assassinations of the czar or the French president Sadi-Carnot by anarchists in 1894. However, he eschewed accounts of collective violence by peasants, workers, or slaves (for example, he did not serialize the Hautefay affair of 1870), perhaps because collective violence often constituted a critique of and protest against certain aspects of its own society, a critique that fell outside his mission of entertaining and instructing, while selling newspapers.

On one level, the Buzançais affair could seem depoliticized and irrelevant to readers in France in the 1950s. It had, after all, happened long ago and in an obscure place in a society that existed no more. Largely forgotten, with all participants long dead and the last popular publication thirty years (plus a world war and a depression) in the past, the event survived only in antiquarian nooks and crannies, such as the faded pages of *Lectures pour tous* and its aged readers.

On another level, however, Buzançais had acute relevance to the 1950s. Recent memories of ten years (1939–49) of wartime and postwar dearth, high prices and lagging real wages, issues of hoarding and price gouging, and outbreaks of protest against these remained fresh in many readers' minds.[31] In this postwar era, the impetus that had long powered and legitimized social protest now marshaled its forces in support of the welfare state. The peasant culture and economy long cherished as the repository of France's soul now seemed imperiled by an exodus from the countryside that reached palpable levels by 1951–52. The 1919 publication of Gilbert Stenger's popular novel *Retour à la terre* (Return to the Soil) had marked this nostalgia for traditional French culture and the values rooted in its agrarian society and village life. The Vichy regime had promoted this association and had tried to stem the movement to cities, but to no avail. After 1945, the flight accelerated. By 1955, 170,000 farms (or 7 percent) had disappeared out of almost 2.5 million. Smaller farms (less than ten hectares) disappeared faster than larger ones. Only those over twenty hectares grew, and these at the expense of the smaller ones.[32]

Domestic politics roiled the 1950s. Poujadism, a political expression of extreme-right populism, attracted some on the margins of the era's economic growth and developments (small shopkeepers, artisans, and farmers).[33] Anticommunism remained acute, fueled by hostility to the Communist Party, which still played a salient role in French politics.[34] Food security issues also troubled French consumers. The recent scandal of the *pain maudit* (bread purportedly contaminated by ergot) that had poisoned consumers in Pont-Saint-

Esprit in southern France in 1951, intoxicating many and killing five, had galvanized public opinion and the press, thereby pushing subsistence issues and their hydra-headed implications to the front of French awareness.[35] Finally, protest roiled through the empire, in Indochina and Algeria, making headline news. Despite the prosperity of the times, acts of collective violence, killings, demands for "rights," and hostility to elites made news every day, news that permeated the pages of *France-Soir* with reports and pictures filed by its own reporters and photographers in Dien Bien Phu and Saigon, Algiers and Oran, Marseilles and Berlin.

Although Gordeaux's declared intent to stick to the past shielded him from engaging with contemporary affairs, a glance at the pages of *France-Soir* in the 1950s reveals a paper obsessed with stories of crime and scandal. Headline after headline, page after page reported ghastly crimes both at home and abroad: thefts, murders, rapes, assassinations, massacres, fraud, and mysterious deaths. Continuing a long tradition of reporting on violence and mayhem, *France-Soir* abandoned the practice of relegating most stories of crime and punishment to the *faits divers* column on inside pages and instead scattered them throughout the paper, even splashing them across the first page. For example, the front page of a January 1956 issue of *France-Soir,* which headlined a story about the recent elections, also broadsided a story about "the body of a man cut into morsels fished out of the Ourcq in Bobigny."[36] All local interest aside (since Bobigny lay in the Paris *banlieu*), the sensational nature of this story, like so many others, attracted readers concerned with the problem of crime and what to do about it. Gordeaux's *Le Crime ne paie pas* series drew upon the past to address a current concern and give reassurance that crime was not new—nor did it go unpunished. The crimes profiled in his series proved as sensational as those reported daily in the press, but less frightening.

By criminalizing Buzançais—as with his other conservative interpretations of crimes against property, female virtue, and constituted authorities—Gordeaux sends a message reassuring to readers uneasy about the implications of collective violence and social protest. Better to see the protesters of Buzançais as savage, drunken, bloodthirsty criminals—an "other" in time and place, but also in nature—than to see their lawlessness as the work of those with legitimate claims, provoked by villains who abused or mismanaged their positions of wealth and power.

Gordeaux benefited greatly from the images supplied by his illustrators.

Like the two interwar illustrators, Mario Simon and B. Leclercq, illustrators of his cartoon strips faced challenges posed by the existence of texts: they had to remain "faithful" to both the plot and affect of the texts; however, the difference between the acts of viewing and reading (acts of interpretation) enabled them to color the reader's perception of the texts they illustrated. Cartoon strips place even greater emphasis on the act of visual interpretation than do illustrated books because the images usually occupy proportionately more space. The 1919 Edouard-Joseph edition of Vallès, *Les Blouses,* offered fourteen images altogether, while the 1925 *Lectures pour tous* articles on "La Jacquerie de Buzançais" by Bouchardon included only six. In comparison, the *Le Crime ne paie pas* series used five panels in each daily strip. Although Gordeaux's text occupied at least equal space, the illustrators found themselves in the privileged position of supplying images that preceded the text and could influence by anticipation the way the viewer/reader received the words that followed.

The cartoon strip genre—even allowing for the greater role of text in a format such as Gordeaux's *Crime ne paie pas* series—constrains both text and image. A single drawing cannot easily represent action in process but must make a particular moment suggest what preceded and what will follow. Moreover, whatever Gordeaux found in texts such as Bouchardon's, the cartoon strip format dictated abridging such sources. In that process of abridgment, Gordeaux, perhaps willingly, risked simplifying narratives and descriptions and changing meanings. In "La Jacquerie de Buzançais," Gordeaux both streamlined the narrative (by omitting certain aspects of the action) and rendered even more starkly Bouchardon's presentation of the *jacquerie* as a confrontation between a criminal mob of protesters and their law-abiding, well-intentioned, propertied targets.

Jean-Albert Carlotti (1909–2002), Gordeaux's illustrator for the Buzançais affair, produced images that reinforce these representations. A professional artist and illustrator, Carlotti had a long career during which he produced sketches, drawings, paintings, and illustrations for books and for multiple comic strips written by Gordeaux and others. As an artist Carlotti could perhaps follow his muse; as an illustrator he had to articulate someone else's, which meant meeting two imperatives: conveying Gordeaux's message and selling newspapers.[37]

Illustrators deploy visual conventions, caricatures, and stereotypes to convey certain meanings to viewers. Carlotti used several of these to hallmark specific characters and to transmit information to the viewers. He graphically delineated differences between the poor Buzancéens who protested and the rich elites who served as both targets of protest and the repressors of it, as well as between characters and acts with which the viewer should sympathize and those the viewer should abhor. His use of visual conventions and symbols enabled viewers to differentiate at a glance between the story's criminal/bad figures and law-abiding/good figures, male and female, reinforcing and even initiating readings of Gordeaux's texts.

Gordeaux opens his story of Buzançais by setting the tone for interpreting the narrative: "The Jacquerie of Buzançais! One of the most tragic, the most terrible manifestations of popular rage in a small town. A sudden fit of bloody drunkenness, a brusque return to ancestral barbarism, and, all that in a population—in the Berry—renowned for its good sense and level-headedness. And this during a time that, with the passage of years, appears to us (wrongly) as peaceful and even fairly well-off, the reign of Louis-Philippe, the citizen-king."[38] The reader cannot mistake Gordeaux's tendentious interpretation. Whatever terrible crime (and crime it must be given the series title) perpetrated in Buzançais occurred because drunkenness had released a savagery that still lurked in the recesses of the popular nature. The image that leads the first episode features three gendarmes, who stand calmly but attentively at an intersection, listening to instructions from another gendarme on horseback. In the background, a (stereotypically) well-dressed woman in a bonnet peacefully carries a pannier to or from the market. The central figures of the gendarmes suggest that public order and security reign in a well-policed town.

In the next frame, Gordeaux explains that bad harvests in 1845 and 1846 have produced shortages in many places. But the real problem lay neither in shortages nor the official response to it. Rather, it lay in popular ignorance and suspicion: "Convinced that exporters without scruples were shipping grain out of France, peasants and workers in many departments in the West and Center of France, where misery was great, used force to oppose the circulation of barges and carts and seized the grain they happened to find. This contagion might attack Buzançais, although the city—situated in a fertile area—had its provision of grain assured, the price of grain was still below six francs, and the municipality had . . . opened a charity workshop . . . in order to alleviate the suffering of the poor class." Gordeaux clearly wants the reader to understand that shortages might have threatened in some places, but not in Buzançais. The

1956 reader—who bought bread from a *boulangerie,* not unprocessed grain from the market, and at controlled current prices, not volatile 1847 ones, but who could easily remember prewar depression, shortages, and high prices, as well as rationing during and immediately after the war—never learns from Gordeaux whether 6 francs for a double *décalitre* of grain meant feast or famine, or whether the charity workshop paid a living wage to those in need. Gordeaux assures the reader that the situation in the "charming" (*coquette*) city of Buzançais did not merit concern, a fact underscored by the preceding image that, he explains, shows Caudrelier, the brigadier of the Buzançais gendarmerie, giving instructions for maintaining order as he prepares to leave on service elsewhere.

So opens yet another interpretation of disorder in Buzançais. Whereas Vallès had empathetically cited issues of social justice and Bouchardon had hinted unsympathetically at revolutionary undercurrents, Gordeaux and Carlotti portray only criminal intent. Their rioters appear neither as subalterns driven to desperation by exploitation and indifference and seeking to alleviate their suffering, nor as dangerous, subversive (but uneducated) insurgents. Instead they appear as ignorant barbarians eager to indulge untamed, primal instincts for violence. The opening days' texts and images set the tone from the outset, and the story never detours far from that basic condemnation of the *jacquerie* at Buzançais as an unambiguously criminal act.

The next image (Fig. 5.1), set in the marketplace, depicts men and women, who look generally well fed and adequately dressed for January, bargaining calmly over stalls displaying food—one full of potatoes. In the foreground, a distinguished-looking older man stands carrying a cane and dressed in a substantial winter coat, collared shirt, pale scarf stylishly tied, and a brimmed felt hat. He has an aquiline nose and hair either white with age—meriting respect —or light colored—which, after the fascist era, might signal racial purity and distinction. He stands next to, but does not look at, a man who stares menacingly at him. The distinguished man lifts his hand slightly as if to buffer himself from the implied threat. The other, stockier and dressed in the smock (*la blouse*) that identified peasants and workers and a stocking cap (possibly the revolutionary Liberty cap or the Phrygian cap associated with the revolutionary *sans-culottes*), portrays the antithesis of the propertied elite. He has unkempt dark hair and sideburns, bushy eyebrows that beetle over wild black eyes, and a snub nose.

Fig. 5.1. *Menace at the Market.* From the archives of *France-Soir,* Paris, by permission of *France-Soir.*

Throughout the story, Carlotti draws upon long-standing visual conventions to distinguish elites from peasants and workers, representing elites with light pen strokes and refined features, the common people with darkened strokes and coarsened features. The first figure evokes the progress of civilization; the second harks back to primitive barbarism.[39] The physical (and particularly facial) attributes of the second figure could have further, particular resonances for French readers in the 1950s. Most immediately, the figure closely resembles the well-known image of the Bolshevik peasant (muzhik) frequently displayed on French political posters and other propaganda from 1919, sometimes referred to as "the man with the knife between his teeth."[40]

This poster, produced by the thousands by the patronal organization the Union des intérêts économiques, sought to defend free trade and private enterprise and to support the Bloc national during the 1919 elections. These posters linked the communist threat to an image of a crazed (foreign) peasantry. Of course, the French did not have to look as far as Russia to recognize another stereotype in this image from "La Jacquerie de Buzançais." This simian figure, swarthy (but not black), could also resonate with stereotypes of the North Africans who had migrated to France in growing numbers to reinforce its depleted labor force and to assist in the rebuilding of the war-torn country. Across the Mediterranean these same people currently waged a war of nationalist liberation against France itself, a war daily spattered across the pages of *France-Soir* in texts and photographic images that conveyed a message similar to that of the *jacquerie* in *Le Crime*: here one sees savagery, not protest. A final resonance came from Nazi representations of Aryan elites as light haired, fair skinned, and fine featured—and their Slavic and Semitic antitheses as dark haired, dark skinned, and coarse featured. Readers fresh from the Occupation press would easily distinguish which figure represented the forces of the law-abiding good and which the mass of criminal savages.[41]

Carlotti made sure the reader perceives the menace implied in the confrontation by having the peasant/worker point at a partially raised felling axe in his hand as he leans forward slightly and glares at the worried distinguished gentleman. The text identifies the first man as Baptiste Bienvenu, a day laborer, soon to emerge as the leader of the savage *jacquerie* hordes. The gentleman, landed proprietor Frédéric Gaulin, offers grain for sale at what might seem a reasonable price to the reader, but Bienvenu, Gordeaux explains, does not think it so. He declares to Gaulin: "Take care! I have a brand-new felling axe. I'll use it to break open the doors of all the profiteers!" The term "profiteers," unknown to people in 1847 (the quotation from the 1847 records specifically used the word "bourgeois"), evoked bitter memories in the postwar era. Gordeaux layers memory upon memory by quoting the by now familiar François Légeron: "I have already seen three revolutions. Let them make another one. I'll turn my scythe upside down and then we will see!" Gordeaux has now prepared the setting by giving the reader/viewer (as Bienvenu has given Gaulin) "something to think about."

Gordeaux and Carlotti interpret the episode of the grain carts as criminality, not desperation. The illustrations show two common people (signaled by their caps) watching heavily laden carts stop before an inn; inside the inn, the carters wine and dine, while outside a mass of people gathers; outside, an official (with the sash of office), seconded by several gendarmes, gestures for calm amid an angry crowd that includes Bienvenu, who points at the mayor menacingly. Gordeaux's text narrates the grain transport through Buzançais, signals the "imprudence" of the carters dawdling at the inn for a "solid meal," and explains that by the time the carters had supped their fill, such an "excited and menacing crowd" had formed that the "old mayor, M. Guesnyer seconded by three gendarmes, found themselves forced to try, in vain, to disperse them."

Later, as men surround a grain cart and escort it away, a dour, possibly older, woman in the foreground stares severely out at the viewer, gesturing toward the cart, seemingly inviting the viewer to follow along. Gordeaux summarizes the situation: "By dint of negotiating, the mayor . . . [gets the crowd to] drive the carts to the school courtyard, next to the town hall." Carlotti's image shows sturdy men unloading heavy sacks from a cart while a wrinkled and hawkish woman with straggly hair glares out from the frame's edge.

The series never mentions the complex interplay between the women who first assembled around the carts or their exchanges with the men at the charity workshop. Carlotti's crowd scenes include both men and women, but the women play a more passive role than men. Women often appear primarily as mediators between the viewers and the frames, looking out at the viewers as if to interrogate them. Using images that visually echo Bouchardon's textual descriptions of women around the bonfire, Carlotti does not portray them as benevolent, welcoming intermediaries in the riot; rather, they are depicted as truculent, even frightening, intruders. Most have severe, wizened faces with sharp, even warty, noses that look evil and witchlike and imbue their interrogatory gazes with menace.

Carlotti exposes his intention to discourage empathy in a frame that shows the bonfire built during the night by those guarding the grain in the courtyard (Fig. 5.2). Flames lick welcomingly upward. In the center, an obviously well-fed, even fat, woman warms herself enough by the flames (and drink) that she can expose a full figure with cleavage. She smiles joyfully out at the viewer, offering a toast. Others nearby also smile congenially. They appear healthy and nourished; none looks starved or wretched. Closer to the fire, one old man and woman do appear thin, even sunken; but the robustness of the other figures denies any general famine or scarcity, and the old couple themselves appear repellent rather than pitiable. They too smile out at the viewer, but the man's bald head looks like a skull; dark circles around the woman's eyes give them a ghoulish cast. They resemble cadavers, and the elderly man wears a suit more appropriate for a funeral than for a riot. Just behind the buxom woman in the center lurks a figure with a face suggestive of a monkey.

Without the guidance of Gordeaux's text, which follows this image and explains that the rioters built the bonfire to stand ready to "thwart a possible counteroffensive from authorities," the viewer might easily imagine a carnival celebration (complete with disguises, masquing, and uninhibited behavior) or a coven of witches and warlocks (with celebrations of death and unnatural

Fig. 5.2. *Carnival Carlotti Style.* From the archives of *France-Soir,* Paris, by permission of *France-Soir.*

temptations), rather than see a cold January vigil mounted in desperate protest. Drinks in hand, the crowd hardly seems likely to starve. Compared with the frontispiece to the 1919 Edouard-Joseph edition of Vallès's *Les Blouses,* this image discredits and denigrates the popular movement.

Carlotti next shows a gentleman trying to negotiate with the crowd (Fig. 5.3). They surround him, gesturing and grimacing, menacing, suspicious, angry, looking even more ghoulish. Gordeaux identifies the gentleman as the justice of the peace, Gaulier, who has arrived to persuade the crowd to "respect the law." However, "they surround Gaulier; they threaten him; he was nearly thrown alive into the fire whose flames gave a reddish gleam to their tense, malicious, disquieting faces."

As the story moves forward, evidence mounts that the rioters have an agenda of violence, not justice; destruction, not subsistence. The "overexcited" "terrifying column" of women and men armed with "scythes, pickaxes, sledgehammers, and felling axes" ignore or threaten authorities, sound the tocsin, devastate the mill, and rampage through town. When the miller, Cloquemin, tries "for the public good" to save his flour and grain from destruction and "of-

Fig. 5.3. *Remonstrance Confronts Reason.* From the archives of *France-Soir,* Paris, by permission of *France-Soir.*

fers it to the rioters for distribution to the poor," the crowd demonstrates that it "doesn't care about the shortage" by splitting open the sacks and "trampling it underfoot, ruining it, wasting it, just for the sake of it."[42] They have sacked and pillaged, forced the gendarmes to disarm (an event completely manufactured by Gordeaux),[43] and "extracted from the town councilors a promise that all grain . . . held by the proprietors will be sold . . . at three francs the double *décalitre.*"[44] "Even these accords at town hall do not interest the true insurgents, those whose declared initial motive for rioting never held more than theoretical importance, and who, considering destruction and rapine as thrilling games, love insurrection for itself."[45] Gordeaux calls the crowd's actions at proprietors' houses "raids" and, even more significantly, "punitive expeditions," language politicians and journalists used to describe clashes in the colonies, especially in Algeria.

The mob has primed itself for the struggle at the Chambert house. Gordeaux and Carlotti make the most of it. Carlotti's initial image features Mme Chambert, a distinguished-looking elderly lady, strikingly different in appearance—carefully coiffed, thin, erect, and composed—from the witchlike harridans who have swelled the crowds of rioters. She sits at a table, looking at two wild-haired men dressed as common people. Behind her stands a younger gentleman, her son, Chambert, who looks serious but holds his hands behind his back, threatening no one. To either side, in the background, two servants (Madeleine Blanchet and Louis Bourgeot) stand, looking worried. Gordeaux explains that, with her son's permission, "Marie-Thérèse Moreau de Bellesourd, a wife living separated from her husband, M. Huard-Chambert," complied with the two delegates' demands that she sign the engagement to sell grain at a reduced price. More than any previous version, Gordeaux's text insists on calling the Chamberts by their more formal, aristocratic-sounding names, a distinction that further distances them from their tormenters to elicit greater sympathy from readers.

Gordeaux and Carlotti hone a pointed narrative from the historically blurred one of the Venin shooting. Finding an appropriate context for Venin's death matters to Gordeaux because *Le Crime ne paie pas* intends to persuade the reader to believe that three beheadings and multiple sentences to the galleys constitute condign punishment. Gordeaux must minimize the mitigating circumstances of Venin's death (just as he has minimized the suffering and injustice leading up to 13 January 1847). In fact, Gordeaux and Carlotti trot out several possible justifications for Chambert to shoot Venin.

First, author and illustrator suggest that Chambert stepped up to defend his loyal male servant Louis Bourgeot. Carlotti portrays the struggle between Bourgeot and the rioter, Venin. At first, Bourgeot has thrown Venin to the ground, while Chambert holds out his arm to restrain the other intruders, including Bienvenu. Mme Chambert stands by his side, clearly distraught.

Below the image, Gordeaux explains that just as Mme Chambert has signed the engagement, Venin and his group barge into the house demanding money. Bourgeot steps up to halt their advance, and Venin yells, "Here is the first brigand to kill." Bourgeot tackles Venin and a fight ensues. Gordeaux writes that "Venin, being younger, gets the upper hand." A second image shows Venin now throttling Bourgeot, who appears on the verge of succumbing. The other intruders have eluded Chambert's restraint and look poised to attack. Chambert, who has armed himself with his rifle, aims from his shoulder directly at Venin's head. Gordeaux explains that, "worried about his servant's life, M. Huard-Chambert grabbed his hunting rifle off its pegs. He aimed it at Venin. The latter let Bourgeot go immediately and headed directly for M. Huard-Chambert, who, loathe to use his weapon, let Venin advance." In the next scene Chambert shoots Venin. However, Chambert has lowered his weapon to a largely nonoffensive position, down by his hip. Venin has grasped its barrel, perhaps to snatch it away or to redirect it. Whatever the intent, he may have aimed it at himself. So, when Chambert fires, Venin receives the blast directly. Angry rioters hold their own weapons ready as they hover nearby. Gordeaux's narrative explains: "In one leap, he [Venin] throws himself on [Chambert], grabbing him by the collar with one hand, while with the other he tries to push the rifle aside. M. Huard-Chambert struggles. The two men wrestle in a confused mêlée. Suddenly, an explosion rings out. Smoke comes out of M. Huard-Chambert's rifle. Venin leaps backward, letting loose howls of pain and he grabs his stomach with both hands." In this, as in so many previous narratives of Chambert shooting Venin, Chambert *does* nothing, except grab his gun. Thereafter the action passes to Venin, and even to the gun itself. Chambert is not the subject of any verb once the struggle begins. The gun itself has more agency than Chambert.

Gordeaux offers a second explanation for Chambert's readiness to use his gun: to defend his mother's honor. Carlotti's images enhance an interpretation that emphasizes a protective son. In various illustrations, Chambert hovers over his frightened and frail mother, shielding her with his body while Venin and Bourgeot fight. In another panel (Fig. 5.4), Carlotti shows the dazed old lady trying to reorient and steady herself after rioters have flung her ruthlessly to the floor. Her female servant, Madeleine Blanchet, struggles valiantly against Bienvenu to prevent greater harm. Other wild-eyed rioters press in from behind him. What son, the story asks, would not seek to protect his mother from such a fate?[46]

Gordeaux does not echo previous explanations that granted Chambert the right to protect his property, with guns if necessary, from incursions. He emphatically recounts the "sack and pillage of several private residences" as part of the litany of crimes committed. But in the Chambert/Venin incident, Gordeaux emphasizes that Chambert's duty to his servant and his mother, the human bonds of loyalty and filial devotion, justified his reaction.

The rioters did not excuse Chambert for killing Venin, however. Gordeaux and Carlotti portray the tracking and killing of Chambert: enraged rioters rampage throughout the Chambert house; Chambert begs for clemency, receives an axe blow to the head, seeks refuge between two beds in saddler Rue's

Fig. 5.4. *Helpless; Heroine.* From the archives of *France-Soir,* Paris, by permission of *France-Soir.*

nearby shop, and gets dragged out into the street.[47] Throughout the fracas, the rioters (with Bienvenu leading or in their midst) look enraged, depraved, and increasingly simian—a symptom of evolution in reverse.

Finally, in a repugnant image of the savage final attack (Fig. 5.5), Chambert sprawls on his back, bleeding from head wounds, while three men and a woman hover.[48] Two men have already pierced his body with a pitchfork and stave; another raises his axe, readying a massive blow. Gordeaux writes: "The sabot-maker, Louis Michot, struck him with his iron sledgehammer; the day laborer Etienne Billaut hit him with his roadman's hammer; the day laborer Jean Foigny hacked at him with a pitchfork that he had turned into a lance, by breaking two tines; a certain Arrouy planted a manure pitchfork in his stomach, then in the head; a woman, Anne Cotteron, as enraged as the men, beat on the wounded man with a heavy sabot."

Gordeaux summarizes the episode as a "savage, barbaric execution." Even this atrocity has not "calmed the insurgents' nerves," so they attack yet another old man, M. Dauvergne, who lies sick in bed. Carlotti illustrates this assault and the intimidation of Dauvergne's wife as the "horde" smashes, "just for the pleasure of it, the beautiful new piano of which she was so proud."[49]

Fig. 5.5. *The Death of Chambert.* From the archives of *France-Soir,* Paris, by permission of *France-Soir.*

More than any previous versions, Gordeaux and Carlotti's version positions both poor and elite women in positions to elicit either fear/disgust or empathy/outrage. Although Bouchardon's account had clearly provided source material and inspiration for Gordeaux and Carlotti's story, they further streamlined and polarized gender roles. For example, Carlotti shows the women who intercepted the shipment of grain on 13 January, but neither his images nor Gordeaux's text acknowledges women's well-documented, provocative role in the event itself.[50] Both Gordeaux's references to and Carlotti's images of women among the protesters function to discredit the entire movement. As we have seen, the first women whose faces appear in Carlotti's images resemble witches. The only alternative figure to appear among the protesters is the provocatively dressed, buxom woman who toasts the viewer from the bonfire. Neither image encourages sympathy, and by suggesting evil intent or undermining claims of privation, both help criminalize the protest itself.

As in Bouchardon's story, women in Gordeaux's text play no strategically important part in the riots. Ironically, however, their striking presence in Carlotti's images may suggest a more influential role. As witch or harlot, they exude potentially bewitching or alluring auras that, coupled with repeated references to ancestral barbarism and savagery embedded in the common people, posit an explanation for the outbreak of disorder unconnected to dearth and exploitation.

No one woman emerges either visually or textually (as they do in Vallès's narrative) from the ranks of the common people to represent the protesters. The one figure who functions as the iconic rioter is male: Baptiste Bienvenu, the day laborer, whose dark, hirsute, axe-wielding form occurs in virtually every crowd image and in most of the texts listing rioters and their deeds. The viewer comes to recognize him as a caricature of a rioter. Gordeaux's textual profile complements the visual one: "Vagabond, homeless, perpetually unemployed, scorned by all."[51] Such an oversimplified portrait, coupled with a visual image that emphasizes his brute strength and robust health, evokes classic conservative images of the able-bodied "undeserving poor": lazy malcontents who would rather riot than work.

Bourgeois or propertied women appear more frequently, and their images serve to elicit sympathy and outrage at the atrocities committed against their class. For example, from the first scene, when the intruders force the distinguished old lady to sign the engagement, to the subsequent assault on her son, to the final image of the brutal attack that flings her to the ground and compels Madeleine Blanchet to interpose herself between the raging Bienvenu (yet again) and her mistress, Gordeaux and Carlotti make Mme Huard-Chambert an object of empathy. As single head of an invaded and desecrated household, as mother of a murdered son, and as elderly prey of physical assault, she symbolizes victimization in many of its terrifying forms.

During the third day of rioting, "maniacs" also abused the "saintly elderly unmarried woman" Mlle Uranie Lindet (Bouchardon's spelling), a woman "known for her inexhaustible charitable spirit" and whose chignon distinguishes her from the straggling witchlocks of the aggressively hostile common women.[52] As she "advanced toward the demonstrators, a sack of money in her hand, to give to each an offering . . . three maniacs threw themselves at her and violently tore her sack away from her." Gordeaux writes that "most . . . people there disapproved of this brutal act. Citizens ran to the scene [and] seized the three culprits, . . . to turn them over to the brigadier Caudrelier." Gordeaux suggests, as had Bouchardon, that this incident stirred the "bourgeois" to emerge from hiding and take a stand against the insurgents.

In pursuit of images to fire outrage about criminal behavior, Gordeaux and

Carlotti turned several stories of female bravery into tales of female victimization. Nevertheless, they do acknowledge the courageous intervention of Mme Chambert's loyal servant, Madeleine Blanchet, although Carlotti's image seems to marginalize Blanchet's selfless act (Fig. 5.4). At its center, Mme Chambert lies on the floor, shaken and terrified. Blanchet is relegated to the background of the frame. In the text that follows, Gordeaux brings her to the focal point: "The rioters seize the elderly Mme Huard-Chambert, née Moreau de Bellesourd, [who is] paralyzed by fear. They drag her into the courtyard, throw her on the ground, and get ready to kill her. But her faithful servant, Madeleine Blanchet, covers her with her body: 'Band of cowards,' the brave woman yells. She has such a resolute air that the rioters, ashamed of their behavior toward the old inoffensive woman, abandon Mme Huard-Chambert."[53] Thus, brave women, like Madeleine Blanchet and the Mlle Lindet, could impose some degree of shame and even restraint on the rioters.

In addition to gendered stereotypes, Gordeaux and Carlotti play upon images about old age to mobilize audience attitudes against the *jacquerie*. Throughout, author and illustrator emphasize the advanced age of the propertied elite who find themselves the targets of popular rage, including the "old" mayor, Guesnyer; an "old municipal councilor, M. Jean Brillant," whom rioters surround and threaten on his way to the town hall;[54] and the Gaulins, referred to as "the old couple."[55] Text and images reveal "old miller Cloquemin" as a terrified geriatric, scurrying around his bedroom while the rioters burst through the door. Gordeaux writes that when he flees, "he soon has a fierce pack on his heels who track him, and catch him just at the moment when, out of breath and exhausted, the old man throws himself into the arms of his sons." Similarly, the crowd attacks the house and property of the "old proprietor," forge owner Bonneau, "aged seventy-two."[56] At the Dauvergne household, the marauders "invade the room where M. Dauvergne, an old man, reposes" and make him pay a 260 franc "ransom" to keep his bed. Carlotti shows an old man frightened in his bed. Gordeaux even mentions that the sergeant who commands the troops that arrive in Buzançais with the Prefect is "old."[57] By contrast, only one rioter, "the old agricultural worker François Légeron," is identified as elderly.[58] All the protesters appear young and vigorous, capable of working and feeding themselves, but instead choose to terrorize and rob venerable, old people.

The theme of old age connects to other preoccupations of the 1950s. First, by the 1950s, the depopulation of the French countryside had stirred widespread concern. Already an issue in the era after World War I, after World War II the accelerating trend exacerbated the anxiety of many observers who saw the French countryside and its agrarian society as fundamental to French national identity and its most important (conservative) values. "Modernization" changed the lifestyles and attitudes even of those who stayed on the land. In many French imaginations, older age and traditional peasant society intertwined in positive and negative ways. Although Gordeaux himself, Lazareff, or the editorial policy of *France-Soir* was unlikely to have found much appealing in the right-wing (and often anti-Semitic) parties of the peasantry or *poujadisme,* the shared sense of a declining countryside and its mutating values could encourage a view of old age as worthy of respect and protection.

Second, this perception of a countryside losing population reinforced observations about the demographic structure of French society in the 1950s. The population distribution of France had changed, with older people constituting an increasing proportion of it. Their visible presence, the conservative critique of a rapidly modernizing France, and a tendency to link that change to the growing younger population resulting from the postwar baby boom[59] might have made depicting the elites of Buzançais as enfeebled by age seem natural to Gordeaux, himself sixty-five years old.

Identifying not only the rioters' victims but also those individuals in positions of power as older men seems to encourage the reader to explain and excuse the ill-preparedness and lack of solidarity and resistance among the Buzançais elite. Too old to staunchly defend their own property, let alone the public order, these geriatrics make easy prey for the youthful, vigorous, undisciplined animals who rise up against them. Small wonder that the lone brigadier of the gendarmerie, Caudrelier, and his tiny complement of men find themselves in such difficult straits.

The series takes on both the question of administrative competence and the lack of elite (or bourgeois) solidarity during the riots. Authorities fail and err repeatedly in the story. The mayor "fails" to stop the interception of the grain carts.[60] Not only does the justice of the peace, Gaulier, fail to get those standing guard around the bonfire to "respect the law," but he actually "overexcites them." The mayor fails to call up the national guard, "although he had the right." When he does ask the fire captain to assemble his men, the captain "takes refuge behind the ill will of his men" and refuses to act. The secretary-general for the prefecture fails to comprehend the seriousness of events at Buzançais and refuses to act on his own account to send troops when the mayor requests assistance the first time.[61]

When the rioters seek to sound the tocsin, the sacristan defers to the parish priest, who "by good fortune is liked by all." In Gordeaux's version, he "has several bottles [of wine] brought, fills glasses, drinks to the health of his nocturnal visitors, and with cheerful conversation, the good-natured man calms them a little, provisionally diverting them from their project to sound the tocsin."[62] Whether his wine helped cool or heat tempers, the likeable Abbé Audoul did not manage to halt the assault on the tocsin for long.

At the town hall, the rioters find local authorities and notables huddled, "overmatched by events, terrorized, panic-stricken." Asked to lower and fix prices, "under threats, the authorities and notables signed anything." Gordeaux concludes that "legitimate government thus passed into the hands of the insurgents."[63] He adds a new (and fabricated) twist that further weakens the possibility of resistance. He explains that "in order to [neutralize] the forces of order . . . they demanded that brigadier Caudrelier and his three gendarmes deposit their arms and hats at the caserne."[64] When twenty-five dragoons arrive, Gordeaux has the lieutenant explain to the prefect that he fears sending his men to engage in street-by-street combat because they would risk massacre. When the prefect asks why, the lieutenant responds, "I have to admit it . . . we left without a single cartridge!"[65]

The prefect ultimately concludes that, without effective protection from the cavalry, he should leave Buzançais. The *procureur du roi,* who has accompanied him, agrees that to stay "would reveal to everyone a flouted authority," and the *juge d'instruction* further admits that "as long as the law cannot be maintained, our presence here diminishes us." In the end, Gordeaux explains, "the magistrates get back into their carriage and, escorted by the dragoons, they leave for the capital. Insurrection thus remains master of Buzançais."[66] Gordeaux's account of disarmed gendarmes and unprepared soldiers makes a mockery of July Monarchy armed forces. But when they return two days later, force restores the law: a squadron of lancers and an entire battalion of infantry clear the way for magistrates from the Cour Royale at Bourges. The repression will strike hard, but by then authority itself has suffered massive humiliation.

Gordeaux also reveals the lack of solidarity among elites in Buzançais. Old age and the surprise factor notwithstanding, they fail to make the slightest effort to rally resistance. Gordeaux explains that not until the "insurrectional fever" had abated on the 15th, when only small bands, composed mostly of women, remained, did "the 'bourgeois' begin to regain their courage." It took the assault on the charitable "saint" Mlle Linguet (Gordeaux's spelling), to get "some 'bourgeois' to leave their houses where for two days they had barricaded themselves." Now they assembled and yelled "To arms!" Then, finally, the mayor did what he should have done at once: "He gave the order to rally the national guard. Immediately, the members of the national guard dressed themselves in their uniforms, took up their arms, and assembled before the town hall under the command of M. Louis-Joseph Huard-Chambert, the father of the unfortunate Eudoxe Huard-Chambert, savagely assassinated on the 14th by the rioters."[67] Gordeaux supplied no commentary and Carlotti no image of the bourgeoisie cowering in their homes, but they clearly emerge as cowards and the mayor as ineffectual. Unlike Bouchardon, Gordeaux does not laud the brigadier, Caudrelier. In Gordeaux's version, Caudrelier makes several errors in judgment. He agrees to disarm himself and his men and argues that, "by not taking them on directly, we conserved the possibility of intervening and preaching calm."[68] In addition, he stationed his small force outside the wrong house, while rioters attacked the Chamberts, recognizing his error only after the deaths of Venin and Chambert.

Carlotti's final image of an authority figure shows Louis-Philippe's wife, Queen Marie-Amélie, reading a letter from *frère* Jean de Dieu de Magallon, asking for intercession. Virtually absent from July Monarchy public life, the queen symbolized bourgeois notions of female difference and domesticity.[69] Passive, pious, and private—the epitome of female bourgeois culture—this "bourgeois Queen" sits in her bourgeois setting, amid her bourgeois furnishings, and reads an appeal "to ask for efforts worthy of her piety to save the three men condemned to death." But in keeping with her apolitical persona, she does nothing. The verdict remains unchanged.

Despite the extensive evidence of non-, mis-, and malfeasance on the part of those in authority in Buzançais, the series directs viewers to conclude that those arrested had to pay. Gordeaux supplies no contextual information to explain why rioters targeted some homes rather than others, or why they reacted more violently to some proprietors than to others. Their actions appear gratuitous and irrational, more terrifying because unexplained, except by instinctual savage barbarism or insanity. Mitigating factors melt away as the series nears its end. The story's last frame and text narrate quite simply the execution of the three men sentenced to death. Only the last line hints that the affair might then have resonated beyond the scaffold, perhaps to 1848. As the last man, Velluet, steps up to meet his fate, "he says nothing. He contents himself with a jest of revolt and despair before being thrown upon the fatal chopping block."[70] For Velluet and his fellow villains, then, crime surely had not paid. For Paul Gordeaux, J.-A. Carlotti, and their boss, Pierre Lazareff, it paid handsomely as *Le Crime ne paie pas,* as part of the dynamic fuel powering the rise of *France-Soir.*

Gordeaux's vertical cartoon series had no mission to inform at the cost of alienating readers. He nevertheless addressed issues that carried political weight; after all, one could scarcely represent love or crime without passing judgments about morality and justice. Even after picking his stories from history, he still confronted choices with every incident he selected. The *Crime ne paie pas* series offered little subtlety. The acts it portrayed led only to punishment: crime did not, must not pay. That the series recounted acts defined at the outset as criminal formed a circular logic that cast the actors as criminals, not righteous protesters, not political revolutionaries. But then most people in France—in that violent era at home and abroad in which they lived—probably felt reassured by such logic, just as stories of superheroes righting wrongs and saving the world from disaster often offered more satisfying solutions to problems than reality did. Whatever weaknesses might lurk in the constituted authorities, however much they had to bumble their way to resolving the problems they confronted, in Gordeaux's series, resolve them they eventually did. That readers and viewers knew from the start how the stories would end may very well have provided one of the attractions of the series. A world in disorder would ultimately find order again.

By the 1970s, *France-Soir* had lost much of its readership. A combination of factors contributed to its decline: the rise of radio and television as alternative news and entertainment sources; the challenge posed by the increasingly successful specialized press of daily newspapers (like *L'Equipe,* the sports daily) and weekly magazines (*Le Nouvel Observateur, Marie Claire,* and *Télé 7,* for example); the failure of *France-Soir* to adapt to changing reading tastes; its close association with Gaullist politics; and its hostile reaction to the spirit of '68.[71] After the death in 1972 of its founder, director, and guiding light, Pierre Lazareff, no subsequent editor managed to adapt to the changing times. After a major labor struggle in the mid-1970s, the paper never really recovered.[72]

By the late 1970s, editors resorted to a variety of strategies, including several relatively "cheap fixes," to rescue *France-Soir* from plummeting toward oblivion. Among these, they opted to recycle Gordeaux's *Le Crime ne paie pas* in 1976.[73] It had proved wildly successful in its first run, and editors now hoped to lure former readers through nostalgia and new ones through novelty. In fact, however, the decision to rerun the series says more about the desperate straits of *France-Soir* than the editors' sense of the reading public, with which they had demonstrably lost touch. Nevertheless, the republication did insert Buzançais yet again into the popular media, and at bargain rates. Since the paper already held the copyrights and the originals, reprinting cost much less than commissioning new work. The editors did not republish all of Gordeaux's strips, nor did they print them in the same order as in the 1950s, but they did select "La Jacquerie de Buzançais." Its first episode appeared in January 1979. With no modification in image or text, it ran for nineteen days, just as it had in 1956.

Some readers may have remembered Buzançais from twenty-four years earlier and read the strip influenced by the context in which they had first encountered it. Others would have read "La Jacquerie de Buzançais" in the current context of 1979. Certainly much had changed. The Fourth Republic had collapsed; France had lost most of its empire, some of it (such as Indochina and Algeria) only after bloody wars and humiliating defeats; de Gaulle had forged a Fifth Republic and then quit when voters had abandoned him after the explosive events of 1968; the oil crisis of 1973 had ended the era of spectacular postwar economic growth, *les trentes glorieuses;* population growth had slowed significantly as the birth rate plummeted; women had entered the full-time labor market in unprecedented numbers, while feminist activists had demanded, and ultimately received, liberalization of divorce laws and reproductive rights that included contraception and abortion; tensions had mounted over the place of immigrants and the citizen-children of immigrants in French society; rising inflation and unemployment had heightened dissatisfaction with government policy. All this, coupled with a series of political scandals, had enabled the Socialist Party to make positive, if uneven, gains during the 1970s; activist intellectuals had drawn on the respect French public opinion had traditionally accorded them to keep issues of human rights and social justice, as well as the people's right to demand these by various means, on the political agenda.[74]

By 1979, readers had grown accustomed to an image of France as an *état providence* and of the French people as legitimately empowered (especially after 1968) to assert themselves, sometimes even violently, in pursuit of social rights. Given that, how might they interpret visual cues such as Carlotti's caricatures of Bienvenu, the women around the bonfire, local authority, or even the image of Queen Marie-Amélie? Drama or satire, serious or puerile, edifying or offensive? We can only speculate that some readers/viewers in 1979 reacted to the texts and images differently than they (or their parents) had years earlier. We know for certain, however, that the return of Gordeaux's series did not reinvigorate *France-Soir.* Burdened by losses, stripped of its once peerless staff, saddled with outdated printing facilities, bought and sold, it drifted into bankruptcy, waning with the century itself.

"LE PAIN ET LE VIN" IN 1978

Meanwhile, back in the TV studio, the burgeoning visual medium of television had discovered, as had other media, that the story of Buzançais lent itself to adaptation. During prime time, on 10 June 1978, Antenne 2, one of France's three television channels, offered a compelling and richly produced dramatization of the Buzançais affair entitled "Le Pain et le Vin" (Bread and Wine).[75] For eighty minutes, the viewing public watched a fictionalized reenactment of both the riot and the trial with dialogue drawn from the affair's transcript and images from the era's paintings and engravings. "Le Pain et le Vin" was the second of five historical *téléfilms* in the series *Les Grands procès témoins de leur temps* (Great Trials, Witnesses of Their Times).

By 1978, the French media had already accustomed their viewers to a steady diet of historical dramas. On the night "Le Pain et le Vin" aired, radio listeners (France-Culture) might have already heard "La Guerre des sabotiers" (The War of the Sabot Makers) about "misery and revolt among the peasantry of the Sologne in the seventeenth century." Alain Decaux's long-running, popular radio history program *La Tribune de l'histoire* ran a show titled "La prise de pouvoir par Henri IV (1589)" (Henry IV's Seizure of Power) at virtually the same time (8:30 p.m.) as "Le Pain et le Vin."[76]

Posing ethically and politically difficult questions about collective or individual acts of violence and their consequences proved a common thread for the entire "Great Trials" series. All the shows addressed contentious political and social moments in history and emphasized their continuing relevance. For example, the first in the series, "Les fusils sont arrivés" (The Guns Have Arrived), which aired in October 1977, revisited a trial that followed a bloody strike in a provincial factory in Haute-Savoie in 1904. The owner's four sons had fired on picketing strikers, killing three and wounding forty-one; the survivors responded by sacking the factory. The owner's sons were charged with murder and six workers indicted for attacking the factory. The jury condemned the shooters to one year of prison and acquitted the workers (defended by Aristide Briand).

Another *téléfilm* in the same series, airing in November 1978, "La preuve par cinq" (Casting Out Fives), considered the case of an early twentieth-century wet nurse suspected of as many as five counts of infanticide. The courts repeatedly acquitted her until witnesses caught her in the act of killing a young boy. When she was finally declared insane, the court sentenced her to a psychiatric hospital. "Coincidence, insanity, or criminality?" the program's publicity inquired.

"Le Pain et le Vin" also had an impressive pedigree. Television and cultural *saltambanque* (impresario) and *papa* (boss) Pierre Desgraupes (1918–93) wrote the script.[77] By the time "Le Pain" appeared, Desgraupes had already established a dominant place and publicly recognizable name for himself in French television.[78] After World War II, he had worked for French radio, reporting and directing the news for Pierre Lazareff at *France-Soir,* and also created a radio literary show with Pierre Dumayet. In 1953, he decided to follow Lazareff and seize the exciting possibilities offered by television.[79] By the mid-1970s, Desgraupes had acquired an impressive record in television: as cohost with Dumayet of the paradigmatic television literary review *Lectures pour tous* (1953–68);[80] as one of Pierre Lazareff's "five pillars" who inaugurated *Cinq colonnes à la une* (1959–68), the first French television show dedicated to investigative journalism;[81] as writer/producer of several successful courtroom drama series; as part of the direction (1969–72) of Office de radiodiffusion-télévision française (ORTF), the state oversight authority for French radio and television; as director (1969–72) of the news for TF1, the first French television channel; and as director of Editel, a production company (1972–81).[82]

Beginning with one state-owned channel after World War II, France added a second in 1964 (renamed Antenne 2 in 1975 after the breakup of ORTF) and a third in 1973 (renamed France-Régions 3 in 1975). As an exclusively state-owned public service (until 1981), French television enjoyed the benefits of commercial-free development but found itself vulnerable to government interference and administrative rigidity. Its original mission sought to "inform, educate, entertain, and cultivate," while "watching over the morality of programming, maintaining respect for the public, and defending the French language."[83] Both Fourth and Fifth Republic governments saw television as a useful "tool in the service of nation building."[84]

In short, government policy mandated television as the locus of "cultural popularization" for the growing mass of French viewers.[85] Through the 1960s and early 1970s, French television producers embedded this imperative in scripts harmonically resonant with French literary tradition. By creating a "visual grammar," they contributed to the construction of moments of "shared memory,"[86] particularly of the rural France so dear to the French soul and so rapidly disappearing.[87]

However, the rapid and uneven pace of technological capabilities, public opinion and tastes, and the explosion of viewership by the mid-1970s exposed the fact that these charges had proved harder to fulfill than many contemporaries had imagined. By 1974–75, after television had played an important part in debates during the presidential race, the Giscard government suppressed ORTF and its unilateral control. The government urged the three channels to nurture pluralism and serve the diverse tastes of television audiences, but it still "considered television an instrument of social unification."[88] Moreover, despite this new emphasis on liberty and independence for the three channels, which included attempts to foster competition among them for audiences, government oversight remained a "permanent feature" of French television, even if outright interference proved rare and, when it occurred, contentious.[89]

Desgraupes's work in French television clearly shared the Lazareff(ian) commitment to take French culture and news to the widest possible audience while still putatively maintaining high standards in content and presentation. Desgraupes had frequently described his target audience as "a female shopkeeper in Périgueux," who "could not tolerate a subject that lasted longer than fifteen minutes, could not support subtitles because she had weak eyes, and required a louder volume when foreigners spoke."[90]

As an "instrument of mass communication," television, Desgraupes explained, "should be the least elitist as possible." Although he insisted that he had no "educational vocation" and he rankled at the idea of generating "cultural programs" for television, he did believe that *téléspectateurs* deserved accessible but high-quality programs, a "link between culture and entertainment."[91] He believed that to produce successful history programs on television, one had to think "not as a historian, but as a producer of spectacles" because to compete with the cinema demanded quality production.[92] Although state ownership of French television in this era still protected it from the type of commercial-driven demands found in American television, the advent of surveys of viewing habits (the Audimat) and post-1974 reforms introducing greater competition among channels had made it more heavily demand-driven than during its first few decades of existence.

Television programming on the night that "Le Pain et le Vin" debuted typified the medium's efforts to fulfill these conflicting mandates. TF1 ran a musical variety show hosted by Mort Shuman, an American singer-songwriter of several popular French songs, such as "Le Lac Majeur." FR3 offered the Verdi opera *Le Trouvère.* A2 may have had a winning combination that night, for immediately after "Le Pain et le Vin" ended, France, rebounding from a bitter loss to host and eventual champion Argentina, beat Hungary in the World Cup.

Whether viewers knew it or not, the *Grands procès* series represented a significantly more sophisticated rendering of issues than the *Le Crime ne paie pas* cartoon strip in Lazareff's *France-Soir,* although the TV rendering of Buzançais manifests a knowledge of Gordeaux's version of the "Jacquerie." Desgraupes—constrained by some mixture of limitations of cost, conventions inherent in the television medium, and artistic choices—also took liberties with the historical record. He filmed "Le Pain et le Vin" in the village of Beaulieu-lès-Loches rather than in Buzançais, showed only fifteen rather than twenty-six accused on the court's bench, reduced the action to a few episodes, allowed one character to represent many others, and introduced two fictitious characters as external observers and commentators. His nuanced script and imagery, however, did locate the riot and trial within a wider cultural and political frame of French history, replete with the interpretive ambiguities the affair raised.[93]

By invoking within the program itself a wide variety of other textual and visual signs known (he hoped) to French viewers, Desgraupes could give the affair a richer context and resonance, as well as compensate for the possibility, if not certainty, that most viewers had no detailed previous knowledge of Buzançais. His work (on *Lectures pour tous,* especially) had long sought to allay fears that television would merely debase French culture; his *Grands procès* series seemed to seek to hearten those who, like Gaullist minister and member of the Académie française Michel Debré, worried that "our history would be known only through historical fiction and television."[94]

From the beginning, the title "Le Pain et le Vin" played with both a literal and figurative set of images. First, the show targeted bread as the primary focus of popular concern and wine as an aggravating factor. The show's summary explained that, in 1847, when three carts had stopped at an inn in Buzançais, "men and women surrounded them, because the sacks were full of grain and grain lacked in the region. . . . Little by little, with the help of wine, spirits heated up and violence rose." The Christian sacrament of communion would also have resonated with a broad audience. But in a third intertextual reference, the title also echoed that of Ignazio Silone's 1936 novel, *Pane e vino,* one theme of which explores the life, ignorance, and desperate struggles of peasants in the Italian countryside under fascism. By suggesting similarities between the common people of Buzançais and those of Silone's Pietrassecca a century later, Desgraupes could play with the contemporary gap that distanced *la France profonde* (in all its ambiguity) from the rest of the country, the role of formal politics in village culture, and the persistence of morally contested issues. "Social drama or an unbridling of the criminal instincts of the crowd?" the show's advertising blurb asked. It continued: "The task of the tribunal will be difficult as witnesses and accused overlap with each other, and where the moral principles asserted seem a thousand leagues removed from life."

Desgraupes further nested the Buzançais affair in a context of other carefully positioned, widely known historical symbols, scholarly and popular. For example, the show opens (and ends) with an image of Honoré Daumier's famous post-1848 painting *The Uprising,*[95] concludes by quoting Karl Marx and Victor Hugo on the affair, and introduces several shots that evoke the Le Nain brothers' paintings of peasant life in the seventeenth century. During the initial sequence foregrounding the shipment interception, the gendarme gently chides the drunken Légeron, who has referred to his past revolutionary experiences, by teasing him that "you still think you are at the Bastille!" (a reference not found in the documents from the era), thus linking Buzançais with one of the most crucial events in French history. All of these allusions contributed to integrating the Buzançais affair (and particularly the issues it raised) more fully into French history—as part of its mainstream, rather than marginalizing it as criminal and outside the accepted metanarrative, as various previous versions had by affiliating it with the September Massacres or the Terror. By leaving questions open rather than resolving them, as trials are intended to do (and as television programs usually do), "Le Pain" invited continued discussion of its issues.

In part, this approach, which makes history relevant to contemporary interests and concerns, is dictated not just by producers or writers seeking to interest audiences in their product but by the nature of the medium itself. Television (like film) has technical difficulty "rendering temporal dimensions with much precision [and tends to] amplify the present sense of immediacy out of proportion."[96] Even during the 1970s and the early 1980s, a golden age for history on television in which professional historians got "a carte blanche" to show historians' history,[97] the sorts of extratextual references characteristic of "popular history" and preprofessional history also helped explain the success of history stories in television.

"Le Pain" also drew inspiration from contemporary French popular culture. Although the script did not treat Buzançais as an essentially criminal affair as Gordeaux's *France-Soir* cartoon had, it drew several images (and representations of certain historical figures) directly from frames found in "La Jacquerie de Buzançais." These included scenes around the initial shipment interception and confrontations between the mayor and rioters. Perhaps even more revealing, the TV program portrayed Bienvenu as remarkably similar to his simian comic-strip counterpart. Unlike Gordeaux's Bienvenu, however, Desgraupes's character performs a more complicated role than simply brandishing an axe.

These sorts of recognizable signs—some known to all audiences, others only to a smaller group—could please viewers who enjoyed both their own capacity to recognize them and the comfort such recognition offers amid the unknown.[98] References to well-known events in French history and images widely circulating in French culture gave viewers with even modest education entry points into the story, while more educated viewers could enjoy their privileged access to yet another set of signs. Although all genres play with or against intertextuality, cinema and television have proved themselves especially capable of mobilizing not only textual but visual and audio referents.

The program also sought to engage viewers by encouraging an intimacy with the characters that creates identifications with the historical actors portrayed. "The smaller screens and privacy of the home" have encouraged "fashioning most fictional and nonfictional historical portrayals in the style of personal dramas or melodramas played out between a manageable number of protagonists and antagonists. When successful, audiences closely identify with the historical 'actors' and stories being presented."[99] At the expense of historical accuracy, "Le Pain" rapidly focuses viewer attention on the plight of four of the accused (Légeron, Bienvenu, *la femme* Coteron, and Michot) by introducing them into virtually every action scene and by offering frequent close-ups of their faces both during the uprising and during the trial, when they confront both interrogation and sentencing.

While steering clear of the potentially "average viewer"-alienating "critical" or "experimental" histories that film producers had sometimes used to fracture viewers' comfort with the past or with conventional production methods, "Le Pain" also avoids monumental (biographies of heroic men or heroic events) or antiquarian (nostalgic representations of days of yore) approaches to history.[100] In this respect, it reflected the influence of the Annales school, an influence already felt in French television in the 1970s—the "golden age for history on television"—with the success of series based, for example, on Fernand Braudel's *La Méditerranée,* André Burguière's "Les Chemins de l'histoire," and George Duby's *Le Temps des cathédrals.*[101] The film achieves this effect in two principal ways. First, it refuses to impose a straightforward narrative on the Buzançais affair. Recourse to two (fictional) characters from 1900, who reconsider events that took place in their hometown in 1847, flashbacks to both the protest and trial, and shots of nineteenth-century engravings or cartoons that illustrate (or challenge) some aspect of the dialogue deflect the viewer from discerning either a dominant narrative of what happened or an unambiguous interpretation of the events.

Second, the film introduces diverse perspectives by scripting multiple voices: observers, protesters, witnesses, authorities, and magistrates all intervene at various points to offer their interpretations of what happened and why. While some of their lines are invented, many others come directly from the trial transcript. For example, the two fictional characters—a young man, Olivier, and a considerably older man, Oudoul—offer two very different voices.[102] The film opens with Oudoul receiving a visit from Olivier, who wants to resolve questions he has carried with him ever since he witnessed the affair as a child of eight. He wonders especially about causes, responsibility, motives for riot, and what sort of justice the trial's verdicts had actually served. Olivier supplies the voice of the naïve child witness who had matured into a thoughtful, articulate young man. Oudoul, in contrast, witnessed the affair as an educated adult with "somewhat advanced ideas for the time." He saw the trial, and, he explains, his subsequent life experiences have made him more cynical about both human nature and the complicated problem of justice.[103] These two interlocutors perform important functions. They bridge time gaps in the narrative and offer reflections (from the perspective of the Third Republic) on more "contemporary" (late 1970s) issues including the proper relationship between social rights and property rights, the appropriateness of collective violence, the proper role of government in crisis, and the character of the judicial process including capital punishment.

By giving voice to protesters and accused, to authorities (the mayor, Guesnyer; brigadier Caudrelier) and proprietors (Brillaut), to the judge (Mater), prosecutor (Didelot), and one defense lawyer (exact identity unclear), as well as to various voices in the crowds, "Le Pain et le Vin" summons a complicated set of answers to the questions of what happened, who did it, and why. Although much of the film takes place in the courtroom and the viewers get extended exposure to the accused, the judge, and the witnesses, the jury appears only briefly, and no courtroom spectators appear or are heard. As in Desgraupes's program *En votre âme et conscience* (1954–68), the viewer becomes a member of the jury, but with two related differences: the viewer has the benefit both of hindsight (assisted by the interlocutors Olivier and Oudoul) and of contemporary values and experiences. Also unlike *En votre âme et conscience,* however, "Le Pain et le Vin" immediately provided the 1847 verdict and did not solicit a contemporary viewer's verdict at the end.

The initial shipment interception occupies almost one-quarter of the film, an emphasis unusual in previous renditions. The sequence begins with the boy Olivier playing among large sacks of grain on carts stopped in the street. The mountainous sacks of grain remain visible throughout most of the protest reenactment sequences until the film turns to the Chambert episode, as if to remind viewers about the point of the protest. As Olivier plays, a woman's voice shouts that "we are dying of hunger." The camera angle widens to show several similar carts stopped before an inn. A crowd mills anxiously and angrily around the carts, and we hear several individuals declare their intentions to seize their load. The innkeeper's wife emerges to tell the crowd to disperse, but a woman retorts that "since she's not in need, she cannot possibly understand their situation." She urges the crowd to go get the men from the charity workshop. Upon reentering the inn, the innkeeper's wife announces to the carters, obliviously enjoying their meal, that they had better leave because "what they have in the sacks isn't grain but dynamite."[104] The gluttonous carters respond that "just because one is carrying grain it doesn't mean that one has to tighten one's belt." The other announces, "I won't leave until you give me a kiss" and grabs her lasciviously. She breaks free, snarling to her passive husband that she "wears the pants around here."

The shipment interception sequence also introduces many of the important characters: protesters, gendarmes, and authorities. From the outset, "Le Pain" shows unarmed, confused, and frustrated people worried about grain, who become angry only when they confront a harsh, uncomprehending, unbending notability. Four of those accused play more important roles as characters in the film than in the affair itself, but their characters voice the concerns of many. For example, *la femme* Coteron's character plays the pivotal role in the shipment interception: she suggests calling for help from the men from the charity workshop; she and Bienvenu lead the crowd escorting the grain carts to the courtyard; and she speaks defiantly to the mayor, who tries to calm and disperse the crowd. When the brigadier attempts to explain that the grain was destined for Issoudun, whose population also needed grain, she huffed, "Issoudun, isn't that in England?" This retort expresses the long-held view that any grain leaving the town constituted an affront to the community and its priorities, as well as the suspicion that merchants conspired with authorities to starve the people and feed the enemy, whom the French had conventionally associated with England.

Bienvenu may have physically resembled his comic strip counterpart, but the film's portrayal of his character marked a significant departure. Like the *France-Soir* depiction and the historical Bienvenu of 1847, he turned up in almost every crowd, but Desgraupes's character carried no axe and spoke—during both the riot and the trial—more assertively for the common people's needs and rights. After the arrival of the men from the charity workshop, Bienvenu emerges as one of the most important leaders. As *la femme* Coteron leads the grain escort toward the courtyard, he joins her to confront the mayor, who proclaims that "force must belong to the law." Bienvenu counters by asserting the popular right to existence: "The grain belongs to the people and must remain with the people." Although Desgraupes frequently sticks to the trial transcript, such as when his Bienvenu reminds the court "that grain was not 'falling' on the market, neither for gold or silver [and] we needed it," his version emerges increasingly as the counterimage to the prosecution's Bienvenu: simple certainly, but articulate, not stupid; hardworking, not lazy; and respected by his peers, not marginal to the community.

Perhaps even more striking, Bienvenu plays two crucial roles in the television program. First, three days after the initial interceptions, he organizes the community distribution of the seized grain in accordance with the "engagement." Bienvenu presides over the measurement of rations from sacks stacked in the courtyard. He announces that there is "enough" grain at 2 francs for everyone who needs it and "free for the poor."[105] He chases away a man dressed "en bourgeois," saying, "This grain comes from you, get away from it!" He gives an additional measure of grain to one person "because you have children." When a man appears with money from the mill's coffers, Bienvenu tells him to pay with it "and we'll see what to do about it later." The mayor and a gendarme stand nearby huffing in frustration.

Second, on several occasions the film character presents himself as an intermediary between people and authority. Not only does he ally with *la femme* Coteron to present the popular cause to the mayor, but he also claims that he had sought permission from the mayor to negotiate (*parlementer*) with the prefect when he arrived in Buzançais on the second day. Upon hearing this, President Mater explodes at Bienvenu, "But you are *not* a *parlementaire*! You lead pillagers and murderers!"

During the sequence involving the shipment interception, François Légeron emerges clearly as the antithesis to the version proffered by both Gordeaux's comic strip and the 1847 prosecution. No rendition ever disputed that he had, indeed, made his incendiary and revolutionary pronouncements—which included claiming he had seen three revolutions, promising to ready his scythe for the next, and denouncing the bourgeoisie. All versions, while admitting that drink may have clouded his judgment, assumed not only that he chose these words intentionally but also, perhaps more important, that they inspired the protesters as well. The Légeron of "Le Pain," however, appears in a different light as a man whom everyone indulges and no one takes seriously.

He first turns up in the inn, where the carters dally stubbornly. As the gendarme sent to urge them on their way agrees to drink with them, Légeron, manifesting signs of drunkenness himself, stumbles to his feet suggesting that they "drink to the revolution." As the screen switches to the action around the carts outside, Légeron's voice denounces the "sacré bon dieu de bourgeois." On this cue, the film's designated spokesman for the bourgeois / property owners, Brillault, appears at the inn to try to establish some order. Brillault brushes off Légeron's promise to get ready for the next revolution with "You are completely drunk as usual. You still think you are at the Bastille!" A little while later, when Brillault is helping the mayor ready himself for the crowd, he explains that "up until now old Légeron has been playing his habitual role of *sans-culotte.*" As the screen switches again to the interlocutors Olivier and Oudoul, the viewer hears the thoughtful Olivier express sympathy for "poor Légeron, after having told his story of the readied scythe so often, they finally started to take him seriously. . . . All this tragedy needs perhaps a buffoon. It was he." Rather than see Légeron as a dangerous revolutionary rousing others to his banner, Desgraupes portrays him as a silly and even tragic old man, dangerous only to himself.

Because the film disrupts the direct narrative structure of previous renditions of Buzançais, the viewer gets more information only later, during the trial sequences, about conditions in the charity workshop. "Le Pain" repeatedly emphasizes the derisory nature of the assistance available during the crisis, contradicting with images what President Mater asserts insistently during the trial. For example, while Mater berates Bienvenu for claiming need when "the government, the administration, the commune gives you assistance" and Bienvenu protests its insufficiency, the screen shows an engraving of a fat, condescending, well-dressed administrator doling out soup rations from on high to a crowd of desperate women. During another sequence involving Foigny, Desgraupes takes his interrogation directly from the record but yet again undermines Mater's imperious dismissal of Foigny's plea that he could not support his family of six on the charity supplied by showing an engraving of downtrodden women and children dismally queued up outside a Parisian *bureau de bienfaisance.* Foigny's words from the record that "we are six people trying to live on six livres of bread and one sou a day" find no sympathy from Mater, who denies him a right to steal. However, the film's Foigny gets one line beyond his 1847 interrogation: "What are we to do, then? Die?"

Similarly, when the voices of authority deride the men employed at the public work project as lazy ne'er-do-wells, visual images counter starkly. During the verbal duel between Mater and Bienvenu over the provenance of his 25 francs, Mater denounces those who chose the workshop over offers by notables to pay 25 sous more a day. He explains to the jury that "at the workshop they lounge about [*on flâne*] and gossip. They pass the time insulting and threatening those who would help them survive. However, if they worked for an individual, they would be supervised and made to work. It is always laziness and dissipation over good conduct and work." As he speaks about the public workshop, an engraving shows men at the back-breaking work of hauling coal up through a narrow tunnel. During his praise of work offered by a local proprietor, an engraving appears of strong, healthy men working in a spacious metalworks—hard work surely, but done in less disagreeable conditions. A similar courtroom exchange with *la femme* Coteron ushers on screen an image of women laboring in a textile sweatshop.

The shipment interception serves to establish the issues at stake (real need and fear of worsening circumstances, local and national notability's incomprehension of the popular plight, and the consequent lack of support) as well as the people involved. These themes recur throughout the program. Through a series of sequences ranging from reenactments of the popular movement and the trial to moments of reflection by Oudoul and the adult Olivier, all punctuated by images drawn from nineteenth-century engravings, the film challenges earlier renditions of the Buzançais affair that embraced—from the left or right—less complicated interpretations. "Le Pain" captures better the cacophony of interpretations offered by the political press of the 1847 era.

The film's rendering of the Chambert/Venin killings also evokes an atmosphere of uncertainty—an approach at odds with the prosecution's version in 1847. The sequence begins with the adult Olivier explaining, "I neither saw nor understood anything . . . happening. I followed the crowd [to the Chambert house], but I only saw peoples' backs." However, he also offers the only characterization of Chambert: "I didn't like Chambert. He was crazy." Instead of the episode beginning with the action surrounding Venin's shooting, the sequence begins with the boy, Olivier, struggling to get a glimpse of the action, while the adult Olivier's voice describes "something flying over my head followed by a cry." He thus begins his story with the attack on Chambert. Oudoul elaborates: the court condemned "Velluet for [throwing the hatchet at Chambert's head], but I never thought he was worse than the others. I knew him well. His protestations of innocence seemed sincere to me."

That those who stood accused were "no worse than the others" remains a constant theme of the program. During the trial President Mater erupts in frustration: "Yet again, I hear that 'someone' did this or 'someone' did that. No one knows this 'someone'?" He complains that witnesses and accused alike have resorted to testifying that "'someone' pillaged, sacked, devastated, visited . . . but everyone else just followed. But who decided to go one place or another? Was there a leader?" To Velluet's response that Venin had led them, Mater retorted, "Thanks, but Venin is dead and cannot deny it."

When the story again shifts to the Chambert episode, Louis Bourgeot, the Chambert servant, stands before the tribunal. As he testifies, the screen shows him serving lunch to Chambert and his mother in a richly furnished house, as a crowd of "mostly women and children" grows outside. Two men enter, carrying the engagement with the "list of grain owners." A struggle erupts as one man slams the table with a stick and Bourgeot wrestles with him. He explains that he lost consciousness for an instant and, when he came to, he heard a shot, followed by people pouring in through broken windows, yelling "Chambert assassin." The reenactment of this episode ends, and the screen shifts to Olivier and Oudoul as President Mater's voice summarizes "what happened next" for the jury. But Oudoul immediately contradicts this narrative of the assault on Chambert. Like the others, he emphasizes the "cruelty" of the violence, but unlike either judge or prosecutor, he has trouble locating blame: "Half the village was there. During the trial they condemned men for murder who had not done any more or less than those who had simply come to watch. They could have traded places with the accused."

"Le Pain" blends the speeches of the defense into one summary that focuses on Chambert's inability to master his actions and "an entire crowd calling for [Chambert's] death." The lawyer concludes that "if one admits that a murder occurred, one has to accept that the whole town committed it." As the judge reads the sentences condemning Bienvenu, Michot, and Velluet to death and others to forced labor, Olivier wonders if "one can really judge such collective acts as one judges a crime of passion committed by a single man."

The character of Louis Michot, the youngest of the accused sentenced to death, offers one of the most effective vehicles for influencing viewer opinion about the harsh verdicts. Olivier explains that he had a special memory of Michot because "he never resembled the others and the town called him 'Louis lunatic.'" The viewer sees him returning home after the Chambert episode. Michot appears sick (perhaps already hung over) and devastated. He cries out, "Now I am like the others!" while his mother accuses his companion—a composite of several 1847 rioters who sports a woman's hat, licks honey off his fingers, and boasts that Chambert had put up a good fight—of having "made a murderer of a child of twenty." When the judge reads the verdicts, Michot weeps, head in hands, misery etched on his face.

Although "Le Pain" powerfully conveys the ambiguities residing in the Buzançais affair, it less effectively engages the questions of gender raised by earlier narratives. The need to simplify both events and characters explains some of this, but except for the amplification of *la femme* Coteron's role and the greater nuance offered by the first shipment interception scenes, women largely disappear from the film. The viewer gets only a brief shot of Mme Chambert's back, while the Gaulin household never appears in the narrative. Glimpses appear of mothers struggling to defend their sons—Michot's mother worrying about his actions and the young Olivier's mother trying to shield him from danger. Oudoul's rendition of the Chambert assault underlines the incomprehensibility of the attack by noting that he had seen "women, *women,* pass their feet between the legs of other attackers to kick him with their sabots."[106] Perhaps the most significant alteration occurs at the expense of Madeleine Blanchet. Not only does the script exclude her from the story, but it also shows Louis Bourgeot receiving the praise for bravery that Mater had in fact showered on her in 1847.

"Le Pain" emphasizes starkly the inadequacy and incompetence of local authorities. The program accentuates their ineptitude so much that this part of the story could have provided comic relief if not for the tragic verdicts. From the gendarme, drinking wine with the carters rather than forcing them to drive on, to the hopelessly confused and fearful mayor, the story indicts the forces of order as equally culpable for the escalation of the affair. After the first sequence involving the shipment interception, the scene shifts to the mayor in his office preparing to confront the protesters. With great difficulty he finally manages to wrap his tricolor sash around his waist. "Does this suffice to prop up my authority?" he asks the lone municipal councilor in the room. The answer proves almost as ludicrous as the question: "Yes, with the hat, it always makes an impression." As the mayor learns that the national guard will not help, an engraving of a cartoonish guardsman struggling with his equipment appears on the screen.

When Mater grills the mayor about his failure to rally support to establish order amid such "anarchy," the mayor explains that "things are much more complicated than they appear on paper." As Mater lectures the mayor about his duty to assert authority and enforce order, engravings flash across the screen of national guardsmen sleeping rather than fighting, firemen trying to act like soldiers, and a guardsman preening himself in a mirror. Coupled with several images mocking the bourgeoisie—one in a coffeehouse and another of notables gathered porcinely around a restaurant table—these seriocomic scenes lay the onus for the tragedy upon the notability.

In the end, "Le Pain et vin" presented not just one version but multiple versions of what happened at Buzançais. In this it resembled journalism—a multivocal journalism, both political and popular—rather than an univocal interpretation. It contested simpler narratives that interpreted Buzançais as a vicious crime and the repression as a matter of public order. However, it also enabled viewers to interpret the uprising as popular protest demanding that need prevail over property rights; it thus suggested to viewers that authorities and the privileged should respond to the imperatives of that need and that collective violence might sometimes play a legitimate role in political process. Although it did not endorse physical violence against individuals—in fact, Oudoul had spoken eloquently against the excesses of cruelty—it did acknowledge that against oblivious or callous disregard of basic human needs, collective violence against authority might constitute an appropriate final recourse. The program achieved this by distorting the historical record: by simplifying the story; creating composite characters; taking imaginative detours from the transcript of 1847; and actively invoking the benefit of hindsight.

On this last point, not only did the presence of Oudoul and the adult Olivier (as well as readings from Hugo and Marx at the end of the program) constitute the obvious workings of post hoc reflection, but the introduction of elements external to the story itself—such as the engravings—also created an extratextual reference. Moreover, by creating dissonance between what the audience heard and what it saw, the *téléfilm* could virtually compel audience participation. The *téléspectateurs* found themselves trying to sort out the contradictions.

"Le Pain et le Vin" seemed to belong to a 1970s trend in television called the "French western," which emphasized a France divided into two antagonistic parties: "the little people versus the influential, the poor versus the rich . . . the left versus the right . . . which offered reflections on the misery of the people, the relationship between power and justice."[107] Despite the persistence of political influence and the heavy participation of Gaullists such as Lazareff, French television had always also attracted participation from the left, including communists.[108] The entire series offered dramas about the underdog in the French past and reflected the prevailing view of French history, at least since the Revolution, as a series of antagonistic struggles. Buzançais offered yet another opportunity to reinforce this picture.

The television program "Le Pain et le Vin" demonstrates more clearly than previous renditions of the Buzançais affair that references to it could amplify the significance (and peril) of other crises, for example, the Revolution of 1848 or the Commune. In addition, the program enhanced the importance of Buzançais by linking it to other crises such as post–World War I shortages, interwar and post–World War II law-and-order and national unity debates, or post-1968 concerns about rapid economic and social change and the uses of social violence. Thus moving back and forth through French history with Buzançais at hand both deepened and broadened French history as narrators added new events and spun them into a thick skein of intertwined causality and context. Invoked at the right time and in the right way, these intertextual references operated to integrate (if not to mainstream) Buzançais into the heritage of France. It helped to build a particular kind of "historical capital," "the cultural heritage of every country and every community," manifested in such things as identifiable places, dates, events, and characters known to all members of that community,[109] that the French could accept as theirs alone.

CHAPTER SIX

Buzançais Rendered in History, Patrimony, and Sound and Light

> The most passionate history is the history of one's home town. . . . Indeed, certain events have marked the history of France, such as the *jacqueries* of Buzançais in 1847. . . . To you, reader, I wish you an enriching visit to the history of Buzançais.
>
> —Mayor Régis Blanchet

During the 1970s, several elements converged in new appropriations of the Buzançais story by such genres as scholarly history and works associated with *la patrimoine* (heritage preservation and promotion) movement. These factors included the success of the "new history" (encompassing the Annales school, social history, and regional and local studies) among professional historians; a long-standing passion for local history among amateur members of local *sociétés savantes* (who functioned as guardians of the local archives and *patrimoine*); and eagerness of municipalities to encourage local culture as a means to restore or maintain healthy communities and economies. Sometimes working together and sometimes at odds, these disparate invokers of the past cast into the limelight places and stories that traditional, national histories had ignored or relegated to the gloaming of *la France profonde,* where they had originated. Battles waged in the 1960s over the interpretation of popular revolts during the early modern and revolutionary eras now migrated into the study of the nineteenth century. Then the events of 1968 energized the study of past revolts as embodiments of resistance to forces of change, alienation, and exploitation.[1]

We have already seen how, between 1848 and the 1970s, political and economic discourse as well as the literary and visual arts had variously deployed the story of Buzançais to edify and entertain. Until the 1970s, only two serious works of local history had substantially explored the event: Eugène Hubert's history of the canton of Buzançais in his 1908 multivolume work *Le Bas Berry: Histoire et Archéologie du département de l'Indre* and Marcel Bruneau's history in honor of the centennial celebration of the Revolution of 1848, *Aspects de la Révolution de 1848 dans l'Indre.*[2] Hubert largely reproduced the 1847 indictment and denounced the rioters as "drunken" workers thirsting to exact "vengeance against the bourgeois for selling their grain too dearly." He concluded that the causes of the riot did not lurk in any previously existing conspiracy and explained that contemporaries had blamed "this criminal riot" on the "weakness of public authorities too slow to act and to quell at the outset the leaders of a crowd that let itself be blindly led to the greatest crimes."[3]

Bruneau's more sympathetic history introduced Buzançais to set a context for the Revolution of 1848. He noted that the "Indre did not escape the general economic crisis [of 1846–47]. One can cite the riot at Buzançais as an example of a *jacquerie,* of peasant misery—but worker misery would be more exact." He reported only briefly the basic incidents of what he called "a story often told": "a load of grain . . . stopped . . . by unemployed workers." They continued by "pillag[ing] a mill and several individual houses." "The movement demanded a ransom from several bourgeois. One of them defended himself. A leader was killed and his adversary was killed with the refinements of cruelty. There were thus two deaths. The prefect hurried to the scene and demonstrated an energetic attitude—the troops arrived. The Assize court quickly liquidated the affair with several sentences."[4] Buzançais served Bruneau as a microcosm of the economic crisis and suffering that lay at the root of the Revolution of 1848. The use of the passive voice avoided most issues of intent and responsibility.

Neither Hubert nor Bruneau lingered long over Buzançais because their real subjects lay elsewhere. In the 1970s, however, historians turned to events like Buzançais with renewed interest and new questions. Given the late twentieth century's historical concerns, neither an uncritical acceptance of the official narrative nor an explanation of the episode as "exceptional" would suffice. Buzançais now attracted historians who sought to understand it by analyzing the structures of economic, social, and political relations that produced it. These historians pursued a broader, more innovative range of sources for answers and focused more on the people who protested than on those whom they confronted. Studying France "from the bottom up," they focused on criminals and deviants, the common people, minorities, and "those without history." They sought to understand forms of conflict and the processes of marginalization and exclusion.[5]

Two graduate students from different universities and advised by different mentors arrived almost simultaneously in the archives in Châteauroux to research the crisis of 1847 in the Indre in general and in Buzançais in particular. In 1976, Solange Gras, working under the direction of Philippe Vigier, completed a thesis, "La Crise du milieu du XIXe siècle en Bas-Berry," for the *troisième cycle* at the University of Paris–Nanterre. The next year, Yvon Bionnier completed his *maîtrise,* "Aspects économiques et sociaux des émeutes de la faim dans l'Indre en 1847," at the University of Tours under Alain Corbin.[6]

Professors Vigier and Corbin then occupied different positions in the profession but shared similar concerns. Vigier, twelve years older, had already established a reputation in nineteenth-century French history and had held several academic posts. His own thesis had focused on the development of political consciousness and opinion at midcentury, especially in the region of the Alps during the Second Republic.[7] He directed attention away from Paris, where most historians of his day had concentrated their work, to argue that 1848 had marked an important turning point in the politicization of alpine inhabitants. This politicization, he argued, had meant different things to different people. To elucidate the diverse political positions that emerged throughout a region so distant from the center, Vigier studied its economic, social, and cultural structures and the stresses it confronted at midcentury.[8]

In the mid-1970s, in contrast, Corbin had only recently finished his own *thèse* and held his first university position as *maître de conférences* at Tours.[9] His doctoral thesis had likewise explored the contours of political culture in a remote, poor part of France, the Limousin, at midcentury. He, too, had applied a careful reading of the society and culture of the region's inhabitants to explain the particular features of their political development. More than Vigier, Corbin explored village sociability and sensibilities. In their resulting studies, both Corbin and Vigier argued that the stresses of "modernization" and the experiences of the Revolution of 1848 and the Second Republic had helped politicize rural inhabitants, although Corbin concluded that the process took most of the nineteenth century to complete.[10]

Vigier and Corbin, both of whom taught at the University of Tours, shared many questions, methods, and objects of study in these early years—which might have encouraged the convergence of their students on the Indre. Of course, both Bionnier (himself a Buzancéen) and Gras surely had their own personal as well as professional reasons for focusing on the Indre during the 1846–47 crisis,[11] but whatever their motives, both produced thoughtful, thoroughly researched studies of the structures and tensions in the Indre at the time of the crisis. While Bionnier focused principally on the canton of Buzançais, Gras ranged more widely, both in time and space. Both concluded that the troubles of 1847 "followed above all from the social situation."[12] Sensitive to differences in local relations and culture, both scholars analyzed the roles these played in local politics. Although principally concerned with the crisis that produced rioting in 1847, both looked to possible subsequent connections between those dislocations and local politics during the Revolution of 1848. Both projects reflect the concerns and methods of social history and the Annales tradition during the 1970s, as well as a deep sensitivity to the ambiguities residing in the Buzançais affair.[13]

Vigier made extensive use of Gras's work in his 1982 book *La Vie quotidienne en province et à Paris pendant les journées de 1848* for the Librarie Hachette's series on daily life, La Vie quotidienne, one of its most successful collections.[14] Begun in 1938, the series reflects a growing influence of the Annales school (further spurred under the Vichy regime by nationalist and conservative —if not fascist—nostalgia for certain aspects of France's past) and, during the 1970s, the even greater impact of the era's ethnographic and sociological interests. In the 1970s, the series manifested its respect for France's *patrimonies* (and its sense of a potential market) by publishing titles such as Henri Vincent's *La Vie quotidienne dans les chemins de fer aux XIXe siècle* (1975). Titles sometimes sold well over 100,000 copies. Vigier's first chapter, entitled "Buzançais, le 13 Javier 1847," presents the riot as paradigmatic of the transitional 1840s.

Vigier begins with the story of the shipment interception, which he quickly contextualizes on a European scale. He describes the crisis as pitting the "Blouses" against the "Habits"; underscores the role the "myth—and reality—of grain hoarding by *le Gros*, the bourgeois," played in its instigation;[15] and critiques the official narrative that had underpinned most stories of the riot until "scholars" had stepped in in the mid-1970s.

He pays particular attention to the silences in the record. When he narrates the Venin/Chambert episode, he explains that "at the corner . . . rose a vast house, inhabited by the dame Huard-Chambert, and her only son, aged about forty. They were among the richest notables in Buzançais, and also the least liked in the popular milieu—they called the son 'the usurer,' without our being able to get more details about his activity in this area, nor about the death threats that, it appears, had for a long time been directed against him: the later investigation proved remarkably discreet about these points."[16] Nor, Vigier explains, do the records provide evidence for why some—the proprietors, not the protesters—designated Venin "the leader of the brigands." Given such omissions, the official record cannot serve as the last word on what happened and why.

Vigier himself reveals assumptions that shaped his narrative. For example, he writes that when the fight broke out between Venin and the servant Bourgeot, Chambert, "*no doubt reckoning that the latter's life was in danger* and in rather confused circumstances, got his gun, and shot at Venin, whom he killed straight out."[17] As we have seen, no clear evidence exists—nor will it ever—to prove one way or another what motivated Chambert to grab his gun.

Except during the initial shipment interception, women play little role in Vigier's story. He does claim broadly that when "insecurity was growing in the countryside . . . bands, composed, of course, of housewives (as is customary in these sorts of troubles), formed to protest the growing price of food stuffs."[18] He also notes their presence in Buzançais, blocking the cargo's departure and appealing to the men from the charity workshop to assist them. Thereafter they disappear: absent from the crowds of "Blouses" who confront the "Habits" over the course of three days, and even absent from the accused and punished. Among the "Habits," only Mme Huard-Chambert makes an appearance to sign the engagement.[19] But then, supposedly, only men wear "Blouses" and "Habits" in the mid-nineteenth century.[20] Vigier's common people, whom he treats with respect and empathy, he clearly genders male. As Joan Scott has observed of E. P. Thompson's working class, Vigier's Buzançais does not entirely lack women, but they figure awkwardly, and rarely.[21]

Vigier emphasizes the impotence of all the authorities—from the mayor and local notables to the prefect—in the face of the growing disorder, contrasting fear and confusion in the officials' ranks with mounting courage among the "Blouses." Vigier explains that they "perceive rapidly that the Prefect does not have the means to enforce his policies."[22] When the "crowd inundates" his twenty-five-dragoon escort, the prefect tells them "to sheath their sabers." Panicked and disorganized, local and departmental authorities can only retreat and convoke the repressive forces of the military and Assize Court.

Vigier explains that the "huge gulf that separated the little people from the big, the Blouses from the Habits in a country [heretofore] considered 'moderate' and tranquil . . . ; and the awareness as well of the weakness, if not the total disappearance of the notables and constituted authorities" led to a precocious *front de l'Ordre,* even before the Revolution of 1848.[23] Vigier uses the story of Buzançais to marshal both the history of local events and the larger processes of long-term social and economic development to explain evolving mid-nineteenth-century political opinion. Although the book features other events to illuminate trends in different parts of France, the fact that his first chapter tells the story of Buzançais mounts it as a template to which others compare or relate.

The success of Hachette's Vie quotidienne series, which targeted both a popular and academic audience, broadly disseminated the story of Buzançais. This time, however, the story reflected more empathy for the protesters than had Bouchardon's version or Gordeaux's *bande dessinée* and, by contextualizing the rioters' plight, elaborated the circumstances that excited such a violent reaction. Vigier observes that even if the convicted rioter, Légeron, did not actually say that "'today is carnival [and] tomorrow we will bury the bourgeois under the ashes' . . . [those in court] believed that he or someone else could have said it. . . . This shows how alive such a mentality (an old dream and ancient terror) of *social inversion* remained even in the middle of the nineteenth century—an inversion that would put the Petits in the place of the Gros."[24]

Authorities from Châteauroux to Paris were shocked, Vigier concludes, that a protest begun over the arrival of several grain carts in the faubourgs of Buzançais had exploded into open revolt there and in some twenty other rural communities "against a liberal order [unconcerned about] its little people." The outbreak stunned officials who had thought "jacqueries" impossible "in a France thought to be civilized." For this jolt to complacency, Vigier explains, the government "made [the rioters] pay dearly."[25] In one chapter, he makes Buzançais an event more intriguingly complex, and the issues it raised more challenging to analyze, than in the earlier popular versions of Bouchardon and Gordeaux, and more factually rigorous than in Desgraupes's version. Vigier's narrative came to play an influential role in situating Buzançais at the center of histories of the mid-nineteenth-century crisis.

British historian Roger Price's impressive study of the impact of railroads on French agriculture in the nineteenth century dedicated an entire section to analyzing subsistence crises in first half of the century.[26] He established a typology of popular protests that began with "verbal protests" and included a scale for assessing the severity and type of disorders. Price featured Buzançais at the end of the section because, he argued, it belonged to "the small number [of disorders] which got out of control and developed into minor insurrections. . . .

These posed a threat of social revolution."[27] Classified under a rubric—"From protest to insurrection"—Buzançais struck Price as "very different in character, in terms of the violence involved and the social animosities which came to the fore." Relying on his own research in the administrative and judicial records in the National Archives and in the substantial reports of the military dispatched to suppress domestic disorders,[28] Price produced a narrative that evinced sympathy for the misery of many of the men (he mentions no women) who protested, but which also stressed their excesses. For example, after briefly noting the interception of the grain transport, he recounts that, "encouraged by their success, many poor people spent the night sitting around camp fires in the town square, persuading themselves . . . to take further revenge against those who had exploited them. They were fortified against the cold by strong drink, some at least provided free by an enthusiastic inn keeper."[29] Price omits that the protesters needed "camp fires" (not just "strong drink") to stay warm in the January night while guarding the grain until the next day, when they anticipated distributing it at a just price.

The narrative dwells on details of the attack on Chambert, while eliding the shooting of Venin. Price writes that "only one individual, a M. Chambert, refused to sign" and, "fearing ill treatment, [Chambert] armed himself with two pistols and fired at the crowd as it broke into his house. He killed one rioter and wounded another, but this only infuriated the crowd. Chambert was cut down by men armed with picks and axes. Subsequently, François Arrouy, a *vigneron,* admitted that he alone had delivered two blows against Chambert with his pitchfork, the first in the stomach, the second in the face. When the fork had stuck in the unfortunate Chambert's mouth he had needed to put one foot on the man's shoulder in order to gain sufficient leverage to pull it out again."[30]

In both narratives, Price supplies juicy details about the rioters' ill-considered behavior (drinking and brutal violence) while omitting similar, relevant details about the immediate context for their actions. Mme Chambert (who appears nowhere in the narrative) had in fact already signed, probably with her son's approval; Chambert did not have two pistols, and no previous account ever reported that he had "fired at the crowd as it broke into his house." These omissions and errors suggest that the protesters posed even more of a threat than really existed, and so Price's version firmly legitimizes Chambert's actions.

Price concludes his chapter on "subsistence crises and popular protest" with a reflection on Buzançais's resonance into other Indre towns and villages. Although he acknowledges that some contemporaries feared that insurrections (*jacqueries*) like Buzançais signaled open class warfare ("War on the Rich!"),[31] he claims that "with the benefit of hindsight it seems clear that these events were produced by widespread and intense misery." Indeed, Price continues, "The year 1847 saw the last of the peasant *jacqueries* and the 1850s the last substantial wave of lesser disorders due to high food prices. Subsequently, popular misery would be eased as a consequence of economic development." Buzançais, despite its alarming aspects, thus found itself shelved as one of the archaic popular movements soon to disappear under the force of modernization.[32]

That same year, Marxist historian Roger Magraw inserted a contrasting slant on the affair in his important textbook on nineteenth-century France by claiming that the event "epitomizes the nature of rural unrest" during the crisis.[33] He described Buzançais as a "market town of rural artisans and agricultural laborers" where "the old hostility to the château was replaced by new hatreds of landowners and grain merchants." Magraw noted the traditional protest behavior of shipment interceptions, and he especially emphasized newer behavior that included "attacks on flour mills, cries of 'Kill the bourgeois' and attacks on threshing machines." His summary of the Venin/Chambert episode exaggerated Chambert's aggression and grouped Venin with those carrying the "engagement."[34] Magraw concluded that "pleased with the verdict, the regime gave it wide publicity. But the case aroused widespread distaste" and he quoted George Sand's comments about the "disgusting spectacle of men 'gorged with money [refusing] necessities to fellow men, and [rubbing] their hands, saying it was an excellent year for making good grain profits.'"

By the 1990s, Buzançais had become the most frequently cited (and sometimes only) example of midcentury popular protest in such politically divergent but standard works as François Furet's *La Révolution, 1770–1880* (1988); Jean-Claude Caron's *France de 1815 à 1848,* in Armand Colin's Cursus collection (1992, 2000); Hervé Robert's study of the July Monarchy for the widely read Que sais-je? series (1994); and Peter McPhee's *Social History of France, 1780–1880* (1992).[35] In a section entitled "The End of Louis-Philippe," Furet writes that amid several other political problems that bedeviled the Guizot administration in 1846–47, "a grave social and economic crisis then occurred to add to its effect, as in 1788–89, to this moral and political discredit." He outlines the bad harvests, "stockpiling and speculation, the poverty of the populace, and here and there, famine—the last in French history" that once again triggered behavior associated with widespread disorder. Buzançais serves as Furet's only example: "The most violent revolt occurred in Buzançais . . . ; in this big Indre township on the Berry borders, dominated by about a hundred property owners and merchants, the rural lower classes—day laborers, farmhands, weavers, craftsmen—maintained insurrectionary rule for three days, with price-fixing and requisition, after murdering a rich bourgeois. Then came the arrival of the troops, arrests; a few dozen unfortunate wretches taken to the court at Châteauroux before a jury of property owners; heavy prison sentences and three executions on 16 April, market days in the main square of the town amid a throng of silent people."[36] Furet omits the fact that the murdered bourgeois had just killed one of the "unfortunate wretches." He declares that these sorts of "activities . . . had no direct relationship with political life properly speaking, although as usual, the government took the blame." Furet implies that the government (whether local, departmental, national is unclear) could have done nothing to ameliorate the hardships caused by that grave economic and social crisis.

Still another version appears in Peter McPhee's text covering the same time period. The story of Buzançais appears at beginning of a chapter entitled "The Mid-Century Crisis, 1846–52," integrating the crisis of 1846–47 into a larger one that included the Revolution of 1848 and the subsequent trauma that characterized the period until Louis Napoleon seized power in 1852. McPhee explains that while "wildly erratic weather had ruined grain and potato crops," real responsibility for prices "higher than at any time since 1817" lay with "merchants and large farmers" who "deliberately withheld stocks to profit from shortages." Added to the collapse of manufacturing and inadequate, "belated government relief," the crisis produced widespread suffering and protest. McPhee continues: "The most extensive direct action originated in the market town of Buzançais (Indre) in January 1847, and began as an example of popular price-fixing, when six carts were stopped and their contents sold. It soon became much more. The crowd forced the mayor, the Justice of the Peace and sixty notables to sign an engagement to provide grain at a fixed price until the next harvest."[37] McPhee briefly describes how the events at Buzançais resonated more widely throughout the region and how swiftly the government responded with retribution. He explains that "the rioters had murdered a large landholder who had killed and wounded several of their number; the three deemed responsible were guillotined in the public square of Buzançais itself." Although McPhee, like Furet, uses Buzançais as the only specific example of protest during the crisis, he contextualizes it more carefully and makes the concerns it reflected central to political affairs at midcentury.

Both Hervé Robert and Jean-Claude Caron have written general histories for a wide public in France, especially students preparing for the baccalaureate and *premier cycle.* The Que sais-je? and Cursus collections have long-standing reputations for providing short but "authoritative" narratives of essential information and interpretations. Robert's last chapter, "From Stability to Sclerosis," concludes with a section entitled "Time of Crisis." Buzançais figures as an example of the "social consequences of such a disastrous conjuncture," which included not simply an agricultural crisis but also an industrial, commercial, and banking crisis related to, but not entirely contingent upon, the bad harvest. He explains that "the rural and urban popular classes suffered first from the agricultural crisis. The ancestral fear of shortage resurfaced in the countryside, and with it endemic agitation, nourished by rumors and old rancor against the *gros* or the *habits.* In Poitou and the Loire valley in particular, to the cry 'death to hoarders,' armed bands attacked grain convoys; bakeries were pillaged. The Buzançais affair struck people's attention: in this capital of a canton in the Indre, the *blouses* made 'insurrection based on taxation and requisition' for three days in January 1847."[38] As he emphasized insurrection, Robert quoted from Furet's survey text but went beyond Furet's conservative assessment of the protest's influence to argue that, together with the other aspects of the economic crisis, the disorders "discredited the regime in the eyes of its partisans," whom he identified as "the middle classes who could blame Guizot's government" for having failed to ensure "material prosperity" and "public order."[39]

Jean-Claude Caron first introduces Buzançais in his second chapter on French society. In a section entitled "Peasants and Politics," he explains that, although it could not vote, the peasantry did act in political ways: "Revolts of misery . . . do fall within the political field: when authorities turned to the guillotine (four people at Montargis in 1817, three people in Buzançais, 1848), it is in the name of order, which is political."[40] Buzançais receives more attention at the end of the book, in a chapter entitled "The Crisis of the July Monarchy and the Revolution of 1848." A bulleted section with the heading "Affair de Buzançais" relies on Vigier's previous study for its narration and even includes a special "box" that quotes from Vigier's citations of commentaries by a troop commander and from George Sand. Caron asks if the affair did not show that what the two "groups or social classes" who confronted each other "had in common was their definitive rejection of a discredited regime," as demonstrated by their lack of support for it in February 1848. He concludes that the crisis, "beyond its social effects," had provoked "notably an awakening of the provincial bourgeoisie confronted with the incompetence of the government."[41] Robert's and Caron's versions share more with McPhee than Furet on both the political ramifications of the 1846–47 crisis (particularly the agricultural crisis) and the importance of Buzançais itself as a salient example not only of popular disorder but also as symptomatic of the mood of many provincial French, both propertied and propertyless.

Most recently, Nicolas Bourguinat's preface to *Les Grains du Désordre* (2002) features Buzançais, and in a novel way.[42] Bourguinat uses Buzançais to help reintroduce the state and cultural elites into the economic and social history of the first half of the nineteenth century. His study of French food rioting centers on the state and the political construction of social and economic relationships, not on the protesters or their targets. He observes that the last years of the July Monarchy marked the last major wave of food riots in France and argues that the translation of protesters' demands to a formal political level contributed to revolution in 1848. Bourguinat suggests that this period also marked the final rupture of already fragile relations between bourgeoisie and lower classes. Not only does Buzançais appear at the very beginning of his story, but Bourguinat also reinvokes it many times to show how contemporaries deployed it in their struggles to produce new post-1789 social and political identities. He argues that authorities believed that Buzançais had "respected none of the known rules for [food] rioting" and therefore found themselves forced to reconceptualize the society in which this happened and to recast ways to restore public order.[43]

Bourguinat begins with a report from the *juge d'instruction* concerning a mysterious character seen by a witness on the outskirts of Buzançais. "Dressed like a bourgeois . . . [he] engaged [the witness] to return to Buzançais, where carts would pass on their way to Châtillon-sur-Indre; he had announced that they would be stopped and there would be a stir. . . . [The mysterious character] expressed himself with facility; he sympathized with the people's misery, but he said nothing bad about the government or the proprietors."[44] Bourguinat argues that although the magistrates doubted this story, they found it troubling because, even as a lie, it introduced new elements: a bourgeois who foresaw the future, absented himself from the arena, deplored the people's misery, but did not incite revolt against constituted authorities or property owners. This story did not fit their image of what proper conspirators should say and do.

Bourguinat identifies other behaviors that troubled the court—murders, random pillaging, and attempts to restore order in ways that had worked in the past—but ended up instead provoking even more disorder. July Monarchy elites had just learned (and Buzançais had played a primary role in teaching them) that "collective action and violence had become unstable and uncertain terrain," no longer part of a traditional and "definitively written repertory."[45] Somehow, they worried, the script and the scenario—the repertory of gestures and players—had changed. In the postrevolutionary era, so much had changed, much of it influenced by the state itself. Those in power found themselves struggling to respond (and consequently exerting more influence, even if unwittingly) and to rethink society and the relationship between state and society.

The July Monarchy increasingly found itself defining French society in terms of class antagonisms, "an uprising of the poor classes against the rich classes . . . of a practical communism."[46] This vision of social relations made it easier for authorities to explain what happened around them and to align themselves with property (rather than Guizot's more fluid "capacity") and the market. This newly delegitimized consumers' *économie morale*—what Bourguinat calls the *contrat social des subsistances*[47]—restricted local intervention in the market and installed more effective means to punish protesters. The effort to find an appropriate language and model, however, had to compete with an increasingly vocal and assertive opposition, secular and religious, socialists and republicans, national and local. The traditional food riot proved capable of breaking its chains of tradition and, with Buzançais as its focal point, propelled France yet again toward revolution. Contrary to Furet, therefore, Bourguinat asserts a strong connection between the crisis of 1846–47 and the Revolution of 1848.

Bourguinat never actually narrates the Buzançais affair. He mentions the grain interception on the 13th (and the fact that women instigated it) and the next day's *taxation populaire,* but he never returns to the episode in any coherent way. We learn of "two murders of property owners," when at Buzançais only one property owner died; the other death involved Venin, the protester.[48] Bourguinat, understandably, concerns himself more with the ways that contemporaries mapped a new vision of their society onto the landscape of food riots than with the course of the riots themselves.

For all the new questions and new methods to answer them that the scholarly historians of the 1970s brought to the study of the Buzançais affair, in the end their work exhibited many of the characteristics of those who had preceded them in the search for a usable past. These included (among other things) an eclectic use of sources; a politicized interpretation of the behavior of contemporary participants, whether bourgeois, common people, or authorities; and a selective and sometimes uncritical use of previous accounts. The pliable Buzançais affair could serve as a flag of convenience for conservative scholars such as Furet and Marxists such as Magraw, just as it had for impassioned "amateurs" such as Bouchardon and Vallès.

The 1970s witnessed not just a scholarly interest in the events at Buzançais but also their adoption by certain local groups as part of their efforts to preserve and promote their *patrimoine,* or local heritage.[49] Whether they embraced it proudly as a legacy or sought to exert something like paternalist control over its narrative, they reproduced the story in multiple local genres.

Although what follows focuses on the recently renewed efforts to write the history of the "Jacquerie of Buzançais" as part of the town's heritage, earlier efforts had appeared. A general interest in local heritage reemerged in France in the 1970s. Its origins lie much further back, especially in the late eighteenth and nineteenth centuries, when local notables and *sociétés savantes* sought to forge a unique identity for their cities in the struggle for privileges and against the centralizing state.[50] Locals had often made a conservative and nostalgic bid to restore past local difference and hierarchy against the revolutionary Republic that proclaimed itself *une et unie.* Local history could also serve factions seeking to dominate local politics. These concerns manifested themselves in a variety of ways: local ceremonies, commemorations, and histories. Such events often provoked conflict because they put individual and family, social, economic, political network interests and reputations at risk.

An attempt immediately after the Revolution of 1848 to organize a commemorative service for the three guillotined Buzançais protesters seemed too hot for even the new government to handle. As we have seen, as early as February 1848, the demands for the release of incarcerated protesters had won considerable support in Limoges and beyond. For those executed, however, amnesty came too late. Upon the later return of those released, some townspeople scheduled a formal funeral ceremony at the local cemetery on 5 March (a Sunday) for the three men buried there after their executions in April 1847. Fearing disorder, the local government canceled the commemoration.[51] To a government that sought class harmony, not class warfare, giving voice to those previously criminalized and silenced seemed too dangerous to the new regime. Challenges to what Pierre Nora has called the "classical model of commemoration"[52] generated by the political center might destabilize the precariously positioned Second Republic.

Throughout the nineteenth century, various unresolved issues of the affair haunted the community. Certainly, compensation for property destroyed and the pardoning of the convicted remained sources of contention into the 1870s. Although no other episodes of collective violence occurred in the region in subsequent decades, even during the economic crisis of the 1850s, to "reactivate and recharge symbolically and materially" the collective memories of 1847, Buzançais's effects continued to resonate in concrete ways,[53] as when Vallès's 1880 serial novel cast aspersions on the reputations of such local notables as the mayor.

Local notables seeking to manage resources and reputations, and having the requisite power and authority, continued to control the context of commemorations and histories—the "official" articulations of collective memory—during the nineteenth century. Property owners had to appear as benevolent victims, local authorities as competent but insufficiently armed and manned, and protesters as barbaric criminals. Hubert's 1908 history of Buzançais virtually reproduced the 1847 indictment, and Pierre's 1911 note on sources offered a military commander's report, both local legitimations of the previous century's dominant interpretation. As Bruno Benoit has argued for Lyon, regardless of which political order controlled local governments, local authorities remained hostile and refused to grant legitimacy to any collective disorder on the grounds that their "security mission" denied them any nuance when responding to violence.[54]

During the twentieth century, whatever firsthand memories of Buzançais had lingered in the nineteenth century disappeared with those who held them. Individual families may have continued to nurture their own tales, inherited along with everything else, but Bionnier found little such evidence.[55] Until the late 1960s and 1970s, interest in Buzançais's nineteenth-century history in general and its *jacquerie* in particular rarely, if ever, surfaced publicly. During the

Third Republic, and particularly after World War II, an agenda concerned with the construction and dissemination of a national narrative dominated—if it did not suppress outright—the production of regional and local ones.

By the 1970s, the resurgence of local interest in the local past may have been rooted in concerns like those of the nineteenth century, but it also flowed into new concerns, and this helped to create more diverse narratives of the Buzançais affair. Local heritage (*patrimoine*) again attracted attention as interest grew in local culture. As with scholarly history, most attention throughout the first half of the twentieth century had focused on "grand narratives" of political history, and within that field national and Parisian history in particular prevailed over social or economic history, or regional or local histories of any genre. Local studies had seemed to offer either too narrow (too small, too detailed, too personal) or too unexceptional a focus for serious scholars. By the late 1960s and 1970s, however, embracing the local—as local identity, local history, local heritage—had become strategically useful to those seeking to stake a claim to reputation, resources, and autonomy.

As Pierre Nora has argued, the previous "unifying framework of the nation-state" had had a "classical model [which] assumed a unified history." That model had "reduced to silence or to private commemoration" all histories that did not fit it. The "dissolution" of that framework permitted the "replacement" of the model by a "loosely organized system of disparate commemorative languages" and "different kinds of relationships to the past."[56] Control of these languages no longer lay with the central government but "passed into the hands of private groups, political parties, trade unions, and other organizations, with a concomitant potential for internal conflict and controversy." Nora explains that this "crisis of the 1970s led to a delving into the depths, a turning inward, a quest for familiar landmarks."[57] He gives many reasons—for example, "a series of apparently unrelated upheavals"—for this dissolution and for locating the shift in the mid-1970s: the sudden end to thirty years of growth, the awareness of the "definitive end of the peasant world," the "collapse of revolutionary marxism," the public success of the Annales school and the related "new history," an awakening to the relegation of France from a "great to a middle-range power," and demands for more emphasis on the "local and cultural perspectives."[58] The Année du Patrimoine celebrations of 1980 proved so diverse, so numerous, and so successful because the "process of realignment" that made it possible had already occurred in the 1970s.

These developments coincided with decentralization and democratization of political power and of culture in its multiple forms away from the central government and Paris, thus enhancing the municipality's stewardship of heritage.[59] Even within the municipalities, political parties debated goals and procedures. Should the government aim to disseminate and encourage the appreciation of "high culture" (basically the canon of French/Parisian culture) or foster the creation of new cultural forms? Should democratization and decentralization not also occur in towns themselves, reaching out to all ages, classes, genders, and races on the periphery as well as in the center? Should the government take an active role in identifying and nurturing certain cultural forms, or simply provide opportunities and spaces for the public(s) to create and support forms of their own choosing? What role should renovation of past forms play, and who should renovate them? What about the promotion of local culture outside the locality? Could (and should) cultural institutions deploy history to address and mitigate social and economic transformation?[60] Hotly debated at each turn, these questions themselves testify to the renewed concern with the definition, promotion, and commodification of local culture.[61]

In the 1970s many French witnessed and participated eagerly in a "return to the local,"[62] including a growing awareness of a "value" inhering in certain local sites, personages, or past events as well as an extension of what *la patrimoine* might signify, even to celebrating a bloody crime in new ways. In this context, the "Jacquerie of Buzançais" yet again found a new niche in a variety of genres: local history, local fiction, local journalism, local pedagogy, and local performance, all "historically tutored" by the new scholarly interest in and scholarship on the episode itself.[63]

Beyond the question of how to interpret its history, Buzancéens might have found aspects of their recent past particularly complicated to contemplate and restore. At the end of World War II, even as Buzancéens expected liberation and had a local artisan making flags to celebrate it, retreating Germans had set fire to the town's center (30 August 1945).[64] Massive damage to the church and château (which had served since before the days of the *jacquerie* as the administrative center for the mayor, justice of the peace, and gendarmes) forced the city to rebuild the space anew, not just renovate it. In its place rose a new town hall, a post office, and a large open center square, named (as so many others) Place de Gaulle. In the 1960s and 1970s, older Buzancéens still remembered the former cityscape, now appreciated as a cherished *patrimoine historique,* but for the postwar generation only the new sites had meaning. The municipality—presided over, until 1995, by the same mayor elected in 1945, Jean Bénard—accompanied this necessary rebuilding with new investment in local culture: a sports complex, *salle des fêtes,* cultural center, club center, and a secondary school.

In December 1968 a cluster of men, several of them local history teachers, established the Groupe d'histoire et d'archéologie de Buzançais (GHAB). Like the guiding spirits of so many such societies, they shared a passion for history, especially for that of their town and its heritage. The *Bulletin* they published involved countless hours spent scouring personal, municipal, parish, departmental, and national archives for anything that shed light on the town's past. They busied themselves with uncovering a substantial history in the written archival records and published the findings in their own journal.

The Buzançais Groupe d'histoire also encouraged others doing local historical research. For example, Yvon Bionnier's work appealed especially to the society: it published his *mémoire* in its journal, urged him to publish a longer book on his research, and raised the money to subvent its publication by a press in Châteauroux. This fund-raising campaign, and the publication of the book itself, attracted the attention of the regional newspaper, *La Nouvelle République* (edition for the Indre), which published an interview with Bionnier.[65]

The 1980s and 1990s saw the continued resurrection of Buzançais as local history and heritage. It has proven useful to genealogists who have, with increased sophistication, sought to root their family trees in a deeper historical context. For example, in 1980, a genealogist and local historian, André Chapu, wrote an article for the Buzançais historical group's *Bulletin* in which he claimed significance for an ancestor by linking her to the 1847 riots. The article, entitled "On the Periphery of the Buzançais Jacquerie: The Stormy Life of a Woman of the People," asked provocatively: "Geneviève Bezard, did she participate directly in the riots begun 13 January" in Buzançais? Unfortunately, Chapu had to answer, "One cannot know." But not all is lost, for he concluded that her husband probably *had* participated.[66] Although the author felt compelled to admit that he was not actually related to the husband (and only distantly to Geneviève), he felt he had increased the significance of his lineage by making a connection, an "exotic enrichment," with an event of historical resonance,[67] linking himself, even if indirectly, to someone who played either a heroic or a criminal role, depending on perspective.

In 1991, when France, and the Indre in particular, suffered under the burden of unemployment and mounting homelessness, the mayor of Pellevoisin, a small village near Buzançais, again invoked the 1847 riots. He published in his newsletter a brief article on Buzançais.[68] The author, a socialist politician, Amédée Renault, introduced the Buzançais riot by commemorating "a double centenary" in labor history: the "fusillade de Fourmies" on 1 May 1891 that killed nine workers and injured many others demanding the eight-hour day, and the papal encyclical *Rerum Novarum,* issued on 16 May 1891, which called for industrialists to aid poor workers.

Renault then links these episodes with the Buzançais affair, an event "closer to us in distance, and which also must find a place among the sad *cortège* of social dramas." The author justifies the connection because of its similarity to other severely repressed protest movements and claims a local tie to one of the participants in the region's extensive rioting, a day laborer from Pellevoisin, Pierre Brault. The narrative assumes that readers have some familiarity with the event itself and with the current map of Buzançais, for he locates the shipment interception before "the inn Boulet (now the 'Soleil d'or')" in the faubourg des Hervaux and the "maison bourgeoise" belonging to the Chamberts on the "current rue Aristide Briand." Most important, the essay reminds readers that the Buzançais affair erupted during "the finest hours of *libéralisme sauvage,*" an ideology that threatened to inflict social injustice in the nineteenth century, much as it threatened similar consequences in 1990s France. Renault continues: "Only a few years earlier, did not the Prime Minister of Louis Philippe, Guizot, proclaim his celebrated formula: enrich yourself!" With these local connections to the past, both Chapu and Renault sought in history a path to awakening social justice.

In the 1990s, the narrative of Buzançais remained malleable, subject to appropriation by different people, in different times, for different reasons, narrated and renarrated to suit the people, the times, and the reasons. Memory, political culture, and history overlapped and intertwined. They encouraged and reinvigorated one another. A 1994 article in a local magazine entitled *Berry* may reflect this process. Its author, Paul Clemente, insisted—flatly contradicting Bionnier less than two decades earlier—that "still today, the memory of this tragedy strongly pervades the collective memory of Buzancéens." He explained why in simple terms: "It is relatively close in time, it touches a sensitive question: hunger, and it features the people."[69]

It appears likely, however, that whatever "memories" existed of the episode constituted the product of almost a century of reworking its narrative. In 1981, the new socialist government under François Mitterrand offered start-up money to encourage small enterprises with a cultural purpose. Among those who took up the opportunity, two men, Thierry Maricourt and Jean-Paul Louis, created publishing houses. Maricourt set up Le Goût de l'Etre in Amiens, and Louis began Editions du Lérot in Tusson. Despite differing reasons for choosing the publishing industry,[70] they gravitated toward reprinting similar books. In 1986, both publishers reprinted the 1919 Edouard-Joseph edition of Vallès's *Les Blouses.* Louis produced a high-quality, limited-edition book, while Maricourt produced a much cheaper volume. Both reinserted the story of Buzançais, and Vallès's sympathetic version in particular, into the broader reading public, assuring that it would remain available for renarrating and creating new memories. After more than a century of exploitation by the political Right, the Buzançais affair, which had appealed to Vallès so long before, now struck the regional and local Left in the 1990s as an attractive episode to appropriate.

In 1996, native Buzancéen Léandre Boizeau wrote a historical novel, *Les Lueurs de l'aube* (The Light of Dawn), set in the Indre in 1846–47.[71] Boizeau wanted to "rehabilitate the memories of the hunger rioters in the eyes of his readers" and "to tell the story from the inside as the principal protagonists lived it."[72] As his main characters, he cast poor working people struggling to survive and to find some happiness in the difficult swamp country of the Brenne south of Buzançais. Boizeau describes their plight and their attempts to make the best of the worst: "They had very young known work, misery, and sometimes injustice . . . all this formed the daily life of the Brennous. Yet they were also known for their lively spirit and good humor: retaining from their brief childhoods a surprising taste for play."[73] Honest but made desperate by the crisis, his characters find themselves, and those they love, caught up in the calamitous disorders in the Indre in January 1847.

Like Vallès, Boizeau blends fictional and historical events and people to create a story that pointedly sympathizes with the plight of the common people by giving voice to the historically voiceless. From the third page, Boizeau paints a picture of grinding hunger and struggle. When a steward urges the workers to guard a pond carefully to prevent "brigands" from stealing the fish, one man suggests that these brigands might suffer from hunger, too. Trying to deflect attention from hoarding and speculation, the steward explains mounting food prices by pointing to bad weather.[74] But he fools no one. These hardworking people realize that human hands play a role in the suffering they endure. A character reports that "the mayor of Buzançais has set up charity workshops. . . . People . . . fill the potholes in the roads [and] clean out the ditches . . . all for 15 sous a day! With that, how can anyone survive! . . . There are children who will die of starvation! . . . and while some starve to death, others hide their grain to make the price go up! And it works: a month ago grain sold for 2 fr. a *boisseau,* now it is up to 4 fr.! Can this go on much longer?"[75]

References to misery and hunger mount relentlessly as Boizeau describes the gulf in experience and culture separating rich and poor. To the poor, poaching amounted to no crime, for the fault belongs to "those who oblige us to do it." One character explains that in Les Hervaux, on the periphery of Buzançais, "everyone is in misery, sometimes they do not even have bread to eat . . . the rich live in the heart of the city and are plenty warm, clean, and well nourished." How, another wonders, could it happen that, in the "present era with its progress, machines, mills, one could die of starvation"?[76]

The novel presents the story of Buzançais through the narrative of several fictional characters, especially two young lovers, Etienne and Rachel. Louis, Etienne's close friend, first recounts the grain shipment interception on the 13th. When the convoy stopped at the inn in the middle of Les Hervaux,

> women from the neighborhood identified it as a grain convoy and called for the men to help them stop it from leaving. Those who did not dare to come . . . had a difficult quarter hour: [The women yelled] "Cowards! Big idlers! Chickens!" . . . some [men] even had rocks thrown at them. . . .
>
> The men finally found their courage and helped to block the convoy. They seized the grain and decided to sell it at the normal price of 3 fr. the double *décalitre* in the presence of the mayor, who was there.[77]

The women taunt and shame the men into acting. But once set on intercepting the convoy, the group, in the presence of the mayor (suggesting his tacit acquiescence), fixes a new "normal" price for its grain. The protesters' *taxation populaire* sets the price at the usual, noncrisis rate.

Louis describes the rioters' state of mind: they with so little, the miller and other "bourgeois" having so much, beyond the poor's wildest imagination, and this in a time of crisis. At the "grain thieving mill [now] wiped off the map," they found 7,000 francs. When Louis saw "the astounded look of his friends, he repeated, yes, seven thousand francs in gold! . . . which was shared out." As the groups visited one house after another, feelings of vengeance came quickly: "Ah! they trembled in their boots, the bourgeois! . . . Green with fear, those tight-fisted starvers, shaking in their shorts, those blood suckers . . . signed everything . . . , they accepted the *taxation* of grain, they promised not to send their grain to the mill anymore."[78]

Louis's narrative of the Venin/Chambert episode describes the participants' reactions to a long history of exploitation and resentment, as well as the flash of rage in the unplanned moment of combustion.[79] He damns Chambert as "worse than all the others: a usurer." When the people arrived at the Chambert household, Chambert "pulled out his rifle and killed Venin. Venin . . . who had led us from the beginning, who forced the bourgeois to sign the engagements." Louis explains that "anger just took hold of us." After a chase, "they finished him off in the street . . . with pitchforks it seems. . . . It wasn't pretty to see!" Although Louis claims that he did not actually participate in Chambert's killing, he expresses powerful feelings: "I can tell you that no one mourned for him! We even drank to it!" Long-standing rage, resentment, and humiliation exploded into violent assault when Chambert shot Venin. Louis never refers to Mme Chambert or the servant Bourgeot. Chambert simply pulls a gun out and shoots Venin. No one tried to puzzle out his intentions or his rights. The usurer gets what he deserves.

The story characterizes the killing of Chambert as "justified" by his murder of Venin. When the court announces its indictments, the people cannot believe the calls for the death penalty: "What happened to Chambert was unfortunate but if he hadn't killed Venin and then threatened everyone around him, it never would have happened." They thought that authorities countenanced some of the requisitioning and price-fixing. Despite these claims, or perhaps because of them, the court does order severe sentences and three executions. The novel dwells on the feelings of those who watched the executions in April 1847 by describing the reactions of another of Etienne's friends, Nonone, who unwittingly finds himself in Buzançais that day. Helpless before such a horror, tempted to flee but afraid that the gendarmes might suspect him of complicity and arrest him, he watches with fear and fascination. The execution of Louis Michot proves particularly distressing because, at twenty, he was "too young to die." Women cried "because he could have been their son."[80]

Boizeau dedicates the novel to the three men guillotined in 1847: "To Louis Michot guillotined at Buzançais 16 April 1847 at the age of twenty. To Baptiste Bienvenu and François Velluet executed the same day. To their companions in misery who died in the galleys." Boizeau, an investigative journalist, relies on research (in both archives and secondary sources) to fill out (plausibly, if imaginatively) the sketchy image of the common person provided in conventional elite accounts.[81]

Boizeau bestows human personalities on the poor and desperate people who experienced the events of 1847. The character Louis proudly gives his struggling mother the few gold coins he received during the distribution of the Golconda found at the mill, an act that Bienvenu might have imagined when he collected 20 francs to help support his own ailing mother. Louis problematizes the label "rioter" by emphasizing that the authorities, not the common people themselves, assigned it to the arrested and punished.[82] Those who had protested in the streets to demand bread and justice did not think of themselves as rioters, nor of their actions as a riot.

Despite all his empathy for the unfortunate, Boizeau casts his female characters in limited roles, primarily as objects of male desire, love, and protection—and as sources of shame when male protection fails. Except for the episode over the grain convoy, historical women as characters appear nowhere in the novel. Fictional female characters abound, but except for Rachel (Etienne's love), none plays any significant role in the story. Unlike in *Les Blouses,* no strong female protesters like Marianne or the Old Woman appear. As in *Les Blouses,* no bourgeois women appear here either, their absence denying readers opportunities to sympathize with them as victims. Only women of the people play the part of victim; in fact, they play no other part.[83]

In his novel, Boizeau offers an empathetic portrayal of people struggling to make lives for themselves despite grinding poverty, social injustice, and periodic crisis, all exacerbated by social polarization and incomprehension. The Buzançais sources offer glimpses of little-known aspects of popular life, usually obscured by the silences that prevail in "normal" times. But even these sources offer at best one-dimensional and biased pictures of popular concerns because elites produced them. Boizeau complains pointedly that "most local historians or erudites navigate in a mode of thought very attached to the established order. They take inspiration from . . . the writings of representatives of the propertied classes." In their hands, rioters become little more than "alcoholic hoodlums."[84] Historical fiction, like Boizeau's *Les Lueurs de l'aube* or Vallès's *Les Blouses,* exploits the historical records generated in exceptional times and applies a wash of imagination to give the characters substance and shading not supplied by these records.

Boizeau's historical novel demonstrates that Buzançais continues to attract new narrators seeking to explore its multiple dimensions, narrators who find the story exciting to tell, and find a market for it. Boizeau's novel, published by his local publishing company, had modest circulation, but nonetheless sold and continues to sell.[85]

By the end of the 1990s, the story also found a place in two very different genres: historical theater and local history. First, in 1995, a local theater club involving schoolchildren and residents performed a history of Buzançais from the Middle Ages to the present in which a reenactment of the riot figured prominently.[86] The director, Patrick Lepas, a local elementary school teacher, actor, and amateur theater director in Buzançais, had students research the city's history, and he produced the performance.

After the play's first casual performance in an indoor theater in 1995, Lepas proposed a major outdoor production for the next year. This rendition remapped Buzançais's history onto its modern landscape by staging it in front of the remains of the Pavillon des Ducs on the Place de Gaulle. Régis Blanchet, the recently elected mayor (and the first new person to hold the position since 1945), eagerly seeking ways to bolster local morale and to attract favorable attention (and hopefully resources) to his economically depressed town,[87] encouraged Lepas to develop the production further. Politicians in Buzançais, as in many towns all over France, had discovered that *spectacles historiques* offered promising opportunities to nurture and even shape community identities and to create economic opportunities by inventing tourist attractions.[88]

In 1996, supported by a newly founded *comité des fêtes,* Lepas presented a much more ambitious production, "Le Pavillon des Ducs raconte l'histoire de Buzançais." This "sound and light show" offered "a fresco" of episodes from the Gallo-Roman era to the present. The actual places where most of the city's history took place—the church, much of the château, and the *place* around which both stood, along with the town hall, *collège,* and garrison for the gendarmerie—had vanished in the fire of 1945, replaced by modern structures. Lepas's impressive show—involving more than sixty actors (all local), several horses and motor vehicles, period costuming, professional "sound and light" effects, intermission entertainment, and seating for spectators—staged a history that gestured (with script and lighting effects) to the departed sites of yore.[89]

Amid stories of Buzançais from its origins in the early Middle Ages, through its lively existence during the Hundred Years' War, to the passage of the young Louis XIV through town, the 1847 riot forms a significant episode. Again, local children and adults enact episodes from the riot, while a narrator describes the hard times caused by the 1846–47 crisis and the mounting desperation of the common people. Bands of peasants and workers (men, women, and children) march through the Place de Gaulle seeking grain and imposing the engagement; Chambert shoots Venin and a crowd kills Chambert, closes in on his prostrate body, and, as the light fades, flails at him with pitchforks and scythes in bloodless slow motion. The forces of repression ultimately descend on the unfortunate town: police, magistrates, and troops. Executions and prison sentences ensue. The last tableau represents the three executions. Dressed in pure white shirts, the condemned men enter with hands bound behind their back. Accompanied by their confessors, each kneels for the last benediction, and then at the unmistakable sound of an invisible falling guillotine blade, they topple forward and the lights go out. From the shadows, the invisible narrator describes the episode as a "dark moment" in the town's history, but the performance itself enshrines it as part of the city's patrimony (funding and support from the municipality, with special thanks to the mayor, Régis Blanchet) on a par with homage to other, more positive memories, such as saving the life of an American soldier in World War II.

More than one thousand people attended the production, twice as many as Lepas and the *comité* had projected. This first success encouraged Lepas to propose a new spectacle dedicated entirely to the 1847 affair, commemorating its 150th anniversary. Mayor Blanchet supported the effort, "even if few people seemed to remember [the event]."[90] Lepas turned to the archives for information, working with Yvon Bionnier. Before Lepas could complete his script, Léandre Boizeau's 1996 novel, *Les Lueurs de l'aube,* had attracted considerable local attention. Finding the story compelling, Lepas decided to combine the "history of the riots with a pretty love story" and contacted Boizeau, who gave him carte blanche to adapt the novel for the spectacle.[91]

The plan to represent the Buzançais riot in theater did not go unchallenged, however. Both Lepas and Boizeau recalled early resistance from the local representative of the National Front (whom they also identify as a descendant of the Chambert family). Showing the enduring potential of the past to inflect the present, the representative worried that the play would resurrect old local social tensions and engender new ones over the issues of an extension of social rights in an era of unemployment, out-migration, and deindustrialization in the region.[92] Despite these concerns, the production received widespread local and regional support. Volunteers provided both the production crew and the cast, and the spectacle received financial support from the town, the department, and the region. Even wretched weather could not deter audiences; the production proved so successful that a more polished version followed the next year.

The spectacle, entitled "Buzançais, 1847," draws heavily on both archival records and Boizeau's novel. A disembodied (off-stage) narrative voice offers authoritative historical context to set each scene. The voice performs multiple roles: describing the crisis and the plight of the peasantry and working class of Buzançais; explaining that one character has better (though still grim) job prospects because he knows how to read; differentiating between the caring and uncaring elites; explicating various moments of the protest; and interpreting the trial that ensues. Individual characters express anguish, desperation, and mounting frustration with hoarding, speculation, and the accompanying high prices.[93] As in Boizeau's novel, children and adults alike seek happiness and love despite the increasingly grim circumstances, from which they hope to escape.[94]

In its presentation of the shipment interception and the Venin/Chambert episode, as well as in its portrayal of central characters, the play follows Boizeau's novel closely. The invisible narrative voice intervenes frequently, guiding the spectator firmly toward empathy for the people. Characters threatening the miller Cloquemin portray "a veritable eruption of popular fury." For these poor people, was not "the essential element of their existence, bread, at stake?" As the people clamor for Chambert's death, the narrator states that by shooting Venin, "Chambert had committed the irreparable."[95] Participants found themselves compelled to protest their misery, then got caught up in the crowd "for which they were mere instruments."[96] By its swift and merciless prosecution of twenty-six individuals, the government sought "to exploit the situation . . . to strike imaginations vividly."[97] The narrator relates that those arrested felt unjustly accused because at least "274 people could be found guilty of the same acts." In his script, Lepas quotes from despairing rioter testimony, the *premier président*'s chastisement of the local elites for their cowardice, and the argument of the defense lawyer who holds Chambert culpable for shooting Venin.[98] In the second to last tableau, the narrator describes the mood in Buzançais as the spectator watches the execution of the three condemned men: "Shock seized the entire region: the first excitement of revolt had given way, first to fear, then to a deep feeling of injustice, and finally to despondency." As the blade drops, the scene darkens. Then one by one, the characters return, each holding a candle, while the narrator explains that "during the execution, most unpunished rioters had preferred to close themselves in their houses [because] they did not want to witness the deaths of those who had died in their stead."[99]

The final tableau offers both a moral for the story and a ray of hope. It opens as the main characters, Etienne and Rachel, discuss the recent executions and repression. Etienne declares that "we must never forget this!" Rachel wishes that "the baby inside me will never know anything like this [and] that misery will never cause blood to spill again." They unite to hope for a "better world," where "men will realize that if everyone is to live, they have to share a little," and "hate and exclusion will not dominate the world." However, the narrator points out that in order to go forward, "it was necessary to forget the drama of 1847." The play ends with a popular festival all the more joyously celebrated because it offers a reprieve from memories of the "villainous époque" of 1847.

Rendered as a sound-and-light spectacular, the history of Buzançais and the 1847 *jacquerie* in particular succeeded beyond anyone's imagination and provided a springboard for an expanded collaboration between Lepas and Boizeau. After a pause in 1999, they undertook a production of another of Boizeau's books, about a late nineteenth-century poacher and his defiance of all authority.[100] Although the first productions made no reference to the 1847 riots, those presented in subsequent years have included ever longer introductory scenes that present the *jacquerie* as prelude to the poacher's story.[101]

Earlier concerns about the possible political ramifications of the production proved somewhat justified. As a recent study of the heritage industry and culture has argued, such efforts often find themselves "hostage" to "outside economic factors or power struggles."[102] Bolstered by common political sympathies with Boizeau on the left and by growing connections with the community, Lepas put himself on the candidate list of the Union de la Gauche during the 2002 municipal elections in Buzançais.[103] He ran against the conservative list of the Union pour le movement popular (UMP) and the Union pour la Democratie française (UDF), with whom Mayor Blanchet and most of the municipal council affiliated.[104] Lepas lost, but the campaign had served to "revive tensions" within the municipality. Boizeau and Lepas hoped, in fact, to encourage political debate around their productions. As Boizeau tells it, "If I occasionally hear that my dialogues are more pernicious and revolutionary than they seem, I take it for a compliment."[105]

In the end, Boizeau and Lepas moved their spectacle outside Buzançais, to the *clairière* de Saint-Suplice in the Parc national régional de la Brenne, where they expanded the operation into a veritable village festival, with displays by local craftspeople, services provided by local restaurants, and other delights supplied by local performance artists.[106] Liberated from the conflicts of Buzançais politics, their productions became increasingly similar to other historical spectacles performed throughout France in recent decades.[107] Moreover their audiences, originally local and "popular" in composition, changed; many spectators came from farther away and seemed more affluent.[108] A national television channel, TF1, reported on the spectacles, with a special focus on Boizeau; tourist offices listed the performances on their agendas.[109]

This experiment in dramatizing the disorders of 1847 suggests two divergent but related developments. The Buzançais affair can still generate and sustain local tensions, which may still involve local personal agendas. The story's conversion into performance, however, also operates as commemoration and perhaps even as an opportunity to reflect more general concerns about contemporary social questions that have animated the political Left in France—socially responsible development, unemployment, social inequities.[110] By presenting the historical protest and the debates it generated, contemporary actors may produce a "usable" history suitable for current politics. By reanimating the bodies of those from 1847 and reenacting their struggles, the actors erase the chasm that separates 1847 from the twenty-first century. For a while, the spectator lives in their time.

In this regard, the translation of the Buzançais affair into spectacle reflects a certain departure from the spirit animating the performances either at Puy de Fou in the Vendée or at Meaux in Seine-et-Marne.[111] Although, like the directors of these other spectacles, those in Buzançais certainly hoped to build stronger local communities by evoking and enacting the past, Lepas and Boizeau diverged from the others in their visions of what those past and the present communities should look like. In the Vendée, the conservative director and politician Philippe de Villiers sought to revive imagined past values (associated with religion and paternalism) that he believed had valiantly resisted but now risked extinction.[112] In Meaux, city administrators hoped that collectively performing the past would create new forward-looking common values among the highly mobile, diverse, and often alienated population that had emerged in the past thirty years.[113]

In Buzançais, Lepas and Boizeau actively rejected any thought of restoring a regretted past; in their deployment of history, they resembled more the animators of the historical spectacles in Meaux than those in Puy de Fou. However, while Buzançais suffered from economic and demographic anomie, it had not undergone the sort of immigrant-driven transformation experienced in Meaux. Nevertheless, the very choice of subjects to perform—from the "Jacquerie of Buzançais" to the oppositional life of a rural poacher—reflected a political commitment to forging new links to the contested past, and with them a local political consciousness that could identify and challenge inequities.[114] Boizeau saw no distinction between his journalism and his other local roles as storyteller, novelist, political activist, and president of the association that organizes the spectacles.

Boizeau and Lepas's purposes extended beyond personal political activism to invigorate the local community (by providing a site for developing social networks) and local politics (by reengaging with social questions), while also stimulating economic activity. Their efforts clearly belong to the larger trend of *patrimonialisation* that has connected interests in cultural heritage and pedagogy, art, tourism, and associational activities.[115]

The very performance of the Buzançais affair, as a sound-and-light spectacle, also had a second, paradoxical effect. Performance depoliticized it and made it available (and palatable) for appreciation by social elites and political conservatives. Supply found demand, and the "Jacquerie of Buzançais" proved marketable. Local postcards and maps that show the locations of historical sites and local businesses include a brief history of Buzançais as a town torn by war but also as a town "bruised by a popular riot in 1847. The guillotine did its job, but it did not resolve the tribulations of misery."[116]

In 2000, retired history teacher, local historian, and cofounder in 1968 of the GHAB Jean Duplaix (1914–2008) published a four-hundred-page history of Buzançais.[117] A resident since 1937 and a longtime denizen of the archives, Duplaix traces the town's history with great affection. As with most local histories, imagining their audiences as interested members of the public seeking a "good read" about the streets they walk, the buildings they pass every day, and the family trees of their neighbors, Duplaix loads his text with local detail, many quotations from documents, and provides virtually no scholarly apparatus such as footnotes to document the information provided or distract the lay reader.

Duplaix dedicates five pages (including two full-page images) to a section titled "Events of 1847 in Buzançais" and relies heavily on Hubert's 1908 local history and Bionnier's work published earlier by the GHAB.[118] His narrative, when compared with his lengthy accounts of less dramatic episodes in the town's history, seems strikingly brief. However, by 2000, after publicity from multiple genres, most Buzançais residents must have known the story. He explains that "the precariousness of life will be the cause of this severe crisis in 1847." As so often with amateur local historians, he seeks to offend the fewest people possible (especially since descendants of participants still lived in town). Furthermore, as a longtime resident, former schoolteacher, and local historian, Duplaix had forged strong ties with the established community and had a great deal of social capital at stake. He laments that "Buzançais, which over the course of its history, was remarkable for its moderation which inhabitants had demonstrated during times of trouble, acquired in 1847 a sad celebrity."

Duplaix notes that "Buzançais was a bourgeois city; if a certain number of the rich were charitable, others gave evidence, mostly through their speech toward the poor population, of a scorn that could only aggravate the hatred." He briefly narrates the usual episodes. When the convoy arrived in Les Hervaux on the 13th, "women gathered around the carts, they called for help to the workers in the charity workshop [and together they] blocked the convoy and prevented it from continuing its route. . . . What did the rioters want? Quite simply, they wanted that grain be requisitioned and distributed at a reasonable price."[119] While the bonfire burned, "wine and brandy was passed around, voices rose, and certain people provoked the crowd by designating targets for popular fury." In fact, no records exist to show that anyone had designated "targets" during the night, beyond sounding the tocsin.

Duplaix recounts briefly the attacks on the mill and other proprietors before lingering over the Venin/Chambert episode: "Mme Chambert . . . received the rioters. She accepted and signed the engagement. . . . Everything seemed regulated. What happened next? One of the rioters, Venin, demanded money, a servant intervened and above all, Chambert fils armed himself with a rifle and aimed it at Venin. It went off and Venin collapsed: he died several hours later in the hospice. Naturally, the rioters charged Louis Chambert who fled, hid himself in an armoire, but was discovered, beaten, struck by pitchforks. He, too, died several instants later at the hospice." Aside from ascribing need and (perhaps even some legitimate) anger to the rioters, Duplaix eschews assigning motive to any participants in the affair.

The narrative says that the prefect arrived from Châteauroux and "in order to pacify the crowd distributed money and grain from the intercepted shipment." Here an error slips into the narrative: the prefect, whatever his weaknesses, adamantly refused to accede to the distribution of grain and, in any case, had left town by the time the distribution took place. Duplaix flays the authorities. A timely intervention on the first day might have "pacified popular anger" and prevented the "excesses" that occurred. Eventually the repression put an end to disorders, and "in government circles those in high places wanted Buzançais to serve as an example," so they levied heavy sentences.

Duplaix concludes that "these events marked life in Buzançais for a long time. The families of the condemned, 'the 47' as they called them, remained marked by popular opinion right up to recent times," but he offers no evidence to support this claim. He notes that revolutionaries in Limoges made the release of the Buzancéens from their prisons a major demand, suggesting that in some circles, at least, popular opinion was favorable.[120]

Duplaix's narrative, by its brevity and its suggestion that no single individual or group could claim victim's status without considerable qualification, provides a centrist version of the affair that received local government approval manifested in the mayor's acclamation on the back cover of the book. Régis Blanchet —the same mayor who endorsed the Lepas/Boizeau historical performances— wrote: "As a native of the city of Buzançais . . . and being convinced that the most passionate history is the history of one's home town, it seemed important to me that Jean Duplaix's diverse research be united in a work consecrated to the history of Buzançais. . . . Buzançais has had an extremely rich past. Indeed, certain events have marked the history of France, such as the *jacqueries* of Buzançais in 1847. . . . To you reader, I wish you an enriching visit to the history of Buzançais. Every Buzancéen or lover of Buzançais, whether he lives here or abroad, should be able to find his roots in this book."

On 21 November 2008, Mayor Blanchet showed his continued interest in, support for, and sense of the commercial potential of Buzançais's story. To commemorate the republication of Yvon Bionnier's book by Léandre Boizeau's

Editions La Bouinotte, Blanchet hosted a reception, followed by a screening of the television show "Le Pain et le Vin." Altogether he achieved an impressive confluence of talents from far and near, national and local media, and disparate political viewpoints in the service of his town and its people.[121]

The Buzançais affair has thus found a place in local as well as national heritage. Genealogists associate descendants with it; local novelists and journalists evoke it; educators make school projects out of it; the community performs it; politicians deploy it as political capital or as a heritage to generate attention and attract resources; some (publishers and authors) may even make (or strive to make) money out of it. For the last of these, as for so many before them, Buzançais has provided a usable past indeed.

Epilogue

In December 2006, while surfing the Web, I discovered that the story of Buzançais had made it into the contested realm of globalization, by way of the blogosphere. "Buzançais, le 13 janvier 1847" appeared in an issue of the monthly cyberzine *CQFD: Ce qu'il faut dire, détruire, dévélopper.*[1] *CQFD* presents itself as an "independent publication . . . committed to social criticism and experimentation."[2] Its mission to publish "refractory" opinions has resulted in articles on the struggles in Oaxaca; a critique of soccer icon Zinedine Zidane as spokesperson for the multinational corporation Danone; a commentary on the repopulation of the French countryside by British vacationers; and political cartoons and music reviews.

The article, by Iffik Leguen, a regular contributor to *CQFD,* unlimbers the Buzançais affair from the mid-nineteenth century as ammunition to debate another journalist, Alexandre Adler, about resistance to liberalizing economies.[3] The article begins with a brief account of the riot in 1847, portraying sympathetically the protesters' plight. Leguen relates that, when the price of bread skyrocketed and "two-thirds of the population was reduced to begging and dependency on 'charity workshops' . . . a crowd of day laborers, servants, workers and artisans" requisitioned—with "women leading"—a shipment of grain. With the complicity of the mayor, they decided to "recuperate" their essential supplies at the home of a "hoarder . . . but a bourgeois nicknamed 'the usurer' ruined the festival by killing an insurgent. He was promptly lynched."[4] The article then fastens on a festive aspect of the affair: "Coincidence or not, the next day was carnival. And the theme is thus found. 'We will bury the bourgeois under the ashes.' Three days of the world turned upside down saw the propagation of the revolt into neighboring villages, at the sound of the tocsin and in the light of fires."[5]

Leguen describes Louis-Philippe and Guizot's dismay that "such a '*jacquerie*' could still occur in a France where liberalism had triumphed to the chant of 'enrich yourselves.'" Force seemed to the government the only possible response. So, despite "the solidarity of *les blouses,* among whom authorities could find no snitches," arrests ensued. The article quotes an incredulous judge who wondered how "people who passed their time in a café could then go break the furniture of others simply because the latter were richer than they were." Such disbelief sent "three insurgents gallantly to *l'Abbaye du monte-à-regret* [the guillotine]" and "henceforth nothing would be as before." Leguen insists that memories remained and "the hatred in the eyes of the proletariat was equaled only by the fear in the bad conscience of the bourgeois." The article quotes Hugo's *Les Misérables,* "who saw in this episode the premise of the February 1848 revolution."

Returning to the present, the article claims that "one hundred and fifty years later," the journalist Alexandre Adler had posited an analogy between "current antiglobal resistance and the waves of conservative resistance against liberal capitalism in nineteenth-century France." Resistance, Adler had declared, had availed nothing in France in the mid-nineteenth century and would prove equally futile in the twenty-first. On the contrary, Leguen counters, Buzançais had left deep scars in France that survived to warn the unreconstructed who still thought repressing resistance a viable strategy. According to Leguen, the lesson dictates the opposite conclusion: repressing resistance intensifies the struggle and heightens tensions. Once again, Buzançais demonstrates its durability and its utility to political debate, this time in the struggles over globalization, surely one of the most "contentious conversations" at the turn of the twenty-first century, particularly in France.

Buzançais again figured prominently in the January 2008 issue of *Marianne,* a weekly national magazine dedicated to political commentary, oriented on the left, but opposed to both the *pensée unique* of neoliberalism and the politics of the *soixante-huitards.*[6] This double issue, entitled "1640–2008, Comment naissent les révolutions?" (How Are Revolutions Born?"), featured four rubrics: "The French Case," "Revolutions for Freedom," "Messianic Revolutions," and the "Neocon Insurrection."[7] "The French Case" focused on five key revolutionary moments: Grenoble's prerevolutionary "Day of Tiles" on 7 June 1788; "the King's Melancholy Wishes" for the New Year 1830 preceding the July Revolution; "The Revenge of the Gray Smocks" (Buzançais) on 13–14

January 1847; the Commune's "Revolution despite Itself" of 18 March 1871; and "the Revolution of the Frustrated" of 10–13 May 1968. Buzançais thus finds itself ranked among the major events of French history.[8]

This version embeds its story of Buzançais deep into the body of revolutionary history.[9] In 1847 "France dreamt of order and prosperity," and revolution seemed unimaginable to most, but "had they listened to the sounds from the provinces," they would have heard "the prerevolutionary rumblings." Parisians such as "Proudhon, Lamennais, and Lamartine," too busy imagining the "return of the Republic," could not interest themselves in "a banal food riot . . . turned bad."

The author, Anthony Rowley, well known for publications ranging from gastronomic history to dictionaries of contemporary French history, invoked Buzançais to set the stage for national revolution.[10] Providing minor details such as the name of the inn where the carters stopped (auberge du père Poulet) and the name of the magistrate, Mater, but sweeping past the names of rioters or even Chambert himself, the essay drives directly toward its point: real but unacknowledged hardship "turned weavers, masons, and ironworkers into masters of the town despite themselves." Their very anonymity makes them seem numerous, and powerful.[11] They "made the rich pay up" and "sign an engagement to guarantee six months of grain at half price." This "social carnival" rolled on "until the death—in confused circumstances—of one of the requisitioners turned the revenge of the little people into insurrection."

Rowley asserts his position unequivocally by declaring the first death a "murder." Describing how people took their revenge against the unnamed "murderer—'called the usurer' . . . tracking him like an animal throughout the town and bludgeoning him to death by clubs, axes, pitchforks, and sabots," Rowley explains that the "usurer" "crystallized ancient hatreds against property owners and new ones against the distant political power held coresponsible for their difficulties." Invoking not previous revolutionary events but the Reformation, this "Saint Barthélemy for the bourgeois" brought on punitive official retribution, Rowley explains. Even if what happened in Buzançais seemed to many Parisians a mere brushfire, others saw it for what it was, a dangerous attack on property that put the "popular revolutionary anger at the center of the political game."

The essay points out "for the readers of *Marianne*" that rather than bravely embrace the message of Buzançais's protest in 1847, the opposition weakly "cooks up . . . banquets" for their notability. The revolution then simmering ultimately boils in February 1848, and this time the "troops fire" and seventeen die on the boulevard des Capucines. Rowley's essay bristles with allusions to the danger of ignoring the calls of the suffering; to the tendency of the notability, political as well as intellectual, to debate rather than act; and to the illusions of social peace beneath which social war seethes. Buzançais showed the "little people crouched behind the curtain" and their looming revolutionary potential.

In these recent invocations, just as at the time of the event and so often since, Buzançais has served different narrators as an object for political debate, a crime story, a morality play, or merely an engaging tale. Over these 160 years, each narrator has manipulated it textually and sometimes visually. Consciously or not, each version has manifested the concerns and attitudes of those deploying it in different media, for different audiences, and with different messages, in the process revealing the diverse ways different media reframe history for ideological ends and the rich ambiguities inherent in such an effort. My story of Buzançais's story shows not only that local and national "memories" rarely operate in the same way at the same time but also that the nature of the media themselves,[12] which ran the gamut from court records to comic strips, from novels to *son et lumière,* transformed the modalities of memories.

Observing the ways different authors and media have represented Buzançais over time raises questions about the relationship between collective and individual memories.[13] During the lifetime of those who experienced the events firsthand, or read contemporary accounts of them, allusions to Buzançais resonated allegorically across France, though the tincture of the response depended on the political hue of the responder. Such circumstances might seem to support Maurice Halbwachs's characterization of all memory as collective and Roland Barthes's obituary for the author, which have rendered defining the role of individual memories difficult.[14] Although for a time at least Buzançais evoked emotions across its contemporary society, it never congealed as part of French collective memory in the same way as the Bastille.

Because the voice(s) of collective memory spoke sotto voce of Buzançais during this period, memories of it proved less constraining, making the affair available to perform different kinds of work. Writers, artists, and publishers on the right, on the left, and in the market saw in it a story less fixed and more open to individual interpretation, despite the fact that it spoke (and speaks) of enduring and collective issues. Between the 1880s and the 1970s, individuals chose to employ the story of Buzançais, to present it in certain ways and in particular media, because it served their specific artistic, didactic, and/or commercial purposes, not because collective memory dictated the choice.[15] This arc of the Buzançais trajectory argues for maintaining both the author and the individual as components of memory studies, however much the work of both local and professional historians has inserted the story into the wider French consciousness since the 1970s.

Just as collective protest has often incorporated and adapted previous forms of collective behavior, so has each rendering reflected an engagement with the ones that preceded it. Identifying the intertextuality of narratives has become a commonplace of literary analysis, and the narratives of Buzançais reflect an ongoing exchange with previous representations of the event, as well as with contemporary texts and images. For example, references to and images of carnival, upturned scythes and pitchforks, the struggle between Chambert and Venin, and bourgeois women recur in many narratives and illustrations, drawn from witness accounts, fiction, and visual depictions. Yet such recurring images can mean different things when set in different contexts. Rioters can appear as righteous starvelings or as murderous scoundrels; women as guardian mothers or menacing harridans; bourgeois as sturdy citizens or craven cowards.

Protesters in Buzançais in 1847 disturbed contemporaries by demanding food at an affordable price, living wages, and social equity at a time when most political elites stressed less rather than more government support for social needs, and by their violence, which alienated even many of the era's socialists. Since 1847 in the West democratization and the welfare state have reconfigured both the context for claim making and the nature of claims made. Although the repertoire of collective claim making has changed in the West, collective violence still occurs often (the Rodney King riots in Los Angeles, G8 violence in Seattle, riots in Paris *banlieue* and other major French cities in the fall of 2005). In addition, while most demands for justice or retribution in the West take more peaceful form as social movements, demonstrations, petition drives, electoral campaigns, and collective lawsuits,[16] France retains a privileged relationship to the politics of the street.

Buzançais belongs to a long national history of collective mobilizations—much of it violent—during which the protesters went "down into the street."

Calls to *descendre dans la rue* have continued to punctuate many nonviolent and violent protests in France, particularly since the events of 1968.[17]

The French have often "descended into the streets," sometimes to dump loads of potatoes, or eggs, or fish, or pigs into them. Activist José Bové has mounted repeated verbal and physical assaults on McDonald's.[18] French factory workers facing layoffs have invoked "boss-napping" and have threatened to set off gas canisters or to blow up plants and machinery: in 2000 at Cellatex in the Ardennes, Kronenbourg in Alsace, and Benard-Faure in the Aube;[19] in 2009 at Nortel in Chateaufort and New Fabris in the Midi, to list a few. A trade union representative, using terms long familiar, declared, "We are not terrorists or bandits, just . . . victim[s] of . . . financial scandal,"[20] claiming a legitimacy of such protests that French from many walks of life acknowledge. A similar comment came from Alba Ventura, deputy chief of "Service politique" at Radio France. Asked "Is social violence legitimate?" she defined it as legitimate if comprehensible, and comprehensible from people losing their businesses or their jobs. These victims focused their anger on the true villains, "the financiers" who "played with fire" and created this "rift" between managers and workers.[21]

An article reviewing the situation five months after the 2005 crisis in the *banlieues* quoted Claude Dilain, the mayor of Clichy-sous-Bois, who described the events as "a *jacquerie,* a social revolt," and Louis Schweitzer, former manager of Renault and president of HALDE, who explained that "as long as there is injustice there will be disorder."[22] Such comments confirm an interpretation of French history as highly contentious, even on the brink of civil war, or *guerres franco-françaises.*[23] Revisiting Buzançais has helped sustain this legacy. Meanwhile, the rest of the world has grown more violent, or at least appears so in the light of global news reporting. Deprivation has not disappeared, not in France, nor in the rest of the world. Calls to remember Buzançais create links to a past that legitimizes the persistence of similar claims in the present and future.[24] In France, bread remains a potent symbol, and bakers hold a special place (revered and reviled simultaneously) despite twenty-first-century fast food ubiquity, supermarkets full of bagged salad and factory-made baguettes, and upscale frozen food emporiums. Fluctuations in the price of bread serve as a surrogate for the cost of living in general.

Even after the post–World War II shortages had subsided, price controls remained on bread. In 1958 the government "liberated" the price of small loaves, in 1978 it freed the baguette, but not until 1986 did the government finally achieve the old liberal *desideratum* of removing all bread prices from control by the state. Despite the supposedly competitive market, the public remains suspicious of price-fixing, and with reason, for the government has prosecuted a few conspiring bakers.[25] On their part, bakers fear that competition will drive prices below costs, especially for small, artisanal establishments.[26] French media and the French public remain ever vigilant, and discussions of rising prices and their legitimacy (or lack thereof) appear often in blogs,[27] and on informational Websites.[28] Continued interest in the role of bread in daily life manifested itself in a France-Culture series "Feeding the City," broadcast on Radio France 4–7 May 2009.[29] The final featured Steven Kaplan, Cornell University professor, the doyen of bread and its history.[30]

Although the twenty-first-century West casts them in a different language than mid-nineteenth-century protesters did, the issues the Buzançais affair poses—between moral and political economy, legitimate protest and crime, the right to existence and the right to property, collective and individual violence, and the proper exercise of authority—remain relevant, especially if we look beyond France and the West into the rest of the world. Food riots still break out with striking frequency, and the politics of provisions plays a major role in contemporary global politics. In recent years, violent protests have often erupted over government subsistence policies and their effects in such diverse locales as Eastern Europe, Venezuela, Egypt, the Sudan, Zambia, Algeria, Morocco, Tashkent, Haiti, and Mexico.[31] Hunger has always demanded not simply charity but political recognition and standing, even leverage. The often brutal effects of forced transitions to market economies in Asia, South America, and Africa have made the story of a small town in an unremarkable part of France during the era of its own painful transition relevant to other times and places. Buzançais has thus endured through multiple renditions: as event and experience; as history and memory and myth; as dialogue for contentious conversations. Like the hungers and fears that spawned it, Buzançais lives on.

NOTES

ABBREVIATIONS

ADC	Archives départementales du Cher (Bourges)
ADI	Archives départementales de l'Indre (Châteauroux)
AESC	*Annales: Economies, Sociétés, Civilisations*
AG	Archives de la Guerre, Archives historiques de l'Armée de Terre
AHR	*American Historical Review*
AHRF	*Annales historiques de la Révolution française*
AHSS	*Annales: Histoire, Sciences Sociales*
ALM	Fonds Albin Michel
AN	Archives nationales
APLI	*Annales politiques et littéraires de l'Indre*
BN	Bibliothèque nationale
FHS	*French Historical Studies*
GHAB	*Bulletin du Groupe d'histoire et archéologie de Buzançais*
GS	Garde des Sceaux (Minister of Justice)
HR/RH	*Historical Reflections/Reflexions historiques*
IMEC	Institut mémoires de l'édition contémporaine (Caen)
JI	*Journal de l'Indre*
JMH	*Journal of Modern History*
JSH	*Journal of Social History*

INTRODUCTION

1. I define a narrative as a story told to recount events that occurred in a temporal sequence. As a historian, I am particularly interested in analyzing these stories and exploring how each story intersects with contemporary discourses about political, economic, social, and cultural relations. Many scholars distinguish between terms such as "story" and "narrative." I do not adhere to this distinction. Instead, I use such terms as "narrative," "account," and "story" interchangeably. Porter H. Abbott, *The Cambridge Introduction to Narrative* (Cambridge, 2002), 13, 17; David Herman, introduction to *Narratologies: New Perspectives on Narrative Analysis,* ed. David Herman (Columbus, 1997); Hayden White, *The Content of the Form: Narrative Discourse and Historical Representation* (Baltimore, 1987).

2. Cynthia A. Bouton, *The Flour War: Gender, Class and Community in Late Ancien Regime France* (University Park, PA, 1993); "'La Liberté, l'égalité, et la libre circulation des grains': Le problème de l'économie morale sous l'Ancien Régime et pendant la Révolution française," *AHRF* 319 (janvier/mars 2000): 71–100; and "French Food Riots: Provisioning, Power, and Popular Protest from the Seventeenth Century to the French Revolution," in *Disturbing the Peace: Collective Action in Britain and France, 1381 to the Present,* ed. Michael Davis and Brett Bowen (London, forthcoming).

3. Balzac claimed that the "law of the *pays*" was "to innovate nothing" and that locals "have a profound horror of any sort of change, even for that which might be in their interests." *La Comédie humaine,* vol. 3, *La Rabouilleuse* (Paris, 1949), 937–38.

4. On the department of the Indre and Buzançais during the July Monarchy, see Ernest Badin, *Géographie départementale classique et administrative de la France: département de l'Indre* (Paris, 1847); Marc Baroli, *La Vie quotidienne en Berry au temps de George Sand* (Paris, 1982); Louis Bénard, *Etude sur les ouvriers agricoles de l'Indre* (Châteauroux, 1907); Marcel Bruneau et al., *Aspects de la Révolution de 1848 dans l'Indre* (Châteauroux, 1948); Daniel Bernard, *Paysans du Berry: La vie des campagnes berrichonnes* (Roanne, 1982); François P. Gay, "La Champagne du Berry: Essai sur la formation d'un paysage agraire et l'évolution d'une société rurale," 2 vols. (thèse doctorat, Université de Poitiers, 1976); Solange Gras, "La crise du milieu du XIXe siècle en Bas-Berry," 2 vols. (thèse de 3e cycle, Université de Paris X–Nanterre, 1976); Alain Pauquet, *La Société et les relations sociales en Berry au milieu du XIXe siècle* (Paris, 1998); Guillaume Lévêque, "La Classe politique du département de l'Indre durant la Monarchie de Juillet," in *Jean-Edmond Briaune: Cultivateur, agronome, économiste,* ed. Jean-Paul Simonin (Angers, 2006), 87–100; and Jacques Bionnier, *Les Jacqueries de 1847 en Bas-Berry* (Châteauroux, 1979). In addition, I have conducted extensive archival research.

5. William Sewell, "Historical Events as Transformations of Structures: Inventing Revolution at the Bastille," *Theory and Society* 25 (December 1996): 841–81, and *The Logics of History: Social Theory and Social Transformation* (Chicago, 2005); Dominique Kalifa, "L'Indignation qui divise: Naissance de la forme affaire," in *Affaires, scandales et grandes causes de Socrate à Pinochet,* ed. Luc Boltanski et al. (Paris, 2007), 197–211; Lloyd Pratt, ed., "In the Event," special issue, *differences* 19, no. 2 (2009).

6. Robert Gildea, *The Past in French History* (New Haven, 1994).

7. Paul Cohen, *History in Three Keys: The Boxers as Event, Experience, and Myth* (New York, 1997). An American example is Jill Lepore, *The Name of War: King Philip's War and the Origins of American Identity* (New York, 1999).

8. Todd Shepard, *The Invention of Decolonization: The Algerian War and the Remaking of France* (Ithaca, NY, 2006); Joshua Cole, "Entering History: The Memory of Police Violence in Paris, October 1961," in *Algeria and France, 1800–2000: Identity, Memory, Nostalgia,* ed. Patricia M. E. Lorcin (Syracuse, NY, 2006), 117–34. For a discussion of the Revolution of 1848 as a "mnemonic *non-lieu,*" see Rebecca Sprang, "First Performances—Staging Memories of the French February Revolution," in *1848—A European Revolution? International Ideas and National Memories of 1848,* ed. A. Körner (London, 2000), 179.

9. Alain Corbin, *Le Village des "Cannibales"* (Paris, 1990); Edward Berenson, *The Trial of Madame Caillaux* (Berkeley, 1992); Alice Kaplan, *The Collaborator: The Trial and Execution of Robert Brasillach* (Chicago, 2000).

10. Pierre Nora, "Entre mémoire et histoire: La problématique des lieux," in *Les Lieux de mémoire,* ed. Pierre Nora (Paris, 1997), 24–25, translated as "Between Memory and History," in *Realms of Memory: Rethinking the French Past,* vol 1, *Conflicts and Divisions,* ed. Pierre Nora, trans. Arthur Goldhammer (New York, 1996), 1–20. Nora's collective project has come under considerable critique.

11. Victor Hugo, *Les Misérables* (Paris, 1862); Gustave Flaubert, *Education Sentimentale* (Paris, 1869).

12. Karl Marx, *The Class Struggles in France (1848–1850)* (1850; New York, 1976).

13. Jules Vallès, *Les Blouses: La Famine à Buzançais, 1847* (juin–juillet 1880).

14. Pierre Bouchardon, "La Jacquerie de Buzançais, I & II," *Les Lectures pour tous* (juin et juillet 1925): 1109–19, 1345–56, and "La Jacquerie de Buzançais," in *Crimes d'autrefois* (Paris, 1926).

15. Philippe Vigier, *La Vie quotidienne en Province et à Paris pendant les journées de 1848 (1847–1851)* (Paris, 1982); republication as *1848, les Français et la République* (Paris, 1998).

16. François Furet, *Revolutionary France, 1770–1880,* trans. A. Nevill (Oxford, 1992); Hervé Robert, *La Monarchie de juillet* (Paris, 1994; repr., 2000); Peter McPhee, *A Social History of France, 1780–1880* (London, 1992); Nicolas Bourguinat, *Les Grains du désordre: L'Etat face aux violences frumentaires dans la première moitié du XIXe siècle* (Paris, 2002).

17. For other such reimplanted memories, see Philippe Joutard, *La Légende des camisards: Une sensibilité au passé* (Paris, 1977), and Yves Lequin and Jean Métral, "A la recherche d'une mémoire collective: Les métallurgistes retraités de Givors," *AESC* 35 (janvier–février 1980): 152–53. Jean-Pierre Rioux, "La mémoire collective," in *Pour une histoire culturelle,* ed. J.-P. Rioux and J.-F. Sirinelli (Paris, 1997), emphasizes "la mémoire de création" (created memories), whose creators include "historians, movie makers, and the media in general" (338).

18. David Lowenthal, "Fabricating Heritage," *History and Memory* 10, no. 1 (1998): 5–24, and *Possessed by the Past: The Heritage Crusade and the Spoils of History* (Cambridge, 1998).

19. Jules Vallès, *Les Blouses: La Famine à Buzançais (1847),* illustrations de Mario Simon (Paris, 1919).

20. "La Jacquerie de Buzançais," in *Le Crime ne paie pas,* in *France-Soir* (janvier 1956), récit de Paul Gordeaux, images de J.-A. Carlotti, reprinted more than twenty years later, in 1979.

21. "Le Pain et le Vin," in *Les Grands procès témoins de leur temps* (10 juin 1978), Antenne 2, produced by Pierre Desgraupes and directed by Philippe Lefebvre.

22. A recent consideration of the problem of violence and its representations in French history and historiography is Jean-Clément Martin, *Violence et révolution: Essai sur la naissance d'un mythe national* (Paris, 2006).

23. Pierre Michel, *Les Barbares: 1789–1848: Un myth romantique* (Lyon, 1981). See also Susanna Barrows, *Distorting Mirrors: Visions of the Crowd in Late Nineteenth-Century France* (New Haven, 1981).

24. Pierre Bourdieu, *Distinction: A Social Critique of the Judgement of Taste* (Cambridge, MA, 1984); *The Rules of Art: Genesis and Structure of the Literary Field* (Stanford, 1996); *Champ politique, champ des sciences sociales, champ journalistique* (Bron, 1996); *Propos sur le champ politique* (Lyon, 2000); *On Television* (New York, 1996); and, with Randal Johnson, *The Field of Cultural Production: Essays on Art and Literature* (New York, 1993). Rodney Benson, "Review: Field Theory in Comparative Context," *Theory and Society* 28 (June 1999): 463–98.

25. Charles Tilly, "Contentious Conversation," *Social Research* 65 (1998): 491–510, and *Stories, Identities and Political Change* (London, 2002).

26. See especially the special issue "Les guerres franco-françaises," *Vingtième Siècle* 5 (janvier-mars 1985).

27. Bronislaw Baczko, *Les Imaginaires sociaux: Mémoires et espoirs collectifs* (Paris, 1984), 54.

28. Scholars of narratives might call the first two episodes "constituent events" or "nuclei" events—central to what happened at Buzançais—that "drive the story forward." Abbott, *Cambridge Introduction to Narrative,* 20–21, quoting Roland Barthes, "Introduction to the Structural Analysis of Narratives," in *A Barthes Reader,* ed. Susan Sontag (New York, 1982), 295–96. The second episode attracted the greatest attention, both at the time and subsequently. While every narrative of Buzançais grapples with the two deaths (even if each does so in particular ways), not all accounts narrate the others ("supplementary events" or "catalyzers"). However, even when absent they are significant.

29. I use the term "renderings" to apply to any subsequent version of these four episodes or facets, regardless of the media in which they appear.

1. THE RIOT AND ITS FIRST RENDITIONS

1. This account relies on the generally accepted narrative of the event, that is, those actions and words that no version disputed substantially. Certain aspects of the affair were contested, and these contested incidents (and words) proved fertile ground for subsequent narrators to fill in gaps in knowledge about what happened, who said what, and why individuals or groups did and said these things, by fabricating a narrative out of their personal perspectives and cultural materials.

2. "A poke with a pickaxe." Testimony of François Théophile Gaulin, juge de paix at Buzançais (Audience, 26 février 1847), reported in *L'Eclaireur* (lundi, 8 mars 1847).

3. Deposition, François Théophile Gaulin, juge de paix, n° 101 (19 janvier 1847), ADI, 2 U 68. (Subsequently reclassified as 2 U 70 and 2 U 70bis.) All the testimonies and interrogations may be found in the same carton. Hereafter, where the source is not noted, it is this carton. Although many were assigned numbers, others were not. I've included numbers where they appeared.

4. Interrogation, Louis Deschamps, 23 ans, manœuvre, n° 14 (21 janvier).

5. Interrogation, Jean Légeron, 27 ans, manœuvre (20 janvier). Fifteen sols equaled 75 centimes. The price of a kilogram of bread at the time had risen to more than 45 centimes (from approximately 28 centimes) for *pain bis* (a lesser quality than more elite white bread). A working person ate approximately one kilogram of bread a day. Thus Légeron's pay bought less than two kilograms of bread a day for a family of four.

6. Deposition, Pierre Frédéric Gaulin, propriétaire, n° 42 (23 janvier); Testimony, Baptiste Bienvenu, Audience (25 février 1847). Here and subsequently, I use "Audience (date)" to refer to the printed (but unofficial) trial transcript published by Typographie et Lithographie de Migné, ADI, 2 U 68. No transcriber's name appears. No "author" (or stenographer) appears. The transcript exists as an independent pamphlet publication, ready for distribution. No publication date appears on it; however, excerpts from it began appearing in the *Journal de l'Indre* with only two days' delay, on Saturday the 27th; in the national papers the following week; and on several broadsides.

7. Interrogation, Baptiste Bienvenu, Audience (25 février).

8. Deposition, Charles Fernand Cloquemin, négociant, n° 98 (20 janvier).

9. Interrogation, Pierre Trémine, *dit* Savoie, 23 ans, journalier, vigneron (24 janvier).

10. Interrogation, Baptiste Bienvenu (19 janvier); Interrogation, Audience (25 février).

11. Deposition, Jean Baptiste Aubert, 35 ans, journalier, n° 25 (24 janvier).

12. Interrogation, Louis Michot (19 janvier).

13. Deposition, Maitre Devers, gendarme, n° 14 (25 janvier); Deposition, Etienne Laurent, 42 ans, gendarme (22 janvier).

14. Interrogation, Jean Foigny (20 janvier).

15. Interrogation, Etienne Billault (14 février); Deposition, François Prouteau, 49 ans, charron, n° 27 (bis) (24 janvier). Honey proved a clear memory marker for witnesses.

16. Interrogation, Jean Foigny (20 janvier).

17. Interrogation, Etienne Billault (24 janvier); Interrogation (14 février).

18. Interrogation, Jean Foigny (20 janvier).

19. Deposition, Etienne Geay de Montenon, propriétaire, n° 9 (25 janvier).

20. Interrogation, Anne Bouchard, *femme* Coteron (21 janvier).

21. Interrogation, Jean Foigny (20 janvier).

22. Interrogation, Jean-Baptiste Rouet-Bézard, maçon, 23 ans (20 janvier).

23. Interrogation, Anne Bouchard, *femme* Coteron (21 janvier).

24. Interrogation, François Arrouy, Audience (25 février).

25. Interrogation, Jean Baptiste, 34 ans, charon (20 janvier).

26. Interrogation, Jean Foigny (20 janvier).

27. Interrogation, Pierre Trémine, *dit* Savoie (24 janvier).

28. Interrogation, Jean Baptiste, 34 ans, charon (20 janvier).

29. Interrogations (three), François Velluet (19 janvier, 27 janvier).

30. Several versions exist of this part of the affair, especially Procès-verbal, transport à Buzançais, flagrant délit, par Paul François Edouard Patureau Mirand, juge d'instruction, arrondissement de Châteauroux (14 janvier), and the unpublished memoirs (1854–56) of the *procureur du roi,* Vasson, "Mémoires," ADI, 1 J 1386 12. My thanks to Marc Du Pouget, Directeur, ADI, for signaling this document.

31. Deposition, Prosper Pinault-Valler, maréchal-ferrant, n° 64 (22 janvier).

32. They still had their bayonets and sabers, of course, and Buzancéens probably knew nothing of this oversight. Procès-verbal, Mirand (14 janvier). Vasson explained that when he heard about Buzançais, he concluded that they must rush there, "bringing all the available forces, ready or not, well or poorly equipped." He also reported that the troops were without cartridges ("Mémoires").

33. Juge de paix to procureur du roi (15 janvier, 11 heures du soir); Pierre-Charles Guesnyer, maire, Buzançais, to Ferdinand Leroy, préfet, Indre (16 janvier, 6 heures du matin), ADI, M 5225.

34., Guesnyer to Leroy (16 janvier, 4 heures du soir), n° 649, ADI, M 5225.

35. Guesnyer to Leroy (17 janvier, 7 heures du soir), n° 656, (18 janvier, 5 heures du matin), n° 648, ADI, M 5225.

36. In several places, authorities attributed the eruption of disorder in their towns to the refusal in Buzançais to distribute grain at reduced prices to those from outside the commune. Maire, Vendœuvres, to Leroy (16 janvier), n° 638, (17 janvier), n° 639, ADI, M 5225.

37. Maire, Vendœuvres, to Leroy (16 janvier), n° 638, ADI, M 5225; Robert de Chenevière, 2e avocat général à Châteauroux, to GS (17 janvier), AN, BB19 37. See also the trial records for the disorders in these towns: ADI, 2 U 68, 2 U 69. The death of M. Rabier at Villedieu never received much investigation, despite early reports that he had been killed by "pillagers." Procureur général à Bourges to GS (20 janvier), AN, BB19 37.

38. Guesnyer to Leroy (30 janvier), n° 932, ADI, M 5225, responding to a circular letter from the minister of the interior to the prefects for distribution to the mayors in January.

39. Guesnyer to Leroy (27 janvier), n° 715, and Guesnyer to préfet (30 janvier), n° 755. See also his letters dated 4, 5, 23 février, ADI, M 5225. On 21 February, he asked for further reinforcements during the period of the trial.

40. Ordonnance de Louis-Philippe (28 janvier), n° 741, ADI, M 5225. The reorganization was not complete until March, however, so the town relied even more heavily on the presence of troops. Commissaire de police, Buzançais, to Leroy (9 mars), n° 811, ADI, M 5225.

41. Marie-Eve Thérenty and Alain Vaillant, eds., *Presse et plumes: Journalisme et littérature au XIXe siècle* (Paris, 2004); Marie-Eve Thérenty, "Pour une histoire littéraire de la presse au XIXe siècle," *Revue d'histoire littéraire de la France* 103 (juillet–septembre 2003): 625–35.

42. For example, on 24 January the *Affiches de Châteauroux* published an "erratum" correcting itself about certain details.

43. William M. Reddy, *The Invisible Code: Honor and Sentiment in Postrevolutionary France, 1814–1848* (Berkeley, 1997), 22.

44. Robert Nye, *Masculinity and Male Codes of Honor in Modern France* (Oxford, 1993), 8; Reddy, *Invisible Code,* 18–64; Jan Goldstein, *The Post-Revolutionary Self: Politics and Psyche in France, 1750–1850* (Cambridge, MA, 2008).

45. Henri Monnier, *Scènes populaires: Les bas-fonds de la société* (1830; Paris, 1984); Louis Chevalier, *Classes laborieuses et classes dangereuses à Paris prendant la première moitié du XIXe siècle* (Paris, 1958).

46. For a discussion of bourgeois class identity issues at midcentury, see Cynthia A. Bouton, "Cowardly Bourgeois, Brave *Bourgeoises,* and Loyal Servants: Bourgeois Identity during the Crisis of 1846–47," *French History and Civilisation* 1 (2005): 172–85.

47. Carol Harrison, *The Bourgeois Citizen in Nineteenth-Century France: Gender, Sociability, and the Uses of Emulation* (Oxford, 1999) and "The Bourgeois after the Bourgeois Revolution: Recent Approaches to the Middle Class in European Cities," *Journal of Urban History* 31 (March 2005): 382–92; Martina Kessel, "The 'Whole Man': The Longing for a Masculine World in Nineteenth Century Germany," *Gender and History* 15 (April 2003): 1–31; Nye, *Masculinity;* Reddy, *Invisible Code;* Bonnie Smith, *Ladies of the Leisure Class: The Bourgeoises of the Nord in the Nineteenth Century* (Princeton, 1981).

48. Rapport sur les événements accomplis dans la ville de Buzançais les 13, 14, 15 janvier 1847 et les jours suivants, ADI, M 2565. On 4 February, the *Journal de l'Indre* refused to publish it but commented on it. The *Gazette du Berri* published it on 10 February and *L'Eclaireur* on 13 February.

49. "Assassinat de M. Louis Chambert," *APLI* 1 (jeudi, 21 janvier), 3. I cannot identify the family connection. The next week's issue featured a second article that offered more about the episode that involved Chambert. "Nouveaux renseignements sur les événements de Buzançais," *APLI* 2 (jeudi, 28 janvier), 3.

50. "Assassinat de M. Louis Chambert," 3.

51. This account appeared on the first page of the official departmental paper, *JI* (jeudi, 11 février) and clearly reflected its editorial stance.

52. This version conflicts radically with the ex post facto unpublished memoirs of the *procureur du roi,* Edouard de Vasson, who accompanied the prefect to Buzançais on this first trip. He wrote that, upon receiving news on the morning of the 14th that circumstances had deteriorated overnight, he hastened to depart, "taking all the forces available from Châteauroux, with the general and forty-one cavalry, ready or not, well or poorly outfitted." However, as he readied to leave, he learned that "the general and cavalry had nothing ready. The general was unfindable. . . . The Prefect himself had not finished lunching." Vasson wrote this sometime after 1854, and with his own interests at stake, so we have no reason to take his word as more truthful than any other account ("Mémoires").

53. Chambert was over forty years old and still dependent on his mother for support.

54. The narrative emphasizes two contradictory points. First, it represents the weapon itself as murderous, not Chambert. Second, even before Venin grabs for it, he had already demonstrated murderous qualities.

55. Acte d'accusation, ADI, M 2565. Raynal, the premier avocat général du parquet, Cour Royale, Bourges, had presented this report to the Chambre d'Accusation on 2 February. The Chambre had pronounced the indictments on 3 February. Raynal to GS (3 février), AN, BB19 37.

56. On narrative in legal discourse, see Sarah Maza, *Private Lives and Public Affairs: The Causes Célèbres of Prerevolutionary France* (Berkeley, 1993), and Bernard S. Jackson, "Narrative Theories and Legal Discourse," in *Narrative in Culture: The Uses of Storytelling in the Sciences, Philosophy, and Literature,* ed. C. Nash (London, 1990), 23–50.

57. Except, perhaps, for the brigadier of the gendarmes, Caudrelier.

58. Italics in the original. In his memoir, Vasson claimed that the prefect had distributed "several coins" to women who surrounded him, "without calculating the consequences of this untimely act of generosity, which, later, his enemies would exploit as a serious complaint against him" ("Mémoires").

59. "Discours de M. de Tocqueville, année 1847," in *Les Prix de Vertu fondés par M. de Montyon: Discours prononcés à l'Académie française,* ed. F. Lock and J. C. d'Aragon, 2 vols. (Paris, 1858), 2:246–75. On the prize, see Jeremy L. Caradonna, "The Monarchy of Virtue: The Prix de Vertu and the Economy of Emulation in France, 1777–91," *Eighteenth-Century Studies* 41 (Summer 2008): 443–58, and Sylvain Rappaport, "Images et incarnation de la vertu: Les prix Montyon (1820–1852)" (thèse de doctorat, Université de Paris I, 1999). Dossier, Madeleine Blanchet, Archives de l'Académie française, 2 E 14.

60. Tocqueville's speeches and writings subsequently extended the critical line that he enunciated in his Académie française speech. In October 1847 he predicted that "one day the political struggle will be between the haves and the have nots. Property will be the great battlefield." "De la classe moyenne et du people," in *Œuvres,* 2 vols., ed. A. Jardin et al. (Paris, 1991), 2:1124. This he blamed squarely on the middle class and its "constant appeal to . . . individual cupidity" and its "indifference" and "egotism," which by 1848 had produced a situation that he described to the Chamber of Deputies as "sleeping on a volcano." Tocqueville to Nassau William Senior (25 August 1847), in *Alexis de Tocqueville: Selected Letters on Politics and Society,* ed. R. Boesche (Berkeley, 1985), 188,

and Discours, to Chambre des Députés (17 janvier 1848), in *Œuvres,* 2:1125–38. This edition mentions Buzançais specifically in an explanatory footnote to the speech. I thank Jeremy Popkin for his assistance with this point.

2. REPRESSION AND REACTION, CHALLENGE AND RESPONSE

1. Even Napoleon had responded to the severe crisis of 1811–12 by issuing his own *maximum* on grain prices and by regulating aspects of the grain trade.

2. For a recent bibliography of the extensive literature on the history of labor protest, see Jeff Horn, *The Path Not Taken: French Industrialization in the Age of Revolution, 1750–1830* (Cambridge, MA, 2006).

3. Edward Shorter and Charles Tilly, *Strikes in France,* 1830–1968 (Cambridge, 1974); Charles Tilly, *The Contentious French: Four Centuries of Popular Struggle* (Cambridge, 1995); William M. Reddy, *The Rise of Market Culture: The Textile Trade and French Society, 1750–1900* (Cambridge, 1984); Roger Magraw, *A History of the French Working Class,* 2 vols., vol. 1, *The Age of Artisan Revolution, 1815–1871* (Oxford, 1992); François Jarrige, "A temps des 'tueuses de bras': Les bris de machines et la genese de la société industrielle (France, Angleterre, Belgique), 1780–1860" (thèse de doctorat, Université Pantheon-Sorbonne, 2007).

4. George Rudé, *The Crowd in History: A Study of Popular Disturbances in France and England, 1730–1848* (New York, 1964); E. P. Thompson, "The Moral Economy of the English Crowd in the Eighteenth Century," *Past and Present* 50 (February 1971): 76–136.

5. Cynthia A. Bouton, *The Flour War: Gender, Class and Community in Late Ancien Regime France* (University Park, PA, 1993), 163–67.

6. Raynal to GS (18 janvier, à minuit), AN, BB19 37.

7. Raynal to GS (n.d. janvier), AN, BB19 37. Didelot, the *procureur général,* characterized the events at Buzançais and its environs as "an organized pillage against those who are owners [of property]." Didelot to GS (20 janvier), AN, BB19 37.

8. Acte d'accusation (7 février), ADI, M 2565.

9. William Beik, *Urban Protest in Seventeenth-Century France: The Culture of Retribution* (New York, 1997), 256; William Beik, "The Violence of the French Crowd from Charivari to Revolution," *Past and Present* 197 (November 2007): 75–110.

10. Raynal to GS (22 janvier), AN, BB19 37. References to Chambert's death as an expression of cannibalism appear in several letters.

11. Acte d'accusation.

12. Jean-Clément Martin, *Violence et révolution: Essai sur la naissance d'un mythe national* (Paris, 2006).

13. Georges Lefebvre, *The Great Fear of 1789: Rural Panic in Revolutionary France,* trans. J. White (New York, 1973); Clay Ramsay, *The Ideology of the Great Fear: The Soissonnais in 1789* (Baltimore, 1992); Michel Vovelle, "Les Taxations populaires de février–mars et novembre–décembre 1792 dans la Beauce et sur ces confines," in *Ville et campagne au 18e siècle: Chartres et la Beauce* (Paris, 1980), 230–76.

14. Raynal to GS (22 janvier), AN, BB19 37.

15. Steven L. Kaplan, *The Famine Plot Persuasion in Eighteenth-Century France* (Philadelphia, 1982); François Ploux, *De Bouche à oreille: Naissance et propagation des rumeurs dans la France du XIXe siècle* (Paris, 2003).

16. Raynal to GS (21 janvier, 11 heures du soir), AN, BB19 37; Rapport, Sous-préfet de l'arrondissement du Blanc to conseil d'arrondissement, session août 1847, AN, F1cVII 26 (Indre).

17. Jeremy Popkin, "Worlds Turned Upside Down: Bourgeois Experience in the 19th-Century Revolutions," *JSH* 40 (Summer 2007): 821–39.

18. See also references to *jacqueries* in Mme de Staël, *Considérations sur la révolution française,* ed. duc de Broglie, new ed., 2 vols. (Paris, 1818), chap. 2, and Prosper Mérimée's play *La Jacquerie: Scènes féodales* (1828).

19. A.-D. Blanqui, *Histoire de l'économie politique en Europe depuis les anciens jusqu'à nos jours,* 3e éd., 2 vols. (Paris, 1845), 1:ix.

20. P. de Barante, *Histoire des Ducs de Bourgogne* (Paris, 1824), 249. Howard Brown, "Echoes of the Terror," *HR/RH* 29, no. 3 (2004): 529–58, and "An Unmasked Man in a Milieu de Mémoire: The Abbé Solier as Sans-Peur the Brigand-Priest," *HR/RH* 26, no. 1 (2000): 1–30; Edward J. Woell, *Small-Town Martyrs and Murderer: Religious Revolution and Counterrevolution in Western France, 1774–1914* (Milwaukee, 2006).

21. Jean-Baptiste Monfalcon, *Histoire des insurrections de Lyon en 1831 et en 1834* (Lyon, 1834), 40; Jeremy Popkin, *Press, Revolution, and Social Identities in France, 1830–1835* (University Park, PA, 2002), 21, 48, 230–32, 235–39.

22. Popkin, *Press,* 236.

23. Joseph-Marie Gérando, Baron de, *De la bienfaisance publique,* 2 vols. (Paris, 1839), 1:168; C. G. de Chamborant, *Du Pauperisme, ce qu'il était dans l'antiquité, ce qu'il est de nos jours; des remèdes qui lui étaient opposés, de ceux qu'il conviendrait de lui appliquer aujourd'hui . . .* (Paris, 1842), 201.

24. *Le Populaire* (27 septembre 1846), 2.

25. Victor Considérant, *Principes du socialisme: Manifeste de la démocratie au XIXe siècle,* 2e éd. (Paris, 1847).

26. Commanded by Lieutenant Colonel Bousquet, the minister of war's aide-de-camp. Raynal to le GS (17 janvier), AN, BB19 37.

27. After the prefect's hasty departure on the 14th, the Cour Royale at Bourges had on the 16th appointed an examining judge, Bazenerye, to the case. Arrêt de la chambre des mises en accusation de la Cour Royale séant à Bourges (16 janvier), ADC, 2 U 338. We know little about Bazenerye, except that he was one of two *conseillers* at the Cour Royale in Bourges. However, his appointment to this high-priority case suggests that his credentials and background resembled those of most July Monarchy magistrates: socially a propertied notable and politically an Orléanist strongly committed to the status quo. Jean-Pierre Royer, Renée Martinage, and Pierre Lecocq, *Juges et notables au XIXe siècle* (Paris, 1982), 13–18, 24, 51, 53–56; Jean-Claude Farcy, *L'histoire de la justice française de la Révolution à nos jours* (Paris, 2001), 216–30.

28. On procedure, see *Code d'instruction criminelle* (Paris, 1808, 1824), livre I, chaps. 6–9. See also A. Esmein, *Histoire de la procédure criminelle en France et spécialement de la procédure inquisitoire depuis le XIIIe siècle jusqu'à nos jours* (1882; Paris, 1978); general discussion of procedures in Farcy, *Histoire de la justice;* and Jean-Pierre Royer, *Histoire de la justice en France,* 2e éd. (Paris, 1996).

29. Didelot to GS (n.d. but probably 20–21 janvier), AN, BB 19 37. The supplementary *juge d'instruction* was Jacques Denis Paul Duhail, président du tribunal civil of Châteauroux.

30. "Affaire de Buzançais," AN, BB 19 37.

31. During this phase, they never heard testimony from the owner of the carts detoured that day or the carters. Aside from the owner of the inn where the carters had stopped, and the local authorities involved, the judges sought very few witnesses involved in the early events on the 13th.

32. For the differences in their competence, see *Code d'instruction criminelle* (Paris, 1824), livre I, titre II, chap. 1, and the Code pénal (1810).

33. Didelot to GS (n.d., but probably 20–21 janvier), BN, BB 19 37.

34. Interrogation, François Velluet (19 janvier).

35. Interrogation, François Velluet (27 janvier).

36. Interrogations, Anne Bouchard, *femme* Coteron (21, 23, 27 janvier).

37. Raynal to GS (3 février), BN, BB 19 37.

38. Arrêt de la Chambre des mises en accusation de la Cour royale séant à Bourges, ADI, M 2565 and ADC, 2 U 376.

39. Raynal to GS (22 janvier), AN, BB 19 37.

40. The first indictment opened the way for the death penalty because it followed Art. 304 of the 1810 Penal Code: Code pénal (1810), in *Bulletin des lois de l'Empire français,* 4e sér., t. 12 (1810), n° 277bis. The prosecutor later introduced the accusation of premeditation during the trial, further encouraging a capital verdict.

41. Those indicted were Louis Michot; Laurent Bonnin; François Velluet; Baptiste Bienvenu; Baptiste Brillant-Godeau; Louis Fauchon; Jean Foigny; François Légeron, père; Etienne Billault; Anne Bouchard, *femme* Coteron; Jean-Baptiste Rouet-Bézard; Jean Baptiste; François Arrouy; Pierre Barraud, fils; Edouard Bataille; François Moneron; Jean Légeron, fils; Louis Deschamps; Désiré Signoret; Giraud-Rouzet; Pierre Laumont; Jacques Venin; Jean Depont; Pierre Treline, *dit* Savoie; Louis Bézard; and Georges Coulon-Cormier.

42. The magistrates of the Royal Court at Bourges and the minister of justice decided to hold an "extraordinary session" of the Assize Court, the trial to begin on 25 February. Ordonnance de Mater, premier président à la Cour royale de Bourges, cited in Leroy (préfet de l'Indre) to GS (12 février), AN, BB 19 37.

43. GS to Mater (11 février), AN, BB19 37.

44. *Code d'instruction criminelle* of 1808 modified only slightly in 1824 prevailed until 1897. On procedure, see R. Garraud, *Précis de droit criminel contenant l'explication élémentaire de la partie générale du code pénal d'instruction criminelle et des lois qui ont modifié ces deux codes,* 14e éd. (Paris, 1926), 802–6; Jean-Marie Carbasse, *Introduction historique au droit pénal* (Paris, 1990), 329–31.

45. The law of 7 pluviose an IX had separated the jobs of examining judge and prosecutor. Jean-Pierre Royer, *Histoire de la justice en France,* 3e éd. (Paris, 2001), 454–55.

46. A. Esmein, *A History of Continental Criminal Procedure with Special Reference to France,* trans. John Simpson (Boston, 1913), 507–10.

47. Interrogatoires and nominations pour conseil (14–15 février), *Bulletin des lois,* n° 332 (1810); *Code d'instruction criminelle* (Paris, 1824), livre I, chap. 3, arts. 294–95; André Damien, *Les Avocats du temps passé: Essai sur la vie quotidienne des avocats au cours des âges* (Versailles, 1973); Bernard

Sur, *Histoire des avocats en France des origines à nos jours* (Paris, 1998); Henri Moreau, *Le Ministère public et le barreau: Leurs droits et leurs rapport* (Paris, 1860).

48. Berton-Pouriat, defense for Rouet-Bézard, Audience (28 février).

49. *Code d'instruction criminelle* (Paris, 1808), art. 372; Esmein, *Continental Criminal Procedure,* 514; Laura Mason, "The 'Bosom of Proof': Criminal Justice and the Renewal of Oral Culture during the French Revolution," *JMH* 76 (March 2004): 29–61. An official procedural *procès-verbal* was required, but it contained no testimony from witnesses or accused. This exists for the Buzançais trial in ADI, 2 U 68.

50. Mason, "Bosom of Proof," 39–40.

51. Ibid., 41–43.

52. Dominique Kalifa, *Crime et culture au XIXe siècle* (Paris, 2005); "Crime Scenes: Criminal Topography and Social Imaginary in Nineteenth-Century Paris," *FHS* 27, no. 1 (2004): 175–94; *L'Encre et le Sang: Récits de crimes et société à la Belle Époque* (Paris, 1995); and "Usages du faux: Faits divers et romans criminels au 19e siècle," *AHSS* 54 (1999): 1345–62. Annie Vienne, "Une Lecture de la Bourgeoisie: Les Romans-Feuilletons du *Journal des débats* (1839–1840)," *Cahiers de l'institut d'histoire de la presse et de l'opinion* 4 (1977): 247–70; Thomas Cragin, *Murder in Parisian Streets: Manufacturing Crime and Justice in the Popular Press, 1830–1900* (Lewisburg, PA, 2006).

53. See chap. 1, n. 6.

54. François Azouvi, "Psychologie et physiologie en France, 1800–1830," *History and Philosophy of the Life Sciences* 6, no. 2 (1984): 151–70; Martin Staum, "Physiognomy and Phrenology at the Paris Athenée," *Journal of the History of Ideas* 56 (July 1995): 443–62; Angus McLaren, "A Prehistory of the Social Sciences: Phrenology in France," *Comparative Studies in Society and History* 23 (January 1981): 3–22.

55. Mason, "Bosom of Proof."

56. "Cour d'assises: Affaire des troubles de Buzançais: Pillage et assassinat: Session extraordinaire," *L'Eclaireur* (samedi, 6 mars), 1.

57. Where the two diverge or where one supplies information not available in the other, I note the source. The Migné transcript appears to have had the greatest (if not the only) national circulation. Historians refer most frequently to this Migné transcript, largely ignoring the ways it differed from the *Eclaireur* version.

58. Mater was assisted by MM Jules Rapin and Frédéric Adolphe Duliège from the Royal Court at Bourges and Jacques Denis Paul Duhail, president of the court at Châteauroux.

59. *L'Eclaireur* (samedi, 6 mars), 1.

60. Didelot to GS (26 janvier), AN, BB19 36. The jury list included 20 proprietors (including the comte de Lancosme-Brèves, whose château rioters had assaulted in the wake of Buzançais), 4 notaries, 1 lawyer, 1 tax collector, 1 judge, 1 retired army major, 1 agent for military provisioning, 1 printer (for the journal *Les Affiches de Châteauroux*), 1 banker, 1 hotel manager (*maître d'hôtel*), 1 merchant (a close relative of Chambert), 1 *marchand roannier* (probably a ribbon merchant), 1 iron merchant, 1 wool merchant, 1 millstone merchant (*marchand de meules*). Two came from Buzançais, and twenty-three came from other places where riots had erupted. The most powerful regional aristocrat, the comte de Lancosme-Brèves, refused to serve and paid the 500 franc fine prescribed by law. Liste des jurés, ADI, 2 U 68. Bernard Schnapper, "Le Jury criminel, un mythe démocratique (1791–1980)," *Histoire de la justice* 1 (1988): 9–18.

61. *La femme* Coteron, only forty-four years old with two dependent children, was older than the average age of thirty-six but younger than the seventy-year-old Pierre Laumont.

62. Testimonies for Michot by Delporte-Degalle, fabricant de draps at Châteauroux, Charles Froteau, sabotier at Châteauroux, and Guillepin, Henri, sabotier at Châteauroux, Audience (27 février).

63. Testimony for Brillant-Godeau by Barrault-Fois, vigneron at Buzançais, Audience (28 février).

64. Testimony for Pierre Barrault by *femme* Molusson, journalier at Buzançais, Audience (28 février).

65. Testimony for Pierre Barrault by Auguste Boucher, manœuvre at Buzançais, Audience (28 février).

66. Mater especially criticized a female witness because "it was one thing for a man to have that sort of curiosity, but [not] for a woman." Testimony for Pierre Laumont by *femme* Dussert, fileuse at Buzançais, and for Pierre Barraud by Pierre Gauluet, journalier at Buzançais, Audience (28 février).

67. Testimony for Pierre Barraud by Pierre Gauluet, journalier at Buzançais, Audience (28 février).

68. Berton-Pouriat protested further that his client's father had designated these witnesses and he had had no chance to vet them before the trial.

69. This exchange followed the testimonies of two witnesses who both declared that the accused, Jean-Baptiste Rouet-Bézard, had admitted to killing Chambert. Pierre Simon, journalier at Buzançais, and Etienne Julien, journalier at Buzançais, Audience (28 février). In response to this sensational testimony Mater responded, "The accused has no need to summon you to say this. We know it already."

70. Both Prothade-Martinet and Rollinat found their performances (which became the two most often reproduced defense summaries of the Buzançais trial) stepping-stones to career advancement. The first achieved regional success immediately after the Revolution of 1848, when elected *procureur* of the republic in Châteauroux. Rollinat, a republican (*un républicain de la veille*) and friend of George Sand even during the July Monarchy, made it to the national scene when he was elected deputy in 1848 and 1849. Solange Gras, "La Crise du milieu du XIXe siècle en Bas-Berry," 2 vols. (thèse de 3e cycle, Université de Paris X-Nanterre, 1976), 2:587, 637, 616.

71. Article 441 of the 1810 Penal Code makes provisions for "provocation." See the defense lawyers' forwarded notes dating 25 février–5 mars, ADI, 2 U 68.

72. Sentences in ADI, 2 U 68, and summarized in Didelot's "Rapport sur la session extraordinaire des assises de l'Indre," AN, BB24 327–47.

73. Extrait des minutes de la Cour de cassation, l'audience du 1 avril 1847, ADI, 2 U 68, and Rapport du ministre de justice: Affaires criminelles et des grains (14 avril), AN, BB24 2018 1.

74. Some jurors may have voted against the majority during deliberations. French jurisprudence then required only a majority vote to convict.

75. Biet, commissaire de police de Buzançais, lettre, (9 mars), ADI, M 5225. On 23 March, however, the prefect argued that the sentiment for clemency had abated and "all the friends of order" are convinced that "the only way to prevent the return of revolt is to uphold the jury's decision and execute the verdict in its entirety." Leroy to GS (23 mars), AN, BB24 2019 1.

76. "Rapport sur la session extraordinaire des assises de l'Indre," AN, BB 24 327–47.

77. Letter, Muret de Bort (1 avril), AN, BB24 2018 1.

78. Michel Foucault on the "ceremony of power" in *Surveiller et punir: Naissance de la prison* (Paris, 1975).

79. Emile Mathieu, letter (14 avril), AN, BB24 2018 1.

80. Frère de Dieu de Magallon, letter (12 avril), AN, BB24 2018 1.

81. Raynal to GS (17 avril), Vasson to Didelot (12 avril), Prefect to GS (20 avril), AN, BB 24 2018 1. Several reports of the execution appeared in local journals: *JI* (samedi, 17 avril); *L'Eclaireur* (samedi, 24 avril); and *Affiches de Châteauroux* (dimanche, 18 avril).

82. Correspondence between the ministers of justice and war (8 avril); letters, Leroy to Raynal (8 avril), AN, BB24 2018 1.

83. Raynal to GS (17 avril), AN, BB24 2018 1.

84. Mercuriale de la commune de Buzançais (16 avril), ADI, M 5225.

85. Leroy to GS (20 avril), AN, BB24 2018 1.

86. Law (7 vendémiaire an IV; 2 October 1795). J. B. Duvergier, *Collection complète des lois, décrets, ordonnances . . . de 1788 à 1824,* 2nd ed. (Paris, 1834–35), VIII (1795–96), 301–3, especially titre IV, arts. 1–2, 6; titre V, arts. 1–2, 4–9.

87. Originally charges ran much higher. Cloquemin alone claimed damages to his mill and other property totaling 103,365 francs 10 centimes. Pierre Claude Martin Cloquemin, négociant at Buzançais, to conseil municipal at Buzançais (21 janvier), ADI, M 2567.

88. The printed Proclamation aux habitants du département de l'Indre (30 janvier 1847) warned that the year IV law made local inhabitants "collectively and personally responsible for any loss experienced by any one person." ADI, M 2569. All over France authorities published this. See the extended correspondence on the indemnity in ADI, M 2566, 2567.

89. See the exchange of letters in the 1870s: maire, F. Cloquemin, de Buzançais to préfet de l'Indre (6 décembre 1876); ministre de l'intérieur to préfet de l'Indre (3 mars 1877), ADI, M 2567.

90. Tableau des condamnés dans le ressort de la Cour Royale de Bourges pour crimes ou délits se rattachant à la cherté des subsistances, qui ont paru dignes d'être proposés à la clemence de SM pour des remises, reduction ou commutations de peines (1847); Letters, Justice, direction des affaires criminelles et des grâces (30 juillet, 7 août 1847), AN, BB24 327–47.

91. Unlike previous episodes of food rioting from the revolutionary period to the eruption of 1816–17, the government did not issue a general amnesty law but rather asked the courts to review each case. Circular letter from the Ministre de la Justice (7 août 1847); Tableau des condamnés, AN, BB24 327–47. On amnesties, see Cynthia Bouton, "French Food Riots: Provisioning, Power, and Popular Protest from the Seventeenth Century to the French Revolution," in *Disturbing the Peace: Collective Action in Britain and France, 1381 to the Present,* ed. Michael Davis and Brett Bowen (London, forthcoming).

92. Comité chargé de l'administration provisoire du département de la Haute-Vienne to Ministre de la Justice (29 février 1848), AN, BB24 327–47. Alain Corbin, *Archaïsme et Modernité en Limousin au XIVe siècle (1845–1880),* 2 vols. (Paris, 1975, 1998), 2:763–64.

93. Prothade-Martinet to membres du gouvernement provisoire (29 février 1848), AN, BB24 2018 1.

94. A local republican wrote that "eleven of the Buzançais condemned were pardoned and have returned home. The fourteen still in the galleys should come home in early May." Thavenet-Bellevue (délégué de l'Indre) to comité révolutionnaire (25 avril 1848), AN, C 938.

95. Commissaire du gouvernement près le département de l'Indre to Ministre de la justice (n.d., 1848), AN, BB24 327–47. The pardons are recorded in Rapport (14 avril 1848).

96. AN, BB24 327–47.

97. Popkin, *Press;* Thomas Ferenczi, *L'Invention du journalisme en France: Naissance de la presse moderne à la fin du XIXe siècle* (1993); Richard Terdiman, *Discourse/Counter-Discourse: The Theory and Practice of Symbolic Resistance in Nineteenth-Century France* (Ithaca, NY, 1985); Marie-Eve Thérenty and Alain Vaillant, eds., *Presse et plumes: Journalisme et littérature au XIXe siècle* (Paris, 2004). Journalists resorted to a *bricolage pragmatique,* a pragmatic assemblage of various genres, usually "mobilizing literary forms" to elaborate their columns: "the chronicle, critique, *fait divers,* political debate, studies of *moeurs,* advertisement." Marie-Eve Thérenty, "Pour une histoire littéraire de la presse au XIXe siècle," *Revue d'histoire littéraire de la France* 103 (juillet–septembre 2003): 626.

98. Sarah Maza, *Private Lives and Public Affairs: The Causes Célèbres of Prerevolutionary France* (Berkeley, 1993); Michel Foucault, *I, Pierre Rivière, Having Slaughtered My Mother, My Sister, and My Brother,* trans. F. Jellineck (Lincoln, NE, 1982; original French, 1973); Anne-Emmanuelle Demartini, *L'Affaire Lacenaire* (Paris, 2001); Kalifa, "Crime Scenes" and "Usages du faux"; Cragin, *Murder in Parisian Streets.*

99. For assessments of mounting critiques of the July Monarchy, see Pierre Rosanvallon, *Le Moment Guizot* (Paris, 1985); David Pinkney, *Decisive Years in France, 1840–1847* (Princeton, 1986); James Livesey, "Speaking for the Nation: Radical Republicans and the Failure of Political Communication in 1848," *FHS* 20 (Summer 1997): 459–80; Jo Burr Margadant, "Gender, Vice, and the Political Imaginary in Postrevolutionary France: Reinterpreting the Failure of the July Monarchy, 1830–1848," *AHR* 104 (December 1999): 1461–96; and Jill Harsin, *Barricades: The War of the Streets in Revolutionary Paris, 1830–1848* (New York, 2002). Although the July Monarchy political press functioned as organs of particular political "parties" or factions that circulated around one or a small number of men who endorsed their positions, no paper reproduces exactly the opinions of only one man, and even less a small group of them. Therefore, while remaining aware of the tight connection between individual and faction, I will attribute the opinions to the papers themselves.

100. The early reports usually claimed to quote directly from either the *Journal de l'Indre, Moniteur parisien,* or the *Moniteur universelle.* The last served as the July Monarchy's official newspaper. It was widely read for its reporting on government affairs. Charles Ledré, *La Presse à l'assaut de la monarchie (1815–1848)* (Paris, 1960), 221. The papers often cross-quoted each other, and although few worried about attribution or exact citation, the thread back to the same first sources is easy to trace. However, later, as more news arrived, some occasionally cited (unattributed) "correspondence" or "letters" that supplied amplifications of reports.

101. The French press served a subscription-only readership. As part of its many efforts to restrict freedom of the press, the July Monarchy prohibited direct sales on the streets of individual issues. Despite these restrictions, readership had increased significantly during the regime, from 73,000 in 1836 (when Emile de Girardin and Armand Dutacq founded their low-cost, "industrial" papers, *La Presse* and *Le Siècle*) to 148,000 in 1845. J.-P. Aguet, "Le Tirage des quotidiens de Paris sous la Monarchie de Juillet," *Schweizerische Zeitschrift für Geschichte* 10 (1960): 216–86; Charles Ledré, "La Presse nationale sous la Restauration et la Monarchie de Juillet," *Histoire générale de la presse française,* ed. Claude Bellanger et al., 3 vols. (Paris, 1972), 2:120. See Aguet, "Tirage des quotidiens," and Ledré, "Presse nationale," for circulation figures for the newspapers cited below.

102. Edward Berenson, *Populist Religion and Left-Wing Politics in France, 1830–1852* (Princeton, 1984).

103. By mid-January, most newspapers referred to the riot in Buzançais as a "Jacquerie." The national press appears to have picked up the reference from the *Journal de l'Indre,* which on 20 January declared: "Insurrection continues. Rioting and pillaging propagate from canton to canton. We are in the presence of a veritable Jacquerie."

104. Rapport sur l'ensemble général des événements de la ville de Mulhouse (3 juillet); Lettres du lieutenant commandant la 5e division militaire au ministre de la guerre (27, 28 juin), AG, E5 156; Roger Price, *The Modernization of Rural France: Communications Networks and Agricultural Market Structures in Nineteenth-Century France* (London, 1983), 164.

105. *Gazette du Berri* 12 (mercredi, 10 février); "La Guillotine à Buzançais," *La Réforme* (mardi, 20 avril).

106. Marcellin de L'Estang, *Haute mission de la France dans l'avenir des peuples* (Toulouse, 1847), 130.

107. Charles-Joseph-Nicolas Robin, *Les Tablettes du Diable* (Paris, 1847), 51–52.

108. Georges-Marie Mathieu-Dairnvaell, *Scandales du jour: Les Ministres jugés par Satan et par un pamphlétaire devenu ministre,* 2e éd. (Paris, 1847), 4, 25. Here Daimvaell continues to associate Jews with the evils of unregulated capitalism and government tyranny when he refers to the suspicious "speculations in subsistence [including] the supplies in grain made by Rothschild in Algeria and Brest." Julie Kalman, "Rothschildian Greed: This New Variety of Despotism," *French History and Civilization* 1 (2005): 215–23.

109. Georges Duchêne, *Actualités: Livrets et prud'hommes* (Paris, 1847), 52–53. He associates the Buzançais executions with a history of labor disputes: *grève à quatre sous* at Anzin in 1833 and a savage strike at Saint-Etienne in 1846. Both resulted in clashes with troops and severe repression.

110. "Discours prononcé à la Chambre des députés dans la discussion d'un projet de loi sur les céréales (18 juin 1847)," in Alexandre Ledru-Rollin, *Discours politiques et écrits divers,* t.1 (Paris, 1879), 311.

3. BUZANÇAIS IN NINETEENTH-CENTURY POLITICS AND LITERATURE

1. Pierre Dupont, "Le Chant du pain" (Paris, 1849), BN, YE-55471 (840). Roger Bonniot, *Pierre Dupont: Poète et chansonnier du peuple* (Paris, 1991), 70–71.

2. In Lille in May 1847, several hundred workers joined women to pillage bakeries, to demand "bread at 5 sols," to attack property, to sing the "Marseillaise," and to accost the national guard and troops. Ninety-four arrests ensued; fifty people ultimately faced judgment in lower courts. Commandant par intérim de la 16e division militaire to Ministre de la guerre (12 mai 1847), and other letters from military personnel (13, 16, 19, 22, 26 mai), AG, E5 158; procureur général à Douai to ministre de la justice (22 mai 1847), AN, BB19 38. A. M. Gossez, *Le Département du Nord sous la deuxième république, 1848–1852: Etude économique et politique* (Lille, 1904), 83; Roger Price, *The Modernization of Rural France: Communications Networks and Agricultural Market Structures in Nineteenth-Century France* (London, 1983), 163.

3. Benoît Voisin, cordonnier en vieux à Sens, "Le Seigneur Candidat," in *La Voix du peuple ou les républicaines de 1848: Recueil des chants populaires, démocratiques et sociaux publiés depuis la Révolution de février* (Paris, 1848), 185–86, verse 3.

4. See the broadside "Boichot, Rattier et Commissaire: Troisième entretien de Jean Pichu avec son sergent, au sujet de la nouvelle Assemblée de 1849" (Paris, 1849): "Louis-Philippe sent [the

military] to defend the hoarders of grain who starved the people in order to enlarge their pile of gold; he had two fathers guillotined at Buzançais who were only guilty of wanting affordable bread for their children."

5. *Le Droit au travail à l'Assemblée nationale: Recueil complet de tous les discours prononcés dans cette mémorable discussion . . .*, ed. L Faucher et al. (Paris, 1848). Thomas Bouchet, "Le droit au travail sous le 'masque des mots': Les économistes français au combat en 1848," *FHS* 29 (Fall 2006): 595–620, and *Un Jeudi à l'assemblée: Politiques du discours et droit au travail dans la France de 1848* (Quebec, 2007), 173.

6. *Droit au travail,* 414.

7. Ibid., 415.

8. François Ducuing, *L'Ordre du jour: Questions sociales* (Paris, 1848), 54. Ducuing was a future Third Republic member of the National Assembly (1871–75), member of the jury for the Exposition universelle in 1867, and contributor to the *Revue des Deux Mondes.*

9. Gustave Du Puynode, *Lettres économiques sur le prolétariat* (n.p., 1848), 221. See also "Agriculture et le libre échange," *Journal des économistes* 18 (octobre 1847): 283–95, 287.

10. Karl Marx, *The Class Struggles in France (1848–1850)* (1850; New York, 1976), 38 and n. 24.

11. Victor Hugo, *Les Misérables* (1862), trans. L. Fahnestock and N. MacAfee (New York, 1987), 1054. Hugo returned to Buzançais at the end of his long poem "Conduite de l'homme vis-à-vis de la société," in *L'Âne* (Paris, 1881): "Your meager economic science fails / It is named Hunger, Despair, Buzançais." Hugo, *Œuvres complètes, Poésies III* (Paris, 1985), 1081.

12. Gustave Flaubert, *Sentimental Education* (1869), trans. R. Baldick (New York, 1964), 142–43.

13. Emmanuel Delorme, "La République sociale," in *Les Chansons,* ed. Auguste Pillette (Paris, 1890), 206–9.

14. For a recent entrée into this vast corpus of references that relied on collective memory, see economist Jean-Pascal Simonin, "Les Emeutes de Buzançais (janvier 1847) sous le regard des économistes et des écrivains" (paper presented at the Journée d'études "Economie et Littérature (1815–1848)" Université de Paris X, 6–7 avril 2006). Simonin mostly considers the evocations of Buzançais by national and local economists during the period 1847–70, although he also quotes Sand, Hugo, Stendhal, and, briefly, Vallès. I would like to thank him for sending me an advance copy of this work. Some of this now appears in *Jean-Edmund Briaune: Cultivateur, agronome, économiste,* ed. Jean-Pascal Simonin (Angers, 2006).

15. Gay Gullickson, *Unruly Women of Paris: Images of the Commune* (Ithaca, NY, 1996), 191. Martin H. Waldman, "The Repression of the Communards," *Canadian Journal of History* 8, no. 3 (1973): 225–45; Pamela J. Stewart, "Invisible Revolutions: Women's Participation in the 1871 Paris Commune" (Ph.D. diss., University of Arizona, 2006); David A. Shafer, *The Paris Commune: French Politics, Culture, and Society at the Crossroads of the Revolutionary Tradition and Revolutionary Socialism* (New York, 2005). Not until the republicans gained control of the National Assembly could they address the question of amnesty.

16. On 3 March 1879, the Assembly voted a partial amnesty law. Although it did not concern most condemned Communards, it did hold out the possibility of an eventual general amnesty and return to France.

17. Jean Dautry, preface to *Les Blouses,* by Jules Vallès, in *Les Œuvres complètes,* ed. Lucien Scheler (Paris, 1957), 121. Clemenceau attended the *lycée* during the Second Empire.

18. The first issue of *La Justice* appeared on 16 January 1880. Clemenceau presided as "political director" and journalist Camille Pelletan as editor. Gregor Dallas, *At the Heart of a Tiger: Clemenceau and His World, 1841–1929* (New York, 1993), 219–23; Jack D. Ellis, *The Early Life of Georges Clemenceau, 1841–1893* (Lawrence, KS, 1980), 77–79; Dautry, preface to *Les Blouses,* 119–45; Roger Bellet, *Jules Vallès* (Paris, 1995), 474, 477.

19. On Vallès's life, see Jules Vallès, *Œuvres,* ed. Roget Bellet, 2 vols. (Paris, 1975), 1:ix–lvii; hereafter cited as Vallès, *Œuvres* (Pléiade).

20. Vallès to Arthur Arnould, première quinzaine de décembre 1878, in Jules Vallès, *Les Œuvres complètes,* ed. L. Scheler and M.-C. Bancquart, 4 vols. (Paris, 1969–70), 4:1068. Also cited by Silvia Disegni, "Jules Vallès face au roman populaire," in *Problèmes de l'écriture populaire au XIXe siècle,* ed. R. Bellet and P. Régnier (Limoges, 1997), 58.

21. Vallès, *Œuvres* (Pléiade), 1:1039–43.

22. He wrote in 1870, "I love the people, the blood of a worker runs in my veins. I remember days of implacable misery." Vallès, to Arthur Arnould, editor of *La Marseillaise, La Rue* (17 mars 1870), in Vallès, *Œuvres* (Pléiade), 1:1147–48.

23. Bellet, introduction to Vallès, *Œuvres* (Pléiade), 1:xix.

24. The term *les petits esprits* belongs to the target audience of the *roman populaire.* These "little minds" belonged to "artisans, seamstresses, and darners." Maria Adamowicz-Hariasz, *Le "Juif errant" d'Eugène Sue—du roman-feuilleton au roman populaire,* Studies in French Literature, 53 (Lewiston, NY, 2001), 8 n. 23.

25. Vallès, letter to the editor, "Le Député des fusillés," *Le Citoyen français* (5 août 1881), in Vallès, *Œuvres* (Pléiade), 2:718.

26. For the discursive construction of class identities, see Alain Pessin, *Le Mythe du peuple et la société française du XIXe siècle* (Paris, 1992), and Bronislaw Baczko, *Les imaginaires sociaux: Mémoires et espoirs collectifs* (Paris, 1984).

27. Vallès, *Œuvres* (Pléiade) 2:4, 5. See also his 22 February 1871 article "Paris Vendu," in *Le Cri du people* in the same volume.

28. On occasion he used *bourgeron* instead of *blouse* to represent workers. This was also a short smock worn by workers and soldiers for certain types of work.

29. Vallès, "A ma bourgeoisie de Paris," in *Cri du peuple* (22 mars 1871), in Vallès, *Œuvres* (Pléiade), 2:44.

30. Jean Dubois, *Le Vocabulaire,* 128–29; Marie-Claire Bancquart, "Jules Vallès et le peuple," *Romantisme* 9 (1975): 121. By 1880, these terms continued to find usage among intellectuals but much less purchase among the political activists. As Dubois and Bancquart both argue, the terms could find currency among the expressly anti- or nonrevolutionary writers such as Flaubert, Zola, or Edmond de Goncourt.

31. Vallès, *L'Insurgé,* in Vallès, *Œuvres* (Pléiade), 2:959. The black flag belonged to the anarchists. See also *L'Insurgé,* ed. Marie-Claire Bancquart (Paris, 1975).

32. Vallès, "Les Mères devant les soldats," *La Marseillaise* (26 juillet 1878), in Vallès, *Œuvres* (Pléiade), 2:108.

33. Roger Bellet claims that Vallès had already begun to write the story of "the last French peasant *jacquerie*" while in London. Bellet, *Vallès,* 477.

34. *La Justice,* vendredi (18 juin 1880). The announcement ran for several days.

35. Michel Winock, *Les Voix de la Liberté: Les écrivains engagés au XIXe siècle* (Paris, 2001).

36. On the serialized novel in France, see Charles Ledré, "La Presse nationale sous la Restauration et la Monarchie de Juillet," in *Histoire générale de la presse française,* 3 vols., ed. Claude Bellanger, Jacques Godechot, Pierre Guiral, and Fernand Terrou (Paris, 1972); Lise Queffélec, *Le Roman-feuilleton français au XIXe siècle, Que sais-je?* (Paris, 1989); and "Le Roman Feuilleton," Special Issue of *Europe, Revue littéraire mensuelle* 52 (Juin 1974).

37. Marie-Eve Thérenty and Alain Vaillant, *1836, l'an I de l'ère médiatique: Analyse littéraire et historique de La Presse de Girardin* (Paris, 2001).

38. "Roman-feuilleton" in *New Oxford Companion to French Literature,* ed. P. France (New York, 1995), 712. See also David Coward, "Popular Fiction in the Nineteenth Century," in *The Cambridge Companion to the French Novel from 1800 to the Present,* ed. T. Unwin (Cambridge, 1997), 72–94.

39. Yvonne Knibiehler and Roger Ripoll, "Les Premiers pas du feuilleton: Chronique historique, nouvelle, roman," *Europe: Revue littéraire mensuelle* 52 (juin 1974): 7–18. On the historical novel, see, among others, Kalikst Morawski, *Le Roman historique moderne en France* (Warsaw, 1962); Wieslaw Mateusz Malinowski, *Le Roman historique en France après le romantisme, 1870–1914* (Poznan, 1989); *Histoire et Roman populaire,* ed. Dominique Kalifa, special issue of *Tapis-Franc: Revue du roman populaire* 8 (1997); and Laure Lévêque, *Le Roman de l'histoire, 1780–1850* (Paris, 2001).

40. Knibiehler and Ripoll, "Premiers pas," 12.

41. Jacques Goimard, "Quelques structures formelles du roman populaire," *Europe: Revue littéraire mensuel* 52 (juin 1974): 19–30.

42. Adamowicz-Hariasz, *Le "Juif errant,"* 9.

43. Disegni, "Jules Vallès," 51. However, Vallès claimed that he would have liked to publish a complete novel (like Hugo did with *Les Misérables*) because he recognized the ways the format of the feuilleton affected the structure and content of the work. With the restrictions of the format in mind, he hoped to write the complete work in advance of serialization in order to avoid the worst of the fragmentation and incoherences that accompanied the genre. Ibid., 61–62.

44. Of course, he could have easily mixed such societies that existed elsewhere in the late 1840s with the secret Montagnard societies (clandestine *démoc-soc* groups) that emerged to resist Louis Napoleon's coup in December 1851 (to one of which Vallès himself might have belonged). Ted W. Margadant, *French Peasants in Revolt* (Princeton, 1977).

45. I follow the version published in *La Justice;* references are cited by installment number and date.

46. On this, see Dautry's notes to *Les Blouses,* in Vallès, *Œuvres complètes,* ed. Scheler, 389 n. 1; Maurice Agulhon, *Marianne into Combat: Republican Imagery and Symbolism in France, 1789–1880* (Cambridge, 1981); Venita Datta, "Sur les Boulevards: Les représentations de Jeanne d'Arc dans le théâtre populaire," *Clio* 24 (2006): 125–47.

47. 6, 26 juin. Fombertot will later say, "All that I know is the corner of my hearth, work all day long, sleep at night, and a little rest on Sunday" (7, 27 juin).

48. 1, 21 juin 1880.

49. 4, 24 juin. On women's roles in finding ways to assure the survival of their household in crises, see what Olwen Hufton calls the "economy of expedients" in "Women and the Family Economy in Eighteenth-Century France," *FHS* 9 (Spring 1975): 1–22.

50. 1, 21 juin.

51. 2, 23 juin.

52. Ibid.

53. Ibid.

54. 7, 27 juin.

55. Quoting from the trial report, Vallès uses the same phrase as had Légeron (7, 27 juin).

56. While witnesses of the 1847 episode suggested that he had contributed heavily to the drunkenness that "excited" even more violence, Vallès has Monneron lecturing those assembled about the dangers of drinking alcohol under these circumstances. "They might drink! They are cold, they are hungry: one drop will get them drunk . . . you have no idea where that will lead!" (5, 25 juin).

57. 5, 25 juin.

58. Later in the story, Monneron explains, "I say 'we' to speak for the poor people. I, myself, have the means to pay the 24 sous for my bread, but that is luck. I don't want others to lack" (6, 26 juin).

59. 4, 24 juin. Vallès further emphasizes the legitimacy of this popular government by describing how, when the people station the grain carts in the courtyard of the *mairie,* the tricolor flag hung above it.

60. 5, 25 juin. She thus launches bundles of distant memories.

61. Accusations that the rich would make the poor eat grass long formed part of the repertoire of rumors associated with the politics of provisions.

62. 2, 23 juin.

63. 9, 30 juin.

64. Ibid.

65. During the actual riot, the brigadier of the gendarmerie, Caudrelier, manages to rescue them from a fire they set and sneak them out of the mill for safe keeping.

66. 11, 3 juillet.

67. In Vallès's version, Velin is neither a rootless scoundrel nor a cipher but a journeyman artisan, a Compagnon du Devoir.

68. 12, 5 juillet.

69. 23, 25 juillet.

70. Vallès never tells us what happened to any children she may have had, nor how the Fombertots became the sole caregivers for their young grandchild.

71. "[Fombertot] had heard everything, but he preferred to let Marianne, the strong head of the household, answer first. He was ready to do immediately whatever she decided."

72. 1, 23 juin.

73. 24, 28 juillet.

74. Vallès, "La Révolution. A Alphonse Daudet," *La Rue* (21 décembre 1879), in Jules Vallès, *Littérature et revolution: Recueil des texts littéraires,* ed. R. Bellet (Paris, 1970), 385.

75. During the Commune Vallès had had firsthand experience with female revolutionaries. See the excellent recent work on the *petroleuses* during the Commune Gullickson, *Unruly Women.*

76. Vallès, "Lettres Républicaines, Le Terme," *La Marseillaise* (8 janver 1870), in Vallès, *Œuvres* (Pléiade), 1:1146.

77. 2, 23 juin.

78. 7, 27 juin.

79. For gender differences in punishments, Cynthia A. Bouton, "French Food Riots: Provisioning, Power, and Popular Protest from the Seventeenth Century to the French Revolution," in *Disturbing the Peace: Collective Action in Britain and France, 1381 to the Present,* ed. Michael Davis and Brett Bowen (London, forthcoming).

80. 23, 25 juillet.

81. Cynthia A. Bouton, *The Flour War: Gender, Class and Community in Late Ancien Regime France* (University Park, PA, 1993), 18–20; Natalie Zemon Davis, "Women on Top," in *Society and Culture in Early Modern France* (Stanford, 1965), 124–46.

82. 2, 23 juin. Doctor Bonnel thus expresses his frustration with failing to recruit Fombertot to the republican conspiracy, which he calls "the conspiracy against hunger."

83. Ibid.

84. 3, 24 juin.

85. 5, 25 juin.

86. Ibid.

87. Ibid. Vallès presents a similar dilemma with regard to the parish priest. Despite wanting to ring the tocsin, most people in the crowd refuse to "string the priests up on the lantern" (invoking the call of 1793). "Most respected the priest because 'he was a decent man'" (6, 26 juin).

88. 23, 25 juillet.

89. 24, 28 juillet.

90. Daniel Bernard, "La Vie quotidienne sous le Second Empire dans les cantons de Buzançais et de Châtillon," *GHAB* 10 (1978): 131–47.

91. See the exchange of letters in the 1870s: F. Cloquemin, maire de Buzançais, to préfet de l'Indre (6 décembre 1876); ministre de l'intérieur to préfet de l'Indre (3 mars 1877), ADI, M 2567.

92. AN, BB24 327–47.

93. Unfortunately, municipal records from the nineteenth century are missing.

94. Vallès to Camille Pelletan, rédacteur en chef de la Justice (vers le 20 juillet 1880), in Vallès, *Œuvres complètes,* ed. Scheler and Bancquart, 4:1474. However, Vallès's followers did not abandon the novel so easily. They reissued it again in serialized form in 1885, not long after his death in February. *Le Cri du peuple* (15 avril–12 mai 1885).

95. Pamela Pilbeam, *French Socialists before Marx* (Montréal, 2000).

96. 14, 10 juillet.

97. Ibid.

98. Ibid.

99. 7, 27 juin.

100. 8, 28 juin.

101. 23, 27 juillet.

102. Roger Bellet, *Jules Vallès: Journalisme et révolution, 1857–1885* (Tusson, 1987), 486.

103. Each issue sold for 5 centimes. It published various genres of popular literature, especially adventure and police stories that had appeared first elsewhere. For example, in 1885 it published Vallès's second volume in his Jacques Vingtras trilogy, *Le Bachelier,* on the first page, and three other police and adventure stories on the following pages: *Mémoires d'un commissaire de police: La Lanterne Rouge* by Pierre Zaccone, *Agence Tircoche et Cacolet,* by Jules Lermina, and *Paris-Bandit: L'omnibus du Diable,* by Fortuné du Boisgobey.

104. *Le Cri du peuple* (samedi, 11 avril 1885), 1.

105. Ibid. (lundi, 13 avril 1885). They ran the same announcement on the 15th.

106. The memory of Buzancéens had thus been honored. It is likely, however, that most readers would have recognized the actual location of the story.

4. POPULAR PUBLISHING BETWEEN THE WARS

1. Jules Vallès, *Les Blouses: La Famine à Buzançais (1847),* illustrations de Mario Simon (Paris, 1919). This same edition was reprinted in 1986 by the editor Du Lérot: Jules Vallès, *Les Blouses: La Famine à Buzançais (1847),* illustrations de Mario Simon (Tusson [Charente], 1986).

2. Pierre Bouchardon, "La Jacquerie de Buzançais, I & II," *Lectures pour tous* (juin et juillet 1925): 1109–19; 1345–56.

3. See, among many others, Jean-Jacques Becker and Serge Berstein, *Nouvelle Histoire de la France contemporaine,* t. 12, *Victoire et frustrations, 1914–1929* (Paris, 1990); Maurice Agulhon, *The French Republic, 1879–1992,* trans. A. Nevill (Oxford, 1993), 179–82, 504; Charles Tilly and Edward Shorter, "Les Vagues de grèves en France, 1890–1968," *AESC* 28, no. 4 (1973): 857–87; and Benjamin F. Martin, *France and the Après Guerre, 1918–1924* (Baton Rouge, 1999). On 1919, see Tyler Stovall, "The Color Line behind the Lines: Racial Violence in France during the Great War," *AHR* 103 (June 1998): 737–69.

4. Paul Hanson, "The 'Vie Chère' Riots of 1911: Traditional Protests in Modern Garb," *JSH* 22 (Spring 1988): 463–81; Tyler Stovall, "Du Vieux et du neuf: Economie morale et militantisme ouvrier dans les luttes contre la vie chère à Paris en 1919," *Mouvement Social* 170 (1995): 85–113.

5. Jean-Jacques Becker, "Union sacrée, l'exception qui confirme la règle," *Vingtième Siècle* 5 (1985): 111–22, and "Union sacrée et idéologies bourgeoises," *Revue historique* 264 (1980): 65–74; Joseph F. Byrnes, "Priests and Instituteurs in the Union Sacrée: Reconciliation and Its Limits," *FHS* 22 (Spring 1999): 263–89.

6. Wheat production had declined to 60 percent of prewar levels. Becker and Berstein, *Victoire,* 181.

7. Philippe Bernard and Henri Dubief, *The Decline of the Third Republic, 1914–1938,* trans. A. Forster (Cambridge, 1985), 39–45; Paul Alexis, *Causes et conséquences de la crise de vie chère, 1914–1920* (Montpellier, 1922), pts. II and III; Michel Augé-Laribé and Pierre Pinot, *Agriculture and Food Supply in France during the War* (New Haven, 1927), 287–314.

8. Martin, *Après Guerre,* 30–31; Becker and Berstein, *Victoire,* 181–83, 186.

9. In contrast, retail traders, manufacturers of goods important to the war effort, and others able to take advantage of market opportunities offered by the war prospered.

10. Parisians called it the "starvation" ration. Martin, *Après Guerre,* 3–4.

11. Law of 10 February 1918 gave Clemenceau's government considerable latitude in regulating French subsistence needs. Bernard and Dubief, *Decline,* 63, 64, 73.

12. Bernard and Dubief, *Decline,* 44; Tom Kemp, *The French Economy, 1913–39: The History of a Decline* (New York, 1972), 3.

13. Jeanne Singer-Kérel, *Le Coût de la vie à Paris de 1840 à 1954* (Paris, 1961), 146–51.

14. By December 1919, it took 11 francs to buy a dollar, compared with 5 in 1914. Bernard and Dubief, *Decline,* 93. See also Kemp, *French Economy,* chap. 6, "Battle for the Franc."

15. Martin, *Après Guerre,* 30. Corinne Jamet, "Pourquoi 'la vie chère' après la Grande Guerre?

Le regard des Français au miroir d'un grand quotidien," *Recherches contemporaines* 1 (1993): 61–72.

16. The Socialist Party's membership leapt from 36,000 in December 1918 to 133,000 in December 1919. Bernard and Dubief, *Decline,* 87. CGT membership rose from 941,000 in 1913 to 1,473,000 in 1919. Martin, *Après Guerre,* 31. On the CGT, see Annie Kriegel, *Aux Origines du communisme française, 1914–1920,* 2 vols. (Paris, 1964) and *La Croissance des effectifs de la CGT, 1918–1921* (Paris, 1967). A total of 2,026 work stoppages in 1919 involving 1.4 million strikers marked the high point to date of the working-class movement. Charles Tilly and Edward Shorter, *Strikes in France, 1830–1968* (Cambridge, 1974); Gérard Noiriel, "Les Grèves de 1919 en France: Révolution manquée ou mouvement d'humeur?" *French Politics and Society* 3 (Winter 1990): 50.

17. Becker and Berstein, *Victoire,* 181.

18. The year 1919 witnessed a resurgence of interest in subsistence questions (especially during the first revolutionary era) among French historians, exemplified by H. Destainville, "Le Problème du ravitaillement dans un district de l'Aube de 1792 à 1793," *Annales révolutionnaires* 11 (1919): 229–41; Albert Mathiez, "L'Application du premier maximum (juin–juillet 1793)," *Annales révolutionnaires* 11 (1919): 495–507 and "Le vote du premier maximum avril–mai 1789," *Annales révolutionnaires* 11 (1919): 292–321; and Henry E. Bourne, "Food Control and Price-Fixing in Revolutionary France, I, II," *Journal of Political Economy* 27 (February 1919): 73–94; (March 1919): 188–209.

19. Raymond Hesse, *Le Livre d'après guerre et les sociétés de bibliophiles, 1918–1928* (Paris, 1929), 30.

20. Gordon N. Ray, "The Art Deco Book in France: The 1985 Lyell Lectures," ed. G. Thomas Tanselle, *Studies in Bibliography* 55 (2002): 21.

21. Henri-Jean Martin, Roger Chartier, and Jean-Pierre Vivet, *Histoire de l'édition française,* t. IV, *Le Livre concurrencé, 1900–1950* (Paris, 1986); hereafter cited as *Histoire de l'édition,* IV).

22. Hesse, *Le Livre d'après guerre,* 29–30; Ray, "Art Deco Book," 21. See also Antoine Coron, "Livres de luxe," in *Histoire de l'édition,* IV, 428, and Elisabeth Parinet and Valérie Tesnière, "Une entreprise: La maison d'édition," in *Histoire de l'édition,* IV, 123.

23. Ray, "Art Deco Book," 21; Noel Clément-Janin, *Essai sur la bibliophilie contemporaine de 1900 à 1928,* 2 vols. (Paris, 1931–32), 2:152–53. A coal miner in 1919 made 14.52 francs a day. *Annuaire statistique de la France, retrospectif,* edition, 1961, cited by the National Bureau for Economic Research (NBER), Macrohistory Database Series from France, www.nber.com/databases/macrohistory/contents/fr.html (consulted 10 April 2008).

24. Hesse, *Le livre d'après guerre,* 35.

25. Ray, "Art Deco Book," 22.

26. Ibid., quoting Raymond Hesse, *Le Livre d'art du XIXe siècle à nos jours* (Paris, 1927), 150 51.

27. The owner, Edouard Henri Joseph, born in 1886, lived above his shop at 31 rue Vivienne, directly across from the Bourse. He called himself *libraire-éditeur* on the 1919 electoral lists. Archives de Paris, Listes Electorales, 1919, 2 MI 19 / 368. The "Bottin de Commerce" for 1919 declared in large, bold type: "Edouard achète les livres, achat de bibliothèques, d'éditions originales et de luxe, romans, volumes en nombre, en solde et de livres en tous genres. Edouard-Joseph." *Annuire du commerce Didot-Bottin,* 122e année, 1919, T. 1 (Paris, 1919).

28. A total of 1,000 copies of *Les Blouses* appeared in 1919: 50 on the finest paper, called "Japon," 100 copies on "Hollande Van Gelder," 100 on "papier rouge," and 750 on paper called "vergé à la forme."

29. The Nobel laureates produced two plays (Belgian writer Maurice Maeterlinck, winner in

1911) and a collection of essays (French author, Romain Rolland, winner in 1915). The French poet and novelist Francis Jammes won the Académie française's Grand prix de littérature in 1917.

30. Balzac was the most frequently published nineteenth-century author. Coron, "Livres de luxe," 428.

31. "Les Lettres et la vie," *Revue de Paris* 26 (novembre–décembre 1919): 841–58. The other two books reviewed are Octave Mirabeau's *Chez l'illustre écrivain* (Flammarion) and Jules Renard's *Les Cloportes* (Crès). Edouard-Joseph, although a small press, merited review in a significant literary journal alongside two major presses of the era, Flammarion and Crès. Fernand Vandérem (1864–1939) was also himself a novelist and playwright.

32. Published in 1899, Le Roy's story recounts a fictional revolt of local sharecroppers (*métayers*) against a cruel and oppressive aristocratic landlord on the eve of the Revolution of 1830. Vandérem states, "I see nothing analogous [to *Les Blouses*]—in sentiment, milieux, episodes—except the dark and powerful book by Eugène Le Roy—a work too little known and whose hour will come" (843).

33. Jacques Sadoul deserted to the Bolshevik regime's Red Army after a court-martial in absentia had ordered the death penalty. The Socialists put him at the head of their list for the 1919 elections in the Paris region. Martin, *Après-Guerre,* 52. Satory was a prison camp for Communards.

34. Charles-Alexandre Picart Le Doux had illustrated for Maeterlinck's *Bourgmestre;* André Deslignères for Maeterlinck's *Miracle* and Jammes's *La Rose à Marie;* Démétrius-Emmanuel Galanis for Rolland's *Voyage;* Gayac for Jammes's *Une Vierge;* and Auguste-Jean-Baptiste Roubille for Jammes's *Le Noël de mes enfants.* All of these illustrators appeared in multiple dictionaries and encyclopedias of illustrators and artists of the era such as René Edouard-Joseph, *Dictionnaire biographique des artistes contemporaines (1910–1930),* 3 vols. (Paris, 1930–34). Many had illustrated for the magazine *Le Rire,* and some had illustrated during the art deco movement for *Le Bon Ton* and fashion magazines, such as *Vogue.*

35. A Mario Simon did make a minor name for himself as an art deco fashion illustrator. He contributed many stencils (*pochettes*) for *Le Bon Ton* in the prewar era (1912–14) and for *Vogue* in the years 1919–23. During the immediate aftermath of the war, with fashion work hard to find, many artists also illustrated books.

36. Hesse, *Le Livre d'après guerre,* 14.

37. Philip Stewart, *Engraven Desire: Eros, Image and Text in the French Eighteenth Century* (Durham, NC, 1992), 2; Edward Hodnett, *Image and Text: Studies in the illustration of English Literature* (London, 1982); Roland Barthes, "The Rhetoric of the Image," in *A Barthes Reader,* ed. Susan Sontag (Chicago, 1982), 30; Alain-Marie Bassy, "Le texte et l'image," in *Histoire de l'édition française,* t. II, *Le livre triomphant, 1660–1830,* ed. R. Chartier and H.-J. Martin (Paris, 1990), 173–200; Wendy Steiner, ed., *Image and Code* (Ann Arbor, 1981) and *The Colors of Rhetoric: Problems in the Relations between Modern Literature and Painting* (Chicago, 1982), 148.

38. Stewart, *Engraven Desire,* xi–xii, 10.

39. Vallès, *Les Blouses* (1919 ed.), 54–58.

40. Stewart, *Engraven Desires,* 37.

41. Vallès, *Les Blouses* (1919 ed.), 80–81.

42. Temma Kaplan, "Female Consciousness and Collective Action: The Case of Barcelona, 1910–1918," *Signs* 7 (Spring, 1982): 545–66; John Bohstedt, *Riots and Community Politics in England*

and Wales, 1790–1810 (Cambridge, MA, 1983); Lynne Taylor, "Food Riots Revisited," *JSH* 30 (Winter 1996): 483–97.

43. Which (as "baton of a Compagnon de Devoir"), according to Vallès's text, he has just "twirled in triumph."

44. Vallès, *Les Blouses* (1919 ed.), 99.

45. *Le Chambard socialiste* (17 Avril 1893), in "Steinlen et *Le Chambard socialiste*," www.steinlen.net/main.php?g2_itemId=416 (consulted 22 December 2008), and "L'Internationale," in Danielle Tartakowsky, "'L'Internationale,' hyme révolutionaire," www.histoire-image.org/site/oeuvre/analyse.php?i=82&d=331 (consulted 22 December 2008). Steinlen contributed regularly to popular illustrated magazines such as *Le Rire* and *Gil Blas,* illustrated political papers such as *Le Chambord Socialiste* and *L'Assiette au Beurre* and various World War I publications. Jacques Christophe, *Theóphile-Alexandre Steinlen: L'œuvre de guerre: Œuvre graphique de 1914 à 1920* (Lyon: 1999); Susan Gill, "Theophile Steinlen: A Study of his Graphic Art, 1881–1900" (Ph.D. diss., City University of New York, 1982); and *Images du peuple* (Limoges, 1986).

46. Margaret Kelleher, *The Feminization of Famine: Expressions of the Inexpressible?* (Durham, NC, 1997), 6, 230.

47. Pierre Bouchardon, *Crimes d'autrefois* (Paris, 1926).

48. Bernard and Dubief, *Decline,* 53–54; Jean-Denis Bredin, *Joseph Caillaux* (Paris, 1980); Edward Berenson, *The Trial of Madame Caillaux* (Berkeley, 1992).

49. Bouchardon, *Le Magistrat* (Paris, 1926), 99, and *Souvenirs* (Paris, 1953), 187. He further refers to the pre-1881 Assize Court president as a "severe god descended from Olympus" (*Magistrat,* 97).

50. Bouchardon, *Souvenirs,* 184–85, 182. Bernard Schnapper, *Voies nouvelles en histoire du droit: La justice, la famille, la répression pénale (XVIe–XXe siècles)* (Paris, 1991), 241–312; Elisabeth Claverie, "De la difficulté de faire un citoyen: Les 'acquittements scandaleux' du jury dans la France provinciale du début du XIXe siècle," *Etudes rurales,* nos. 95–96 (juillet–décembre 1984): 143–66; Françoise Lombard, *Les jurés: Justice représentative et représentations de la justice* (Paris, 1993); Renée Martinage and Jean-Pierre Royer, *Les destinées du jury criminel* (Lille, 1990). I am grateful to an anonymous reader for LSU Press for suggesting these works.

51. "The jury, it is universal suffrage." Bouchardon, *Souvenirs,* 183.

52. Ibid., 204, 182, 200–201, 203–4. The law of 25 November 1941 reduced the number of jurors on the Assize Court from twelve to six and ordered the three magistrates to participate with them in deliberations.

53. Ibid., 193, 191.

54. Joseph Caillaux, *Mes prisons* (Paris, 1920), 83; Bredin, *Caillaux,* 249.

55. Joseph Caillaux, *Mes mémoires,* 3 vols. (Paris, 1942–47), 3:203. In 1923 Bouchardon admitted he took great pleasure in a positive review of his work in *L'Action française.* Bouchardon to editor of Michel Albin (12 février), ALM 2545–20, IMEC.

56. Becker and Berstein, *Victoire,* 199.

57. Bouchardon, *Souvenirs,* 179.

58. He claims in his memoirs that he even asked the minister of justice, Camille Chautemps, to explain his obvious "excommunication." He learned, "from his own mouth, that they held everything against him" from his time on the Conseil de guerre. Ibid., 180.

59. Ibid., 419–20.

60. Becker and Berstein, *Victoire,* 186, 208–10; Ron Kedward, *La Vie en Bleu: France and the French since 1900* (London, 2005), 107; Kriegel, *Origines du communisme* and *Croissance.*

61. Bouchardon, *Souvenirs,* 254–55.

62. Ibid., 257.

63. Ibid., 50.

64. Bouchardon loved this quotation from Balzac's novel *Modest Mignon.* See the publisher Albin Michel's publicity page on Bouchardon in the Fonds Albin Michel: ALM 2545–20 (n.d.); "Les Grandes Causes Criminelles: L'œuvre de Pierre Bouchardon," *Vie Littéraire,* n° 11, ALM 188–11; and an interview with him in *Le Journal littéraire* (20 décembre 1924), ALM 188–11, IMEC.

65. Pierre de Pressac, "Littérature criminelle: L'œuvre de Pierre Bouchardon," *Opinion* (1 juin 1934), clipping held in ALM 188–11, IMEC.

66. Bouchardon, *Souvenirs,* 257.

67. Publishing houses Michel Albin and Perrin published most of Bouchardon's books.

68. Bouchardon, *Souvenirs,* 257. Gregory K. Shaya, "Mayhem for Moderns: The Culture of Sensationalism in France, c. 1900" (Ph.D. diss., University of Michigan, 2000); Robin Walz, *Pulp Surrealism: Insolent Popular Culture in Early Twentieth-Century Paris* (Berkeley, 2000).

69. Eileen Sposato DeMarco studies Hachette's market-conscious strategy in *Reading and Riding: Hachette's Railroad Bookstore Network in Nineteenth-Century France* (Bethlehem, PA, 2006).

70. Claude Bellanger et al., *Histoire générale de la presse française,* t. III, *De 1871 à 1940* (Paris, 1972), 387.

71. National Bureau for Economic Research (NBER), Macrohistory Database Series from France, www.nber.org/databases/macrohistory/contents/fr.html (consulted 25 November 2009), retail price of bread per two kilograms, City of Paris, 1925.

72. This history published in *Lectures pour tous* (June and July 1925) is hereafter cited by part number (I or II) followed by page number. Leclercq sometimes appeared as one of the featured illustrators on the title page. Since Hachette used him regularly, Leclercq knew how to cast images that resonated with the public. Though he had already achieved a certain public prominence, Bouchardon in 1925 was a tyro in the publishing business, only one of a stable of Hachette authors, and in no position to dictate the choice of illustrator (or illustrations).

73. I, 1108.

74. I, 1117. Bouchardon had clearly referred to the *acte d'accusation* (either the archival version or the version reprinted many times in various newspapers) for his information. It nevertheless varies in tone and detail from the official narrative.

75. Alain Corbin revisits this episode in *Village of Cannibals.*

76. I, 1110.

77. I, 1111. Italics in the original.

78. I, 1111. Italics in the original. However, Bouchardon misquotes the dossier. No witnesses actually reported that François Légeron had said, "Let them make another one."

79. I, 1111, 1113; II, 1348. Italics are mine.

80. I, 1112.

81. Ibid.

82. I, 1115, 1116–17. During his account of the trial, Bouchardon also repeats the severe reproaches the magistrates leveled at the local, cowardly bourgeois. II, 1352.

83. I, 1117.

84. I, 1118.

85. Ibid.

86. I, 1119.

87. Ibid.

88. I, 1120, 1119.

89. II, 1348.

90. Referring to them as *lâches* (cowards) (I, 1118). He did later reproduce President Mater's words of praise for Blanchet during the trial (II, 1352).

91. I, 1115.

92. I, 1116, 1120.

93. II, 1348.

94. II, 1350, 1356.

95. I, 1111.

96. II, 1112, 1346.

97. II, 1347. Timothy Tackett, *When the King Took Flight* (Cambridge, MA, 2003).

98. Regarding the story of Varennes, Bouchardon concluded: "We know what happened next; let us return to Buzançais." Ibid.

99. II, 1348.

100. II, 1349.

101. II, 1357.

102. II, 1352.

103. I, 1118; II, 1346, 1355. Italics in original.

5. *JACQUERIE* AS CARTOON AND TELEVISION DRAMA

1. "La Jacquerie de Buzançais," *France-Soir* (janvier 1956), récit de Paul Gordeaux, images de J.-A. Carlotti. I first discovered one day's episode in the ADI cataloged as Doc. Hist. "Buzançais, Jacquerie" n° 6.

2. Press circulation in post–World War II France was 9.6 million in 1952 and 11.4 million in 1958. Jean-Pierre Rioux, *The Fourth Republic, 1944–1958,* trans. Godfrey Rogers (Cambridge, 1987), 441.

3. Robert Soulé, *Lazareff et ses hommes* (Paris, 1992); Yves Courrière, *Pierre Lazareff, ou, Le vagabond de l'actualité* (Paris, 1995); Jean-Claude Lamy, *Pierre Lazareff à la une* (Paris, 1975); Charles Baudinat, *Le petit homme et le grand journal* (Paris, 1973); Robert Salmon, *Chemins faisant,* 2 vols. (Paris, 2004); Benoit Hopquin, "*France-Soir* du triomphe à l'oubli," *Le Monde* (30 octobre 2005); Patrick Eveno, "*France-Soir,* déclin d'un journal populaire," *Le Monde* (11 avril 2006).

4. Jean-Marie Charon, *La Presse en France de 1945 à nos jours* (Paris, 1991), 93. The active collaboration of many papers with the Occupation and the suspect nature of the "news" reported by others discredited many papers during the war. The suppression of many papers (or the purging of their administration) by the government after Liberation meant that 188 of the 206 daily papers published in 1939 disappeared and their property was transferred to new groups. Ibid., 126–30; Clyde Thogmartin, *The National Daily Press of France* (Birmingham, AL, 1998), 223–24, 242; Eveno, "*France-Soir.*"

5. Henri Filippini, *b.documents: Les années cinquante* (Grenoble, 1977), 123.

6. Robert Gildea, *France since 1945* (Oxford, 2002), 195; Charon, *Presse,* 131. Veteran American newsman Daniel Schorr once said that *France-Soir*'s staff could have put out the *New York Times.* Charles Gombault, *Un journal, une aventure: Des relations avec le pouvoir ici et ailleurs* (Paris, 1982), 51.

7. Son of an industrialist near Nice, Gordeaux (real name Paul Gordolon) worked on several local and regional papers in Nice, fought in World War I and got a job immediately for the *Echo de Paris* after demobilization. He wrote several plays and operettas. He helped start a new theater review, *Le Soir,* and asked Lazareff to join him in the enterprise in 1925. Courrière, *Lazareff,* 60–61.

8. Filippini, *b.documents,* 123, 163–64.

9. *France-Soir* (11 février 1950).

10. Thierry Groensteen, "Why Are Comics Still in Search of Cultural Legitimization?" in *Comics and Culture: Analytical and Theoretical Approaches to Comics,* ed. Anne Magnussen and Hans-Christian Christiansen (Copenhagen, 2000), 30.

11. "La Fornarina" featured the life and loves of the woman best known as the painter Raphael's lover.

12. Samedi, 28 janvier 1956.

13. Mallat regularly employed the same illustrators as Gordeaux. In 1970, the paper stopped publishing *Le Crime ne paie pas,* and in 1971, Mallat introduced a new verticle strip, *Histoires mystérieuses.*

14. Patrick Gaumer, *Larousse de la BD* (Paris, 2004), 197.

15. Rioux, *Fourth Republic,* 435–45. Eveno, "*France-Soir.*"

16. Rioux, *Fourth Republic,* 445. See also Gildea, *France since 1945,* 191–204; Robert Tombs, "Culture and the Intellectuals," in *Modern France, 1880–2002,* ed. James McMillan (Oxford, 2003), 195; and Serge Berstein and Pierre Milza, *Histoire de la France au XXe siècle* (Paris, 1995), 801.

17. Alain Fourment, *Histoire de la presse des jeunes et des journaux d'enfants (1768–1988)* (Paris, 1987).

18. One of these "collaborators," Jean Ache (real name Jean Huet), also illustrated frequently for Gordeaux's cartoons in the 1950s.

19. Filippini, *b.documents, 7.*

20. Tombs, "Culture and Intellectuals," 195; Rioux, *Fourth Republic,* 84; Richard Joby, "Tarzan under Attack: Youth, Comics, and Cultural Reconstruction in Postwar France," *FHS* 26 (Fall 2003): 687–726.

21. Fourment, *Presse des jeunes,* 285; Filippini, *b.documents,* 8.

22. Law no. 49–956 of 16 July 1949. Henri Filippini, *Dictionnaire de la bande dessinée* (Paris, 2005), 12; Fourment, *Presse des jeunes,* 302–29, 400–406. See the brief commentary in Filippini, *b.documents,* 8.

23. Filippini, *Dictionnaire,* 12. Quotation largely verbatim from the law itself. Fourment, *Presse des jeunes,* 401.

24. Loi du 29 novembre 1954. In Fourment, *Presse des jeunes,* 401.

25. Fourment, *Presse des jeunes,* 329; Filippini, *Dictionnaire,* 12.

26. *France-Soir* (15–23 février 1950). The first *Amours Célèbres* story began in November 1950, with "Juliette et Romeo," illustrated by Reschofsky.

27. The affair led to a law prohibiting prosecutions for supernatural witchcraft. See Jean-Christian Petitfils, *L'Affaire des poisons: Alchimistes et sorciers sous Louis XIV* (Paris, 1977).

28. Other cartoon strips from the postwar period adapted previously published stories: *Destins hors série, Le Tribunal de l'Histoire, Histoire de Paris.* Filippini, *Dictionnaire de la bande dessinée,* 15

29. Courrière, *Lazareff,* 513–14.

30. Deborah E. Hamilton, "The French Detective Fiction Novel 1920s to 1990s: Gendering a Genre" (Ph.D. diss., Penn State University, 1994), 27–34; Y.-O. Martin, *Histoire du roman populaire en France de 1840 à 1980* (Paris, 1980); Roger Chartier, ed., *Histoire de l'édition française, le livre concurrencé, 1900–1950,* vol. 4 (Paris, 1986).

31. Megan Koreman, "The Cherry Riots of 1945: Food and Politics in the Après Guerre" (paper presented to the Western Society for French History, Orcas Island, WA, 1992). Even by 1954, Paris real wages had not reached their prewar levels. Jeanne Singer-Kéral, *Le Coût de la vie à Paris de 1840 à 1954* (Paris, 1961), 164.

32. Rioux, *Fourth Republic,* 383–89; Henri Mendras, *Les Paysans et la modernisation de l'agriculture* (Paris, 1958) and his *Sociologie de la campagne française* (Paris, 1959); M. Gervais, M. Jollivet, and Y. Tavernier, *La Fin de la France paysanne,* t. V of *Histoire de la France rurale,* ed. G. Duby (Paris, 1985); Annie Moulin, *Les Paysans dans la société française: De la Révolution à nos jours* (Paris, 1988).

33. Stanley Hoffman, *Le Mouvement Poujade* (Paris, 1956); Dominique Borne, *Petits Bourgeois en révolte? Le mouvement Poujade* (Paris, 1977).

34. The Communists held 150 seats in the National Assembly after the January 1956 election, in which it garnered 25.9 percent of all votes, making it the largest single party.

35. Steven L. Kaplan, *Le pain maudit: Retour sur la France des années oubliées, 1945–1958* (Paris, 2008), demonstrates how much the subsistence issue—the grain-flour-bread nexus—continued to preoccupy French politics and public opinion. Alessandro Stanziani, ed. *La qualité des produits en France (XVIIIe–XXe siècles)* (Paris, 2003).

36. *France-Soir* (jeudi, 5 janvier 1956). The day that the first story was announced, the headlines read: "Quatrième aggression des gangsters mondains à Neuilly." *France-Soir* (dimanche–lundi, 12–13 février 1950). The day that it began, headlines signaled a pending strike by railwaymen organized by the CGT and a story about the destructive power of the H-bomb. *France-Soir* (mercredi, 15 février 1950).

37. For a *Comiclopedia* sketch of Carlotti, see lambiek.net/artists/c/carlotti_jean-albert.htm (consulted 22 July 2009). See also Alain Vollerain and René Dérouille, *Jean-Albert Carlotti: Donner une forme à sa vie intérieure* (Lyon, 1995).

38. "La Jacquerie de Buzançais," *France-Soir* (samedi, 28 janvier 1956); hereafter cited by episode number and date.

39. Susanna Barrows, *Distorting Mirrors: Visions of the Crowd in Late Nineteenth-Century France* (New Haven, 1981), esp. 191; Pierre Michel, *Les Barbares, 1789–1848: Un myth romantique* (Lyon, 1981).

40. The poster reads "Comment voter contre le bolchevisme?" See image in "De l'antibolchevisme à l'anticommunisme," www.histoire-image.com/site/etude_comp/etude_comp_detail.php?analyse_id=681 (last consulted 1 August 2009). Jean-Jacques Becker and Serge Berstein, *Nouvelle histoire de la France contemporaine,* t. 12, *Victoire et frustrations, 1914–1929* (Paris, 1990), 191; Jean-Jacques Becker and Serge Berstein, *Histoire de l'anti-communisme* (Paris, 1987), pt. 2, "Le temps de l'homme au couteau entre les dents, 1917–1921."

41. See also Carlotti's portrayal of an 1861 murderer in his first story for Gordeaux, "Dumollard, l'assassin des bonnes" (mercredi, 5 juillet 1950). In postwar France, teasing out good from bad in the Aryan/Nazi versus peasant/communist representations might have proved more complicated

because the Nazis were now the "bad guys." Racialization may have helped simplify decoding and played upon the heterophobia of many French by collapsing poor, communist, and immigrant others into one recognizably criminal image. For recent sensitive and sophisticated representations of the racialized other, see the essays in *The Color of Liberty: Histories of Race in France*, ed. Sue Peabody and Tyler Stovall (Durham, NC, 2003), and Elisa Camiscioli, *Reproducing the French Race: Immigration, Intimacy, and Embodiment in the Early Twentieth Century* (Durham, NC, 2009).

42. 5 (jeudi, 2 février 1956).

43. 7 (samedi, 4 février 1956).

44. 8 (dimanche–lundi, 5–6 février 1956).

45. 7 (samedi, 4 février 1956).

46. 17 (jeudi, 16 février 1956).

47. 9–11 (mardi–jeudi, 7–9 février 1956).

48. 12 (vendredi, 10 février 1956).

49. Ibid.

50. Even Bouchardon discusses their independent role in this event. Vallès emphasizes the old woman's role in organizing the interception.

51. 5 (jeudi, 2 février 1956).

52. 16 (mercredi, 15 février 1956).

53. Carlotti's image, however, clearly situates the scene indoors, not in a courtyard.

54. 3 (mardi, 31 janvier 1956).

55. 6 (vendredi, 3 février 1956).

56. 4 (mercredi, 1 février 1956); 7 (samedi, 4 février 1956).

57. 12 (vendredi, 10 février 1956); 13 (samedi, 11 février 1956).

58. 1 (samedi, 28 janvier 1956).

59. Michel-Louis Lévy, "Les cinquante ans du baby boom," *Population et sociétés* 311 (mars 1996): 1–4.

60. 1 (vendredi, 28 janvier 1956).

61. 2 (dimanche-lundi, 29–30 janvier 1956).

62. 3 (mardi, 31 janvier 1956).

63. 6 (vendredi, 3 février 1956).

64. 7 (samedi, 4 février 1956).

65. 15 (mardi, 14 février 1956).

66. Ibid.

67. 16 (mercredi, 15 février 1956).

68. 13 (samedi, 11 février 1956).

69. Isabelle Paris, *La reine Marie-Amélie, grande-mère de l'Europe* (Paris, 1998); Robert Burnand, *Marie-Amélie, reine des Français, 1782–1866* (1947; Paris, 1973); Jo Burr Margadant, "'La Monarchie impossible' revisitée: Les mères royales et l'imaginaire politique dans la Restauration et la Monarchie de Juillet," in *Pour la Révolution française: Festschrift for Claude Mazauric*, ed. C. Le Bozec and E. Wauters (Rouen, 1998): 411–20, and "Representing Queen Marie-Amélie in a 'Bourgeois' Monarchy," *HR/RH* 32 (Summer 2006): 421–51.

70. 19 (samedi, 18 février 1956).

71. All the national papers suffered during this period; some even disappeared. The provincial press grew, however, suggesting that failure to adapt to changing demand probably played one of the most important roles.

72. Recently (January 2009) purchased by Alexandre Pugachev, twenty-three-year-old son of Sergei Pugachev, Russian billionaire "cashier to the Kremlin," *France-Soir* appears to have a new lease on life, as witness its recently acquired Champs-Elysées offices. See www.timesonline.co.uk/tol/news/uk/article3177619.ece (consulted 23 July 2009).

73. The issue for Tuesday, 12 October 1976, announces on the first page that both *Le Crime ne paie pas* and *Les Amours célèbres* would begin publication the next day. They recycled Gordeaux's stories, not Mallat's.

74. Gildea, *France since 1945;* James McMillan, ed., *Modern France* (Oxford, 2004); Ron Kedward, *La Vie en Bleu: France and the French since 1900* (London, 2005); Maurice Agulhon, *The French Republic, 1879–1992,* trans. A. Nevill (Oxford, 1993); Charles Sowerwine, *France since 1870* (New York, 2001); Jean-Jacques Becker and Pascal Ory, *Crises et alternances, 1974–2000* (Paris, 1998–2002).

75. "Le Pain et le Vin," in *Les Grands procès témoins de leur temps* (10 juin 1978), Antenne 2, produced by Pierre Desgraupes and directed by Philippe Lefebvre. The TV production of "Le Pain et le Vin" can be downloaded (for 6 euros) or an excerpt seen free on the Web at boutique.ina.fr/video/economie-et-societe/justice-et-faits-divers/CPB88015689/le-pain-et-le-vin.fr.html (consulted 20 July 2009).

76. *Télérama* (samédi, 10 juin 1978) covered both radio and television schedules. *La Tribune de l'histoire* ran weekly from 1951 to 1997. Alain Decaux (1925–), historian and prolific author (and, after 1979, member of the Académie française), also hosted a popular television show, *La caméra explore le temps,* that ran on TF1 from 1957 to 1966, followed by *Alain Decaux raconte* (1968–88). Isabelle Veyrat-Masson, *Quand la télévision explore le temps: L'histoire au petit écran, 1953–2000* (Paris, 2000).

77. The important players in early French television were divided into the *saltambanques* (the creative acrobats) and the *géomètres* (the administrative, financial, and political organizers). Desgraupes self-identified as a *saltambanque:* Pierre Desgraupes, *Hors Antenne: Entretiens avec Annick Peigné-Giuly and Marions Scali* (Paris, 1992), 41. Anne Grolleron described him as "the mythical figure of the patron of television." "Pierre Desgraupes," in *L'Écho du siècle: Dictionnaire historique de la radio et de la télévision en France,* ed. Jean Noel Jeanneney et al. (Paris, 2001), 380.

78. Desgraupes, *Hors Antenne;* Commission nationale de la communication et des libertés, *Douze ans de télévision, 1974–1986* (Paris, 1987); Sophie de Closets, *Quand la télévision aimait les écrivains: Lectures pour tous (1953–1968)* (Brussels, 2004); Jeanneney et al., *L'Écho du siècle;* Christian Bosseìno, *200 téléastes français* (Condé-sur-Noireau, 1989); Jérôme Bourdon, *Haute fidelité: Pouvoir et télévision, 1935–1994* (Paris, 1994).

79. As Desgraupes described Lazareff, "[Although he] knew nothing about television [when he first got involved], he knew how to find topics beyond current events that 'spoke' to people" (*Hors Antenne,* 79).

80. This long-running television program introduced the French public to contemporary authors, such as Mauriac, Aragon, Céline, Duras, Borges, and Nabokov. By the 1970s, the show had achieved the reputation of *une émission culte* (Closets, *Quand*) and *émission phare* (flagship program); Degraupes and Dumayet were known as "the philosophers of television." Desgraupes, *Hors Antenne,* 69; Tamara Chaplin, "From Text to Image: Philosophy and the Television Book Show in France, 1953–1968," *FHS* 28 (Fall 2005): 629–59, and *Turning on the Mind: French Philosophers on Television* (Chicago, 2007), esp. 52–58.

81. In 1960, Lazareff invited Desgraupes, Pierre Dumayet (his cohost on *Lectures pour tous*), Igor Barrère, and Elaine Victor to join him, hoping to achieve in television the same sort of success he had had with *France-Soir. Cinq colonnes à la une* lasted until 1968. Soulé, *Lazareff,* 329–38; Lamy, *Lazareff,* 254–77.

82. Desgraupes, *Hors Antenne,* 126.

83. Commission nationale de la communication et des libertés, *Douze,* 31–32.

84. Chaplin, *Turning,* 2.

85. Pascale Goetschel, "Les dramatiques télévisées, lieux d'apprentissage culturel et social dans la France des Trentes Glorieuses," in *La Télévision des trentes glorieuses: Culture et politique,* ed. E. Cohen and M.-F. Lévy (Paris, 2007), 133. By 1984, 92 percent of all French households owned a television set. Isabelle Gaillard, "De l'étrange lucarne à la télévision: Histoire d'une banalisation (1949–1984)," *Vingtième siècle* 91 (juillet–septembre 2006): 9.

86. Evelyne Cohen and Marie-Françoise Lévy, introduction to Cohen and Lévy, *Télévision des trentes glorieuses,* 9, 11, 12.

87. Maryline Crivello, "Des *Croquis* aux *Conteurs,* un sensibilité au passé: Mise en images, mise en récits, 1957–1974," in Cohen and Lévy, *Télévision des trentes glorieuses,* 186.

88. Commission nationale de la communication et des libertés, *Douze,* 36. Gaillard, "De l'étrange lucarne à la télévision," 14.

89. Gaillard, "De l'étrange lucarne à la télévision," 13, 14. For example, the government appointed the directors of each channel, mandated minimum percentages of certain kinds of programs, ordered that between 50 and 60 percent of all programs be French productions, and assured that government spokespersons had ample airtime.

90. Quotation by Pierre Dumayet, in Desgraupes, *Hors Antenne* (56–57), reprinted in *Les Nouvelles littéraires* (juillet 1981). Desgraupes also referred to her in his interview with Pierre Assouline, "TF 1, A 2, FR 3: L'histoire dans les coulisses de la TV," *L'Histoire* 51 (décembre 1982): 135. For more on this "classic conception of television that programs should be understandable to all, even if they are aimed at a particular audience," see Commission nationale de la communication et des libertés, *Douze,* 198. For a critique of assumptions underpinning television as a "field," see Pierre Bourdieu, *On Television* (New York, 1996).

91. Desgraupes, *Hors Antenne,* 135, 24. He claimed that *Lectures pour tous* was a "news," not a cultural, program. For a discussion of the "lien culture-distraction" see Commission nationale de la communication et des libertés, *Douze,* 36.

92. Desgraupes interview with Assouline, "TF 1, A 2, FR 3," 78. Desgraupes was serving as president of Antenne 2 at the time.

93. Film is a collective, and not always harmonious, endeavor. Jérôme Bourdon, "Les professionnels: Conflits, triomphes et decline," in *La grande aventure de petit écran: La télévision française, 1935–1975,* ed. J. Bourdon (Paris, 1997), 30–33. However, I credit Desgraupes with more influence than others for several reasons. First, for the *réalisateur* (director), Philippe Lefebvre (1941–), "Le Pain et le Vin" was his first directorship. Second, Desgraupes had already been a researcher and scriptwriter for historically themed programs such as *En votre âme et conscience.* Also, financial limitations surely influenced choices of certain sequences over others. Desgraupes interview with Assouline, "TF 1, A 2, FR 3," 78.

94. Michel Debré's article in *Le Monde* (3 septembre 1979), cited by Veyrat-Masson, *Quand,* 9.

One of the earliest and most successful television series treating popular protest was the entirely fictional *Jacquou le croquant* in 1969. Jacques Baudou and Jean-Jacques Schleret, *Les Feuilletons historiques de la télévision française* (Paris, 1992); Veyrat-Masson, *Quand,* 319.

95. See this painting at (among many places on the Web) "L'Emeute," www.honore-daumier.com/daumier/oeuvres/detail.asp?arId=1721 (consulted 1 August 2009).

96. Gary R. Edgerton, "Television as Historian: A Different Kind of History Altogether," introduction to *Television Histories: Shaping Collective Memories in the Media Age,* ed. Gary R. Edgerton and Peter C. Rollins (Louisville, 2001), 3. Marcia Landy, ed., *The Historical Film: History and Memory in Media* (New Brunswick, 2001).

97. Edgerton, "Television as Historian," 3–4; Brian Taves, "The History Channel and the Challenge of Historical Programming," in Edgerton and Rollins, *Television Histories,* 261–82. Veyrat-Masson, *Quand,* 481. Jacques Baudou and Jean-Jacques Schleret called it the "golden age" (*Feuilletons historiques*).

98. Umberto Eco, "Innovation and Repetition: Between Modern and Post-modern Aesthetics," *Daedalus* 115, no. 4 (1985): 161–84, esp. 172.

99. Edgerton, "Television as Historian," 3.

100. See Marcia Landy's review of Nietzsche's articulation of dominant forms of historical construction in her introduction to *Historical Film,* 3.

101. Veyrat-Masson, *Quand,* 36, 206, 212, 227, 236–39, 323–25.

102. Desgraupes may have drawn these two characters from actual inhabitants of Buzançais. Olivier has a local family name, Barreau, and Oudoul is the name of both the town pharmacist and the parish priest.

103. The viewer comes to imagine that Oudoul may have served as lawyer or judge under subsequent governments. The two have arranged to meet in a courtroom, and Oudoul gestures to the judge's bench, anouncing, "I have spent as much time here as at the witness bar." This gives Oudoul's voice particular authority.

104. Dynamite was not invented until 1863.

105. The engagement had actually settled the price at 3 francs.

106. Oudoul repeats the word "women" loudly for emphasis. I have highlighted the second usage to reflect this.

107. Veyrat-Masson, *Quand,* quoting Marcel Bluwal, 321; Baudou and Schleret, *Feuilletons historiques,* 11. However, unlike most such *westerns à la française,* "Le Pain et le Vin" did not elevate a lone cowboy to the rank of defender of the underdog. Bienvenu could hardly carry that banner.

108. Desgraupes had expressed a certain predilection for communism in his early years, without "carrying the card," but recent historians have situated him among the more moderate "progressives." Veyrat-Masson, *Quand,* 142. See also Desgraupes, *Hors Antenne.*

109. Pierre Sorlin, "'Historical' Film," in Landy, *Historical Film,* 37, excerpt from his *The Film in History: Restaging the Past* (New York, 1980).

6. BUZANÇAIS RENDERED IN HISTORY, PATRIMONY, AND SOUND AND LIGHT

1. The reasons for this convergence take us away from concerns here, but a quick survey would include the rise to virtually hegemonic status of the Annales school and a parallel and often related

Marxist social history, the expansion of the number of university students, the changing structure of French university education, and the modest but real decentralization of government support for local culture. The literature on this is immense; see, for example, the contributions by Michel Denis, Arlette Farge, and René Rémond in *L'Histoire et le métier d'historien en France, 1945–1995*, ed. François Bédarida (Paris, 1995); Pierre Nora, "The Era of Commemoration," in *Realms of Memory: Rethinking the French Past*, vol. 3, *Symbols*, ed. Pierre Nora, trans. Arthur Goldhammer (New York, 1996), 609–707; Robert Gildea, *The Past in French History* (New Haven, 1994); Jean Boutier and Dominique Julia, *Passés recomposés: Champs et chantiers de l'Histoire* (Paris, 1995); and Christian Delacroix et al., *Les Courants historiques en France, 19e–20e siècles* (Paris, 1999).

2. Eugène Hubert, *Canton de Buzançais*, t. 3, *Le Bas Berry: Histoire et Archéologie du département de l'Indre*, 3 vols. (Paris, 1908); Marcel Bruneau, "L'Indre en 1847," in *Aspects de la Révolution de 1848 dans l'Indre*, ed. Marcel Bruneau, et al. (Châteauroux, 1948). Two older works merit mentioning: Victor-Albans Fauconneau-Dufresne, *Histoire de Déols et de Châteauroux*, 2 vols. (Châteauroux, 1873), 1:586, which touches the affair only briefly, and J. Pierre, "Les événements de Buzançais en 1847," *Revue du Berry et du Centre* 16 (1911): 25–27.

3. Hubert, *Canton de Buzançais*, 436, 438.

4. Bruneau, "L'Indre en 1847," 5.

5. Arlette Farge, "L'Histoire sociale," in *L'Histoire et le métier d'historien en France, 1945–1995*, ed. François Bédarida (Paris, 1995), 281–300.

6. Solange Gras, "La Crise du milieu du XIXe siècle en Bas-Berry," 2 vols. (thèse de 3e cycle, Université de Paris X–Nanterre, 1976); Yvon Bionnier, "Aspects économiques et sociaux des émeutes de la faim dans l'Indre en 1847," 2 vols. (mémoire de maîtrise, Université de Tours, 1977, a part of which he published as *Les Jacqueries de 1847 en Bas-Berry* [Châteauroux, 1979]).

7. Philippe Vigier, *La seconde République dans la région alpine: Etude politique et sociale* (thèse de doctorat, Université de Paris, 1959; published, 2 vols., Paris, 1963). He followed that with *Essai sur la répartition de la propriété foncière dans la région alpine* (Paris, 1963). He ultimately served as president of both the Institut français d'histoire sociale and the Société d'histoire des révolutions du XIXe siècle.

8. For this shift of attention away from high politics and Paris, as well as the increasingly perceived importance of the period 1848–52, see Philippe Vigier, "Un quart de siècle de recherches historiques sur la province," *AHRF* (1975): 622–45.

9. Alain Corbin, *Archaïsme et modernité en Limousin au XIXe siècle* (thèse de doctorat, Université de Paris, 1973; published, 2 vols., Limoges, 1975). Corbin, *Historien du sensible: Entretiens avec Gilles Hervé* (Paris, 2000).

10. Eugen Weber analyzed the problem of peasant politicization in "Comment la politique vint aux paysans: A Second Look at Peasant Politicization," *AHR* 87 (April 1982): 357–89; Ted Margadant, "Tradition and Modernity in Rural France during the Nineteenth Century," *JMH* 56 (December 1984): 667–97; Edward Berenson, "Politics and the French Peasantry: The Debate Continues," *Social History* 12 (May 1987): 213–29.

11. Bionnier currently serves as *administrateur-adjoint, chef de section*, at the Bibliothèque au Sénat in Paris.

12. Gras, "Crise du milieu," 1:7.

13. Bionnier quickly used his master's thesis for a *mémoire* for the D.E.A. in law: "L'affaire de Buzançais" (University of Poitiers, 1977). "L'Affaire de Buzançais," *GHAB* 9 (1977): 63–86, and

Les Jacqueries de 1847 en Bas-Berry (Châteauroux, 1979). Gras's unpublished thesis has become a widely acknowledged point of departure for all those doing research on the mid-nineteenth-century Indre.

14. Philippe Vigier, *La Vie quotidienne en province et à Paris pendant les journées de 1848,* in the series La Vie quotidienne (Paris, 1982). Vigier credits both Gras and Bionnier (342–43 n. 1). When Hachette decided to publish a new edition, Alain Corbin wrote the preface. Hachette retitled it *1848, les Français et la République* (1998); I use this edition.

15. For example, Vigier emphasizes that "about one hundred families held large reserves of grain, of which half was held by seventeen proprietors alone" (*1848,* 37).

16. *1848,* 44.

17. Ibid. Italics are mine.

18. *1848,* 37.

19. However, Madeleine Blanchet never appears in Vigier's drama.

20. With all due allowances for George Sand.

21. Joan Scott, "Women and the Making of the English Working Class," in *Gender and the Politics of History* (New York, 1999), 68–92. Bonnie Smith, *The Gender of History* (Cambridge, MA, 2000).

22. *1848,* 46.

23. *1848,* 51.

24. *1848,* 45. Italics in original.

25. *1848,* 48.

26. Roger Price, *The Modernization of Rural France: Communications Networks and Agricultural Market Structures in Nineteenth-Century France* (London, 1983). See also his "Poor Relief and Social Crisis in Mid-Nineteenth-Century France," *European Studies Review* 13 (October 1983): 423–54, and "Techniques of Repression: The Control of Popular Protest in Mid-Nineteenth-Century France," *Historical Journal* 25, no. 4 (1982): 859–87.

27. Price, *Modernization,* 177; for typology, chap. 5: "Subsistence Crises and Popular Protest," 126–95.

28. He also cites Bionnier's work and the reports in the *Gazette des tribunaux.*

29. Price, *Modernization,* 180. For this, Price relies on the report of the indictment read in court.

30. Ibid.

31. He quotes a military commander at Tours who claimed that the subsistence crisis provided a pretext for an open "War on the Rich!" Ibid., 184.

32. Ibid. For a critique of the modernization model with regard to popular protest in nineteenth-century France, see Peter McPhee, *A Social History of France, 1780–1880* (London, 1992), 275–77.

33. Roger Magraw, *France, 1815–1914: The Bourgeois Century* (New York, 1983), 118.

34. He wrote that "A local 'usurer' was killed after he had shot two men who presented him with a petition urging sale of grain at lower prices." Ibid.

35. Charles Tilly's *The Contentious French* (Cambridge, MA, 1986) is the only major study of collective violence in France not to make Buzançais a prominent example. But Tilly focuses on the provinces of Anjou, Burgundy, Flanders, the Ile-de-France, and Languedoc, and not France's center. It is not my intention to cite every reference to Buzançais, just to emphasize that it became the

paradigmatic example for historians of the nineteenth century and that it served multiple uses in these diverse works. Some salient but representative examples follow.

36. François Furet, *Revolutionary France, 1770–1880,* trans. Antonia Nevill (Oxford, 1992), 379–80. French edition, *La Révolution, 1770–1880* (Paris, 1988).

37. McPhee, *Social History,* 174–75.

38. Hervé Robert, *La monarchie de juillet* (Paris, 1994; repr., 2000), 117.

39. Ibid., 118.

40. Jean-Claude Caron, *La France de 1815 à 1848* (Paris, 1993, 2000), 45.

41. Ibid., 166, 164, 167.

42. Nicolas Bourguinat, *Les Grains du Désordre: L'Etat face aux violences frumentaires dans la première moitié du XIXe siècle* (Paris, 2002). See my brief review of this book in the *Revue d'histoire moderne et contemporaine* 53, no. 3 (2005): 185–87.

43. Bourguinat, *Grains,* 446–47.

44. Bourguinat introduced his book with this quotation, which appears at the top of his "Presentation" (ibid., 9). The full quotation can be found in Raynal to GS (25 janvier 1846, although he surely meant 1847), AN, BB19 37.

45. Bourguinat, *Grains,* 11.

46. Ibid., 447.

47. Ibid., 22.

48. Another property owner in the Indre did die, but not at Buzançais, nor in the same way. A section in part III explores the "repertory" of behaviors common to nineteenth-century food riots, the role of women in them, and the response of authorities. Ibid., 311–72.

49. David Lowenthal, "Fabricating Heritage," *History and Memory* 10, no. 1 (1998): 5–24, and *Possessed by the Past: The Heritage Crusade and the Spoils of History* (Cambridge, 1998).

50. Robert Schneider, *The Ceremonial City: Toulouse Observed, 1738–1780* (Princeton, 1995) and *Public Life in Toulouse, 1463–1789: From Municipal Republic to Cosmopolitan City* (Ithaca, NY, 1989). For eighteenth- and nineteenth-century developments, see Stéphane Gerson, *The Pride of Place: Local Memories and Political Culture in Nineteenth-Century France* (Ithaca, NY, 2004), and Bruno Benoit, *L'Identité politique de Lyon: Entre violences collectives et mémoire des élites (1789–1905)* (Paris, 1999), especially the preface by Maurice Garden. For the twentieth century, see Anne-Marie Thiesse, *Ils apprenaient le France: L'exaltation des régions dans le discours patriotique* (Paris, 1997); Claire Andrieu, Marie-Claire Lavabre, and Danielle Tartakowsky, eds., *Politiques du passé, usages politiques du passé dans la France contemporaine* (Aix-en-Provence, 2006); Maryline Crivello, Patrick Garcia, and Nicolas Offenstadt, eds., *Concurrence des passés: Usages politiques du passé dans la France contemporaine* (Aix-en-Provence, 2006); and Stéphane Gerson, "*Une France locale:* The Local Past in Recent French Scholarship," *FHS* 26 (Summer 2003): 539–59.

51. On what follows, see Rapport, Chassinet to GS (2 avril 1848), AN, BB30 359, n° 477. Chassinet, a former lawyer in Orléans and Buzançais and, after 1848, democratic candidate for local elections, had proved a vocal advocate for the release and amnesty of the Buzançais prisoners.

52. Nora, "Era," 614.

53. Maurice Garden uses this phrase to explain how the resurgence of collective violence in Lyon in 1830 and 1870 harked back to the "original" collective violence of 1793. Garden, preface to Benoit, *Lyon,* 15.

54. Pierre, "Les événements de Buzançais"; Benoit, *Lyon,* 22.

55. Bionnier, "Aspects," vol. 2, annexe n° 7.

56. Nora, "Era," 614. Studies of commemorations have appeared in great numbers in recent years. See Patrick Garcia's bibliography, *Le Bicentenaire de la Révolution française* (Paris, 2000).

57. Nora, "Era," 616, 624.

58. Ibid., 617–27. See also Gerson, "*Une France locale,*" and Brian Jenkins, "Reconstructing the Past: In Search of New 'National Identities'?" in *Recollections of France: Memories, Identities, and Heritage in Contemporary France,* ed. Sarah Blowen, Marion Demossier, and Jeanine Picard (New York, 2000), 16.

59. Jean-Pierre Rioux and Jean-François Sirinelli, *Les Politiques culturelles municipales: Eléments pour une approache historique,* Cahier n° 16, Cahiers de l'institut d'histoire du temps present (Paris, 1990). See also André-Hubert Mesnard, *L'Action culturelle des pouvoirs publics* (Paris, 1969), 357–75. The supranational European Union has also moved the focus away from the nation-state, giving new voice to local and regional entities.

60. Themes identified as "démocratisation, décentralisation, rénovation, [and] rayonnement culturel." Françoise Taliano-Desgarets, "Les Politiques culturelles à Bordeaux de 1945 à 1975," in Rioux and Sirinelli, *Politiques culturelles municipales,* 101. See also Sarah Blowen, Marion Demossier, and Jeanine Picard, introduction to Blowen, Demossier, and Picard, *Recollections,* 1–9, who argue that "the decentralisation of cultural decision-making has been the most significant catalyst for change."

61. One sign of this trend appeared in the decline of the national press (such as *France-Soir*) relative to the provincial press.

62. Gerson, "*Une France locale,*" 471.

63. Paul Connerton, *How Societies Remember* (Cambridge, 1989), 16–21; Susan A. Crane, "AHR Forum: Writing the Individual Back into Collective Memory," *AHR* 102 (December 1997): 1372–85; Maurice Crubellier, *La Mémoire des français: Recherches d'histoire culturelle* (Paris, 1991), esp. 279–311; Kerwin Lee Klein, "On the Emergence of Memory in Historical Discourse," *Representations* 69 (Winter 2000): 127–150.

64. Jean Petit and René Desécure, "Des maquis de Sainte-Gemme au bataillon Casal," *GHAB* (1986) 17–19; Jean Duplaix, *Buzançais à travers les âges* (Vendœuvres, 2000).

65. Pierre Josse, interview with Yvon Bionnier, *La Nouvelle République* (18 septembre 1979).

66. André Chapu, "En marge des Jacqueries de Buzançais: La vie mouvementée d'une femme du peuple," *GHAB* 12 (1980): 75–76. Emphasis added.

67. Lowenthal uses the phrase "exotic enrichment" (*Possessed by the Past,* 218).

68. Amédée Renault, "Une Révolte de faim et de la misère des événements de 1847 à Buzançais," *Pellevoisin Info Plus* 17 (mai–juin 1991): 27–29.

69. Paul Clemente, "Les Emeutes de la faim en 1847 à Buzançais," *Berry* 29 (février 1994): 52–54.

70. Louis publishes high-quality books (well printed on fine paper) and works on the margins of the mainstream literary genres (notebooks, correspondence, essays, and less famous works) by known authors of the late nineteenth and early twentieth centuries or contemporary writers. "Niches éditoriales du Poitou-Charentes: Jean-Paul Louis, Histoires et recherches littéraires," *L'Actualité Poitou-Charentes* 66 (n.d.); my interview in Tusson (Monday, 24 April 2006). Maricourt

created the Goût de l'Etre as a successor to an earlier publishing house, Editions de Quat'sous (1982–85). All the books he published reflected his commitment to anarchism and the politics of resistance.

71. Léandre Boizeau, *Les Lueurs de l'aube* (Châteauroux, 1996).

72. Written communication from Léandre Boizeau, 18 December 2006.

73. Boizeau, *Lueurs,* 22–23.

74. Ibid., 11, 17. See also references on 49–50, 74–75, and 82.

75. Ibid., 91–92.

76. Ibid., 70, 84.

77. Ibid., 98–99.

78. Ibid., 101.

79. On what follows, see ibid., 104–5.

80. Ibid., 134, 152–54.

81. Boizeau, schoolteacher, leftist militant, and storyteller, through an earlier book, *Ils sont innocents* (1980), reopened a murder case with new evidence and thereby reversed the guilty verdict. Boizeau also directs a magazine, *La Bouinotte: Le magazine du Berry,* founded in 1982, and a publishing house, Editions La Bouinotte. Both cater to regional interests.

82. "From among the hundreds arrested at first, the gendarmes retained approximately fifty 'rioters' as they called them." Boizeau, *Lueurs,* 127.

83. Rachel, more than the other women, plays a victim in multiple ways. Attacked and raped early in the story, she is rescued by Etienne.

84. Correspondence with Léandre Boizeau, 18 December 2006.

85. In my multiple interviews and correspondence with Boizeau, he did not disclose sales figures but demonstrated a strong sense of market as well as a commitment to political activism.

86. What follows comes from interviews with participants in and producers of the historical spectacles of the riots at Buzançais and from articles in the daily newspaper, *La Nouvelle République du Centre-Ouest,* and the regional magazine, *La Bouinotte.*

87. Blanchet has a doctorate in economics. Under the banner of the Radical faction of the UDF, he was elected mayor in 1995, reelected in 2001 and again in 2008. In 1999 Buzançais had a 10.9 percent unemployment rate, slightly lower than France overall at 12.9 percent, but still a contentious issue. Institut national de la statistique et des études économiques (Insee), 1999. Susan Milner, "Cultural Policies and the Definition of Urban Identities," in Blowen, Demossier, and Picard, *Recollections,* 187–207.

88. The first major historical spectacle took place in the Vendée in 1977, with what ultimately became one of the most successful productions in France, *Le Puy du Fou.* Jean-Clément Martin and Charles Suaud, *Le Puy du Fou, en Vendée: L'histoire mise en scène* (Paris, 1996).

89. Lepas arranged for a professional video recording of the performance. I thank Mayor Régis Blanchet for supplying a copy of it.

90. Written exchange with Patrick Lepas, 14 December 2006.

91. Written correspondence from Patrick Lepas, 14 December 2006, and letter from Léandre Boizeau, 18 December 2006.

92. Interviews with Lepas and Boizeau, July 2004, and correspondence with Lepas, 14 December 2006, and Boizeau, 18 December 2006.

93. Lepas divides the play into "tableaux" of particular moments over a six-month period, beginning in fall 1846.

94. The play takes the spectator through the winter festival calendar: the Fête de Saint-Martin (11 November), Christmas, and the New Year. It juxtaposes attempts to find occasions for celebration with the increasingly difficult circumstances.

95. Tableau 10.

96. Tableau 14.

97. Tableau 12.

98. Tableau 14.

99. Tableau 17.

100. Léandre Boizeau, *Villemont, le Raboliot berrichon* (Châteauroux, 1986).

101. Written exchange with Patrick Lepas, 14 December 2006, and letter from Léandre Boizeau, 18 December 2006. In the summer of 2004, I attended a rehearsal of "Villemont," which opened with a reenactment of the riot.

102. Blowen, Demossier, and Picard, introduction to *Recollections*, 9.

103. Boizeau had served for six years as mayor-adjoint in the nearby town of Le Blanc, also representing the Union de la Gauche. Correspondence with Boizeau, 18 December 2006, and Lepas, 14 December 2006.

104. "Régis Blanchet, candidat de principe," *La Nouvelle République du Centre-Ouest* (samedi, 25 mai 2002).

105. Correspondence with Boizeau, 18 December 2006.

106. The park offers a link to the spectacle. See www.parc-naturel-brenne.fr/index.htm. (consulted 20 May 2007).

107. Such as the long-standing Puy de Fou spectacles in the Vendée. Although still heavily reliant on volunteers and financing derived from their own ticket sales, Boizeau and Lepas retained considerable control and continually developed a more structured bureaucracy. Each activity (village, restaurant services, technical affairs, security, artistic production, costumes, and communications) is overseen by "commissions."

108. Lepas and Boizeau had arranged for buses to transport the spectators, now numbering more than 1,000 a night.

109. The budget for the spectacle had, as of 2006, risen to 85,000 to 90,000 euros. The tickets still cost 10 euros for adults and 5 euros for children. Lepas had just started receiving a 2,000 euro fee for his services, a testimony to his arrival as a professional director rather than a mere amateur.

110. Development seems to pose a threat to the vitality of town center. The Buzançais Demain Party (with whom Lepas allied) opposed Buzançais's construction of a supermarket (and cafeteria) outside town for fear that local restaurants would suffer. "Parole aux élu: Buzançais 'ville morte,'" in *Buzançais: Bulletin municipal* (juillet 2004), 19.

111. Martin and Suaud, *Le Puy du Fou*; Sylvie Rouxel, *Quand la mémoire d'une ville se met en scène: Etude sur la fonction sociale des spectacles historiques: L'exemple de Meaux* (Paris, 1995). See also the study of historical spectacle in Provence by Maryline Crivello, "Du passé, faisons un spectacle," *Sociétés et representations* 12 (Octobre 2001): 225–34, and Crivello, Garcia, and Offenstadt, *Concurrence des passes.*

112. Martin and Suaud, *Le Puy du Fou.* For de Villiers, the counterrevolution constituted a pivotal moment in both revealing and activating those values. To attempt to preserve culture and to

invent it are, as Eric Hobsbawm and Pierre Nora have argued (even if from different paradigms), interrelated phenomena. See Hobsbawm, *The Invention of Tradition* (Cambridge, 1983, 1992).

113. In the mid-1990s, more than 63 percent of the population of Meaux came from outside the European Union, but the participants in the historical spectacle did not even begin to reflect this demographic. One of the titles of a local performance was "Meaux en marche vers l'Europe."

114. For example, they used proceeds from one of their performances to erect for the poacher, Villemont, a real tombstone to mark his previously anonymous burial in a potter's field. Letter from Boizeau, 18 December 2006.

115. Sylvie Rouxel has offered what she considers an incomplete list of the fields brought together by the historical spectacle: "la culture patrimoniale (monuments historiques), le tourisme culturel (industrie, commerce), le social (solidarité de groups, intégration), l'artistique (mise en scène et théâtre), le politique (collectivités locales, Etat), l'histoire (pédagogie, éducation), la communication médiatique (publicité, média, etc.)" (*Quand,* 26). See also Milner, "Cultural policies," 205–7.

116. Quotation from a text written by André Bochin; it appears on a recent postcard "historique de Buzançais" and on a city directory/map. The next line assures the reader that the "city has become peaceful."

117. Duplaix, *Buzançais.*

118. Ibid., 269–75.

119. Ibid., 270, 271,

120. Ibid., 277.

121. He kindly sent me an invitation, but I unfortunately could not attend.

EPILOGUE

1. Iffik Leguen, "Buzançais, le 13 janvier 1847," *CQFD* (15 décembre 2006). www.cequilfautdetruire.org (consulted 20 May 2008). This "tabloid" also sells a hard copy in some kiosques in France.

2. *CQFD*'s fuller description of itself: "a journal dedicated to social criticism and experimentation. . . . An independent publication belonging to neither Lagardière nor Dassault. Familiar with the terrain of social disintegration present in the struggles important to it (unemployment, antimilitarism, immigration, resistance to policing, and the right to be lazy . . .), its team, which has no chief editor, is comprised of journalists who have broken with the accepted code of conduct, genetically modified illustrators, militants, the unemployed, one prisoner, and one post office worker. . . . Its tools are curiosity, the desire to report, and the search for news that is not pre-chewed by those under the influence of the community of multinationals." Its first issue appeared in May 2003.

3. Alexandre Adler, a former writer on international affairs for the *Libération, Le Monde, l'Express,* and the *Courier international,* author of an award-winning book on the post-9/11 world, *J'ai vu finir le monde ancien* (2003), and chronicler for a morning news show on radio station France-Culture, had provoked Leguen with a radio report (in October 2006) on the situation in Oaxaca, Mexico. He had dismissed resistance there as "a spectacle of revolutionary-populist folklore" in a region "reaching toward modernity." Adler concluded that, while the region thought it could resist the pull of the "North-American market," in fact, "they would realize one fine day that there was no other solution."

4. Vallès's novel seems to permeate this version of the *jacquerie*. For example, the cyberzine identifies itself with refractory ideas, just as Vallès had often referred to himself and those who resisted ideological purity as *réfractaires*. Vallès had portrayed a mayor ready to negotiate and comply, one whom the rioters had even elected to join the delegation led by the Old Woman.

5. Although historians have often noted festive aspects (in language and behavior) of popular protest, this misidentification of the actual celebration of carnival with the eruption of the riot at Buzançais might suggest how much contemporary forms of protest (such as 1968) consciously perform both the festive and aggressive aspects of protest and a tendency to interpret literally such a statement as what one witness reported hearing a rioter say: "We will bury the bourgeois like carnival."

6. Founded by Jean-François Kahn in 1997 and directed by Maurice Szafran, *Marianne* has a regular circulation of more than 200,000 per issue. Kahn, a reporter during the Algerian war, participated in the investigation of the disappearance/assasination of the anticolonial revolutionary Mehdi Ben Barka in Paris in 1965 and later worked for *L'Express* and *Le Monde*. Less than a month (14 February 2008) after the issue in which Buzançais figured prominently, *Marianne* launched a petition calling for "Republican vigilance" against the Sarkozy's personal, "monarchist" self-attribution of power and for "lacitié," "freedom of the press," and the "protection of national independence." The petition's signatories included a spectrum of prominent French political leaders including Dominique de Villepin, Ségolène Royal, Jean-Pierre Chevènement, Corinne Lepage, Bertrand Delanoë, Noël Mamère, and François Bayrou. www.marianne2.fr/L-Appel-republicain-de-Marianne_a83903.html (last consulted May 2008). Regular contributors to *Marianne* include Nicolas Domenach, Daniel Bernard, Patrick Besson, and Alan Rémond. Kahn retired in 2007 at age seventy.

7. *Marianne,* n° 557–58 (22 décembre 2007 au 4 janvier 2008), 62–129.

8. Michael Winock wrote "The Day of Tiles," and Anthony Rowley penned the rest. Each moment features two to three images from the era. The essays ran three to four pages.

9. Anthony Rowley, "La Revanche des Blouses grises," 78–81.

10. Rowley, who teaches occasionally at Sciences Po, has authored *A table! La fête gastronomique* (Paris, 1994) and *Histoire mondiale de la table* (Paris, 2006); he coauthored, with Jean-Michel Gaillard, *Histoire du continent européen de 1850 à la fin du XXe siècle* (Paris, 1998), and, with Bernard Droz, *Histoire générale du XXe siècle* (Paris, 1996). He challenged assumptions about the nature of the crisis of 1846–47 in "Deux crises économiques moderne, 1846 et 1848," *1848, révolutions et mutations au XIXe siècle* 2 (1986): 81–90.

11. Declaring most illiterate, Rowley wonders if the accused "even understood French." Five of the twenty-six were literate, and no record exists to suggest dialect issues.

12. The media become "vehicles of memory." On this, see Alon Confino citing Yosef Hayim Yerushalmi, "AHR Forum: Collective Memory and Cultural History: Problems of Method," *AHR* (December 1997): 1386.

13. See Susan A. Crane, "AHR Forum: Writing the Individual Back into Collective Memory," *AHR* 102 (December 1997): 1372–85.

14. Maurice Halbwachs, *The Collective Memory,* trans. R. J. Ditter and V. Y. Ditter (New York, 1980); Roland Barthes, "The Death of the Author," in *Image, Music, Text,* trans. Stephen Heath (New York, 1977). See also Paul Connerton, *How Societies Remember* (Cambridge, 1989), and Daniel J. Sherman, *The Construction of Memory in Interwar France* (Chicago, 1999), among many others.

15. They perhaps also left a lingering trace of the story in the memories of those who read *Lectures pour tous* or *France-Soir's Le Crime ne paie pas.*

16. Social movements and other forms of peaceful collective claim making have become an object of considerable scholarly interest. See, for example, Sidney G. Tarrow, *Power in Movement: Social Movements and Contentious Politics* (New York, 1998), and Charles Tilly, *The Politics of Collective Violence* (New York, 2003).

17. For a serious analysis of contemporary rebellious France, see *La France rebelle: Tous les mouvements et acteurs de la contestation,* ed. Xavier Crettiez and Isabelle Sommier (Paris, 2006). The English-language press has also often emphasized this discourse and behavior as a particularly French construct. See, for example, the transcript of Margaret Warner's 1995 interview for PBS's MacNeil/Lehrer News Hour about the ongoing national strike in France with *Le Monde* journalist Daniet Vernet and George Washington University's professor of international affairs Harvey Feigenbaum: "Winter of Discontent" (8 December 1995). Professor Feigenbaum explained that, "traditionally in France, one has gone to the streets . . . [as] a traditional way of expressing discontent."

18. www.newsweek.com/id/123330 (consulted 6 August 2009); Nicolas Chevassus-au-Louis, *Les Briseurs de machines de Nedd Ludd à José Bové* (Paris, 2006).

19. Jose-Alain Fralon, "Dans les Ardennes, les grévistes de l'usine Cellatex s'insurgent contre la liquidation de leurs emplois," *Le Monde* (17 juillet 2000); Nicolas Weill, "Les grèves de l'été, retour de luddisme 'briseur de machines'?" *Le Monde* (5 août 2000).

20. Jean-Baptiste Chastand, "Nortel: 'Nous ne sommes pas des terroristes,'" *Le Monde* (15 juillet 2009); John Lichfield, "Pay Us Off or We Blow up the Plant, Say French Workers," *The Independent* (16 July 2009).

21. www.rtl.fr/fiche/5924723024/la-violence-sociale-est-elle-legitimate (consulted 1 August 2009).

22. Luc Bronner and Mustapha Kessous, "Des cités à la cité," *Le Monde* (23 mars 2006). See the inciteful article by Joshua Cole, "Understanding the French Riots of 2005: What Historical Context for the 'Crise des Banlieues'?" *Francophone Postcolonial Studies* 5:2 (2007), 69–100. HALDE stands for Haute Autorité de lutte contre les discriminations et pour l'égalité. See also, for example, Olivier Fillieule, *Stragégies de la rue: Les manifestations en France* (Paris, 1997), and Danielle Tartakowsky, *La manif en éclats* (Paris, 2004).

23. Special issue "Les guerres Franco-françaises," *Vingtième Siècle* 5 (janvier–mars 1985), and more recently, Jean-Clément Martin, *Violence et révolution: Essai sur la naissance d'un mythe national* (Paris, 2006). Micah Alpaugh challenges a common connection between revolution and violence in France. "The Politics of Escalation in French Revolutionary Protest: Political Demonstrations, Non-violence and Violence in the *grandes journées* of 1789," *French History* (forthcoming) and his dissertation, "The Emergence of the Parisian Political Demonstration: Developing Non-violent Protest in the French Revolution, 1787–1795" (University of California–Irvine, forthcoming).

24. As Jonathan Boyarin points out, "those elsewhere on the planet living in drastic relative deprivation are not 'behind' us or temporally 'backward.' They are contemporaries of the professional-managerial class in the 'first world,' and no amount of temporizing will enable us to deny the equal priority of their humanity." "Space, Time and the Politics of Memory," in *Remapping Memory: The Politics of TimeSpace,* ed. Jonathan Boyarin (Minneapolis, 1994), 10.

25. www.autoritedelaconcurrence.fr/user/standard.php?id_rub=13 (consulted 10 August 2009).

26. boulangerie.org/journal/historique.htm (consulted 11 August 2009).

27. For example, cognac-citoyen.blogspot.com/2008/03/le-prix-de-la-baguette.html (consulted 11 August 2009).

28. www.lexpress.fr/actualite/economie/prix-du-pain-la-polemique (consulted 10 August 2009).

29. sites.radiofrance.fr/chaines/france-culture2/emissions/fabriquene (consulted 1 September 2009).

30. And a polished media performer. See him discussing bread with Conan O'Brien on *Late Night*, 22 February 2007, www.noob.us/humor/conan-obrien-and-the-bread-professor (consulted 1 September 2009), promoting his book, *Good Bread Is Back: A Contemporary History of French Bread, the Way It Is Made, and the People Who Make It* (Durham, NC, 2006).

31. John Walton and David Seddon, *Free Markets and Food Riots: The Politics of Global Adjustment* (Cambridge, 1994). Recently, protest marches have occurred in Mexico over the skyrocketing price of tortillas.

INDEX

Algeria: war, 5, 135, 140, 143, 145, 154; food riots in, 208
Annales school, 161, 171, 174, 185
Antenne 2 (television channel), 7, 155, 156
Arrouy, François, 16, 35, 41, 48, 50, 56, 118, 146, 177
Aryans, representations of, 138, 140

Baczko, Bronislaw, 9
Balzac, Honoré de, 4, 69, 95, 110
Baptiste, Jean, 16, 17, 118
Barthes, Roland, 205
Bastille, 5, 159, 165, 205
Bazenerye (*juge d'instruction*), 38–42
Bellet, Roger, 89–90
Bénard, Jean, 187
Berenson, Edward, 5
Bienvenu, Baptiste, 12, 13–14, 16, 17, 45, 46–48, 53, 73, 119–20, 123, 140, 144, 145–46, 148, 155, 160–61, 163–64, 165, 167, 192
Bionnier, Yvon, 173, 174, 184, 187, 188, 194, 199, 200
Blanchet, Madeleine, 16, 28–29, 117, 119, 144, 145, 148–49, 168
Blanchet, Régis, 1, 171, 193, 194, 196, 200, 201, 245n87, 246n104
Blouses, Les (1880), 6, 65, 66, 69, 70, 71–84, 86–89, 90, 93, 95–96, 106, 189, 193; class in, 67, 82, 86–89, 138; elites and authorities in, 82–85, 184; gender in, 68, 80–82, 119, 148; social violence in, 67–68, 70–74, 78, 80, 82, 86–90, 98, 106, 112, 124, 138
Blouses, Les (1885), 90
Blouses, Les (1919 illustrated edition), 91, 97–106, 112, 136, 142; class in, 97–98, 100–01, 103–04; elites and authorities in, 101; gender in, 102–103, 104–05; social violence in, 98, 101–02, 106
Blouses, Les (1986 editions), 189
Boisin, Benoît, 63
Boizeau, Léandre, 189–93, 194–98, 200–01
bonfire, 12, 31, 75, 97–99, 115–16, 118, 141–42, 147, 150, 155, 199
books, illustrated deluxe (*livres de luxe* and *demi-luxe*), 93–94, 96
Bouchardon, Pierre, 6, 91, 130, 133, 136, 183; life of, 106–11. *See also* "Jacquerie de Buzançais, La" (Bouchardon and Leclercq, 1925)
Bouinotte, La (publishing house), 200–01
Bourdieu, Pierre, 8, 57
Bourgeois/bourgeoisie, 9–10, 18, 20–21, 27, 31, 36–37, 48–49, 54, 59, 68, 71, 72, 74, 76–77, 78, 81, 82, 89, 116, 119–20, 121–22, 123, 140, 148, 150–52, 164, 168, 172, 174, 176, 178, 179, 181–82, 183, 188, 190–91, 192, 199, 202, 203, 204, 206
Bourgeot, Louis, 15, 77, 117, 144, 145, 167, 175, 191, 199
Bourguinat, Nicolas, 6, 181–82
Bové, José, 207
bread, 14, 18, 51, 52, 59, 60–65, 68, 72, 75–77, 79, 80–81, 83, 85, 87, 90–92, 111, 126, 134, 135, 138, 159, 165, 180, 190, 192, 195, 202, 207–08
Brillaut, Jean, 13, 47, 164–65
Bruneau, Marcel, 172
Buzançais, evocations of: as crime, 3, 6, 7, 26–27, 35, 46, 58–59, 106, 112, 116–18, 119, 124, 126, 135–37, 138, 140, 145–47, 153, 172, 205, 208; as legitimate protest, 3, 32, 54, 55, 57–59, 60, 62–63, 78, 87–88, 155, 167, 169, 190, 205, 207–08; as symbol and synecdoche, 5, 8–9, 38, 59, 60, 61, 62, 70, 159, 184; first narrations of (1847), 20–30; sentences, appeals, and executions, 52–53, 55

"Buzançais, 1847" (spectacle), 195–96, 197
Buzançais riot of 1847, 1, 11, 19, 32–33; civil suits following, 55, 85, 184; repression of, 17–19, 34, 36, 38; trial of rioters, 38–53. *See also* key episodes, of Buzançais riot

Caillaux, Joseph, 107, 108
Caillaux, Madame, 5
Carlotti, Jean-Albert, 138–39, 140–53; life of, 136–37
Caron, Jean-Claude, 178–81
cartoons, 2, 6, 8, 36–37, 126, 127, 128–33, 136–37, 153–54, 158, 160, 161, 176, 202, 205
Caudrelier, Desiré, 12–14, 18, 21–22, 48–49, 75, 83–84, 116, 121, 138, 148, 150, 151, 152, 162–63
Chambert, fils, Eudoxe-Louis-Joseph, 11, 15–16, 20, 21, 22–23, 25–26, 27, 28–29, 34–35, 39–41, 46–49, 51, 52, 54, 58, 71, 73, 77–78, 79, 80, 87, 97, 103, 104, 116, 117–18, 119, 124, 143–46, 147, 152, 162, 166–67, 168, 174–75, 177, 178, 188, 191, 194–96, 199–200, 204, 206
Chambert, Mme (Marie-Thérèse-Florence-Moreau de Bellesourd; Mme Huard-Chambert), 15, 16, 17, 23, 25, 26, 28–30, 41, 78, 117–19, 143–46, 148–49, 167, 168, 174–75, 177, 191, 199
Chapu, André, 187, 188
charity, 18, 25, 28, 30, 36, 41, 47, 54, 72, 74–75, 81, 87, 118, 120, 148, 152, 165, 199, 208
charity workshops, 11, 18, 19, 30, 47, 52, 58, 79, 82, 114–15, 137–38, 141, 162, 163, 165, 175, 190, 199, 202
Châteauroux, 12, 17, 18, 22, 42, 43, 44, 54, 55, 77, 83, 84, 114, 120, 123, 173, 176, 179, 187, 200
class(es), understandings of, 7, 8, 9–10, 20–21, 27, 31, 34, 37, 43–44, 48–49, 59, 64, 68, 71–72, 76, 82, 110, 120, 140, 150, 152, 172, 174, 177–82, 184, 192–93, 199, 203
Clemenceau, Georges, 5–6, 66, 68, 71, 88, 92, 93
Clemente, Paul, 188
Cloquemin, Pierre, 12, 13–14, 34, 46–47, 48, 73, 76, 82, 85, 97, 101, 102, 104, 112, 116, 119, 142, 149, 164, 172, 178, 190–91, 192, 195, 199
Cohen, Paul, 5
comic strips. *See* cartoons
commercialization, 6, 33, 52, 111, 131, 158, 198, 200, 206
Commune, Paris, 6, 65–67, 68, 69, 70, 90, 95, 170, 204
communism, 36, 50, 57–58, 71, 86, 109, 131, 134, 139, 169, 182
Confédération générale du travil (CGT), 91–92, 93, 109
Considérant, Victor, 37, 57
"contentious conversations," concept of, 8, 32, 57, 203, 208
Corbin, Alain, 5, 173
Coteron, Anne (née Bouchard), 13, 16, 35, 40–41, 45, 48, 78–79, 118, 156, 161, 163, 164, 166, 168,
CQFD: Ce qu'il faut dire, détruire, dévélopper (cyberzine), 202–03
crime: stories of, 6–7, 43–44, 57, 106, 108, 109–11, 125, 126, 129–30, 131–32, 133, 135, 153–54, 155–56, 205
Crime ne paie pas (cartoon series), 7, 126, 129–30, 132–33, 135–36
crisis of 1846–47, 1, 3–4, 33, 172, 173–74, 178–81

Dauvergne, Jean Baptiste Narcisse, 17, 24, 39, 118, 120, 146, 149
Dauvergne, Mlle, 28, 29, 120
Dauvergne, Mme, 28, 29, 120
Delorme, Emmanuel, 65
Desgraupes, Pierre, 7, 157, 176; *En votre âme et conscience,* 162 ; *Lectures pour tous,* 158; life of, 156–58
Didelot (*procureur général*), 26–27, 39, 42, 44–46, 47–48, 50, 53, 73, 124, 162
Dreyfus affair, 5, 108, 133
Duchêne, Georges, 61
Ducuing, François, 64
Dumayet, Pierre, 156
Duplaix, Jean, 198–200
Dupont, Pierre, 62–63
Du Pynode, Gustave, 64

Edouard-Joseph (publisher), 91, 94–96, 94n 27, 97, 99, 100, 102, 104, 105, 106, 124, 136, 142, 189
elites, 1, 5, 7, 9, 20–23, 27–28, 30, 32–33, 34, 35, 36, 37–38, 43, 54, 58, 59, 71, 81, 82, 103, 106, 112, 116, 121–24, 135, 137–40, 147, 149, 150, 151, 181–82, 192, 195–96, 198, 206. *See also* notables
"engagement," the, 15, 17, 18, 19, 22, 24, 54, 77, 103, 116, 117, 144, 148, 164, 167, 175, 178, 179, 191, 194, 199, 204

Fifth Republic, 154–55, 157
Flaubert, Gustave, 5, 64, 65, 117
Foigny, Jean, 14, 16, 35, 41, 45, 48, 51–52, 146, 165
food riots: of 1846–47, 1, 3, 33, 36; other, 1, 3, 4, 31–32, 92, 181–82, 208. *See also* crisis of 1846–47
Fourth Republic, 130–32, 154, 157
France-Soir, 7, 126–30, 131, 135, 140, 150, 153–55, 156, 158, 160, 163
free trade, 33, 58, 61, 131, 139
Furet, François, 6, 178–79, 180, 181, 182, 183

Gaulin, François Théophile, 12, 15, 21, 22, 24, 48, 83, 142, 150, 179, 186
Gaulin, Frédéric, 14, 28, 29, 47, 48, 119–20, 140, 149, 168
Gaulin, Mme, 28, 29, 119–20, 149, 168
gendarmerie, 11, 12, 14, 18, 21–22, 35, 45, 48, 75, 80, 83–84, 85, 112, 115–16, 118, 120, 121, 122, 137, 138, 140, 143, 150, 151, 159, 163, 164, 168, 186, 191
gender, 3, 7, 8, 21, 45, 68, 121, 133, 137, 167, 175, 177, 186; in Buzançais riot, 1, 9, 11–18, 28, 39, 41, 45, 48, 52; female, 21, 28–30, 49, 72, 73–74, 78–82, 102–05, 118–21, 133, 135, 141–42, 147–49, 152, 157, 168, 175, 192; male, 20–21, 25, 49, 68, 72, 79, 81–82, 104, 112–13, 115, 119, 121, 138, 141–42, 148, 175, 192
genealogy, 6, 126, 187, 201
Gildea, Robert, 5
Gordeaux, Paul, 7, 128–30, 132–34, 135–36; *Amours célèbres, Les*, 129–30, 132–33
Goût de l'Etre, Le (publishing house), 189
grain, 1, 11–15, 17–19, 24, 46–47, 50–51, 54, 58, 64, 72–77, 82–83, 88, 91 95, 103, 111, 114, 116, 137–38, 140–41, 142–43, 159, 162–64, 172, 174, 179, 190–91, 194, 199, 200, 204
Grands procès témoins de leur temps, Les (television series), 155–56, 158
Gras, Solange, 173–74
Groupe d'histoire et d'archéologie de Buzançais (GHAB), 187, 198, 199
guerres franco-françaises, 9, 207
Guesnyer, Pierre-Charles, 11–12, 15, 17, 18–19, 21–24, 28, 32, 55, 74–76, 82–84, 85, 115, 120, 121–22, 140–41, 149, 150–51, 152, 160, 162, 163–65, 168, 175, 179, 184, 190, 202
Guizot, François, 60, 178, 188

Hachette (publishing house), 6, 91, 109, 111, 124, 127, 133, 174, 176
Halbwach, Maurice, 205
Hautefaye affair, 5, 13
heritage, 6, 170, 171, 174, 183, 185–87, 194, 196–98, 201
historical fiction, 69–71, 82, 86, 90, 133, 158, 189–93
histories: local, 6–7, 126, 171–72, 186–88, 198–201; popular, 6–7, 67, 91, 106, 111, 160; scholarly, 6–7, 126, 160, 171, 172–83
Huard-Chambert, Louis-Joseph, 117, 144, 152
Hubert, Eugène, 171–72, 184, 199
Hugo, Victor, 5, 64–65, 128, 159, 169, 203
hunger and famine, 1, 30, 36, 38, 60–61, 62–65, 69, 72, 74–75, 77, 80–81, 82, 84–85, 86–88, 90, 93, 95, 97–98, 100–01, 105, 138, 141, 162, 178, 188, 189–90, 208

inter-war era, 2, 91–94, 96, 106, 107–09, 112, 120

jacquerie, 4, 7, 36–37, 59, 62, 91, 95, 106, 111–12, 113–14, 118, 124, 126, 136, 137, 138, 140, 171, 172, 176, 178, 188, 202, 207
"Jacquerie de Buzançais, La" (Bouchardon and Leclercq, 1925), 6, 91, 106, 111–24, 136; class in, 112–13, 114–15, 116, 120–21, 148; elites and authorities in, 114, 121–24, 152; gender in, 115–16, 118–21, 141, 147, 148; social violence in, 113–14, 118, 136, 138, 176
"Jacquerie de Buzançais, La" (Gordeaux and Carlotti, 1956), 7, 129–30, 133, 135–53; aging in, 149–50; class in, 133, 136–38, 140, 143–44, 148, 151–52; elites and authorities in, 135, 140–41, 150–53; gender in, 133, 135, 137, 141–42, 147–49; race and ethnicity in, 7, 139–40; social violence in, 133–34, 135, 136–38, 142–43, 146
"Jacquerie de Buzançais, La" (Gordeaux and Carlotti, 1979), 153–55
Jacquou le croquant (Le Roy), 95, 113, 158n94
July Monarchy, 1, 4, 20, 27, 31, 33, 36, 37, 59, 63, 121, 151, 152, 178, 180, 181–82
Justice, La, 6, 66–69, 85

Kaplan, Alice, 5
Kaplan, Steven, 208
key episodes, of Buzançais riot: elites and authorities' responses to disorders, 9, 11–15,

key episodes *(continued)*
17–18, 21–22, 24–25, 35–36, 59, 71, 74, 82, 84–85, 106, 121–24, 149–52, 168, 175, 181, 195–96, 200; interception of grain shipment, 9, 11, 21, 27, 28, 30, 39, 71, 73, 74–75, 103, 114–16, 140–41, 162–66, 174–76, 177, 178, 179, 182, 188, 190, 194, 195, 199, 202, 204; Venin-Chambert fatal incidents, 9, 15–16, 21, 25–26, 34–35, 71, 77–78, 103, 116–18, 143–46, 166–67, 174–75, 177, 178, 179, 182, 191, 195–96, 199–200, 202, 204; women in local scuffles, 9, 16, 17, 18, 21, 28–30, 71, 78–81, 104–05, 118, 120–21, 146–49, 167–68, 175, 192

labor movements, 3–4, 66, 91–92, 93, 109, 153, 175, 188
Lazareff, Pierre, 7, 127–28, 130, 133, 150, 153, 156, 157, 158, 169
Leclercq, B., 6, 111, 112, 113, 114, 115, 116, 118, 121, 122, 136
Lecomte, Jean, 14
Lectures pour tous, Les, 6, 91, 106, 136, 109, 111
Ledru-Rollin, Alexandre, 58, 61
Lefebvre, Philippe, 7, 238n75, 239n93
Légeron, François, 14, 48, 74, 114, 119, 140, 149, 159, 161, 164–65, 176
Légeron, Jean, 11
Leguen, Iffik, 202–03
Lepas, Patrick, 193–98, 200
Leroi, Ferdinand, 12, 17, 20, 21–25, 28, 36, 38, 47, 54–55, 89, 114, 118, 122–23, 149, 151, 164, 172, 175, 200
Lérot, Editions du, 189
liberalism, 4, 7, 33, 92, 176, 188, 202–03, 208
Limoges, 54, 56, 59, 183, 200
Liniet, Uranie, 28, 120, 123, 148, 149, 152
Louis, Jean Paul, 189
Louis-Philippe, 19, 56, 86, 137, 178, 202
Lowenthal, David, 6
Lueurs de l'aube, Les (Boizeau), 189–93, 194; class in, 189–91, 192; elites and authorities in, 190, 192; gender in, 190, 192; social violence in, 191–92

magazines, popular, 2, 6, 91, 106, 109–10, 111, 125, 131, 153, 188, 203
Magraw, Roger, 178, 183
Mallat, Robert, 130
"man with the knife between his teeth," 139
Marianne (magazine), 203–05
Maricourt, Thierry, 189
Marie-Amélie (queen, wife of Louis-Philippe), 152
Marx, Karl, 5, 64, 67, 159, 169
Mater, Claude-Denis, 29, 42, 44, 46–53, 123–24, 162, 164–67, 168, 204
Mathieu-Dairnvaell, Georges, 60
maximum (government price controls), 4, 27, 36, 92, 207–08
McPhee, Peter, 6, 178, 179–80, 181
Meaux, historical spectacle at, 197–98
memory (memories): role of, 3, 5, 6, 8, 10, 23, 34, 37, 59, 60–61, 62–65, 66, 70, 74–76, 85, 89, 91, 97–98, 112, 134, 140, 157, 184, 188–89, 194, 196, 203, 205–06, 208
Michot, Louis, 13, 14, 16, 35, 45, 46, 49, 50, 53, 120, 123, 146, 161, 167–68, 191–92
Moneron, François, 12, 45, 74–75, 78–79, 82, 83, 84
Monfalcon, Jean-Baptiste, 37
moral economy, 3, 32, 88, 182, 208

national guard, 18–19, 25, 35, 58, 120, 121, 123, 124, 150, 152, 168
newspapers. *See* press
Nora, Pierre, 5, 184, 185
North Africans, 139–40
notables, 15, 19–25, 28, 29, 31, 35, 39, 45, 48, 54, 81, 113, 151, 165, 168, 174–76, 179, 183, 184. *See also* elites

Office de radiodiffusion-télévision française (ORTF), 156–57

"Pain et le Vin, Le" (television show), 126, 155, 156, 158–69; class, 7, 162, 163–65; elites and authorities in, 7, 165–66, 168–69; gender and, 7, 162–63, 167–68; interpretive ambiguity in, 7, 158–60, 161–62, 165–67, 168–69; social violence and, 7, 159, 163–64, 168–69
Pane e vino (Silone), 159
patrimoine, la. See heritage
"Pavillon des Ducs raconte l'histoire de Buzançais, Le," 193–94

Pierre, J., 184
political economy, 3, 4, 208
Poujadism (*poujadisme*), 134, 150
press, 1, 2, 4, 19–20, 21, 30, 38, 43–44, 56–60, 69–70, 86, 92, 126, 132, 135, 140, 153–54, 166, 187; in 1847–48, 19–20, 30, 43–44, 56–61
Price, Roger, 176–78
prix de vertu (Académie française), 29
property, 1, 3–4, 14, 17, 18, 20, 26, 27, 31, 32, 33, 34–35, 46–47, 50, 54, 55, 57–58, 61, 64, 85, 116, 124, 133, 135, 145, 162, 169, 182, 184, 204, 208
property owners, 3–4, 12–15, 17–19, 23–25, 31, 34–35, 37, 39, 46–47, 51, 54, 58, 63, 77, 82, 87, 92, 100, 101, 112, 114, 116, 119, 124, 136, 138, 140–43, 145, 148, 149, 150, 152, 162, 164, 166, 175, 179, 181–82, 184, 192, 199, 204
protest, popular, 2, 3–4, 6, 7, 9, 18–19, 31–37, 57, 65, 71, 86–87, 90, 102–03, 106, 114–15, 133–35, 140, 147, 153, 169, 175–83, 188, 190, 192, 195, 197, 204, 206–08. *See also* violence, social and collective
Prothade-Martinet, Jean-Baptiste, 50–51, 52, 52n70, 56
public assistance, 19, 33, 47, 58, 74–75, 81, 165. *See also* charity
"Puy de Fou" (spectacle), 197–98
Pyat, Félix, 63–64

Que sais je? (series), 6, 178, 180

Raynal, Louis de, 31, 34–35, 36, 38, 41–42, 55
Renault, Améde, 188
republicanism, 36, 56, 57–58, 61, 64, 65, 66, 67, 71–72, 73, 78, 82, 86–89, 93, 96, 106, 182, 183, 204
revolution: of 1789, 4, 23, 27, 31, 32, 33, 42, 43, 55, 68, 74, 76, 86, 98, 159, 181, 203–04; of 1848, 1, 4, 32, 56, 59, 62–64, 67–68, 70, 88, 170, 172, 173, 174, 178–81, 182, 183, 203, 205
Robert, Hervé, 6, 178, 180, 181
Robin, Charles, 60
Rollinat, François, 51–52, 52n70
Rowley, Anthony, 203–05

Sand, George, 44, 81, 180
Scott, Joan, 175
Second Empire, 64–65, 69
Second Republic, 56, 63–64, 65, 70, 173, 184, 204
serial novel (*roman-feuilleton*), 69–70
Sewell, William, 4
Simon, Mario, 6, 91, 96–106, 112, 136. See also *Blouses, Les* (1919 illustrated edition)
socialism, 37, 57–58, 65–68, 86, 89, 91–92, 93, 103–04, 108–09, 154, 182, 188, 189, 206
social justice and rights, 9, 27, 30, 33–34, 37, 51, 57, 59, 60, 61, 62, 75, 80–82, 84, 86–89, 93, 96, 98, 101,106, 107–08, 109, 112, 116, 124, 135, 138, 142, 144, 153, 154–55, 161, 162, 163, 169, 188–89, 192, 195, 196, 206–07
social question, 7, 34, 37, 60, 197, 198
spectacle ("sound and light"), 2, 36, 126, 158, 193–94, 196–98
Steinlen, Théophile-Alexandre, 103–04
Stewart, Philip, 96–97

taxation populaire (popular price-fixing), 1, 3, 12–13, 15, 18, 22, 24, 27, 31–32, 54, 59, 77, 87, 103, 144, 151, 175, 177, 179–80, 182, 190–91, 199, 204, 206
televison, 7, 126, 155–58, 160–61; and historical drama, 155
text: confronting with images, 7, 8, 10, 91, 96–97, 103, 128, 132, 136–37, 155, 158, 160, 205, 206
theater. *See* spectacle ("sound and light")
Third Republic, 56, 65–66, 85, 88, 90, 93, 107, 121, 124, 162, 184–85
Thompson, Edward P., 175
Tilly, Charles, 8. *See also* "contentious conversations," concept of
Tocqueville, Alexis de, 29, 116
Trémine, Pierre, 13, 16, 50
troops, use of, 3, 18, 12, 21–22, 24–25, 35, 54–55, 59, 81, 112, 114, 118, 120–23, 149, 151, 172, 179, 194

Uprising, The (Daumier), 159

Vallès, Jules, 6, 62, 95–96, 106, 112; life of, 65, 66–69, 89, 90; on Buzançais, 70–71, 84–85, 113, 124, 183. See also *Blouses, Les* (1880)
Vandérem, Fernand, 95–96
Vasson, Edouard Girard de, 17, 44, 84, 151
Velluet, François, 16, 17, 39–41, 53, 123, 153, 166, 167, 192

Venin, Louis, 14, 15–16, 21, 25–26, 40, 51, 52, 54, 71, 77–78, 80, 103, 116–17, 119, 144–45, 152, 166, 174–75, 177, 178, 182, 191, 194, 195–96, 199, 200, 206
Vichy regime, 107–08, 131, 134, 174
Vigier, Philippe, 6, 173–76, 180
Villiers, Phillipe de, 197–98
violence, social and collective, 1, 3, 4, 8–9, 20, 31, 32, 34, 35, 43, 57, 60, 62, 89, 134–35, 155–56, 162, 169–70, 182, 184, 206, 207, 208. *See also* protest, popular
web publishing, 202–04
welfare state, 155, 206
women. *See* gender
World War I, 91–94, 95, 99, 106–07, 108, 109, 111, 150, 170
World War II, 126, 127–28, 131, 134, 138, 150, 170, 186, 194, 198

Zola, Emile, 84, 95